ASPIRATION AND AMBIVALENCE

ASPIRATION AND AMBIVALENCE

STRATEGIES and REALITIES of COUNTERINSURGENCY and STATE BUILDING in AFGHANISTAN

Vanda Felbab-Brown

BROOKINGS INSTITUTION PRESS

Washington, D.C.

Copyright © *2013*
THE BROOKINGS INSTITUTION
1775 Massachusetts Avenue, N.W., Washington, D.C. 20036
www.brookings.edu

Library of Congress Cataloging-in-Publication data are available

ISBN: 978-0-8157-2441-4 (hardcover : alk. paper)

9 8 7 6 5 4 3 2 1

Printed on acid-free paper.

Typeset in Sabon

Composition by Cynthia Stock
Silver Spring, Maryland

Printed by R. R. Donnelley
Harrisonburg, Virginia

*To those who have struggled to make Afghanistan
a more peaceful and prosperous country*

Contents

Foreword

Bruce Riedel

The United States has been at war in Afghanistan off and on since January 1980, when the first shipment of U.S. arms arrived in Karachi, en route to the *mujahideen,* less than two weeks after the Soviet Union invaded Afghanistan. At first it was a covert war, fought only by a small number of CIA officers, but after the terrorist attacks of 9/11 the war came out of the shadows and American boots arrived on the ground. Twice in the last quarter-century the United States has squandered great victories achieved in Afghanistan by failing to follow up battlefield success with an enduring commitment to help build a stable government in the country and provide the resources necessary to do so. Both times the cost to the United States of taking its eye off the ball in Afghanistan was high. It is imperative not to make the same mistake a third time, or most likely the outcome will again be costly.

In the late 1980s, after the most effective covert operation in the nation's history, American-supported Afghan *mujahideen* defeated the Soviet 40th Red Army; following that, the Berlin Wall fell, Eastern Europe was liberated, and the Soviet Union itself collapsed. The *mujahideen,* however, were badly divided, and Afghanistan quickly fell into civil war. The United States could have led an international effort to restore order and rally key players like Pakistan and Saudi Arabia to try to end the conflict. Instead, Afghanistan got virtually no attention from the White House or from Congress. By the late 1990s the radical Taliban movement, with the help of Pakistan, which felt abandoned and had lost faith in America, had taken power in most of Afghanistan and was hosting the even more radical al Qaeda terrorist group, which attacked America, first in 1998, then again in 2000, and most painfully on September 11, 2001.

In late 2001 the CIA led a campaign to topple the Taliban with the support of the Northern Alliance, the Taliban's foe inside Afghanistan. Again the results, which came very quickly, were spectacular. By early 2002 the Taliban were routed, al Qaeda was on the run, and both were retreating to Pakistan. Al Qaeda probably would have been destroyed and an Afghan state created that could exercise control over the Pashtun belt, where the Taliban are strongest, if a concerted international effort to do so had been made in 2002 and 2003. Instead, American resources and attention shifted to Iraq and the Afghans got marginal support from the United States. By 2006 the Taliban had come back with a vengeance, again with Pakistani help. Once again, American resources surged toward Iraq. By the end of 2008, the increasingly confident Taliban controlled much of the rural countryside in the southern part of the country, where Pashtuns are a majority. Meanwhile, the Taliban and al Qaeda's leaders were hiding out comfortably in Pakistan. President Barack Obama inherited a disaster in Afghanistan.

Americans' reasons for being tired of the war in Afghanistan are understandable. The mission is expensive and difficult, and far too many people have died or been wounded in pursuing it. But the majority of the problems that the United States faces in Afghanistan are the result of its own errors, not the strategic genius of its foes. Vanda Felbab-Brown, my colleague at Brookings, has written a brilliant new book that explains those mistakes and errors in depth and offers recommendations for how America can still get it right.

Vanda's book is based in large part on considerable field research inside Afghanistan. She has traveled extensively around the country, sometimes with the NATO forces in country but more often on her own. The result is a unique collection of insights based on firsthand experience. These insights, drawn from close observation and tough questioning, are backed up by her years of research on the problems of failing states and drug cultures. She is critical of U.S. failures but hopeful that the United States can still make them right, for both itself and Afghanistan. This book is not only good research and analysis—it is a sparkling good read.

The timing of this critical investigation of the war is propitious. NATO is committed to drawing down the bulk of its combat forces in

Afghanistan by 2014 and transitioning to an Afghan-led military operation. In addition, Afghanistan will hold its third presidential election by 2014. President Obama and President Karzai have promised that the United States and Afghanistan will conclude a long-range military agreement to detail their mutual commitments under the Strategic Partnership Agreement, a critical step toward ensuring that America does not abandon Afghanistan for a third time.

These are enormous challenges. It is a bold gamble to turn over responsibility for Afghanistan's security to the Afghans, but it must be done sooner or later. It would be a far easier task if the Taliban were to show a serious interest in a political process to end the fighting, with Pakistani support, but today that appears unlikely. Moreover, it will be a robust challenge to hold free and fair elections in this complex environment. And it will take creative diplomacy to forge the elements of a long-term, sustainable American-Afghan partnership.

This book makes a major contribution to efforts to meet all of those challenges. Not every expert will agree with every assessment and recommendation, but few have written as vigorous and provocative an analysis as Vanda has here. It is a rich contribution to understanding one of the greatest challenges facing America today.

BRUCE RIEDEL
Washington

November 2012

ASPIRATION AND AMBIVALENCE

Bullets over Kabul's Broadway

On the bright and breezy Sunday morning of April 15, 2012, my colleagues and I left NATO's International Security Assistance Force (ISAF) headquarters in Kabul to meet with Afghan journalists, government officials, and civil society leaders to discuss the security and political situation in Afghanistan and the transition to a much reduced international presence after 2014. For once, I was participating in an official, NATO-sponsored trip of five researchers, whom NATO called "opinion leaders," from the United States, Europe, and Australia.

After several days under NATO auspices, I would stay on in Afghanistan and travel around the country on my own, as I did on previous trips—continuing my research, unencumbered by formal security restrictions and free to interact with many different Afghan interlocutors. This book, in its policy analysis and personal reflections, is based to a large extent on that fieldwork in Afghanistan and recounts some of my experiences that are emblematic of the political and social contentions, violent struggles, and mafia rule with which Afghanistan is grappling on the cusp of the new post-2014 situation, when most Western soldiers will have departed. Many Afghans fear this impending change, even as they are tired of Western presence in their land.

My analysis is well introduced by what transpired on that day, April 15, as we met or were affected by the behavior of many of the types of actors that have Afghanistan's future in their hands. The experience would turn out to be a micro example of what life in Afghanistan after a decade of Western intervention has become: a combination of social

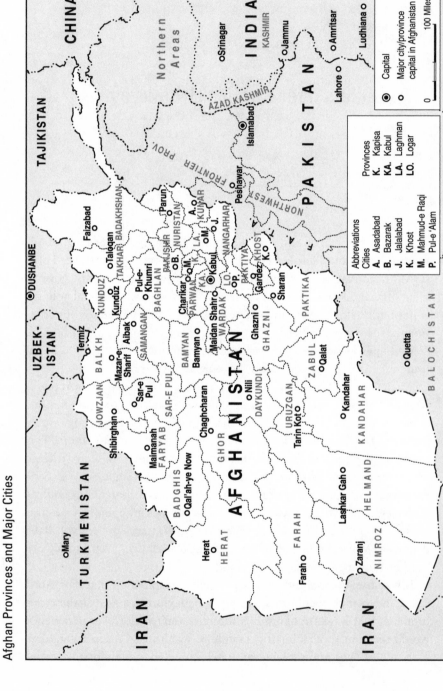

Afghan Provinces and Major Cities

progress, an uncertain and worrisome economic outlook, politics and intrigue, violence by insurgents and terrorists, and fighting back by Afghan security forces.

One of the brightest developments in Afghanistan since 2002 has been the growth of vibrant media in Afghanistan, which increasingly have been able to expose government corruption, abuses by power brokers, and the brutality of the Taliban; challenge oppressive but deeply ingrained social mores; and seek greater accountability for the Afghan people. Yet the morning meeting with Afghan journalists, even though carefully supervised by Afghan government officials, revealed not only the life-threatening pressures that Afghan journalists face from Afghanistan's armed groups and power brokers but also the increasing effort by the Afghan government to undermine and muzzle independent media and other critics of its rule.[1] Moreover, since many independent media outlets in Afghanistan are still fundamentally dependent on Western financial support for their economic survival, the likely decrease in Western funding after 2014 could severely hamper their ability to challenge those who hold formal and informal power and to demand truth for the Afghan public.[2]

Later in the morning, our research group's planned meeting with the secretary-general of the High Peace Council, an institution established to support the Afghan government's negotiations with the Taliban and other insurgents, was canceled. A delegation from one such insurgent group, Gulbudin Hekmatyar's Hezb-i-Islami, had arrived for meetings with the secretary-general. Negotiations with Hekmatyar have been on and off over the years as part of an effort to bring a negotiated solution to the intense insurgency that, by the end of the post–9-11 decade, had swept across Afghanistan and which the Afghan government and ISAF had struggled to suppress during that same period. But as with the Taliban, the negotiations had failed to achieve much traction, despite the fact that many politicians and power brokers associated with Hezb-i-Islami have positions of official and unofficial power in Afghanistan. Unlike some of its key allies in Afghanistan, such as the United Kingdom, the United States had long been reluctant to embrace negotiations with the Taliban, believing that it first had to significantly weaken the insurgents militarily before negotiations could produce any lasting positive results. Yet by the middle of 2012, military progress on the battlefield turned out to be far more elusive than Washington and ISAF had hoped. Negotiations did start in 2010, but as of fall 2012, they were stalled with little achieved.

Still, the morning was cheerful; and after a snack of roadside kebab, our group headed to the Ministry of Mines to meet with the deputy minister, Mir Ahmad Javid, an impressive young man determined to steer the ministry toward good governance and sustainable development. Under the leadership of Minister Wahidullah Shahrani and Mir Ahmad Javid, the Ministry of Mines was working hard to transform itself from a notoriously corrupt government institution—the pervasive characteristic of governance in post-2002 Afghanistan—to one that could support the emergence of a robust, legal economy in the country. One of the poorest, most underdeveloped countries in the world and ravaged by three decades of war, Afghanistan would benefit enormously from being able to extract the large mineral riches—worth as much as $1 trillion—that lie beneath its soil.[3] And indeed, Western budgeting for economic assistance to Afghanistan after 2014 has been banking on Afghanistan's ability to generate substantial economic revenues from the mining sector, which, under optimistic scenarios, the government of Afghanistan estimates will grow from a meager $100 million in 2009 to as much as $1.5 billion in 2016 and $2.3 billion in 2025.[4]

An effective, corruption-free investment of the potential financial profits, focused on community and human-capital development, could be the economic engine of the country, reducing its grinding poverty. But for that to happen, Afghanistan would have to develop its nonexistent infrastructure, establish the rule of law, tame the corruption that makes it the third most corrupt country in the world after Somalia and North Korea, and significantly reduce the insecurity and violence that have wracked the country and its people since the late 1970s.[5] Otherwise, the mineral riches, just like the influx of foreign aid and other money into Afghanistan, could stimulate violent conflict instead of equitable economic growth, mimicking the detrimental outcomes of such mineral riches in countries like the Congo, Sierra Leone, and Liberia.

That morning when we were at the ministry, its officials and Western advisers were drafting new mining laws, seeking to reinforce anticorruption provisions and incorporate a development component into tender rules, all while trying to balance these considerations with incentives for foreign companies to invest in their highly insecure country, such as establishing some guarantees that a company that conducts exploration would get to exploit what it found. A few weeks later, a group of other senior Afghan cabinet officials objected to the new legislation, arguing that the proposed law yielded too much of the profits and influence to foreign companies, thus placing the legislation and five open tenders in limbo.[6] That decision caught off guard Western governments, who were eager for Afghanistan's mining to expand rapidly and thereby avert a massive economic crisis in the country after 2014.

As we were leaving the Ministry of Mines building, we were stopped by guards who informed us that militant attacks were under way in the area, Wazir Akbar Khan, the select, "Broadway" center of Kabul, where ISAF headquarters, foreign embassies, and Afghan government buildings are located and where security is the tightest. This launch of the Taliban and Haqqani network (an affiliate insurgency) yearly spring offensive would strand us at the ministry for the next eight hours. Although we were only about 400 meters away from ISAF headquarters, the streets were deemed too insecure to cross; and, anyway, both ISAF headquarters and much of Wazir Akbar Khan went into immediate lockdown. No foreigners and few Afghan civilians remained on the streets. In fact, no locals should have been moving around during a militant strike either; but after several years of periodic insurgent attacks, many Afghans are no longer all that fazed by such terrorist incidents. Thus, although rocket-propelled grenade explosions and shootings were occurring throughout the quarter—with the Afghan parliament and the Kabul Star Hotel under the most serious attack and various nearby embassies receiving fire—at least some Afghans continued digging ditches (which somewhat eerily resembled graves), selling their wares, and going about their lives, however fraught with peril, insecurity, poverty, and injustice.

Six hours later, despite the firefights still going on in the city, most of the ministry employees left to be with their families. But since NATO headquarters were still under lockdown, our international group had to stay in the ministry, confined to a room where we could watch Al Jazeera's television coverage of the attacks continuing around us in Kabul. Eventually, however, the ministry guards moved our group out of that room, significantly reducing our access to information (by then most of our smartphone batteries had run down) and increasing our frustration. Eight hours after the beginning of the attacks, even our charade game of Taliban impersonations or sharing of spy stories could no longer relieve our confinement-induced boredom.

After yet another hour, we were running out of not only entertainment and patience but also water. Dinner too began to seem like a really good idea, with lunch a faint memory. Not being battle- and hardship-toughened ISAF or Afghan soldiers or guerrilla fighters, we attempted to persuade the ministry guards to allow our two Afghan drivers to leave the compound, go to a kebab place, and come back with food and water. That request, however, ended our stay at the Ministry of Mines since it brought us to the attention of the Afghan National Army (ANA) unit commander just outside of the ministry's gate. For the first time in nine hours, the ANA commander became aware of the fact that several VIP *farangis* (outsiders, an expression used for Westerners) were holed up in the ministry. That discovery extremely displeased the commander. He strongly berated the forlorn ministry guards, who had been as undisturbed by the attacks as the Afghan civilians on the streets, for not informing him of our presence. Then he ordered us out of the compound, not wanting responsibility for protecting six foreigners.

That set off a round of back-and-forth calls with ISAF headquarters. Our NATO handlers continued to be under lockdown and still considered the streets too risky for movement, especially with unexploded ordnance lying around. Perhaps the greatest security danger came from accidently provoking friendly fire from Afghan National Security Forces (ANSF) patrolling the streets while major buildings continued to be under attack and rumors of more suicide bombers in the city persisted.

Clearly determined that no foreigners would be his headache, the ANA commander wanted us off his hands irrespective of NATO's instructions and insisted that we vacate the building immediately. Over the course of the previous several hours, I had repeatedly suggested that we move to Serena Hotel, one of the luxury hotels in Kabul frequented by foreigners and also only 400 meters from the Ministry of Mines—in the opposite direction of ISAF headquarters. Although the Serena had been a popular target for the Taliban in the past (in 2008 the Taliban attacked the hotel and killed six people and injured another six), ISAF security now had no choice but to agree to our being moved there. Promptly we jumped into our two cars and made a mad dash for the hotel a short distance away down the now dark and deserted streets, narrowly avoiding a crash with another vehicle that was also barreling along at high speed. Near the front gates of Serena Hotel, the Afghan National Police (ANP) officers became extremely agitated and pointed their machine guns at us—understandably, since our two cars had arrived right in the middle of a siege and could have been driven by suicide bombers. Rolling down the car windows, we shouted that we were Westerners and the police should not shoot. After a few tense moments, all was resolved and we got safely into the hotel.

In a somewhat surreal scene, given that firefights were raging all around, we spent about half an hour negotiating with the Afghan receptionist over whether we could get NATO's discount rate for the Serena's pricey rooms. The young man, at least overtly oblivious to the mayhem outside, remained perfectly composed yet intransigent over the price. This behavior epitomized the Afghans' tough bargaining about the terms of the Westerners' presence in their country until and after 2014, such as during the protracted negotiations with the United States over the U.S.-Afghanistan long-term Strategic Partnership Agreement, even as their country continues to be deeply troubled by insecurity and dependent on the Western security and economic assistance.

After a rather opulent dinner—considering the circumstances of the firefight and Afghanistan's persisting poverty—we checked into our rooms. As luck would have it, I wound up alone in a junior suite in a distant wing of the hotel, far from the rest of my colleagues. While a more luxurious accommodation, it also happened to be on the side of the hotel closest to major explosions, machine-gun fire, armored truck movements, and chopper flyways—all just outside my windows. Renewed military action against the Haqqani attackers by ANSF kicked off just after midnight and lasted until about 6:30 a.m., guaranteeing I would not get one minute of sleep.

Moreover, in the first hour of that firefight, the gunfire was so close that I wondered if the Serena itself was under attack. Given the attractiveness of the hotel as a target for the Taliban and the Haqqanis, I decided to lie in bed fully dressed, just in case a quick getaway was needed, and watched Al Jazeera's coverage of the war in Sudan and the environmental problems in Australia, punctuated by the sounds of the battle taking place outside my windows. At eight in the morning, bleary eyed, I met up with my colleagues for breakfast. All of them were outrageously well rested, having slept through the night and not having heard one single gunshot.

The April 15 attacks were spectacular in their level of coordination and the sheer number of terrorist actions that the Taliban and the Haqqanis were able to carry out simultaneously in Kabul and across Afghanistan. The attacks also clearly exposed a serious intelligence failure. In what had become his standard political ploy, Afghanistan's President Hamid Karzai (earlier in the decade a close interlocutor of President George

W. Bush but now an embattled leader deeply alienated from and suspicious of Washington) blamed the intelligence failure on ISAF. But given that Afghanistan was well into the so-called transition—the NATO-Afghanistan agreed process to transfer control of the country's security, economic development, and governance to the Afghans, after a decade of Western presence—responsibility for the failure to prevent the attacks lay just as much with the Afghan intelligence and security services. (The term transition is at times used differently by various stakeholders in Afghanistan policy. NATO frequently uses the term in a restricted sense as a military phase to be followed by redeployment. The U.S. government often uses the term more broadly as one pillar of a larger political engagement with Afghanistan. And President Karzai sometimes uses the expression to denote the period through 2014, after which he talks about "transformation." My use of the term refers more broadly to the entire process—before and after 2014—of handing responsibility for security, political, and economic affairs over to the Afghan government, as well as any changes in the security, political, and economic order in Afghanistan resulting from that process.)

During the several weeks following the April 15 attacks, the ANSF managed to prevent at least two other large-scale attacks on Kabul but were unable to prevent a dramatic attack on the nearby Spozhmai resort hotel at Lake Qargha, which Kabulis use for a little bit of recreation.[7] The ANSF were also unable to prevent an attack by a female suicide bomber near the Kabul airport in September 2012 in response to a video mocking the Prophet Mohammad made by several individuals in the United States. Although such attacks do not alter the balance of power on the battlefield, they do significantly affect Afghans' perceptions of security—which of course is the intent of the insurgents. And indeed, although the April 15 attacks took the lives of less than a dozen Afghan security forces and only six Afghan civilians (the attackers let over ten civilians walk away unharmed), they did have a significant, if complicated, psychological impact. They demonstrated that even the most secure parts of Kabul can be breached. At the same time, the reaction of the ANSF for once inspired Afghans.[8] In particular, the special commando forces of the Afghan National Police who responded to the April 15 attacks performed well, demonstrating a real growth in capacity in the ANSF, our own group's experience with the Afghan National Army commander notwithstanding. The Afghan National Police forces managed to maintain better personal security than they did during a previous terrorist attack in Kabul on the Intercontinental Hotel when they charged headlong into fire and certain death. This time, throughout the day and night of the attacks, they were able to maintain command and control. Two months later, however, the Afghan National Security Forces' performance at the Spozhmai resort hotel attack was more mixed. The Afghan forces managed to evacuate over 250 hotel customers—no small feat—but ultimately needed to lean on their Western counterparts to end the Taliban siege.[9]

After a decade of fighting—starting with the relatively easy victory over the Taliban in 2001 and then featuring increasingly tough fighting against a reemergent Taliban insurgency—the growth of the Afghan security forces has become the lynchpin of the U.S. and NATO strategy to achieve success in Afghanistan and extricate themselves from the war there. As yet, however, the Taliban and its jihadi cohorts—the Haqqanis and Hezb-i-Islami—remain entrenched and robust. Although their influence has been weakened by the 2010 "surge" of U.S. military forces, they still exercise substantial sway over large parts of Afghanistan. The Afghan security forces are clearly making progress, but they still continue to be dependent on NATO's assistance for critical assets and capacities; and dangerous ethnic rifts and competing patronage networks continue to run through the Afghan National Security Forces.

In response to so-called insider attacks by ANSF members against ISAF soldiers, ISAF announced in late September 2012 that it would curtail the partnering of ISAF units with ANSF units below the battalion level, unless a special permission for a specific operation were obtained from a two-star regional command ISAF general in Afghanistan.[10] ISAF maintained that this policy did not fundamentally alter its strategy or the effectiveness of its military and training campaigns and that it was only temporary in response to the feared Afghan reactions to the U.S.-made video mocking Prophet Mohammad.[11] However, if these new rules of engagement and force protection requirements remained in place, if they were not temporary or substantially revised, they would, in fact, have widespread—and largely negative—implications for the counterinsurgency effort and for training the ANSF, since the vast majority of all counterinsurgency operations, from village patrols to military encounters with the Taliban, take place at below the battalion level.

Even before these ISAF strategy changes were announced and despite previous real improvements in the Afghan security forces, few Afghans believe that a better future is on the horizon after 2014. NATO and U.S. officials remain cautiously optimistic about the success of the counterinsurgency and stabilization campaign, even if acknowledging that progress is hard.[12] Thus Ambassador Ryan Crocker, who headed the U.S. Embassy in Afghanistan between July 2011 and July 2012, stated at the time of his departure that he considered the outbreak of another civil war in Afghanistan after 2014 unlikely.[13] But many Afghans fear there will be a renewed outbreak of civil war after 2014, when the NATO presence will be much reduced. This prospect of civil war and ethnic infighting after 2014 was foremost on the minds of most Afghans with whom I spoke on my last trip before writing this book—in April 2012.[14] As on my previous trips to Afghanistan over the past decade, these individuals included former and current Afghan government officials, both in Kabul and in various districts and provinces; journalists; civil society members and businessmen; officers of the ANA, ANP, and Afghan Local Police; Taliban and Hezb-i-Islami members; and ordinary Afghans, such as street vendors or truck drivers.[15] The success of the Afghan National Security Forces' response to the April attacks notwithstanding, most of my Afghan interlocutors were profoundly doubtful that the ANSF would be able to fill the security void created by the drawdown of ISAF forces and their far smaller and circumscribed presence after 2014.[16] To a degree, such a perception is driven by the Afghans' short time horizons. Experience has taught them not to trust promises; and the unstable security and economic environment they have faced over the past four decades leads them to make decisions based on immediate realities and to discount plans offered by Westerners. Continual robust performance and improvements of the ANSF, should they in fact materialize, will likely improve how Afghans perceive their forces. But as of the middle of 2012, few Afghans believed the ANSF capable of standing on their own after 2014 and preventing a significant deterioration in security and escalation of violence.

Worse yet, Afghans have become disconnected and alienated from the national government and the country's other power arrangements. They are profoundly dissatisfied with Kabul's inability and unwillingness to provide basic public services and with the widespread corruption of the power elites. They intensely resent the abuse of power, impunity, and lack of justice that have become entrenched over the past decade. The initial post-Taliban period of hope and promise did not last, as governance in Afghanistan became rapidly defined by weakly functioning state institutions unable and unwilling to uniformly enforce laws and policies. Characteristically, official and unofficial power brokers issue exceptions from law enforcement to their networks of clients, who are thus able to reap high economic benefits and even get away with major crimes. Murder, extortion, and land grabbing, often perpetrated by those in the government, have gone unpunished. At the same time, access to jobs, promotions, and economic rents has depended on being on good terms with the local strongman rather than on merit and hard work. The political patronage networks too have become more exclusionary. Local government officials have had only a limited capacity and motivation to redress the broader governance deficiencies.

The level of infighting among elites, much of it along ethnic and regional lines, is at a peak. The result is pervasive hedging on the part of key power brokers, including through the resurrection of semiclandestine or officially sanctioned militias. The hedging is equally pervasive on the part of ordinary Afghans, many of whom are looking for a way out of Afghanistan. Meanwhile, especially in the Pashtun areas that constitute the Taliban heartland, families will often send one son to join the ANA and another to join the Taliban—and possibly a third son to join the local strongman's militia—in an attempt to maximize the chances of being on the side of whoever wins control of the area where they live after 2014.

In short, most Afghans with whom I have talked are deeply skeptical and outright afraid of the post-2104 future. "After NATO forces are reduced, people will be so insecure that they will not even dare to leave their shoes outside of their door," a Pashtun tribal elder in the northern province of Baghlan told me.[17] There are many convincing reasons to doubt the stability of Afghanistan after 2014 and the success of the decade's efforts. After so much sacrificed blood and treasure, why should the continuing fragility of any painstaking achievements and the ominous destabilization of Afghanistan still matter to the United States and the international community?

The principal objective of U.S. policy in Afghanistan since the 9-11 attacks has been—and continues to be—to ensure that the country does not again become a haven for virulent *salafi* (ultraconservative Muslim) terrorist groups like al Qaeda. The premise underlying this policy is that if any part of Afghan territory once again comes under the control of salafi groups, or a Taliban sympathetic to such groups, it will provide them a safe haven for training and planning, increase the lethality and frequency of their terrorist attacks—including attacks against the United States—and enable them to more easily escape retaliation by the West.

There is a debate among scholars as to how closely the Taliban and al Qaeda are aligned today and how definitively the Taliban has learned that its association with al Qaeda generates the wrath of the United States and is extremely costly for the group.[18] Clearly, the two groups are not identical and do not have identical objectives. As detailed in chapter 11, many Taliban commanders seem to have soured on al Qaeda.[19] However, fully breaking with al Qaeda may nonetheless generate costs for the Taliban with other jihadi groups and with at least some of its members, and the movement needs to balance those costs against the costs of U.S. and international military pressure on the Taliban in retaliation for any persisting international terrorist links.

Though the Arab Spring may have severely eroded al Qaeda's influence and possibly demoralized some of its members, and though it is now largely displaced from Afghanistan to Pakistan, it has lost none of its zeal to strike Western countries and undermine governments in Asia, the Middle East, and Africa.[20] The group continues to look for opportunities to exploit and territories to colonize, even if only vicariously though proxies, as in Western and Eastern Africa, and even if some of its local alliances are only fleeting and unreliable.[21]

Suppose Afghanistan once again becomes inflamed by violence, or that the writ of Kabul weakens further and the country becomes even more atomized, with various insurgent and power broker networks controlling different parts of the country. In such an environment, anti-Western terrorist groups may once again establish a dangerous foothold in Afghanistan—whether with the support of the Taliban or without. On a small scale, an anti-Pakistan jihadi group led by the commander Fazlullah has already been able to do so in the rugged and highly contested terrain of eastern Afghanistan. There can be little confidence that in a violent, chaotic, and highly contested post-2014 Afghanistan, the Taliban would pick a fight with other jihadi groups, such as al Qaeda.

Irrespective of any support from the Taliban, al Qaeda remains a major concern and prime target. But there has been disagreement all along about the broader implications of this U.S. counterterrorism interest for U.S. strategy in and toward Afghanistan and its neighbors, especially Pakistan.

Four years into the Obama administration, the debate appears to have been won by those who argue that what happens on the ground in Afghanistan matters only to a limited degree for the successful prosecution of the anti–al Qaeda campaign, and that the needed counterterrorism operations against al Qaeda and its allies can be effectively conducted from the air, reducing the need for a foreign presence in Afghanistan itself.

But is this minimalist strategy sound? In fact, there are limits to what counterterrorism from afar and from the air can accomplish. To be sure, Predator drone attacks can be effective in eliminating terrorist leaders and disrupting operations. But human intelligence and cooperation from local actors on the ground are often critical for the success of counterterrorism operations, including intelligence input for the drones. Moreover, few Afghans, including the power brokers in charge of militias that have been cooperating with the United States, will have an interest in persisting in the effort if they believe that they will be abandoned to the mercy of the Taliban.

A strategy that in effect dismisses stability and state-building as objectives for Afghanistan also ignores the serious and very likely risk that an unstable Afghanistan will further destabilize Pakistan and, consequently, the entire Central and South Asian region. Pakistan's tribal areas as well as Baluchistan have been host to many of the salafi groups, and the Afghan Taliban uses these areas as safe havens. Thus Pakistan's cooperation in tackling these safe havens has been important for U.S. and ISAF operations in Afghanistan (even if such help is often not forthcoming, as explained in chapter 10). But if Afghanistan is unstable and harbors salafi groups that infiltrate into Pakistan, then Pakistan itself could become deeply destabilized and distracted from tackling its other crises, including militancy in the Punjab and a host of domestic calamities, such as intense political instability, economic atrophy, widespread poverty, and a severe energy crisis.

Still fearing encirclement by India, the more Pakistan feels threatened by a hostile government or instability in Afghanistan, the less likely it will be capable of dealing with its massive domestic challenges. The Pakistani state is already hollowed out, its administrative structures undergoing a steady decline since independence. Major macroeconomic deficiencies have increased, and deep poverty and marginalization persist amid a semifeudal distribution of power, often ineffective and corrupt political leadership, internal social and ethnic fragmentation, and compromised security forces.[22] The internal security challenge is far more insidious than that recently encountered by the Pakistani military in the tribal and Khyber-Pakhtunkhwa areas. In actuality, it is the Punjabi groups, such as the Punjabi Taliban, Lashkar-i-Taiba, and Sipah-i-Sahaba, who pose a deeper threat to Pakistan.

Extreme internal fragmentation in Pakistan and a loss of central control, particularly if it extended to the military, could set off one of the most dangerous security threats in Asia and in the world. After all, Pakistan is a large, nuclear-armed Muslim country that coexists in only a precarious peace with its neighbor India.

A disintegration of the Afghan state after 2014 or an outbreak of intense fighting will be a great boost to salafi groups in Pakistan and throughout the world: once again, a great power will be seen as having been defeated by the salafists in Afghanistan. From a strategic communications standpoint, few areas are as important as Afghanistan. The perception that the United States has been beaten there does not require that the Taliban take over the country. From the salafi perspective, merely a gradual but steady crumbling of the Kabul government, with a progressively greater accretion of territory and power by the Taliban, would be sufficient to claim victory. An outbreak of civil war after 2014 would feed the same perception, even if the Taliban did not rapidly take over Kabul and still could not control the majority of Afghanistan's territory.

Finally, switching to a minimalist strategy that is indifferent to stability inside Afghanistan has implications for America's reputation—and self-image—as a country that can be relied upon to honor its commitments. In mobilizing support for Operation Enduring Freedom, the United States made a pledge to the Afghan people to help them improve their difficult condition and not abandon them once again. Although often caricatured as anti-Western, antigovernment, antimodern, and stuck in medieval times, Afghans crave what others do: relief from violence and insecurity; sufficient economic progress to escape dire, grinding poverty; access to justice; and a significant say in how they are governed. Concern by the United States for the well-being of the people of Afghanistan would not in itself justify continuing what has turned out to be an immensely costly effort. But since the United States did intervene—albeit for other reasons—it has an obligation to help deal with the elemental needs of the people whose lives its actions have so profoundly altered. As Secretary of State Colin Powell argued in the summer of 2002, when warning President George W. Bush about the consequences of invading Iraq, with intervention comes responsibility for the lives of the local population. "You are going to be the proud owner of 25 million people," he said with purposeful irony. "You will own all their hopes, aspirations, and problems. You'll own it all."[23]

This range of considerations—not just the threats and worries but also the aspirations of the Afghan people—should have animated and guided U.S. policy. But an analysis of the evolution of Washington's strategies in Afghanistan and of their ambiguous and unsteady character reveals an insufficient appreciation of the stakes and interests as well as of the desires of the Afghan people.

How is it that this enterprise—which started out with a rapid toppling of the Taliban regime and a delighted embrace by the Afghans of their liberation from its brutal rule—now, more than a decade later, hangs by a thread, and many Afghans believe that a civil war is on the horizon?

Many will answer that the United States and the international community tried to do too much in Afghanistan: they got bogged down in a "nation-building" mission that attempted to bring "Valhalla" to a people who wanted to be left untouched by the outside world.[24] The foreigners expended resources on a state-building task alien to the locals, who did not want a central government and were satisfied with their tribal ways— a mission that therefore was bound to fail.[25] The United States and its allies should have concentrated on simply destroying the Taliban regime and al Qaeda's capabilities and safe haven in Afghanistan.[26]

This book argues the opposite: the United States and the international community never strongly and consistently demanded that the Afghan government give the people what they crave most in addition to security—namely, justice, the rule of law, and an accountable government. Instead, the post-Taliban state has frequently failed to deliver the elemental public goods and services the people desire, and has also been outright malign from the perspective of many of the country's citizens. The emergent regime has been characterized by rapaciousness, corruption, tribal discrimination, and predatory behavior on the part of government officials and power brokers closely aligned with the state. Crime—including land theft; corrupt, nepotistic, and unfulfilled contracts; and embezzlement—has spread rapidly throughout the country.

Meanwhile, since being routed from Kabul in 2001, the Taliban has managed in many places to step into the lacuna of effective and accountable state power and good governance. It has offered itself as a protector to marginalized communities and those unable to capture rents from the post-2001 windfalls, acting as a patron capable of redressing these deficiencies. Although brutal and repressive, the Taliban nonetheless appeals to those alienated from the Afghan government and provides its own brand of draconian—but predictable—order. At the same time, more often than not, the Taliban insurgents have simply imposed their rule on the population through the barrels of their Kalashnikovs. Although the causes of the group's emergence and reemergence are multiple and varied, the weakness of the state and the poor functioning of official governance have been crucial enablers of the movement's ability to gain traction with local populations.

The United States and the international community have not adequately focused on restraining pernicious power brokers and corruption, nor have they used their leverage to promote accountability. Rather, they systematically underemphasized good governance and subordinated it to short-term battlefield priorities, pushing it aside and postponing focus on it, unable to muster the resources and persistence needed to improve governance. Throughout the decade's effort, Washington thus remained ambivalent about whether to define the mission in Afghanistan in narrow counterterrorism terms or to genuinely embrace a state-building effort. Although the latter was occasionally emphasized, the difficulties of trying to improve governance in an increasingly corrupt system and the perceived needs of short-term military imperatives constantly eroded Washington's commitment to any broad state-building effort. At other times, the international community often defined good governance in ways that were contrary to the notions of good governance held by many Afghans. And as President Karzai lost legitimacy not just internationally but also domestically, he would try to shift the responsibility for bad governance in Afghanistan onto the international community, blaming it for corruption and a host of Afghanistan's other problems.

To be clear, whatever the many shortcomings of the U.S. and international efforts, the blame for bad governance in Afghanistan lies first and foremost on the shoulders of the Afghan government and the many problematic Afghan power brokers. However, this does not absolve the United States and its allies of their mistakes—which have been "sins" of omission as well as commission.

In short, the United States never really embraced the aspirations of the Afghan people. The Bush administration over-promised what it could accomplish in Afghanistan, under-reached in its goals, and under-resourced its efforts, creating expectations both in Afghanistan and the United States it could not fulfill. The Obama administration, on the other hand, mostly defined its goals and expectations in Afghanistan in ways that were indifferent to Afghan aspirations. Thus, having started in 2001 as Operation Enduring Freedom to effect a presumably swift regime change to drive the al Qaeda–harboring Taliban from power, the U.S. military intervention in Afghanistan morphed by the mid-2000s into a full-blown counterinsurgency effort against the Taliban's drive to retake control of the country. In 2009 the Obama administration inherited the U.S. and international mission there in a condition of deep crisis. The Bush administration's economy-of-force, minimal-input approach for Afghanistan and its prioritization of Iraq had left a structural vacuum in Afghanistan that motivated national and local power brokers to return to their narrow pursuit of immediate power and profit maximization, at the expense of building effective and accountable governance. Although the Obama administration tried to reverse this negative syndrome, its imposition of a time limit on the deployment of U.S. forces only reinforced the short-term, what's-in-it-for-me calculus of the Afghan power brokers. The result has been a continuing uphill struggle to devise mechanisms to improve governance and sustain security gains. Henceforth, and still prevailing at the time of this writing, the United States and its allies have been wrestling with a fundamental predicament: the Taliban insurgency feeds on the condition of inept and corrupt governance, yet the United States and its international partners have been unable and often unmotivated to induce better governance from the Karzai regime and unofficial power brokers.

The Obama administration came into office determined to make the war in Afghanistan and its spillover into Pakistan a key focus of its foreign policy. In comparison with the Bush administration, the Obama administration significantly increased the military, economic, and civilian resources available for the war; yet it has found itself facing some of the same dilemmas and challenges as its predecessor.

Insufficient security has prevented many of the civilians in ISAF and those working for coalition governments from interacting fully with the Afghans. Isolated at the bases, they have had to acquire information and intelligence from problematic interlocutors who often distort their reports to serve their own interests. Consequently, as detailed in chapters 5, 6, and 7, Washington has often been unable to identify those responsible for discriminatory and abusive policies or to persuade Kabul to crack down on such behavior.

Throughout the preceding decade, including during the Obama administration, the United States and the international community struggled to resolve whether the mission in Afghanistan is one of narrowly defined counterterrorism or whether it also includes broader state-building, and hence needs considerably more resources. Oscillation between the two definitions of the U.S.-ISAF mission both raised and disappointed the expectations of the Afghan population (see chapters 2, 3, and 4). In this context, the Taliban was able to exploit the unredressed government deficiencies to gain traction with local populations (see chapter 3 and 4).

The limited willingness of the United States and its allies to devote the necessary resources for the larger state-building mission, including the military aspects of counterinsurgency, has led to various problematic shortcuts on the battlefield—crucially the reliance on manipulative power brokers and controversial paramilitary forces, such as the Afghan Local Police, both of whom undermine governance in Afghanistan, in the present and the long term (see chapters 5, 6, and 8). Just like in Woody Allen's *Bullets over Broadway* movie, it was the various Afghan power broker mafias who in many ways ended up writing the script of the Afghanistan stabilization effort. But unlike in Allen's movie, the outcome has not been uplifting, let alone funny. Mafia rule, especially if it does better than the state in providing security, regulatory services, and socio-economic benefits, can gain a great deal of legitimacy and political capital among the population.[27] But a fundamental problem with Afghanistan's post-Taliban political and economic arrangements has been that the mafias that have emerged have been highly abusive, capricious, and critically deficient in the provision of either security or economic benefits to the wider population. And since many of the mafia-like power brokers have been linked to the Afghan government and even frequently held official positions in the government, many Afghans have come to see the state itself as a thuggish mafia racket without benefits. At the same time, Washington has continually remained conflicted over whether and how to tackle corruption (see chapters 2, 5, and 6). Efforts to work through the national government in Kabul or through local officials often failed to redress the governance deficiencies.

Often, the international definition of good governance in Afghanistan—particularly suppression of poppy cultivation—has remained at odds with the human security needs of the Afghan people. Although the Obama administration's counternarcotics strategy, at least in design, broke with previous counterproductive policies, its implementation often problematically mimicked the Bush strategy, as chapter 9 shows. Chapter 9 also reveals how, far from uniformly encouraging needed economic development, the large amounts of economic aid that flowed into Afghanistan without effective monitoring instead generated their own problems. Often designed as short-term programs to buy love rather than catalyze sustainable development, the aid flows themselves encouraged some of the predatory and rapacious behavior that underlies bad governance in Afghanistan.

The Obama administration also took office resolved to design a regional framework conducive to a stable and prosperous Afghanistan, one that would transform Washington's relationship with Pakistan from a transactional one to a strategic partnership. But Islamabad turned out to be as problematic an ally for the Obama administration as for the Bush administration, and by 2012 the U.S.-Pakistan relationship reached one of its historic lows. And although they are far less pernicious for the stabilization effort than Pakistan, most of Afghanistan's neighbors are still competing with one another and persist in interfering in Afghan affairs, as described in chapter 10.

As discussed in chapters 2 and 11, the military plan of the Obama administration originally assumed that by the time the United States and ISAF began scaling down their presence, they would hand over to the Afghans large parts of the country's territory secured. Four years later, some real progress had been achieved, such as in central Helmand and Kandahar—both of which used to be either intense battle zones or under the Taliban's sway. But as this book goes to press, the territory cleared that is being handed over to the Afghans is much smaller than had been projected. Furthermore, the United States and ISAF are not only handing the Afghans a stalemated war, they are attempting to increase the Afghan National Security Forces' capacity enough to beat back the Taliban insurgency while simultaneously restricting their own capacity to operate in Afghanistan. Meanwhile, as also detailed in chapter 11, negotiations with the Taliban have so far not gained any real traction.

Yet despite all of these negative developments and problematic trends, and despite the deep anxiety with which many Afghans look at the 2014 transition, a failure of the international effort to leave Afghanistan with a stable government is not preordained. Afghanistan is a complex place, where local realities are often highly diverse. There are glimmers of hope. Security has improved in some parts of the country. Afghan security forces exhibit growing capabilities, even as they continue to be challenged by many deep problems. And a new generation of Afghans is rising, many of whom are motivated to take on the problematic power brokers, rise above ethnic cliques, and bring the rule of law to Afghanistan.

Yes, the United States and its international partners in Afghanistan are exhausted and focused on getting out of there. At the end of the four years since Bush turned the problem over to Obama, Washington's talk on Afghanistan has mostly been about irretrievably winding down the war.[28] However, the United States and the international community still can—and should—attempt to empower those Afghans who are determined to pursue the broader interests of the people over narrow power and profit maximization.

At the July 2012 Tokyo Conference on Afghanistan, the international community's insistence that the Afghan government start seriously combating corruption and improving governance as conditions for continued economic support induced President Karzai to once again publicly commit himself to tackling corruption. Whether he will actually enforce any of the provisions from the grab bag of policies he announced and whether the international community will have the wherewithal to hold him to his word remain highly uncertain. The reshuffling of key cabinet posts and governorship positions that Karzai undertook in late summer and fall 2012 seems to indicate that once again he was privileging personal loyalty and ethnic kinship over competence.[29] Such signs are not auspicious.

The faster the United States scales back its efforts in Afghanistan and the more rapidly ISAF forces reduce their presence before 2014, the more the leverage of the international community will be diminished as well. Any improvements in Afghan military and police capacities also will be jeopardized and increases in security undermined. But equally, without major improvements in governance, it is difficult to see how lasting stability after 2014 could be achieved, whatever the balance of remaining military forces on the ground. Without adequate governance in Afghanistan, the international stabilization effort will at most delay the crumbling of the current Afghan state and the outbreak of yet another phase of civil war.

As this analysis shows, the United States and the international community have yet to make various decisions that will have an impact on many trends in Afghanistan. Despite a reduction in leverage due to upcoming drawdowns, these decisions can encourage or discourage stability, and they will influence the country's—and the region's—security, political, and economic developments. In the concluding chapter, I provide a detailed set of recommendations based on the premise that the United States and its allies still have the capacity to significantly affect the situation in Afghanistan, for better or for worse. These recommendations include

—emphasizing U.S. and international engagement with Afghanistan from 2015 onward,

—maintaining an international military presence and robust training and advisory capacity until 2014 and beyond,

—reducing corruption and improving governance,

—reining in the warlords,

—reining in the Afghan Local Police and other militias,

—synchronizing counternarcotics efforts with good governance,

—prioritizing economic sustainability and capacity building, and

—using negotiations with the Taliban as another mechanism to improve governance.

Devoting whatever capacities and will that can still be gathered in the West to emphasize and encourage good governance does not guarantee success: many of the larger and deeper trends in Afghanistan may now be outside the control and beyond the leverage of the international community. But exiting fast, defining the mission from 2015 onward only in very narrow counterterrorism terms, and writing off good governance will only guarantee failure.

Washington's Strategies in Afghanistan since 2001

U.S. policies toward and operations in Afghanistan since the terrorist attacks of September 11, 2001, have been largely a sequence of reflexive reactions in search of a strategy. President George W. Bush stated reasons for driving the Taliban from power, the military undertook operations, Congress committed troops and dollars, and goals for Afghanistan's future were proclaimed by administration officials, but often the U.S. actions—and words justifying them—did not derive from or add up to a comprehensive and systematically prioritized set of ends-means relationships. At other times, when the White House actually articulated a broad strategy, its price tag was severely underestimated, resulting in either inadequate resourcing or a recasting of the strategy to match the limited means Washington was willing to devote. And in general, neither the strategies nor the operations took serious account of the aspirations of the Afghan people and their need and desire for good governance.

Lack of Clarity and Consistency in Defining the Mission

From 2001 onward, the U.S. government and other members of the international coalition have struggled with how to define the mission in Afghanistan. For the allies, the question for years was whether to characterize the effort as a peacekeeping operation (which many chose to do despite the level of insecurity in the country and a lack of peace to keep) or a counterinsurgency and counterterrorism mission. For the United States, the question was whether to set the objective as state building that

results in a stable central Afghan governing entity or as limited counterterrorism that could be accomplished without ensuring that a stable
Afghan government was in place.

The Bush administration vacillated between the two characterizations
of the mission's scope. It conceived of and resourced Operation Enduring
Freedom as a limited military intervention, confined to the removal of
the Taliban government in order to destroy al Qaeda's capabilities and
deprive it of a safe haven. But the Bush administration ultimately recognized that it could not simply leave the country after driving the Taliban
from Kabul. Moreover, the need to generate public support in America
for the war, even in the wake of 9-11, led the Bush administration to
adopt much broader rhetoric about its goals in Afghanistan, including
bringing democracy to a brutally oppressed people and emancipating its
suffering women. At the same time, however, it continued providing slim
resources for the military and economic efforts in the country, inadequate
for either responding to the growing insurgency or for effective reconstruction. [1] The under-resourcing worsened as the White House shifted
its focus to Iraq. Thus, although U.S. policy in Afghanistan was evolving
increasingly into state building even during the Bush administration, the
war in Iraq, with its demands on troops and budgets, constantly pushed
the effort in Afghanistan in the opposite direction. The Iraq war drained
away resources for Afghanistan, stretching them thinner even as goals for
Afghanistan grew, thus guaranteeing that the capabilities would continue
to be insufficient and that implementation would suffer.[2]

Moreover, even while the effort in Afghanistan took on the trappings
of a state-building effort, the policies adopted did not sufficiently focus on
promoting good governance. Instead, the lack of U.S. and international
military resources led to reliance on warlords with a long record of serious
human rights abuses for continuing military operations against the remnants of the Taliban, strengthening these power brokers and weakening
Kabul's already tenuous writ.[3] The early intervention policy of handing
out bags of cash to the warlords for their counterterrorism services had
the same effect.[4] The visible embrace of the warlords by the U.S. military
and Washington's unresponsiveness to President Karzai's early requests
that Washington disarm, neutralize, and disempower the warlords progressively led the Afghan president to seek accommodation with them and
gutted his will to challenge them. Instead, Karzai became conditioned to
strike bargains with the warlords and appease them. The early minimal

troop deployments to Afghanistan necessitated collaboration with the anti-Taliban warlords, but often Washington also chose to ignore their misbehavior. Thus, from the very beginning of the intervention, when there was the largest window of opportunity to embrace Afghan aspirations for good governance and shape the outcome, Washington neglected to commit itself to rebuilding Afghanistan in the right way.

The Obama administration inherited the war at a time when the military situation on the battlefield was going very poorly. The Taliban and Haqqani insurgencies had ramped up (see the next chapter), and the quality of Afghan governance was progressively deteriorating. Afghanistan was experiencing the greatest insecurity since 2001 as well as intense corruption.[5] During his 2008 presidential campaign, Barack Obama emphasized Afghanistan as the important yet unfinished "war of necessity," unlike the "war of choice" in Iraq that he promised to terminate as quickly as possible.

But despite the election rhetoric, from the moment the Obama administration took over, it struggled with some of the very same dilemmas that perplexed the Bush administration. Since al Qaeda was the primary source of terrorist threats against the United States, was it also necessary to continue combating the Taliban? Could an effective counterterrorism mission be prosecuted essentially just from the air and offshore? Or was it necessary to defeat the resurgent Taliban on the ground and build up a stable Afghan government? Should the U.S. military engagement be intensified—with the all blood, treasure, and domestic ramifications that would entail—or should the U.S. military engagement be significantly scaled back?

These competing definitions of the objectives embodied very different policies, force postures and military strategies, and civilian components, such as economic development programs. They were premised on very different behavior from the Afghans and created different expectations in Kabul, the rest of the country, and Pakistan. They also generated different expectations from the domestic constituencies of governments contributing forces to the international coalition. The persistent wavering about objectives continued to complicate the Afghanistan campaign even during the Obama administration.

One important source for the ambivalence and oscillation during the Obama administration was the unresolved, serious tensions and disagreements about and varying perspectives on Afghanistan among the advisors and policymakers. There were also disagreements during the Bush years, but in the Obama administration, they became highly visible. [6] The purpose of this book is not to recount these internal debates and the policy process in Washington but rather to analyze the impact of the decisions made, and not made, on developments in Afghanistan. It is useful, however, to identify two broad camps that emerged early in the Obama administration and have continued to shape the options being considered. One camp included Vice President Joseph Biden and members of the National Security Council, such as Dennis McDonough and Ben Rhodes, who contended that the sole objective in Afghanistan should be to destroy al Qaeda's capacities in eastern Afghanistan and western Pakistan, and that this limited objective could be effectively accomplished through the use of drones and Special Operations Forces with a small number of U.S. ground troops. A second camp, reportedly including Secretary of State Hillary Clinton and having many supporters in the Pentagon, argued that a serious and expanded counterinsurgency effort was critical even for the success of the counterterrorism mission. Meanwhile, the assistant to the president and deputy national security advisor for Iraq and Afghanistan, General Douglas Lute, whom President Obama retained from the Bush administration, kept compiling documents on how the war in Afghanistan was going badly.

Even though the Obama administration ultimately did decide to increase the amount of military and economic resources devoted to the war, its rhetoric about the goals in Afghanistan became far more circumscribed than that of the Bush administration. President Obama first announced his Afghanistan-Pakistan strategy in March 2009, after a two-month crash review to establish a strategy in time for NATO's April 2009 summit in Strasbourg.[7] The strategy consisted of a broad counterinsurgency effort that sought to reverse the worsening security situation in Afghanistan and to create the necessary environment for a large-scale economic development effort, including a strong agricultural program that would also reduce the Afghan population's economic dependence on poppy cultivation. Yet, despite its multifaceted and comprehensive approach, the policy was couched in fairly narrow counterterrorism terms, emphasizing mainly the need to prevent the reestablishment of al Qaeda safe havens in Afghanistan.

Although Secretary of State Hillary Clinton would occasionally express strong commitment to women's rights in Afghanistan, human rights overall and democracy were emphasized far less in the rhetoric of the Obama administration than in that of the Bush administration.[8] Even before the completion of the Afghanistan early review, Secretary of Defense Robert Gates told the U.S. Congress that "if we set ourselves the objective of creating some sort of Central Asian Valhalla over there, we will lose," maintaining that there was not enough "time, patience, or money" to pursue overly ambitious goals in Afghanistan.[9] He also insisted that as the Bush administration goals for Afghanistan evolved, they became "too broad and too far into the future" and that instead the United States should focus on narrower goals: "My own personal view is that our primary goal is to prevent Afghanistan from being used as a base for terrorists and extremists to attack the United States and our allies, and whatever else we need to do flows from that objective."[10]

Starting with the president's speech on the findings of the March 2009 review that officially launched his Afghanistan policy, the White House kept describing the mission as counterterrorism, rarely uttered the word governance, and never dared speak about state building. The actual March 2009 review document contained rather extensive language on improving governance in Afghanistan, but such emphasis was hardly ever reiterated by the president in public speeches.[11] The nearly total emphasis on counterterrorism in the public declarations by the White House about the war was driven by fear that the U.S. public, particularly the Democratic base, believing Operation Iraqi Freedom to have been a fiasco and harboring strong doubts that reforming governance in Afghanistan was necessary or feasible, could easily sour on the whole very expensive undertaking in Afghanistan.[12]

However, this extremely narrow, U.S.-centered definition of the objectives failed to resonate with the Afghan people. The increase in the military effort—justified to the American public as a preventive against more attacks on the U.S. homeland—for them meant more fighting, more civilian casualties, and more disruption to their lives.[13] What they wanted to hear was how the sacrifices ahead would improve their condition—not only by reducing the brutality and oppression of the growing Taliban insurgency but also by reducing the venality and abuse they experienced from the Afghan government and its power-broker cronies. Instead of building upon and energizing the aspirations of Afghan people, the March 2009 White House Afghanistan policy announcement dashed their expectations and hopes.

Worse yet, 2009 turned out to be a year of lost opportunities. While momentum continued to be wasted in countering the insurgency and corruption in Afghanistan, apathy in Washington deepened. The 2009 presidential election in Afghanistan that ultimately resulted in the reelection of President Karzai critically soured the White House on the Afghanistan effort. As detailed in chapter 6, the fraud and corruption that pervaded the election further damaged President Karzai's standing with President Obama and weakened an already frail relationship. It also damaged the already poor relationship of President Obama and the White House with Richard Holbrooke, the special representative for Afghanistan and Pakistan.[14] Tasked with coordinating Afghanistan and Pakistan policies in Washington and getting all the different agencies and stakeholders on the same page, Holbrooke was brought into the administration by his long-time friend, Secretary Clinton. But from the start, President Obama was cool to him, and the National Security Council sought to undercut him.[15] Holbrooke did manage to compel certain agencies, such as the United States Agency for International Development and the Department of Agriculture, to adopt development policies they did not like but that were pushed by the Pentagon (as detailed in chapter 9).[16] But Holbrooke never succeeded in getting on the same wavelength with the White House. Instead, President Obama blamed him for the handling of the 2009 election fiasco—both for failing to stop the fraud and for exposing that Washington was impotent to stop the fraud.[17] Critically, the failure to avert the cheating in the elections further reinforced the belief of many Afghans that the United States was not serious about demanding and enforcing accountability and better governance in Afghanistan.[18]

It also soon became obvious that the March 2009 review did not adequately assess the resources needed to severely weaken the Taliban's military capacity. The White House was shocked by the August 2009 report from the U.S. and ISAF commander General Stanley McChrystal that he lacked the resources to accomplish the mission and reverse the continually deteriorating security situation in Afghanistan. And far more than the March review, McChrystal's assessment keenly focused on the poor state of governance in Afghanistan.[19] Although Obama was wary of the military drawing the United States into another open-ended war, he could not discount McChrystal's systematic and insightful analysis, which was the product and synthesis of authoritative civilian as well as military experts on Afghanistan. The report thus precipitated a second

Obama administration review and subsequent fundamental reconsideration of the administration's Afghanistan policy.

President Obama was, of course, right to undertake due diligence and carefully study the increases in U.S. blood and treasure that implementing the McChrystal report would require, so as not to blindly fall into a potential quagmire. But the amount of time Obama's second review took—hawks and doves alike claimed he was "dithering"—further undermined the already fragile confidence in the United States, among allies, and within the Afghan population that major progress in Afghanistan would be achieved and that Washington would have the stamina to see it through.

The outcome of the second White House review of U.S. Afghanistan policy was unveiled in December 2009. The new policy agreed to "surge" U.S. forces further—by another 30,000. Along with the increase in military capabilities, the beefing up of resources that the United States was dedicating to Afghanistan also included a significant increase in U.S. civilian capacities, the so-called civilian surge that was to more than triple the U.S. government's civilian presence in Afghanistan.[20] But the increase in military resources in particular was far smaller than General McChrystal hoped. Although the requested number of troops remained classified, the press widely reported that the maximum sought was another 80,000, with 40,000 being the minimum number for which the general would settle; instead, he ended up with 25 percent less than that.[21] Moreover, the second White House review also imposed a timeline on how long the surge troops would stay in Afghanistan: not past the 2012 summer.

The second review did publicly stress governance. After the Afghanistan election fiasco, the widespread corruption and poor quality of governance in Afghanistan were very much the subject of focus in the Obama administration, the U.S. Congress, and news coverage of Afghanistan. Moreover, a memorandum from then U.S. ambassador to Afghanistan Karl Eikenberry that was leaked to the press described in excruciating detail the venality and incompetence in Kabul and argued against an increase in U.S. troop levels in Afghanistan.[22] Accordingly, the December 2009 Afghanistan review statement by President Obama did underscore governance, with some sharply worded language: "The days of providing blank checks are over. . . . And going forward, we will be clear about what we expect from those who receive our assistance. We'll support Afghan ministries, governors, and local leaders that combat corruption and deliver for the people. We expect those who are ineffective or corrupt to be held accountable."[23]

But despite the language of the moment, the Obama administration did not manage to hold badly performing government officials in Afghanistan accountable. Instead, it struggled to design and implement robust, effective anticorruption efforts and policies to improve governance. Furthermore, prioritizing governance was never uniformly embraced by all key U.S. agencies and actors, and, as described in chapter 6, soon the exigencies of the military campaign seemed to push against devoting a lot of energy to the knotty governance problems in Afghanistan.

At the end of the day, the dominant theme of the December 2009 review was not governance but timelines: the timeline on implementing the surge of U.S. troops and an unspoken but very strongly implied time *limit* on any extensive U.S. military presence in Afghanistan. The White House meant to use the timelines to Afghanize the war, so as to avoid miring the United States in "another Vietnam" and to pressure the Afghan government to step up to the challenge of providing for its security and effectively governing in Afghanistan. But the imposition of the timeline did not induce Afghan government officials to reduce corruption and improve governance. Instead, it risked jeopardizing the military gains of the surge and contributing to a sense among the Afghans that the United States may not succeed in the effort and would abandon them. Officials and policy mavens around the world became preoccupied with guessing how fast the United States (and hence also its allies, whose resolve critically depended on Washington's) would get out. Unfortunately, the timeline announcements and conjectures and the subsequent talk about "winding the war down" perpetuated and intensified the kind of Afghan behavior that privileges short-term horizons and immediate efforts to maximize power and profit as quickly as possible before it all comes down.[24]

The back-and-forth on what the mission in Afghanistan was all about and which strategies and resources were necessary and sufficient for the accomplishment of the objective also generated a profound uncertainty within the Obama administration as to whether a negotiated solution with the Taliban was possible and appropriate. Since the middle of the decade, several U.S. allies, including the United Kingdom, have privately called for and explored ways to negotiate with the Taliban, arguing that the conflict could not be brought to an end in the absence of a political process and a negotiated agreement.[25] But the Bush administration had

branded the Taliban as an enemy it was vital to defeat, not to legitimize. After all, it was the Taliban who provided Osama bin Laden and al
Qaeda, the perpetrators of 9-11, with safe havens for many years.

However, even in the early days of his administration, President
Obama expressed a willingness to engage in talks with the Taliban, even
if only to split off elements that could be reconciled.[26] Still, the Obama
administration also questioned whether the Taliban could be trusted to
uphold any agreement to break with al Qaeda. The question was animated by the previous bad outcomes of British negotiations with the
Taliban in Musa Qala, Afghanistan, in October 2006 and a series of
Pakistani government negotiated ceasefires with Pakistani Taliban and
other jihadi insurgents in South and North Waziristan between 2004
and 2008.[27] In each case, the Taliban groups, given almost free rein in
the area of the ceasefire, ended up violating the terms of the ceasefire.
As a result, the insurgents' power was strengthened while local tribal
structures opposing the Taliban were weakened.[28] In the case of Pakistan's negotiations, the weak terms of the ceasefires and the lack of their
enforcement by the Pakistani military stemmed from the fact that the
Pakistani military and intelligence services long supported and coddled
the various militant groups.[29] Given how vigorously the United States
had previously opposed Pakistan's negotiations with Pakistani Taliban
groups and their affiliates, it was particularly sensitive for Washington to
accept strategic negotiations with the Afghan Taliban.

The Obama administration also was conflicted as to what other red
lines the United States could not compromise in any negotiations. Would
the Taliban have to disarm, call off its armed struggle, and accept the
Afghan constitution as a precondition for negotiations or would those
be the desired outcomes? How important were women's rights for a successful outcome in Afghanistan to be achieved from the U.S. perspective?
How far advanced would the counterinsurgency campaign need to be to
exert maximum pressure on the Taliban? When would the United States,
international community, and Kabul have the strongest hand: before the
surge was finished and when it still threatened the Taliban, or after it had
degraded the Taliban's capacities but U.S. troops were on their way out of
Afghanistan?[30] What was the relationship between strategic negotiations
with the Taliban and "reintegration," that is, luring individual Taliban
fighters and hostile tribes away with economic incentives and amnesty?[31]
Would the "reintegrated" be given jobs, however generated for them,

and sent back to their villages, or be rearmed under the various militia programs in Afghanistan and sent back to fight the Taliban?[32] What kind of confidence-building measures would be tolerable for the United States: a release of Taliban prisoners from Guantanamo into someone else's custody, a ceasefire zone, or something else? Should Pakistan be brought into the negotiations, and if so, how?

After much deliberation, the Obama administration finally decided to pursue prospects for negotiations. In January 2010, Secretary Clinton publicly endorsed talking to the Taliban: "You don't make peace with your friends," Clinton stated at the time. "You have to be willing to engage with your enemies if you expect to create a situation that ends an insurgency or . . . marginalizes the remaining insurgents."[33] Still, questions and tensions continued about the modalities of the negotiations. Holbrooke was eager to move into negotiations quickly whereas the U.S. military, including General David Petraeus, who replaced General McChrystal as the commander of U.S. and NATO forces in Afghanistan in July 2010, argued that the military surge would first have to run its course and the Taliban's capacities be degraded before any talks could fully get under way.[34] The military prevailed, and U.S. overtures for negotiations were thus delayed for several months. Even after the Obama administration reconciled itself to negotiating with the Taliban, the process has been sluggish and fitful, and so far has gained little traction, largely due to similar ambivalence within the Taliban about its own need to negotiate and how.[35]

Moreover, as the subsequent chapters show in detail, all the strategic questions—even when seemingly resolved at the highest policy levels—became immeasurably more complex at the operational and implementation levels. When there appeared to be strategic clarity, imperatives and exigencies in the field often intruded and subverted the strategic decisions. Ground-level complications and contradictions also added to the accumulated exhaustion and frustration from nine years of war. The resolve to encourage and demand better governance in Afghanistan became one of the first imperatives to wither, and the standards for defining good governance got rapidly downgraded.

By the end of 2010, even before the military surge could take full effect on the battlefield, the mindset in the White House and in the capitals of allies was all about handing the war over to the Afghans. Thus, at the November 2010 NATO Summit in Lisbon, the Unites States, its allies, and the Afghan government agreed on a formal "transition" process wherein responsibility for security would be gradually transferred to the Afghan government. That process included intensifying and speeding up the training of the Afghan National Security Forces (ANSF) and increasing their size to take on a Taliban that was expected to be weakened but still present after 2014. The transition process would begin in early 2011 and be completed by the end of 2014, with all the U.S. surge forces removed from Afghanistan by the end of September 2012. Afterwards, the pace of further drawdowns would be "steady" and the mission would switch from "combat to support."[36]

At the May 2012 NATO Summit in Chicago, the United States and NATO confirmed that the ISAF mission in Afghanistan would be completed by the end of 2014, even though the United States and its allies committed themselves to an additional ten-year period of "transformation," the exact shape and scope of which was yet to be specified. By mid-2013, however, Afghans would assume lead responsibility for security throughout their entire country.

The Unanswered Questions of the U.S.-Afghanistan Long-Term Strategic Partnership

The run-up to the May 2012 Chicago conference featured, once again, a redefinition and narrowing down of U.S. goals and also, paradoxically, a mad dash to complete the protracted negotiation with the Afghan government on a long-term "strategic partnership" with the United States. The partnership was to reassure the Afghans that the United States would not abandon them once again and that it would not completely pull the plug on the Afghanistan effort at the end of 2014. In seeking to outline the parameters of the continuing U.S. engagement in Afghanistan, including militarily, the agreement was meant to be a confidence-building measure for the Afghans. But facing both skilled diplomacy and sheer obduracy from the Afghan government, the United States almost had to plead with Karzai to sign the agreement meant to make the Afghans feel better about their future.

Two issues had been major obstacles to signing the deal: night raids and prisons and detentions. Night raids had become a favorite tool of the U.S. military and ISAF, allowing them to catch unsuspecting Taliban commanders as they rested in the shelter of a house overnight. But they were strongly opposed by the Afghan people, who intensely resented having their houses invaded—a matter of particular social sensitivity—and their men taken away and detained for weeks, months, or years, on what the families often claimed was faulty intelligence. Cultural norms of extending hospitality, even to strangers, often make Afghans feel obliged to provide overnight accommodations to visitors or passers-by. Many Afghans thus deeply resent being arrested for this kind of contact with the Taliban, all the more so given that the constant presence of Taliban members in bazaars and around mosques in particular areas makes it difficult for civilians to avoid interacting with them.[37] Under the Strategic Partnership Agreement (SPA) signed by President Karzai and President Obama on May 1, 2012, it was finally agreed that the night raids were to be Afghan led and Afghan designed, with Afghan forces initiating the entry into a suspect's house. But the United States would provide the intelligence and have to approve the conduct of an operation.[38] Very quickly, however, what the arrangement actually meant in practice came under dispute.

The second major snag in negotiating the U.S.-Afghanistan Strategic Partnership Agreement concerned the detention of Taliban suspects and the operation of prisons, both of which the Afghan government wanted to control. ISAF was more than reluctant to hand over control, suspicious that its Afghan partners might release many hardcore Taliban detainees and doubtful of the Afghans' ability to run the prisons securely. There had been regular breaks from prisons under Afghan control, with hundreds of Taliban detainees escaping.[39] Moreover, serious human rights abuses had been prevalent in Afghan-run correction facilities.[40] Nonetheless, the United States ultimately agreed to relinquish control over the prisons and hand the lead on detentions over to the Afghans, while retaining the right of strong input and monitoring. Thus, after more than a year-long process and a great deal of persistence, patience, and skill on the part of U.S. diplomats, the SPA was finally signed a mere few days before the Chicago Summit.

But just as with the night raids, implementing the memorandum of understanding on detentions has been challenging, and disputes between the U.S. forces in Afghanistan and the Afghan government over detentions quickly emerged. Fearing that the Afghan government did not share its interpretation of the memorandum, the U.S. military refused to hand over all of its detainees at the Bagram detention facility to the

Afghans, much to the outrage of the Afghan government. Some Afghan officials also protested the U.S. system of no-trial detentions at Bagram, an arrangement upon which the United States had insisted to allow for continuing incarceration of prisoners too dangerous to release but too difficult to prosecute.[41] And uncertainties and contentions also emerged over the hundreds of prisoners captured by the United States since the memorandum of understanding was signed but whose status apparently was not covered by that agreement.

The subsequent implementation problems notwithstanding, the signing of the SPA was an important step in the continuing struggle to stabilize Afghanistan. Although the document does not carry the weight of a formal, full-fledged defense treaty and hence does not obligate the United States to treat an attack on Afghanistan as an attack on itself, it nonetheless places Afghanistan in the same special position as other U.S. allies, such as Japan, Australia, Israel, and Pakistan.[42] It stipulates that the United States will continue to train and equip the ANSF. Building closely on the language of the earlier 2005 Strategic Partnership Agreement between the two countries, it confers on Afghanistan a range of benefits, such as preferential access to U.S. military surplus supplies and the use of U.S. loans to finance weapons purchases.[43]

Most important, however, the 2012 Strategic Partnership Agreement was meant to give a fillip to the Afghan people and to help convince them that the United States would be less likely to desert them after 2014 and that such a continuing engagement could lessen the chances of another civil war breaking out.[44] After a decade of muddling through an intensifying insurgency, Afghans were tired of the U.S. and international military presence and of persistent insecurity and fighting. But they were even more wary of another civil war. The vast majority of my Afghan interlocutors did not want the United States to leave after 2014, even if they sought limits to the scope of U.S. military operations and demanded greater accountability for U.S. actions, including detentions and night raids. In fact, house prices in Kabul were reported to have jumped 20 percent within two days of the signing of the SPA, indicating a boost in Afghan consumer confidence, as well as a likely huge housing bubble.[45] (Since then, real estate prices have come down again, hovering between 40 and 60 percent of their value in 2011.)[46]

Yet even as the SPA was designed in large measure to lift the spirit of the Afghans, the phrasing that President Obama employed in his speech announcing the SPA reflected all the persisting ambiguities and ambivalence of U.S. policy. The president juxtaposed America's long-term commitment to Afghanistan's security and well-being with his determination to finally "end the war," meaning (although such explicit wording was politically awkward) U.S. *participation* in it.[47] And as before, the narrow counterterrorism objective of preventing the reemergence of al Qaeda safe havens in the country did not give the Afghan people what they really wanted to hear—namely, a U.S. commitment to end the pervasive insecurity that the Afghan people experience daily and that stems from many sources (the various Taliban groups, criminal bands, militias, and predatory power brokers and Afghan government officials) and has very little to do with al Qaeda per se.

Signing the SPA was also meant to strengthen allies' resolve to persevere in Afghanistan, at least in some limited capacity. ISAF and allied government officials feared that a failure to finalize the U.S.-Afghanistan SPA would have made it more difficult for Western governments to persuade their publics to support any further military or robust economic engagement in Afghanistan after 2014. Profound questions about a continuing U.S. military deployment in Afghanistan after 2014 could have precipitated a race for the exits among the allies, with many seeking to pull out their forces from Afghanistan as rapidly as possible and thus jeopardizing the stabilization effort.[48] (Even with the SPA signed, the French government announced at the Chicago Summit that it would withdraw all of its forces from Afghanistan by the end of 2012.)

The SPA did lay down some of the groundwork for the United States to maintain a continuing military presence in Afghanistan after 2014, the basis and details of which were still to be hammered out. In describing the deal, President Obama stated that some U.S. forces would remain in Afghanistan beyond 2014, pending the outcome and completion of a bilateral security agreement to pursue "two narrow security missions": counterterrorism and training of the ANSF.[49] In the year ahead, the United States would also seek to sign a status of forces agreement and renegotiate continued access to military facilities—bases—in Afghanistan. Afghan government officials expect these two agreements to clarify the number of U.S. troops remaining in Afghanistan after 2014; the number of bases where they will stay and who controls the bases; "the nature, scope, and obligations" of the U.S. mission in Afghanistan after 2014; and the degree of immunity that U.S. soldiers enjoy for their actions in

Afghanistan.[50] Afghan officials have indicated that they would seek to strip U.S. soldiers of immunity for at least certain crimes and subject them to local Afghan trials for religious violations, such as burning the Koran.[51] (Previous incidents of Koran burning by either ISAF soldiers or even Americans outside of Afghanistan have caused outrage among Afghans and triggered violent riots.)

Thus many critical questions, such as how many U.S. soldiers would remain in Afghanistan in 2013 and after 2014 and for what purposes, as yet remain unanswered. If the forces are mainly restricted to military bases to provide training for the ANSF, a policy change for which President Karzai has repeatedly called, they will have little impact on how secure or insecure the Afghan population feels, regardless of whether 5,000 or 20,000 U.S. troops remain after 2014.[52] Similarly, if the September 2012 ISAF restrictions on ISAF-ANSF partnering remain in place—instead of being temporary, as NATO insisted after the new rules of engagement generated consternation within Afghanistan and the international community—the effectiveness of the training mission will be undermined. If until 2014 and beyond ISAF forces are restricted to their bases, only allowed to undertake narrow counterterrorism missions, and cannot partner even in just an advisory-support role with the Afghan forces in the field, their ability to train the ANSF will be seriously hampered. The U.S. ability to provide critical specialty enablers, which the ANSF lack and without which they cannot function, would also be undermined.[53]

To satisfy the Afghan craving for sovereignty, the signed SPA prohibits the United States from using Afghan territory to attack another country, without specifying any one in particular. Kabul (as well as Islamabad) was eager for this clause. The Afghan and Pakistani governments were concerned that after 2014 the United States would reduce its efforts in Afghanistan to an absolute minimum to remain consistent with the SPA, but be tempted to keep using Afghan territory to conduct drone strikes in Pakistan. Kabul in turn feared that such a U.S. policy would continue to provoke Pakistan's meddling in Afghanistan's affairs and encourage Islamabad's continued support of anti–Afghan government militant groups. At the same time, the agreement is couched in terms that allow considerable room for maneuvering and permit U.S. military actions against actors outside of Afghanistan if they are connected to terrorist actions in Afghanistan—that is, insurgents operating out of Pakistan. Given Iran's limited support for the Taliban (see chapter

10), that clause could also be interpreted to permit a retaliatory attack on Iran if its support of the Taliban became more aggressive. Yet Tehran has been as eager as Islamabad to prevent a U.S. military attack on its territory out of Afghanistan, putting pressure on the Afghan government since the middle of the decade to guarantee that.[54] But the language of the SPA does not explicitly answer some of these key questions, such as of what use, if any, could U.S. military bases in Afghanistan be during a U.S.-Iran military confrontation or in the eventuality of the Pakistani state crumbling.

The SPA also contains a continued U.S. commitment to Afghanistan's long-term economic development—at least until 2024. But as before, governance is still the weakest element of the document's emphasis. In his address, President Obama did talk about transparency, accountability, and human rights in Afghanistan.[55] But the governance section of the SPA is the shortest and vaguest, with the Afghan government promising to reform itself and the United States promising to help—without any details or conditions. At the Chicago NATO Summit there was talk about governance in Afghanistan, but just as with security, it was contained in language implying that it was something the Afghans would now do for themselves.

The July 2012 Tokyo Conference on Afghanistan resurrected to some extent international focus on governance in Afghanistan. In exchange for pledging $16 billion in economic development aid to Afghanistan between 2013 and 2017, international donors demanded commitments from the Afghan government that it would adopt stronger anticorruption measures and strengthen rule of law in Afghanistan. Secretary Clinton explicitly called on Kabul to undertake "fighting corruption, improving governance, strengthening the rule of law, increasing access to economic opportunity for all Afghans, especially for women."[56] For the first time, the announced Tokyo Mutual Accountability Framework also explicitly conditioned 20 percent of the international aid on the Afghan government meeting the anticorruption and rule of law demands of the international community.[57] In response, President Karzai issued in late July 2012 a "decree on administrative reforms," some of which focused on tackling corruption, patronage, and nepotism.[58] It is too early to say whether President Karzai will indeed robustly enforce the decree and punish violators, including those powerful officials who regularly violate existing laws and abuse power but whom he had been unwilling to confront in the past.

Previously the Afghan president often made emphatic proclamations but delivered little.

And indeed, the Tokyo Conference language notwithstanding, the international community has a poor record of holding the Karzai administration accountable to its promises. The Afghan government and international community have a long history of setting a plethora of vague benchmarks at international conferences on Afghanistan, which they then do not meaningfully monitor.[59] The benchmarks announced at the Tokyo meeting seemed to be informed by problems with how conditions and metrics were set at previous Afghanistan-focused conferences.[60] But it remains to be seen whether international donors this time around will in fact demonstrate the resolve to use their financial leverage to induce Kabul to fulfill its commitments.

The messages coming from the Obama administration, including the White House, in the run-up to the Tokyo Conference did not augur well for its ability to effectively stimulate and enable Kabul's commitments to strengthen the rule of law. Even as Secretary Clinton was exhorting the Afghan government at the Tokyo summit, other members of the Obama administration had been undercutting the weight of her message. They suggested that the Obama administration's goals for Afghanistan had shrunk to something called "Afghan good enough"—a vacuous and unclear phrase that borders on being pejorative toward the Afghan people.[61] That expression, more than anything else, captured how so much of the strategic debate in Washington about Afghanistan had remained unresponsive to the aspirations of the Afghan people, as if Washington could achieve strategic clarity without taking into account the dust of Afghan realities on the ground.

3

Insurgency in the Context of Poor Governance

The emergence in the 1990s and reemergence after 2002 of the Taliban movement and other militant groups on the Afghan side of the Durand Line separating Afghanistan from Pakistan have been driven by several factors. Although the causes of the Taliban's emergence and persistence are multiple and varied, the weakness of the state and the poor functioning of official governance have been crucial enablers of the movement's ability to gain traction with local populations.

Collapse of Governance in Afghanistan in the 1990s: The Taliban's Rise and Fall

The Taliban originated as a religious fundamentalist movement that became notorious not only for its religious fanaticism but also for its ruthless oppression and unrestrained brutality. It emerged on the political and military scene in 1994 in the context of and in reaction to the basic governance deficiencies of post-Soviet Afghanistan. After the Soviet withdrawal in 1989, the country rapidly plunged into civil war, with former *mujahideen* factions and commanders fighting each other over territory and control of Kabul and the central state. The warlords' inability to reach a stable deal that could prevent the disintegration of the country into predatory warlordism and unstable fiefs created a key opening for the Taliban.[1] The Afghan population was facing an ever more capricious and unpredictable environment, with elite self-enrichment, corruption, major human rights abuses, and constant infighting running high. The lack of governance was so acute that even informal and outright illegal economies not dependent on long-term investments (such as lucrative trucking and smuggling of goods from Pakistan) suffered under the warlords' "stewardship" and at times were paralyzed by uncontrolled theft along roads and exorbitant fees.[2] Various warlords charged such high and constantly increasing tolls that even smuggling across the Afghanistan-Pakistan border was disrupted.[3] Since trucked goods were frequently stolen even when tolls were paid, high transaction costs significantly reduced profits and created a business environment difficult for all enterprises—legal and illegal.[4]

The legal, mainly agricultural, economy had been destroyed as a result of the Soviet occupation during the 1980s. The chaos, violence, and economic deprivation of the civil war made the exhausted population desirous of peace at any price. The Taliban's declared agenda promised to do just that: restore peace in Afghanistan, disarm the combatants, enforce *sharia*, and defend the integrity and Islamic character of Afghanistan.

Although led by Afghans, specifically Mullah Mohammed Omar and his disciples, the Taliban was formed as a transnational network, organizationally present in both Afghanistan and Pakistan. In Pakistan, it drew primarily on a sectarian network of *madrasas* that were educating Afghan refugees and on political parties belonging to the Deobandi movement. Kandahari Pashtuns dominated its leadership and also most of the rank-and-file, but the movement did not simply represent a particular ethnicity. Rather, it represented the rural *ulema* (religious leadership) and their students affiliated with the Deobandi movement.[5] Highly centralized, secretive, and dictatorial, the movement presented itself as motivated by Islam and the desire to pacify and purify Afghanistan. Fundamentally antimodernist, the religious students of the Taliban sought to reconstruct the Afghan state and society by imposing a very strict and almost backward interpretation of Islam on the country as a puritanical relief from the chaos of the era.[6]

Pakistan's support was crucial for growth of the Taliban's physical capabilities. At the outset, the Taliban's forces numbered in the hundreds and were poorly armed, frequently running out of ammunition. But within months, their numbers swelled to 15,000 as students from madrasas in Pakistan poured into Afghanistan. In addition to encouraging the influx of volunteers, Pakistan provided the Taliban with money, weapons, and military support. Early in the fall of 1994, a Pakistani artillery barrage helped the Taliban seize the important border town of Spin Boldak and the arms depot at Pasha, a major weapons cache with rockets, artillery ammunition, tank ammunition, and small arms.[7] The Taliban was also receiving extensive logistical and infrastructural support from Pakistan, as well as money from groups in Saudi Arabia.[8] By October 1996, the Taliban fielded at least 25,000 men, complete with tanks, armored vehicles, helicopters, and fighter aircraft. The equipment was manned, in part, by veteran pilots, tank drivers, and technicians from Pakistan refugee camps who were paid in U.S. dollars and recruited with the help of Pakistan's intelligence service.[9]

Pakistan had two primary reasons for supporting the Taliban. First, the government preferred to have Afghanistan under the control of a pro-Pakistani force rather than one that was close to Russia, India, or Iran. The goal was to protect Pakistan's western flank from encirclement. At the same time, Pakistan's military doctrine called for the use of Afghanistan's territory to give Pakistan strategic depth in a military confrontation with India so that its forces could recoup there should India break through on Pakistan's eastern border. This objective is still foremost in the minds of the Pakistani military and intelligence establishments.[10] Second, Pakistan sought to secure trade access to and through Afghanistan and to end the constant harassment of its truckers by Afghan warlords, who charged ever-increasing tolls on trade routes and sometimes took hostages.[11] Without Pakistan's support, the Taliban would have encountered much greater difficulty in its efforts to take control of Afghanistan.

The Taliban in the 1990s—as well as today—was also able to obtain large financial resources as well as extensive support from the local Afghan population through its sponsorship and regulation of various illicit economies in Afghanistan.[12] Its embrace of the thriving opium poppy economy was particularly important for the growth of its political capital and physical resources.[13]

With support from Pakistan and multifaceted resources from Afghanistan's illegal economies, the Taliban gradually conquered the warlords and expanded its control. By 2000 it had consolidated its power over most of the country and pushed the remaining opposition forces of Ahmed Shah Massoud's Northern Alliance into Panjshir Valley, where that group was barely hanging on until the October 2001 U.S. invasion.

The Taliban succeeded not only in defeating, co-opting, and controlling the various warlords but also in reducing certain forms of insecurity that previously plagued the lives of Afghans during the warlords' rule. The tolls were removed from roads, and physical movement (for Afghan males) became much simplified. Crime, such as kidnappings, murders, rapes, robberies, and land theft, was dramatically reduced. Over the years, whenever I have visited Afghanistan, I would always make it a point to ask my Afghan interlocutors how their lives compared with their condition during the Taliban era. And in the latter half of the 2000s decade, I would get a remarkably consistent answer. "We didn't like the Taliban," many of my Pashtun interlocutors would say. "They were brutal and vicious. But when they were in power, there was order. There was no crime. We could travel with a million rupees [the currency in use at that time] from Kandahar to Kabul, and no one would rob us. Now we are robbed at every corner, and our women are raped in broad daylight."[14]

The Taliban in the 1990s was able to deliver such order and predictability by relying on a reign of terror and a highly restrictive form of sharia. It forbade women from attending school, working outside of the home, or obtaining access to medical care, and imposed *purdah*, the mandatory veiling of women from head to toe with a *burqa* and only a slit for the eyes. Engaging in sports, flying kites, playing music, dancing, and reading anything published outside of Afghanistan were outlawed to ensure that the population was not distracted from prayer. Religious police from the Ministry for Promoting Virtue and Preventing Vice patrolled the streets, looking for offenders, including men who failed to grow sufficiently long beards. Women caught walking on the streets without a male relative or whose ankles were showing were lashed on the spot, frequently by boys or men wielding car antennas or electrical cords. Punishments administered by the Taliban for some offenses were exceedingly brutal: stadiums were frequently packed with crowds of tens of thousands to witness amputations, floggings, and executions. Thieves had their right hand and left foot amputated; murderers were killed, sometimes by members of the victim's family; and adulterers were stoned to death while their children had to watch from the front of the crowd. Along with women, certain minorities, such as the Hazaras, suffered some of the greatest oppression. The order that the Taliban instituted and enforced was draconian, but it was predictable.

The Taliban regime, however, completely failed to alleviate the impoverishment of the population and satisfy its economic aspirations. Even worse, by systematically destroying the vestiges of government institutions left behind in the wake of the 1990s civil war, the Taliban contributed to the extensive socioeconomic deprivation of the Afghan people. The only economic benefit that the Taliban could deliver was its sponsorship of the opium poppy economy, which earned it crucial political capital with the Afghan population. Yet even with respect to poppy, the Taliban record in providing for the basic economic needs of the population was problematic. Its 2000 ban on opium poppy cultivation greatly emiserated the population and deeply alienated even key Pashtun supporters.[15]

What ultimately brought about the demise of the Taliban regime was its coddling of al Qaeda. The personal connection between al Qaeda's leader and creator, Osama bin Laden, and the Taliban's leader, Mullah Omar, dated back to the 1980s when the two men were among the mujahideen sponsored by Pakistan and the United States to fight against the Soviet occupation of Afghanistan.[16] When the Taliban seized territory in Afghanistan in the mid-1990s, bin Laden and al Qaeda moved there to use the Taliban-controlled area to train for operations and plan attacks, including those against U.S. embassies in Tanzania and Kenya in 1998, which killed more than 200 people and wounded over 5,000.[17] Throughout the 1990s, the United States repeatedly tried to persuade the Taliban to hand over bin Laden, but each time the Taliban leadership remained unresponsive. Nor did the Taliban restrict the operations of al Qaeda and its use of Afghanistan's territory for preparation of further terrorist attacks. The ability to enjoy the safe haven in Afghanistan critically augmented al Qaeda's base of operations and capabilities for organizing and directing sophisticated and bloody terrorist plots, including ultimately the 9-11 airplane crashes into the Twin Towers and the Pentagon.[18]

As a result of 9-11, the Taliban was deposed by the United States in coalition with the Northern Alliance warlords and those Pashtun tribal chiefs opposed to its regime. After several years in power during the 1990s, the Taliban was deeply discredited among the Afghan population, including its core base, the Ghilzai Pashtuns, as a result of its brutality and backward, harsh ideology, as well as its inability to generate any socioeconomic improvements for the people.[19] In 2001 most Afghans were happy to get rid of the group, and the Taliban fell without the population lining up on its side to defend the country against "Western infidel occupiers." At the outset, there was no insurgency driven by nationalism against "the occupation" or a desire to restore the Taliban. Indeed, the population welcomed the U.S. and the international community's intervention and applauded the promise of a united, well-governed Afghanistan on a path toward economic development.[20]

The Reemergent Afghan Taliban Insurgency

Despite its fall from power, the Taliban was able to rebuild itself and since 2004 mount an intensifying insurgency in Afghanistan.[21] While principally located in the Pashtun south and east of the country, by the end of 2010 the insurgency had also deeply destabilized Afghanistan's north. Although throughout most of the decade since 2002 the north has been the most stable and secure part of Afghanistan, Taliban militancy (and other forms of insecurity) also flared up there after 2008. Were it not for the presence of the U.S. forces and ISAF, the Taliban probably would have been able to retake much of the south and east and even threaten Kabul. Indeed, General Stanley McChrystal warned in his report to President Barack Obama in August 2009 that without additional troop increases of as many as 80,000 soldiers beyond the 103,230 U.S. and NATO troops already deployed in Afghanistan, the coalition might not succeed in defeating the insurgency.[22]

By the summer of 2012, near the end of the temporary deployment of the additional 30,000 U.S. surge troops, with close to 100,000 American soldiers and another 50,000 ISAF forces from allied countries, the United States and ISAF found themselves in a stalemated war. Security in parts of the south that received the bulk of the surge forces was palpably improved, but the robustness of the improvements, often in fairly small pockets of territory, has yet to be seen. Since the McChrystal strategy was launched, the north too saw a reversal of the Taliban momentum. But many of the security improvements resulting from greater ISAF troop presence there have been proving to be fragile, as poor governance in key parts of the north has kept generating new instability. Meanwhile, the security challenges in eastern Afghanistan have grown increasingly more complex. How they are or are not addressed before NATO hands primary security functions to the Afghan National Security Forces (ANSF) by the end of 2014 will have critical repercussions for the security of Kabul and Highway 1 connecting Kabul and the city of Kandahar, which is the most important locus of Pashtun political power after the capital and a key hub of the Taliban insurgency.

And even though ISAF became more optimistic—at least about the input side of its efforts, pointing to important local progress in central Helmand and around Kandahar City—few Afghans today believe that NATO in combination with the ANSF could truly defeat the insurgency before 2014. Despite the announced U.S. and NATO commitment to retain combat forces in Afghanistan at least throughout 2014, the Afghan leaders and population continue to doubt the persistence of NATO's strength and policy effectiveness as its forces begin to thin out and hand security over to the ANSF. Afghans point to high-profile NATO operations that, despite initial progress, were unable to avert a deterioration of the security situation, such as in Marja and Arghandab in the first part of 2010.[23] Even when the deterioration was subsequently reversed, as in Marja, it left behind essentially a "security pocket."[24] In some cases, such security pockets may be fairly robust; in other cases, as in northern Helmand, to the extent that they exist at all, they are small and fragile, ruled by thuggish warlords with little meaningful Afghan government presence, and surrounded by intense conflict or areas controlled by the Taliban. Even in areas supposedly cleared of insurgents, the Taliban assassination campaign against Afghans interacting with ISAF and the international community—be they Afghan government officials or ordinary people—often paralyzes the community and NATO's efforts to win over the population.[25]

Few Afghans—the exceptions being mostly young, well-educated Kabulis, many of whom returned to Afghanistan after 2001—believe that a better future is on the horizon. Instead, many predict that a civil war between the Pashtuns and the northerners, and also within those broad factions, will break out once NATO presence in Afghanistan is significantly transformed after 2014. Many Afghans are already liquefying their assets, and the more affluent are also relocating them abroad, such as to Dubai, so as to be ready to run away across Afghanistan's borders.[26] Talk is rife about how "quickly Kandahar will fall to the Taliban," how "much of the country will be engulfed in civil war," and which warlords will be able to keep which stable fiefs.[27]

How is it that the Taliban, after its swift defeat in 2002 and with minimal support, has been able to make such a comeback, to so demoralize the population and persuade many in the international community that the counterinsurgency is unwinnable?

Afghans themselves are in fact asking the same question. Enamored of conspiracy theories, many assume a degree of complicity on the part of the United States. After all, they question, how is it possible that the greatest power in history could defeat the Taliban so rapidly in 2001 and then subsequently would have to struggle so much to keep the Taliban at bay? The answer these suspicious Afghans frequently offer is that the Americans do not want to defeat the Taliban because that would eliminate the U.S. excuse for maintaining bases in Afghanistan and using their country as a launching pad for prosecuting the new "Great Game" in Central Asia.[28] Afghans' tendency to attribute purposeful willfulness and omnipotence to the United States also comes through in the second explanation frequently given for the reentrenchment of the Taliban: namely, that the United States installed thuggish mafia rule after 2002.[29]

To seriously explore what accounts for the robustness of the Taliban insurgency, it is important to distinguish between the motivations of the insurgents and the motivations of the wider population among whom they exist.[30]

Characteristics and Motivations of the Taliban and Associated Insurgencies

There are three principal, comingled, but distinct insurgency groups that challenge the Afghan government and ISAF: the Kandahar-centered Quetta Shura led by Mullah Omar and made up of the original Taliban, the Haqqani network, and Gulbudin Hekmatyar's Hezb-i-Islami.[31] These groups were able to rebuild their physical capabilities by enjoying sanctuaries in Pakistan's Federally Administered Tribal Areas and the Khyber-Pakhtunkhwa and Baluchistan provinces. After being pushed out from Afghanistan in 2002, they generated revenues by fundraising in Pakistan and the larger Middle East and by participating in various cross-border illicit enterprises, such as smuggling legal goods, gems, minerals, marble, and timber across the Durand Line, or extorting money from businesses in their areas of operation.[32] The Taliban often denies its participation in criminal activities, claiming that while it collects donations throughout Afghanistan, its members are not permitted to engage in criminal activities such as forcibly collecting *zakat* (religious donations), hijacking, or extortion. However, there is much evidence to the contrary, though there are important differences in the scope and level of involvement in criminal enterprises among the three insurgent groups.[33] The Quetta Shura Taliban, in particular, tends to be far more concerned about appearances and to moderate the level of abuse it inflicts on the population, including in its forms of extortion. Nonetheless, although the donations it receives are supposed to be "voluntary," the presence of dangerous men with guns tends to eviscerate the concept of free will.

Despite intense pressure and a large amount of economic and military aid from the United States over the past decade, Pakistan has allowed key Taliban, Haqqani, and Hezbi leadership as well as rank-and-file fighters to continue operating, organizing, fundraising, and mobilizing in Pakistan.[34] Although Pakistan denies it, there is credible evidence that its Inter-Services Intelligence (ISI) agency continues to provide logistical and financial assistance and strategic advice to the Quetta Shura Taliban and to the Haqqanis.[35] In addition, the ISI steadfastly refuses to robustly take on these groups.[36] The Taliban also networks with a wide array of ISI-sponsored Punjabi and other jihadi groups, such as Lashkar-i-Taiba, who now also operate in Pakistan's Federally Administered Tribal Areas and Baluchistan province.[37] Major attacks by the Haqqanis, with whom the ISI has the tightest relationship, have been linked back to their advisers (or perhaps even controllers?) in the ISI.[38] Based in eastern Afghanistan (the provinces of Khost, Paktia, and Paktika) and in North Waziristan, Pakistan, and anchored in the Zadran tribe and its centuries-old cross-border smuggling networks, the Haqqani group is renowned for some of the most spectacular and vicious attacks in Afghanistan and accounts for perhaps 15 percent of ISAF casualties.[39]

That does not, however, mean that the interests of any of the three insurgent groups and Pakistan's military intelligence establishment are always aligned. Interrogations of captured Taliban members reveal that Pakistan attempts to exercise control over the groups by arresting their members and leaders who are deemed uncooperative. Taliban personnel—from low-level fighters to senior leaders—regularly describe the government of Pakistan as "manipulative," "untrustworthy," "controlling," and "indifferent to the interests of Afghanistan."[40] Such sentiments are apparently even shared by senior Haqqani leaders.[41] Indeed, according to some reports, Pakistan may well be pressuring members of the Taliban to continue fighting.[42] The extent of Pakistan's support for the militant groups led the former U.S. director of national intelligence Dennis Blair to state that "disruption of the insurgent presence in Pakistan is a necessary condition of making substantial counterinsurgency progress" in Afghanistan, an assessment shared by many ISAF commanders and civilian analysts.[43]

But even though Pakistan's support for the insurgents augments their resources, it is the deficiencies of the Afghan government that are an important factor motivating the insurgents and allowing them to gain traction with the Afghan population. The motivations and recruitment tools of the insurgent groups are of course varied.[44] In the case of the Taliban in particular, ideology certainly plays a prominent role. It is rather well defined, even while emphasizing different elements at different times, such as a mixture of nationalism and opposition to infidels' presence in Afghanistan, religious fundamentalism, and affinity with the global jihadi cause. But the macro drivers of conflict and especially the personal motivations among the top leadership, mid-level commanders, and foot soldiers are diverse.

The top level of the Afghan Taliban structure, the Quetta Shura led by Mullah Omar, is probably the element of the Taliban most intensely driven by an ideological compulsion based on a fundamentalist vision of Afghanistan that harkens back to the 1990s and that places a strictly doctrinaire interpretation of sharia at the core of its sociopolitical project.[45] At the same time, the leadership has taken care to publicly announce the moderation of at least some elements of its ideology and practices that were strongly resented by the Afghan population, including the banning of television, highly intrusive strictures (such as requirements for the length of men's beards), and even some restrictions on women.[46] Displaying a "mea culpa" recognition, many Taliban members believe that any future Taliban government should take far greater interest in education and infrastructure than it did in the 1990s.[47] Taliban leaders engaged in negotiations with the United States defined their political project and objectives in Afghanistan in 2012 in a TV interview in the following way:

> We, after the end of occupation, want an Islamic, independent, and sovereign Afghanistan, and a restoration of lasting peace. We are giving special attention to reconstruction, particularly the reconstruction of hospitals, highways, and natural resources. We will pay special heed to education within the framework of Islamic principles and national interests, and give full rights to the women. We have a special focus on extracting natural resources and mines, the

revival of agriculture, trade, and industry, to pave the way for foreign investors to make investment and do trade. We want to have
good political, economic, technical, and educational relations with
the entire world on the basis of mutual respect, and want to benefit
from their progress and development, especially in education, technical, and economic fields. We want complete eradication of narcotics and corruption and the appointment of competent people.[48]

However, many such proclamations remain just that: rhetoric.
Moreover, the Taliban's old determination to enforce rigid sharia rules
through brutal means has far from completely abated. Members of the
Taliban continue, for example, to target women leaders and politicians,
as well as to execute women for alleged adultery and other presumed
violations of sharia.[49] The Taliban, particularly its eastern, Pakistani, and
foreign factions, has targeted schools and sought to prevent even boys,
not just girls, from attending primary schools. The denial of education
to boys is a major irritant to the Afghan population, and in the summer
of 2012, such anti-education policy by the Taliban sparked a widespread
anti-Taliban rebellion in Ghazni province.[50] To mask its own brutality
and proclivity for violence, the Taliban has also embraced the language
of "human rights" and "peace," describing the United States and foreign forces as violators of peace who engage in "antihuman" activities
while casting itself in the role of the just who take up arms to protect
the embattled population.[51] Mullah Omar's 2011 Eid al-Fitr (celebra-
tion of the end of Ramadan) message called on Taliban commanders to
minimize civilian casualties, an edict amplified in his 2012 Eid statement
after the Taliban killed sixty-three civilians in a spate of suicide bombings
within one week of August 2012—including by throwing grenades into
a mosque compound.[52] Its record notwithstanding, the Taliban has also
attempted to coordinate the placement of mines by village *maliks* (chiefs)
to decrease civilian deaths.[53] The Taliban has also reduced its practice
of widely publicizing videos showing the beheading of its prisoners—an
intimidation tactic modeled on jihadi practices in Iraq and Pakistan to
which it had resorted rather frequently before 2011.[54]

Although contradicted by facts, Taliban propaganda has been often
remarkably effective. In Afghanistan's north, historically not a natural
area of Taliban mobilization, the Taliban has not only exploited ethnic
rifts to mobilize the Pashtun minority but also used religious themes to

spread its recruitment even beyond the Pashtuns there.[55] The Taliban's claim to be protecting "Afghan traditional values" continues to be a potent recruitment and support-generating theme across ethnic lines.[56]

How operationally and ideologically close the Quetta Shura Taliban is to al Qaeda is hotly disputed. Some scholars believe that the two groups' shared refuge in Pakistan and their perception of common enemies—the United States, NATO, and the NATO-supported Afghan government—facilitated close cooperation and led Mullah Omar to emphasize and embrace the global salafi cause.[57] Others maintain that the two distinct groups continue to be divided by divergent interests, conflicting organizational and leadership structures, and different objectives.[58] Among at least some Taliban leaders, there is a sense that the tight embrace of al Qaeda in the 1990s precipitated the movement's demise and should not be repeated.[59] Regardless, out of the three groups, the Quetta Shura–based Taliban clearly maintains and regularly enunciates the most developed yet evolving and adaptive ideology, one emphasizing different themes at different times to maximize appeal.[60]

Even absent such a detailed promulgation of their ideology, the eastern Afghanistan network led by Jalaluddin and Sirajuddin Haqqani is rather strongly motivated by the global salafi jihadist cause.[61] Due to its sanctuary in Pakistan, the network came into close contact with al Qaeda and assorted international jihadists and absorbed much of the salafi worldview. The population of Kunar and Nuristan provinces also has historically been sympathetic to Arabs and salafi ideologies. Yet just like many armed Afghan actors—whether on the side of the Afghan government or against it—the Haqqanis also have strong economic interests that drive their determination to perpetuate instability in their areas of operation.[62]

Another key insurgent group operating in eastern and northern Afghanistan, Hezb-i-Islami, is perhaps less motivated by ideology, or its ideology and alignments are extremely flexible and used as justification for the accumulation of personal power by its leader, Gulbudin Hekmatyar. A former anti-Soviet guerrilla commander and a favorite of the United States and Pakistan's Inter-Services Intelligence among the mujahideen they sponsored, Hekmatyar fought both the Northern Alliance and the Taliban over power in Kabul in the 1990s.[63] After 2001, however, he aligned himself with the Taliban to fight the NATO forces, even while sending periodic signals about his possible willingness to reach a deal with NATO and the new Afghan government. Many members of

Hekmatyar's Hezb-i-Islami hold official positions of power in Karzai's government and the Afghan parliament.

At the tribal level, the decision whether groups within a tribe do join the Taliban is frequently driven by a variety of grievances. Although tribal structures have been weakened and tribal affinities are far from definitive for determining allegiance and identity, Afghans do maintain a strong sense of tribal and subtribal belonging and operate within tribal networks, as well as many other kinds of networks.[64] Thus, although Afghans clearly make decisions as individuals, their preferences and choices are also informed by group belonging and dynamics. Many Pashtuns, including both the Ghilzai and Durrani subgroups, felt discriminated against by the composition of the early post-Taliban government that heavily favored the non-Pashtun Northern Alliance. This post-2002 power redistribution only reinforced the historic Ghilzai Pashtun anger at having been marginalized by Durrani Pashtuns. During the 1990s in particular, the Taliban drew heavily on Ghilzai Pashtuns for membership.[65] At the same time, the movement still succeeded in portraying itself as pan-Pashtun and above tribal divisions. However, beyond the crude divisions of Pashtuns versus non-Pashtuns and Ghilzais versus Durranis, there are many other tribal affinities and rivalries—such as Popalzai versus Barrakzai, Achezai versus Noorzai—which influence whether subgroups within a tribe align themselves with the government or with the Taliban. Many of these rivalries are acutely felt and result in feuds, if not outright warfare. Motivated by such rivalries, district and provincial government officials frequently discriminate against communities of different tribal affinity, thus generating recruitment opportunities and support for the Taliban. For example, the discrimination against the Ghilzai in Uruzgan province by Durrani power brokers Jan Mohammad and Matiullah Khan throughout much of the post-2002 period drove entire Ghilzai communities into the hands of the Taliban.[66]

Throughout Afghanistan, the Taliban adroitly exploits such discrimination and rivalries and inserts itself into the local tribal conflicts. It seeks both to mobilize communities that feel discriminated against and to provide alternative governing structures that purport to redress these kinds of grievances. Yet when the Afghan government redressed these grievances and appointed officials seen as fair (frequently only as a result of prodding from the international community), the groups were often willing to give up their support for the Taliban.[67]

However, it would be a gross mistake to try to determine alignments with or against the Taliban simply on the basis of tribal affiliation. Membership in the Taliban crosses all tribal boundaries and rarely includes all members of even a subtribe.[68] Decisions whether to support the government, side with the Taliban, or avoid choosing between them are acutely driven by expectations of which side will ultimately prevail in the area. Without confidence that the ANSF and NATO forces will be able to protect the community from Taliban retaliation, many will not risk cooperating with the Afghan government and NATO. Similarly, without sufficient resources, including a deep bank of ready males to fight against the Taliban for a long period and replenish lost fighters, many Afghan communities will not dare to militarily take on the Taliban on their own.[69] Furthermore, patronage networks and economic interests in Afghanistan, also key determinants of alignments and their flexibility, often cut through and across tribal structures. Much of ISAF's political effort in southern Afghanistan focused on "getting the tribes right."[70] Yet that focus frequently missed how misgovernment, patronage, and mafia networks did not necessarily follow tribal lines and how the tribal label often hid different and complex cleavages.

At the individual level, many Taliban foot soldiers are not motivated by a specific religious doctrine either, even if nationalism frequently runs strong among them. The notion of "ten-dollar guerrillas"—men and boys willing to rent themselves to the Taliban for a pittance—is another gross oversimplification. The vast majority of Taliban members, particularly low-level fighters, do not receive salaries or other financial incentives and must keep their jobs to support themselves and their families. Even commanders at the district or provincial level tend to suffer financially (at least within the Quetta Shura branch of the Taliban, as opposed to the Haqqanis or Hezbi), yet another policy that allows the Taliban to extol its "virtues" by comparing the frugality of its members with the greed of non-Taliban power brokers and government officials.[71] Indeed, as with most insurgencies, many rank-and-file combatants are motivated by highly personal concerns, such as revenge, friendship and family ties, and solidarity with mosque and madrasa networks.[72] Being a victim or family relative of a victim of someone in power can be a particular potent motivator. In Kandahar abuse from those in government drove back into the insurgency even those who had gotten out of it.[73]

Motivations of the Afghan Population: Failure of Governance in Post-2001 Afghanistan and Insurgent Strategies

The complex motivations of active insurgents who joined the Taliban are frequently not identical to the motivations of the wider populace, which simply supports or tolerates the Taliban. Yet a factor common to both and one that critically has allowed the Taliban to gain traction with Afghans has been the country's tradition of state weakness and the failure of the post-Taliban state to deliver good governance. The new state under Karzai failed not only to meet the expectations of the population in terms of economic development and service delivery but also to maintain elemental security.

The absence of Afghan national as well as international forces from large swaths of the country, including much of the strategic provinces of Kandahar and Helmand, allowed the Taliban to return and reestablish itself in its former base by the rule of its Kalashnikovs.[74] Intimidation by the Taliban and a calculation of who will prevail on the battlefield in any given area fundamentally determine with whom the population aligns or whether it sits on the fence. Especially if the Afghan government and NATO forces are unable to protect a community from retaliation by the Taliban, and the Taliban specifically targets those seen as cooperating, or even merely interacting, with the Afghan government or ISAF, few may be motivated to risk resistance. Instead, they will passively acquiesce to the Taliban's presence and even to its rule.

But the persistent inability to establish good governance, even in areas repeatedly cleared by ISAF and the ANSF, has often made any security gains highly ephemeral. The state's manifestation, though meager, has often been outright malign from the perspective of many Afghans. It has been characterized by rapaciousness, nepotism, corruption, tribal discrimination, and predatory behavior from government officials and power brokers closely aligned with the state. Since patronage has been a key determining factor in whether one gets access to resources, those who run afoul of powerful men can face an abject lack of economic opportunities and even experience significant economic hardship.[75] Crime—such as land theft by rival tribes and land grabbing by corrupt power brokers, nepotistic and unfulfilled contracts, and embezzlement—has spread throughout the country. Officers of the ANP, an institution seen by Afghans as one of the most corrupt, along with the official Afghan judicial system, have frequently perpetrated various crimes.[76] Just like in the early 1990s, warlords have become the source of much infighting and physical insecurity.[77] As security significantly deteriorated after 2005, many warlords-cum-government officials began clandestinely rearming and abused their power to discriminate against tribal and economic rivals, thus generating new tensions and violent flare-ups. From its inception in 2002, the new state has been critically challenged in its most fundamental and indispensible function of providing public safety and has depended upon outsiders and private entities for even the sporadic and patchy delivery of security.

The dearth of a multifaceted state presence, including effective law enforcement and formal judicial processes, has exacerbated the pervasive lack of rule of law. Many communities have been left without reliable mechanisms for dispute resolution and the dispensation of justice. At the same time, conflicts over land and water and tribal feuds have escalated due to the absence of the Taliban mailed fist, the lack or venality of formal courts, and a weakening of informal (tribal) dispute resolution codes. Old warlords, now frequently officials at all levels of the Afghan government, have often usurped power for personal enrichment. They regard their positions as governors, police chiefs, and members of provincial development councils (the key governing body at the provincial level), once again, as personal fiefs.[78]

Corruption has become rampant and deeply embedded. It is intensified by the bourgeoning illegal poppy cultivation but also fueled by the structural deficiencies of state institutions, the predatory behavior of official and unofficial power brokers, and the influx of vast, often unmonitored, sums of foreign aid.[79] Corruption in Central and South Asia is hardly restricted to Afghanistan; indeed, it is pervasive and notorious in the area. Nonetheless, the degree of corruption and lack of rule of law in Afghanistan greatly surpasses that of its neighbors and other countries in the region: Transparency International ranks Afghanistan as the third most corrupt country in the world after Somalia and North Korea, tied with Myanmar for that infamous standing. Thus, while Afghanistan lies at the bottom of Transparency's index, ranking number 180 out of 182 countries, Nepal ranks 154; Tajikistan, 152; Pakistan, 134; Kazakhstan and Iran, 120; and India, 95.[80] The national government in Kabul has been, at best, impotent in redressing the causes of this embarrassing status and, at worst, deeply complicit in them.

The overall governance situation in the post-Taliban era has been one where weakly functioning state institutions are unable and unwilling to uniformly enforce laws and policies. Influential power brokers have the capacity to subvert laws and their enforcement for personal benefit by issuing exceptions from law enforcement to their network of clients for payback, thus reaping high profits. At the same time, the new regulations are not necessarily seen as legitimate by the population, and citizens often systematically distrust the capacity or will of state institutions to equitably enforce laws and allocate resources.

The degree of corruption during the 2009 presidential elections and the extensive fraud in the 2010 parliamentary elections further undermined the legitimacy of the Afghan government. Indeed, the authority of the government has sunk so low that even high-level officials, such as provincial governors appointed by Kabul, have found it convenient and necessary to distance themselves from the national government and complain about its venality.[81]

Underlying the profound legitimacy crisis are the short time horizons with which many Afghans have been conditioned to operate after thirty years of warfare and the consequent tendency of the Afghan population to discount the future in favor of the present. The 2014 transition—whatever its ultimate shape and scope—has further abridged the time horizons of the power brokers and population alike, augmenting other drivers of short-term profit- and power-maximizing behavior. Profound and widespread pessimism about the future after 2014 is reflected in the pervasive sense that one has to benefit from today's opportunities now, and provides disincentives for undertaking long-term institutional and economic investments and submitting to the rule of law.[82]

In this environment of uncertainty, pessimism, and unpredictable or absent rule of law, the Taliban has employed four key mobilization strategies and messages.

First, the Taliban has stepped into the lacuna of good governance by disbursing its own "justice" and order—however harsh and arbitrary—adjudicating disputes, such as over land and water, and acting against crime.[83] For mediating tribal, criminal, and personal disputes, the Taliban does not charge money. Afghans report a great degree of satisfaction with

Taliban verdicts, unlike those from the official justice system where they frequently have to pay unaffordable and unreliable bribes.[84] The Taliban also has put a great effort into building a shadow government system that includes its own provincial and district governors and civilian commissions. The Taliban's code of conduct, the so-called Taliban La'iha, promulgated by the Quetta Shura, is designed both to maintain control of Taliban ranks and minimize the emergence of rogue elements as well as to encourage coordination of Taliban shadow government personnel with local leaders to minimize the appearance of outside intrusion.[85] The Quetta Shura has even established teams of specifically designated personnel to travel throughout Afghanistan and elicit complaints from local populations against the Taliban—about corruption, brutality, or other mistreatment—as well as to mediate conflicts among Taliban commanders. It has also distributed phone numbers throughout Afghanistan for the reporting of such abuses.[86] How much the local population trusts this reporting system and actually experiences any redress of its complaints varies greatly, of course. Often the population is simply intimidated by the Taliban and abused. Nonetheless, it is significant that the Taliban has felt it advantageous to establish such a system at all. Even its nominal provision of mechanisms of redress for the population lies in stark contrast to the absence of accountability mechanisms for non-Taliban power brokers and government officials.

Second, the Taliban has attempted to mobilize the Pashtun population by emphasizing its marginalization in the post-2001 period. Particularly the first Karzai government was often seen as being dominated by non-Pashtun northerners. Although that ethnic imbalance was subsequently changed to favor the Pashtuns, the Taliban continued to beat the Pashtun drum. The Taliban has particularly tapped into subgroups that have been discriminated against, marginalized, and otherwise oppressed by government administrators or unofficial power brokers with strong ties to government officials. ISAF's own interrogations of Afghan civilians suspected or accused of collaborating with the Taliban, as well as detained Taliban members, confirm that Afghan civilians frequently prefer Taliban governance over that of the Afghan government due to the latter's corruption and ethnic bias.[87]

The Taliban has employed a similar strategy in the north where Pashtuns are a minority. It has fanned the resentment of northern Pashtuns at the Tajiks' seizure of Pashtun lands in the north and in Kabul in late

2001 and 2002. Elsewhere, the Taliban has stepped into local disputes over leadership and local resources, even among the same branch of tribes and communities.[88]

The third key Taliban strategy for mobilizing support from the population has been through protecting poppy fields from the eradication efforts of the Afghan government and its international sponsors.[89] Amounting to between a third and a half of the country's GDP since 2001, the poppy economy represents the economic lifeline of much of Afghanistan's rural population and underlies much of the economic activity in urban centers as well.[90] Consequently, eradication drives and bans on poppy cultivation have been economically devastating for local populations and thus have severely alienated them from the national government and its international sponsors.[91] Conversely, the Taliban has triggered some of the greatest anger among the population, at times even resulting in rebellions against Taliban presence in particular communities, when its restrictions on the population's movements or economic markets have interfered with the economic way of life and jeopardized a community's ability to secure a living.[92]

Fourth, as the international presence in Afghanistan became increasingly associated with civilian casualties because of the initially sparse NATO troop deployments and the subsequent reliance on drone attacks and close air support, the Taliban came to champion Afghan nationalism, in addition to a violent jihad against the "Western infidels." The surge of U.S. troops and General McChrystal's 2009 guidelines for minimizing civilian casualties considerably constrained the use of airpower. But the restrictions proved unpopular with U.S. troops, who complained that the new rules exposed them to excessive danger by preventing them from attacking civilian compounds where the Taliban would frequently hide and which it used as bases for attacking Western troops.[93] After General McChrystal left Afghanistan and the command of the war was transferred first to General David Petraeus and then to General John Allen, the prosecution of the counterinsurgency campaign gradually retreated from its primary focus on securing the Afghan population (as the McChrystal 2009 review advocated) to dismantling the Taliban's mid-level structures and incapacitating its commanders. Although the goal of protecting the population remained, the tactical priority of disrupting the Taliban's mid-level structures was now elevated. This offensive emphasis, along with the unpopularity among the troops of the air support restrictions, resulted in a renewed resort to air attacks and hence inadvertent civilian casualties—even as Petraeus continued to emphasize the need to minimize those very consequences.[94] President Karzai would often seize upon the issue of civilian casualties and rail against ISAF rules of engagement as a way of diverting attention from his collapsing legitimacy and deflecting international pressures on his government to tackle corruption and improve governance. At the end of May 2012, following yet another vitriolic outburst by President Karzai in response to a particularly bad incident in which over eighteen civilians were killed, NATO once again issued tightened constraints on air strikes against civilian structures, though not halting them altogether, as Karzai had sought.

It needs to be noted, however, that despite the Taliban's propaganda, it is the Taliban and other insurgent networks that have been the source of the vast majority of civilian victims. At least since 2009, the Taliban and other antigovernment elements have been responsible for more than 75 percent of the civilian casualties.[95]

In order to drain the sea where the insurgents swim (to paraphrase Mao Zedong's famous dictum) and deprive the Taliban of popular acceptance, it is necessary to address the chronic and severe governance deficiencies. In the absence of at least adequate governance in Afghanistan, military and civilian efforts at best amount to putting out acute outbreaks of militancy while being unable to address its root causes in a lasting way. But pushing for good governance never has been fully and strongly embraced by Washington. Instead, policies have oscillated between inconsistent efforts to substantially improve governance and ignoring the issue altogether, often with the seductive justification that Afghans do not want government intrusion in their lives anyway.

4

The Myths of (Non)Governance in Afghanistan

The failure to prevent governance in Afghanistan from deteriorating to levels of abuse and impunity intensely grating to the Afghan people has been more than a matter of incompetence by the Afghan government, unresolved strategic dilemmas within the U.S. government, and difficult policy tradeoffs. True, to a critical degree, Afghan elites ruling the country since 2002 are responsible for the dismal record. However, the poor state of governance in Afghanistan is also a result of mistaken assumptions by the United States and the international community about Afghan attitudes toward foreigners and about the role of tribes in the Afghan polity. One such widespread but fallacious notion is that Afghans are basically allergic to any foreign presence, especially to outsiders trying to get them to practice good governance, toward which the supposedly highly fragmented and fractious Afghan polity is inherently inhospitable. A corollary and also mistaken conviction is that to prevent the Taliban from returning to power, the country should be left to the rival tribes and warlords to run or misgovern in their own fashion.

The Fallacy of the "Just Leave Them Alone" Arguments

The argument for not intervening in Afghanistan's politics and not emphasizing good governance practices is based on the belief that Pashtuns, in particular, are uninterested in improved governance, that they want to be left alone with minimal interaction with the outside world, and that they resent central state interference in their lives and foreign presence in their territories. This characterization frequently emphasizes orientalist notions of Pashtunwali ("the social and ethical code of the Pashtuns") and assigns an intensely tribal and antimodern identity to Pashtuns.[1] Presumably, the principal, and frequently only, source of political legitimacy and affinity for them is the tribe. From this set of assumptions about Pashtun attitudes, it is deduced that the cause of the insurgency and popular support for militancy is not the absence of an effective central state and good governance but rather the presence of an imperious central state and foreign troops, which cuts against the grain of Afghan culture. Accordingly, any effort to deliver improved governance is at best futile or directly counterproductive.[2] The contention is that a scaled-down U.S. and international presence in Afghanistan, like that planned for after 2014, will reduce militancy and encourage stable local solutions, such as tribal or local strongman rule.[3] In other words, the international community's travails in Afghanistan have not been caused by it doing too little to promote good governance; they have resulted because it has tried to do too much.

This view was one of the principal drivers of the early decision of the Bush administration to adopt a "light footprint" approach in Afghanistan and served as a convenient justification for devoting no more than minimal resources, especially military, to the Afghanistan effort.[4] The United Nations Assistance Mission in Afghanistan (UNAMA) adopted a similar minimalist approach, seeking to limit its involvement and to encourage Afghans themselves to assume responsibility for the reconstruction of their country. Paradoxically, an underlying rationale for UNAMA's "light footprint" approach was to force donor nations to accept responsibility for assisting Afghanistan and not simply hand the burden over to the United Nations, which is precisely what many of the intervening nations wanted to do.[5]

However, the conventional *cultural* analysis of Pashtuns and Afghanistan is incorrect. While it is true that the vast majority of the Afghan Taliban insurgents are Pashtuns, hardly all Pashtuns support the Taliban. Nor are the Pashtuns or the Afghans in general inherently anti-foreign or anti-Western. Indeed, what was striking about the first half of the post-Taliban decade was the warm welcome that the United States and the international community received from the Afghan population, including the Pashtuns. In the 1950s, 1960s, and 1970s, Afghans grew accustomed to and welcomed a limited foreign presence in Afghanistan, in the form of development aid, technical assistance, and Western tourists. Kabul had Western bars, cafes, hippies, and development workers, even Afghan women in miniskirts. And the Afghan government became rather skilled at playing off the United States against the Soviet Union and letting both court the country with foreign resources.

Neither are the Afghans a collection of tribes without a real nation. While it is true that ethnic and tribal identities are important and the writ of the central state has frequently been minimal and fragile, Afghans do have a sense of nationhood and define themselves as Afghans.[6] Indeed, a common offense that foreigners commit is to ask an Afghan simply what tribe he is from, with the overwhelming reply being that "I am Afghan." Many of Afghanistan's conflicts have been fought over who controls the central state and how much the central state can dictate to local entities, but they have never been about parts of the country seceding, unlike in Pakistan, for example.

Afghans are of course acutely aware of each other's tribal and subtribal affiliations, as the tribe is indeed a critical political unit, intimately linked to a region from which one's family originates. In response to the question of what part of Afghanistan a person comes from, Afghans will often name an area where their great-grandparents lived, even if they themselves may never have lived there. But tribe and region are far from the sole sources of identity or political affiliation. Moreover, the tribal structures today hardly exercise the same level of control and influence that they did before the 1970s. Rather, on both sides of the Afghanistan-Pakistan border, the tribal structures have been severely weakened by multiple factors.[7] In Afghanistan, Communist rule, Soviet counterinsurgency policy, the anti-Soviet jihad, the 1990s civil war, and the Taliban policy of assassinating maliks (tribal elders) going back to the mid-1990s have all severely eroded many of the traditional tribal structures. While they still provide an aspect of one's identification, exert a degree of political and social clout, and can sometimes be mobilized for political and military action, many tribal structures lack the capacity and authority to effectively resist violent criminal or insurgent challenges or to deliver economic improvements and rule of law to the tribe's members. As a result of the Taliban assassination campaign, maliks often leave violently contested areas and retreat to provincial capitals or Kabul, from which they can only influence local governance in limited ways. One of the challenges for the ISAF counterinsurgency campaign and for the transition to Afghan ownership is that even after ISAF-ANSF clearing operations, maliks tend to be reluctant to return to their districts. Often they cannot be relied upon to deliver effective governance in the absence of a robust state. Similarly in Pakistan, political agents have compromised many maliks while others have been assassinated by the militant groups.[8] Indeed, the rise and entrenchment of the Taliban and other insurgent groups in Afghanistan and Pakistan are a manifestation of the erosion of traditional and local governing mechanisms, not of their strength.

Nor are Pashtuns acculturated to shun interactions with the outside world. Indeed, they frequently have intense exchanges with the world outside their valleys and dust plains. And there is a worldwide Afghan Pashtun diaspora, whose members maintain close contact with their communities of origin in Afghanistan. In the same way, the Pakistani Pashtun diaspora is extensively present in Karachi, Islamabad, and Dubai. In fact, more Pakistani Pashtuns live outside of the Federally Administered Tribal Areas (FATA) and Khyber-Pakhtunkhwa than live inside them. Pashtuns thus do not exist in isolation: despite the underdevelopment of their homelands, they are deeply plugged into multiple highly modern and globalized transnational networks (including those of global illicit economies). Even without the foreigners' presence in their lands, the Pashtuns would not be isolated from the rest of the world.

Moreover, the presence of foreign jihadists is as "alien" and disturbing to local ways of life as the presence of Western foreigners and the central state. Indeed, some of the fighting in eastern Afghanistan (as well as in the FATA) has been between foreign jihadists (Arab, Chechen, and Uzbek) and local tribes since the former have sought to dominate local decisionmaking structures and violently impose alien, often socially restrictive, ways.

By and large, Western withdrawal from an Afghan locality will not usher in an eighteenth-century-like happy isolation, free from encroachment by outsiders, with the locals content to be left to their own devices. Instead, what will remain will be an intense comingling of Afghan diaspora flows, returning refugees (many of whom lived outside of Afghanistan for decades and were even born elsewhere), Pakistanis, Iranians, foreign jihadists, and the locals—all of them shaping the identity and evolution of communities.

Pashtuns on either side of the Durand Line are not inherently antistate. In Afghanistan, the Durrani Pashtuns have dominated the central state for centuries. In fact, some of the principal political contestations have been between the Durrani Pashtuns seeking to retain control over the central state and its resources and the Ghilzai Pashtuns and non-Pashtun minorities seeking to obtain such control. During the 1950s and 1960s, an era that many Afghans revere with nostalgia as the golden age of Afghanistan, the central state functioned fairly effectively and peace prevailed. Agriculture, including agricultural exports, was booming. Nonetheless, although nominally highly centralized, formal state authority beyond key provincial and district centers was greatly limited. Governance was mediated via religious leaders, customary law, and the tribes. Tensions over the extent of the central state's sway and the independence of traditional tribal structures were not absent: various modernizing efforts, regarding, for example, women's rights and compulsory primary education, were often resented by tribal leaders and religious scholars. There were also limits to the state's taxation capacity and to its delivery of services. Most state revenues came from foreign aid and customs.[9] Although the central government made efforts to improve infrastructure and schools, the local, including tribal, governing structures often provided dispute resolution processes both for individual quarrels, such as domestic disputes, and tribal conflicts, such as over land and water. Nonetheless, despite periphery-center tensions and the incomplete writ of the central state, the two forms of governance—the state and the tribe—were able to coexist without major violence and essentially satisfy the elementary needs of the people.[10]

In Pakistan, the vast majority of the Pashtuns in the FATA have been largely excluded from control or enjoyment of any central state resources. Nonetheless, during the 1990s when development aid was extended to the FATA and Khyber-Pakhtunkhwa as part of a counternarcotics package, the local population welcomed the assistance. Beyond small-scale rural infrastructure projects, the immediate development benefits proved largely ephemeral and failed to create permanent jobs. Still, at the height of these efforts, many local tribesmen and -women identified themselves for the first time as Pakistanis, even principally as Pakistanis.[11] The greatest identification with the nation and state came at the time of the greatest state presence. Crucially, of course, the state was not simply present; it was present in a positive way, delivering improved governance and public goods, as opposed to generating physical and food insecurity, forcing people to flee, or stealing from their development funds or other resources.[12]

Naturally, when the principal manifestations of the state or foreigners are negative, a rejectionist reaction toward the state and foreign presence does develop and nationalism increases. It is not surprising that Afghan civilian casualties have generated antagonism toward foreign troops. Nor is it surprising that Predator drone attacks in Pakistan and the civilian casualties they cause (however high or low these actually are) are stimulating a nationalist backlash in Pakistan and are exploited by the frantically anti-American Pakistani media and jihadi preachers.[13] But none of this should be taken to mean that the anti-Western, antistate antipathies are static and can only be mitigated by the retreat of the state and the disappearance of Western foreigners.

Similar to the "let the tribes handle it" argument have been proposals for the "warlords" to provide governance to local communities. Many of the war commanders who emerged during the anti-Soviet jihad were outsiders to the traditional tribal structures and challengers to the maliks, presenting themselves as the new *khans* (rulers and notables) and alternative distributors of patronage to their clients.[14] During Operation Enduring Freedom, the United States crucially relied particularly on the Northern Alliance warlords for security, intelligence, logistics, and actual anti-Taliban and anti–al Qaeda operations. Since then, the international community at first and later also President Karzai have been largely unwilling to confront these power brokers and wean themselves off of their dependence on the warlords for counterinsurgency services and political control.

In the first years after being appointed president of Afghanistan in 2002, Karzai initially sought Western assistance in countering the country's numerous powerful warlords and power brokers and eliminating them as obstacles to the authority of the Arg Palace (the presidential seat). But with Washington's help not forthcoming, he quickly adapted by co-opting the warlords. On his own, the Afghan president arguably had few tools to take on the power brokers. He controlled only a minimal force; it was the United States and ISAF that controlled the preponderance of military assets in Afghanistan, and Karzai's relations with the Ministry of Defense and Ministry of Interior that international actors were helping to stand up were often distant.[15] The Arg Palace had little money to buy off anyone directly. The tool available to Karzai to ensure his political—and perhaps even his physical—survival was to offer the various power brokers appointments in the national and subnational levels of the government, thus buying them off indirectly and allowing them to use their positions of power to seek their own rents. He quickly learned to handle the power brokers indirectly via rule by co-optation and by divide-and-subdue approaches.[16] If the warlords' abusive, discriminatory, and incompetent governance became too noxious for Karzai's Western sponsors, he would usually just shuffle the warlords around and give them different influential government jobs, with the manipulation of appointments being his principal tool. Although many of such co-optation deals have been fragile, the increasingly indecisive Afghan national government has preferred to reach such temporary, even if unstable, accommodation with the power brokers rather than to confront them. This approach to ruling, elicited by the early embrace of and indifference to warlords by Washington and coalition forces, became a lasting habit that President Karzai often proved unable to break, even when his international sponsors developed distaste for the power brokers. Thus he has remained often deaf to the calls of the international community to fire and prosecute problematic power brokers. As a result, by the second half of the 2002–12 decade, Kabul was delivering governance that was as corrupt and inadequate as that provided by the power brokers themselves.

The United States, ISAF, international contractors, and other international actors have become complicit in perpetuating the power of the warlords, failing to progressively marginalize them within Afghanistan's political system and remaining dependent on them for the provision of assorted services, including counterinsurgency. Yet the power brokers often have complex relations with the Taliban and other insurgent and criminal groups: on the one hand, deferring to such militant groups threatens the power of the warlords, but on the other hand, the continuing instability ensures the value of the power brokers to the Arg Palace and the international community. Thus the warlords often reach various types of accommodation with the Taliban and other armed actors— for example, by transferring a part of their proceeds to the Taliban in exchange for the latter's modulation of insecurity in their areas. At times the power brokers will even intervene with the government to get senior captured Taliban leaders released from prison, just like they intervene to secure impunity for criminals, their cronies, and themselves.[17]

As a result, warlords-cum-government officials, such as Atta Mohammad Noor in Balkh, Ismail Khan in Herat, Ahmed Wali Karzai and General Abdul Raziq in Kandahar, Jan Mohammad and Matiullah Khan in

Uruzgan, and Gul Agha Shirzai in Kandahar and Nangarhar, once again became entrenched in the new political, economic, and power arrangements of post-2001 Afghanistan.[18] Such power brokers have perpetrated electoral fraud and tribal discrimination; abused and usurped political power, local resources, and international aid contracts; and participated in illegal economies, such as drug smuggling. Far from facilitating good and stable local governance, the reliance on these unaccountable warlords has encouraged massive corruption and discriminatory and rapacious behavior by elites.

What Governance Deficiencies Matter Most to Afghans

Criticisms from the United States and the international community of the governance deficiencies in Afghanistan have frequently lumped together Afghanistan's corruption, absence of public goods and rule of law, and extensive drug trade as equal manifestations of poor governance.[19] Yet not all governance deficiencies are equally important to local populations or are seen as necessarily pernicious in the way that Westerners frequently perceive them. Many Afghans, for example, do not consider poppy cultivation as particularly problematic or a governance deficiency at all; indeed, while it may be illegal, much of the population regards the poppy economy as legitimate.[20]

So then, what governance deficiencies do matter most to ordinary Afghan citizens?

Physical Insecurity and the Absence of Rule of Law and Dispute Resolution Mechanisms

The governance problems that matter most to local populations are the ones that most directly affect their personal security. Uppermost among them is the lack of physical safety from either politically organized violence or violent crime. Of course, the Taliban and other insurgent groups are a frequent source of both targeted killings of local political leaders and government officials and indiscriminate civilian casualties. But as long as the counterinsurgency forces are either incapable of holding territories cleared of insurgents so that these areas are repenetrated by militant groups, or unable to provide effective governance following their clearing operations so that violent crime and government abuse rise, the population does not feel that greater security has been established. Then, too, reducing or eliminating Taliban presence may enable the return of problematic power brokers and their abusive behavior, which can mean even more complex insecurity than when the Taliban ruled the area. In these ways, the presence of the state and counterinsurgency forces come to be associated with a *lack* of security, such as by drawing Taliban attacks or enabling the criminality and predatory behavior of power brokers. Human security is thus insufficiently improved, and the population sits on the fence, at best, or sides outright with the insurgents.

ISAF's tendency to discount threats generated by crime and predatory local power brokers explains why it consistently reports higher levels of security from areas of its operations than local Afghan populations do: ISAF tends to measure security as the number and intensity of Taliban attacks.[21] Locals, on the other hand, experience and evaluate security by the complexity, predictability, and stability of negotiations with powerful actors in their locality with whom they must engage to ensure their personal safety and secure their elementary everyday transactions. A predictable order like that provided by the Taliban—even if brutal and authoritarian—may be far easier for locals to navigate than a complex and unstable security environment. What people who live in areas violently contested by unaccountable powers often crave the most is predictability because that at least would enable them to adopt coping strategies.[22]

A failure to establish public safety and prevent violent street crime not only compromises human security and weakens the allegiance of the population to the state, it also undermines stability and weakens counterinsurgency operations in other ways. Locally contested power abuse and criminality often pull in the Taliban insurgents. On the one hand, insurgents are not averse to making tactical alliances with criminal groups, such as smuggling mafias or drug trafficking organizations, to share in their profits and logistical networks. Symbiotically, many criminal groups prefer to legitimize and glorify themselves by calling themselves "the Taliban" rather than, say, "the three thieves from the road to Tirin Kot." On the other hand, intense and extensive criminality provides key opportunities for militant groups to penetrate and mobilize communities and outperform the government by disbursing their forms of "justice" and order.[23]

Crime can be as much a threat to one's safety and economic survival as outright military conflict. Indeed, crime—such as kidnapping, robbery, and unofficial tolls—is one of the top grievances and frustrations of Afghans today. While the Afghan National Police have improved at handling potential suicide bomber threats and other terrorist actions, at least in major cities (no doubt an important accomplishment resulting from greater training and mentoring by ISAF forces), they are unable to systematically address and prevent crime.[24] Nor are they focused on tackling it: they function mostly as light counterinsurgency forces. Worse yet, the police are frequently implicated in serious crime, such as extortion, murder, and kidnapping.[25] Anticrime efforts remain largely confined to a few high-level, anti–organized crime initiatives, such as the Major Crime Task Force, or sporadic mentoring of a few Afghan police officers, such as via the Law Enforcement Professionals program, but they have not received the focus, priority, and urgency required to reduce crime and improve the population's safety from crime.

Lack of physical security and public safety in turn jeopardizes and frequently paralyzes legal economic development (and, if very severe, even illegal economies, as was the case in Afghanistan in the early 1990s). During the past decade, unofficial checkpoints have proliferated once again. Manned in places by the ANP, unofficial militias of the power brokers, various official paramilitary structures (such as the Afghan National Auxiliary Police and other precursors to the current Afghan Local Police), and security companies that until March 2012 legally operated in Afghanistan, such checkpoints nominally provide security for a particular stretch of road, but meanwhile their operators also shake down those who want to use the road. In more insecure areas, such as in the country's south and east, checkpoint operators frequently pass a cut of the profits to the Taliban.[26] In these areas, the tolls also are higher and more numerous. Depending on the level of security in different parts of the country, these additional illegal transaction costs can vary as much as 33 percent. In other words, as a result of extortion at the check posts, it costs a third more to travel in insecure areas of the south than in the secure areas of the north.[27] In parts of the south during the post-Taliban period, extortion along roads has at times been so high that it became unprofitable for farmers to attempt to transport any legal crops to market, an outcome that severely hampers legal economic development and precludes all but subsistence farming and illegal economic activity in many insecure areas. (Since opium, unlike legal crops, can be picked up by traders directly at the farm gate, it is not subject to these extra transaction costs and expenditures.) Central areas of the southern provinces of Helmand and Kandahar, which received the bulk of the U.S. surge forces in 2010 and 2011, often registered significant improvements in road security and a reduction in toll extortion at the checkpoints. One important test of the transition to ANSF control will be whether or not extortion increases once again. Meanwhile, however, other areas, such as parts of the northern provinces of Baghlan and Kunduz, saw a growth of road extortion during the same period.[28]

The population's alienation from the central government intensifies when the police and other state-sanctioned entities, such as the Afghan Local Police, participate in such extortion. The Afghan National Police not only charge "extra" tolls, they also frequently fail to provide the paid-for services that should have been provided without extra compensation. Many Afghan roads, including the Ring Road, the main artery that links major Afghan cities with Kabul, are too insecure to be used without protection and are regularly attacked by the Taliban, criminal groups, and rogue militias. Even in late spring 2012, almost at the end of the U.S. military surge in Afghanistan and despite clearing operations continually focused on the Ring Road, large parts of it south of Kabul were deemed too insecure for land travel. Occasionally, Afghan government officials would dare to use it, but many trucks would still only travel on the road in large convoys accompanied by the Afghan National Police, Afghan National Army, or unofficial militias. Truckers tend to be most reluctant to travel with the ANP since unlike the army, the police demand extra "taxes" for providing protection and often still run away if the Taliban attacks. The militias, and previously security companies, also charge large protection fees, but they either fight the Taliban or bribe it with parts of the collected payments.[29]

The failure of the formal Afghan judicial system to deliver effective— that is, swift and accountable—justice compounds physical insecurity. The lack of robust anticorruption and anticrime measures only encourages the intensification of both: in the absence of deterrence and effective prosecution, crime and corruption are cheap and easy. At the same time, property disputes tend to escalate quickly to violence—all the more so given the frequent weakness of traditional tribal dispute resolution mechanisms, such as the *shura* (council) and *jirga* (assembly of elders). Not infrequently, existing shuras and jirgas are manipulated by unscrupulous power brokers and become inadequate in resolving disputes.[30] Which is not to argue that no tribal dispute resolution mechanisms work, only that they are substantially weakened and can supplement, but not always be relied upon to replace, formal justice institutions. Several attempts have been made during the post-2002 decade to link existing tribal justice mechanisms with formal courts, such as by allowing disputes resolved through tribal mechanisms to be registered with a formal court. Often facing opposition from the Afghan Ministry of Justice as well as Afghan women's groups, the policy has not been consistent and depends on the provincial governor accepting the program as well as the latest attitude toward the issue within the Ministry of Justice.[31]

The absence of predictability, assured property rights, and contract enforcement in turn deeply undermine any legal economy, compounding the problems generated by physical insecurity. Such deficiencies are detrimental to illegal economies as well. Although illegal economies frequently have lower institutional requirements for their operation than formal legal economies, they nonetheless cannot operate without some level of predictability and contract enforcement. It is precisely the lack of formally sanctioned processes to guarantee property rights and assure contract enforcement as well as government suppression of illicit economies that create space for organized crime groups and other nonstate actors to become sponsors of illicit economies and providers of regulations to facilitate and control them.[32]

In short, crime, unmitigated and unpredictable corruption, and tribal violence provide key openings for the Taliban to exploit.

Economic Insecurity: The Danger of Defining Good Governance in Opposition to Elementary Needs of the Local Population

The second crucial aspect of human security and a key criterion against which Afghans judge the quality of governance is the assurance of elemental livelihoods: food security, economic survival, and prospects for economic development. Yet Western conceptions of good governance for Afghanistan, featuring the suppression of its opium poppy economy, often have been at odds with the elementary economic needs of many of the country's rural communities. For much of the population, cultivation of poppy is the basic source of economic survival and food security, and frequently the sole source of livelihood. Consequently, when, in the absence of alternative livelihoods and hence adequate economic security, the international community demands a drastic reduction in the harvesting of poppy—whether through eradication or bans on poppy cultivation—it defines good governance in a way that is directly detrimental to the fundamental interests of the population.

Alarmed by the spread of opium poppy cultivation in Afghanistan, the United States began in 2004 calling for a strong poppy eradication campaign, possibly including aerial spraying.[33] As a result, between 2004 and 2009, manual eradication was undertaken by central Afghan government units trained by DynCorp as well as by regional governors and their forces. When it was first launched in Kandahar, the campaign almost caused a regional revolt and was halted after only 217 hectares of poppy were eradicated, a tiny portion of the overall area of cultivation in the province.[34] Elsewhere around the country, strikes and social protests against eradication broke out. Another wave of eradication was implemented in 2005. It was lauded as a major success since it decreased the area of cultivation by 21 percent, even though the actual ton output of opium shrank only by 2 percent (because of better yields that year). Most of the reduction in cultivation was achieved due to suppression in Nangarhar province in 2005 where, through promises of alternative development and threats of imprisonment, production was slashed by 90 percent.[35]

For many, however, alternative livelihoods never materialized. The cash-for-work programs reached only a small percentage of the population in Nangarhar, mainly those living close to cities. The overall pauperization of the population there was devastating.[36] Unable to repay debts, many farmers were forced to sell their daughters as young as three as brides or abscond to Pakistan. In Pakistan, the refugees frequently have ended up in the radical Taliban-linked Deobandi madrasas and have begun refilling the ranks of the Taliban.

Apart from incorporating the displaced farmers into their ranks, the Taliban once again began to protect the opium fields of the farmers, in addition to protecting drug smuggling traffic.

The Taliban first learned to exploit the illicit poppy economy for obtaining political legitimacy in the 1990s. Seeing drug production as anti-Islamic, its original impulse was to prohibit it. When, in late 1994 and early 1995, the Taliban moved out of Kandahar west to the Helmand Valley, the main poppy-growing region in Afghanistan at the time (as it is today), it denounced the drug trade and banned poppy cultivation. The emergence of the Taliban on the political and military scene in the poppy-growing regions halved the acreage allocated for poppy for the following growing season, a trend that farmers attributed to the fear of reprisals from the Taliban.[37] Both the United Nations and the United States were hopeful that the Taliban would stem Afghanistan's opium and heroin production. The Taliban also cracked down harshly on hashish addicts.

But the Taliban's prohibition on opium cultivation did not last since it alienated local populations from the Taliban and created military and political problems for the group. Indeed, the Taliban's efforts to end poppy cultivation quickly threatened its position in Helmand, despite the close family and ethnic ties between the Taliban's Pashtun fighters and the local population. Throughout 1995, control over the region shifted back and forth between the Taliban and the Akhundzada power brokers, who had been sponsoring poppy cultivation for over a decade.

By 1996 the Taliban adopted a laissez-faire approach to drug cultivation that progressively evolved into taxing the farmers as well as providing security for and taxing the traffickers and heroin labs. By the end of the 1990s, the 10–20 percent zakat was bringing in between $45 million to $200 million a year.[38] Just like the trucking mafia in Afghanistan, the drug traffickers benefited from the Taliban's sponsorship of the illicit narcotics economy. Compared to the greedy and unpredictable local power brokers, the Taliban significantly lowered many transaction costs, preventing constant power shifts. Thus, with the exception of the initial first few months and its 2000 ban on poppy cultivation (described below), the Taliban when in power supervised a steady expansion of the drug industry in Afghanistan. By the late1990s, under the Taliban's rule, Afghanistan surpassed Burma as the world's biggest producer of opium.

Despite the increase in the Taliban's revenues and physical resources that taxing the opium economy brought, the Taliban's change in its approach to the drug economy was not driven by any acute financial need or logistical problems. The estimated profits from another illegal economy that the Taliban taxed—smuggling legal goods across the border with Pakistan traffic—were $75 million, a number large enough to comfortably sustain the Taliban's military effort.[39] Rather, the Taliban changed its policy toward the illicit narcotics economy to compensate for what its sponsorship of the illicit smuggling of legal goods could not provide: a widespread, if very tenuous, legitimacy. Sponsorship of the illicit narcotics economy boosted the Taliban's legitimacy because it provided a reliable source of livelihood to a vast segment of the population. Ruined by the war against the Soviet Union in the 1980s, Afghanistan's economy crept along on illicit poppy cultivation and assorted smuggling. Embrace of the drug economy was one of the few instances in the 1990s when the otherwise doctrinaire and dogmatic Taliban learned to be highly pragmatic.

The 2000 ban on opium poppy cultivation that the Taliban adopted in order to placate the international community and perhaps finally acquire international recognition, however, lost the group its political capital with the Afghan population. It led to the largest reduction of opium poppy cultivation in a country in any single year, causing a 75 percent fall in the global supply of heroin for that year.[40] The ban severely affected the prospects for economic survival for vast segments of Afghanistan's rural population and alienated them from the Taliban.

But the insurgent group learned that lesson well. So when the international community started demanding eradication and bans on poppy cultivation in the post-2002 decade, the Taliban was ready to step in and offer itself as a protector of the poppy farmers as well as drug traffickers. In fact, the antagonized poppy farmers came to constitute a strong and key base of support for the Taliban. The post-2002 eradication efforts were plagued by massive corruption problems, with powerful elites able to bribe or coerce their way out of having their opium poppy fields destroyed while the poorest farmers, most vulnerable to the Taliban's mobilization efforts, bore the brunt of eradication. Political power brokers in charge of eradication frequently and systematically have used eradication and interdiction to score points with the international community while at the same time undermining their tribal and drug business competition. Their own stocks and access to trafficking would often remain unaffected, and their market power and approval by the international community would be strengthened.[41]

One of the key and highly counterproductive consequences of the resulting alienation of the population from the government and of the strengthening of the bonds between the population and the Taliban was the substantially decreased willingness of Afghans to provide intelligence on the Taliban to NATO and the ANSF.[42] Accurate, timely, and actionable intelligence, of course, is the lynchpin of a counterinsurgency.

Although it pleased the international community and was hailed as an example of good governance, the government's eradication program deeply discredited the central state in the eyes of the local population. Areas without effective alternative livelihoods efforts became politically restless and prone to Taliban mobilization. They were the scene of physical attacks on eradication teams by both angry locals and the Taliban acting on their behalf. Conflicts over land, water, and access to resource handouts from the international community frequently intensified in such areas, as did the movement of militants through them.

The Obama administration tried to adjust counternarcotics policies in Afghanistan to make them consistent with the needs of the Afghan people in an attempt to break the bond between Afghan farmers and the Taliban that was strengthened by eradication.[43] But this salutary change has been beset by numerous problems, and ultimately, the effects of Obama's counternarcotics policies have not been radically different from the policy outcomes of the Bush years. Moreover, on the cusp of the change in political and security order in Afghanistan, the abuse of government power and resources, corruption and state-sponsored criminality, and generalized impunity are as pervasive and intense as ever. Mafia rule in Afghanistan has become deeply entrenched.

5

Power, Impunity, and Legitimacy in Eastern and Southern Afghanistan: Learning to Love Mafia Rule

Dodging trucks, donkeys, pedestrians, and a police convoy transporting someone of importance, my driver Ahmed (an alias to protect him from Taliban reprisals) slowly forged a path through the madness of Afghanistan's traffic as he transported me from Kabul to Jalalabad in the eastern province of Nangarhar.[1] In an effort to travel in low profile, I was in full Afghan garb, wearing a black *salwar kameez* and keeping a burqa on the seat next to me in case I quickly needed to minimize my exposure further. The only aspect of my attire that would give me away as a foreigner was my footwear—Merrell shoes. I prefer them to the Chinese plastic low-heel shoes that most Afghan women wear. When I am out on the street, the Merrells are a dead giveaway that I am not Afghan even when I wear the burqa, but I told myself that if I were to be kidnapped during the two-hour drive to Jalalabad, I would rather be kidnapped in comfortable shoes. Although Nangarhar is a key business center of Afghanistan and relatively close to Kabul, the main road connecting the city with Kabul still had enough security problems at the end of the surge of U.S. forces in late spring 2012 that few foreigners would dare to travel on it.

In Kabul the roadside images alternate between shacks and the modern buildings that the post-2002 reconstruction brought. Men peddle carpets, tires, and vegetables; women are thronged by children. Outside of Kabul, one no longer sees the Western garb of Kabul girls—jeans and tight jackets "legitimized" by a headscarf. Instead, burqas predominate. In the almost ever-present Afghan dust and against the brown-gray mountains,

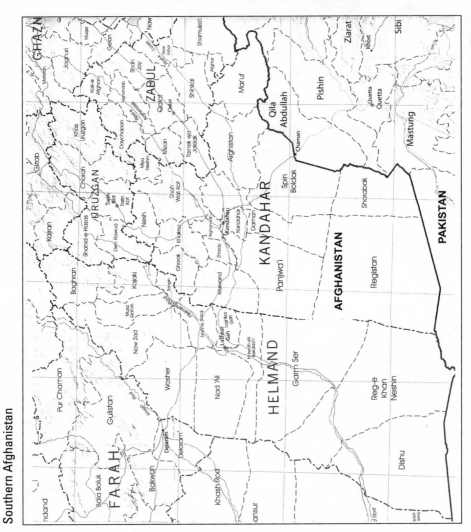

Southern Afghanistan

orange tarps of roadside shacks shade colorful wares for sale—a brilliant splash of color in an otherwise monochromatic landscape. Whenever Ahmed would enter a small town, I would take off my sunglasses, which allow me to see in the sharp Afghan sunlight but ruin my Afghan disguise. Afghans strongly dislike it when a foreigner interacts with them while wearing sunglasses, as most ISAF soldiers often do, since it prevents them from assessing how sincere their interlocutor is. But in the brightness of the Afghan sun, Westerners unused to its piercing quality often find it hard to see without sunglasses. Nevertheless, not wanting to call further attention to myself in the stalled traffic, I would take mine off.

The road to Jalalabad cuts its way through the Koh-e-Paghman Mountains and follows the Kabul River as it meanders through Afghanistan into Pakistan. It is yet another waterway that flows to Pakistan from outside of its borders. The other main waterways originate in or flow first through India, increasing Pakistan's fear of hostile encirclement, including being deprived of its already insufficient water supplies by thirsty or bloodthirsty neighbors.[2] After the unusually heavy rains in the spring of 2012, the rocky and normally gray-brown mountains were covered by delightful yellow, white, and orange wildflowers, and smatterings of wild red poppy and pink bushes. I was reminded of wildflower tourism in Colorado; alas, one could only dream of that in Afghanistan. Perhaps one day tourism will revive in Afghanistan, and the breathtaking mountains and valleys of Wakhan, the blue mosques of Herat and Mazar-i-Sharif, the symbolic Torkham Gate, and the wildflowers of the eastern mountains will again attract visitors.[3] A friend, a first-rate expert on Afghanistan and an Obama official responsible for Afghanistan and Pakistan policy, would occasionally remind me that he remained optimistic about the future of Afghanistan: "I don't know whether it will take two years or two hundred," he would say, "but peace and prosperity will come to Afghanistan one day."

As I traveled further on the Jalalabad road, birds would often cross the road, and I wished once again that I had my binoculars with me. I gave up carrying them to Afghanistan in 2005—just try explaining to ISAF soldiers and Afghan National Police officers what a female *farangi* (a general term Afghans use for foreigners) in a salwar kameez is doing with binoculars. "You're doing what? Looking for birds? What birds—you mean planes? You are with the Taliban?" And a burqa is way too clumsy for bird watching. I've tried it and know firsthand that it is pretty much impossible to focus the binoculars on the bird through a burqa's mesh visor.

Eastern Afghanistan and Border with Pakistan

Wildflower spotting in Colorado is wonderful; but Colorado does not have Afghanistan's wonderfully painted trucks hauling goods and contraband from Pakistan, and providing a major lifeline for the otherwise unemployed locals. Despite Afghans' resentment of Pakistan's incessant meddling in their affairs and continuing sponsorship of the Taliban, many eastern Afghan communities, including the major transport hub of Jalalabad, rely on the trade with Pakistan as their main source of economic activity. Assorted vegetables and fruit are exported from Nangarhar to Pakistan, along with opium and heroin. Consumer goods of all kinds are imported into Afghanistan. The trucks, decorated with bucolic images of lakes and trees, are both a source of amusement and a major menace, Afghanistan being a country that treats road traffic as the ultimate game of chicken and Russian roulette combined.

Nor do Colorado's roads have the caravans of Kochi people trying to squeeze their way on the one-lane highways. One van in front of us, topped with a load of bags and five turbaned Pashtun men bravely clinging to the roof, seemed especially determined to run the Kochis over. These poor and often oppressed nomads, in their stunning pink, purple, orange, and green clothes and long hair braids, move in the spring with their sheep, goats, and the occasional camel from the hot Jalalabad area to Kabul's outskirts or the Shomali plain.

The people of eastern Afghanistan are often embroiled in land disputes—one of the pervasive characteristics of post-2002 Afghanistan and one of the key sources of conflict. The Taliban exploits these tribal land disputes by aligning itself with the losing tribe or promising to correct land grabbing by power brokers. From Kabul to the arid plains of Balkh to the fertile lands of the Helmand Valley, land grabbing has typified politics and economics in Afghanistan since 2002. In Jalalabad itself, it has greatly intensified over the past several years, my Afghan interlocutors told me during the April 2012 trip.[4] In interview after interview, people complained about being dispossessed of their land through fake deeds, by bills of sale listing people long deceased as recent sellers, or simply by the barrel of a gun. Government officials would wrongly designate land as public and then sell it for high profit to their cronies. "Afghans are not used to investing in bonds or stocks," one prominent Logar malik explained. "In land is money and prestige. And those in power just steal it."[5]

Since 2011, house prices have been collapsing all around Afghanistan; in Jalalabad, they were reported to shrink by as much as 50 percent.[6]

The price collapse was attributed largely to the tremendous uncertainty and fear of the 2014 transition and the reduction in foreign troop presence, but the drop was also connected to the widespread land grabs and speculation, both of which go unchecked. The pervasive lack of titles has also made it difficult to get credit for land development. For many farmers in Nangarhar, the only available source of credit would be unofficial moneylenders who demand guarantees in opium. This requirement to repay debts in opium is one of many reasons why people feel compelled to cultivate poppy.[7] In the spring of 2012, the United States Agency for International Development launched an effort to improve cadastres (land registers) in Afghanistan, including in Nangarhar, but the process has been slow going and often stirred a political hornets' nest.[8]

In Sarobi town, which lies on the Kabul-Jalalabad road, I tried to persuade my driver to stop at one of the stalls hawking Kochi clothing so I could buy myself a Kochi shawl. Although I had an assortment of headscarves and shawls from different regions of Afghanistan typical of the country's various ethnic groups, I lacked a Kochi one. Ahmed, however, was vehemently against the idea of stopping and my getting out of the car, even though there were many Afghan National Police officers around. Even as the process of transitioning security from ISAF to the Afghan National Security Forces was well under way, the Sarobi district, where the French ISAF contingent had fought some tough battles against the Taliban and suffered serious casualties, did not have a reputation for tranquility—at least in the eyes of my driver. He was probably too cautious—I hardly thought that I would be kidnapped or that we would be attacked during a ten-minute transaction over the shawl, even with the obligatory bargaining over the price. And I doubted that the ANP, despite their notoriety for corruption, would dare extort a bribe from us so blatantly in the midst of so many people. But then again, with cell phones ubiquitous in Afghanistan these days, I supposed that there was a chance that the police observing me could phone ahead to the next checkpoint behind a mountain curve that a juicy source of "tolls" was coming their way.[9] Deciding to respect Ahmed's judgment, I forwent buying the scarf. After all, Ahmed was taking substantial risks, including attacks from the Taliban and extortion threats from criminals, in transporting a lone female farangi around Afghanistan.

As we entered Jalalabad, I pulled my headscarf tightly around my head to keep as low a profile as possible in the dense Jalalabad traffic. I just never got the hang of fastening it even remotely as well as Afghan women do. Mine inevitably loosens and starts slipping down.

A major business hub, second perhaps only to Kabul, Jalalabad has become notorious for kidnapping and extortion over the past several years. In April 2012, that reputation was stronger than ever. Ransom charges for relatives of prominent businessmen reached between $200,000 and $300,000, a source in Jalalabad told me, looking around furtively to make sure that he was not overheard.[10] Prominent power brokers were widely believed to be behind the criminal gangs. Just like in other parts of Afghanistan, such power brokers include high government officials, who have always enjoyed impunity. Even when criminal or corruption charges have been levied, many have escaped prison terms.

Some of Nangarhar's most influential power brokers in the post-2002 period have been Zahir Qadir and Jamal Qadir, the sons of Abdul Qadir, an influential Pashtun malik of the Arsala clan—a feared anti-Taliban fighter who ran Nangarhar for many years. His power and prominence secured a large tomb for him in the mausoleum of several Afghan royals in the city. Although he was assassinated in 2002, his photograph is still plastered on many a Jalalabad corner and lamppost.

Unlike many of Afghanistan's provincial capitals, Jalalabad does have electric street lights. But in the spring of 2012, as in the years before, they did not light up at night. Mostly only the rich and influential have access to electricity, either from private generators or because they manage to divert the meager electricity generated by a government dam next to town for their private use.

Rumors of criminal activities, including land grabs, kidnapping, extortion, and other brutality, long surrounded Abdul Qadir's son, Jamal, the former head of the Nangarhar provincial council, a key provincial governing body.[11] He was finally arrested on corruption charges in March 2012, but immediately the prosecutor was pressured to release him.[12] Jamal's brother, Zahir Qadir, a former general in Afghanistan's border guard, was serving as the first deputy speaker of the Wolesi Jirga, the lower chamber of Afghanistan's weak parliament.

Since 2005 the Qadir clan has shared power over Nangarhar's lucrative economic markets and political life with another one of Afghanistan's major power brokers, Gul Agha Shirzai. Although hailing from Kandahar, where he was governor between 2002 and 2004, Shirzai was moved to the post of Nangarhar's governor by Karzai in reaction to complaints of the international community about Shirzai's misrule in Kandahar.[13] In Nangarhar, Shirzai has managed to keep many in the international community happy with his strongly enforced ban on opium poppy cultivation in the eastern province (thus making Kandahar's flourishing poppy economy all the more profitable).[14] He has relied on Nangarhar's maliks—those he managed to buy off and co-opt—to communicate his edicts to the population and enforce them.[15] But in doing so, he has critically undermined the influence and legitimacy of the maliks. Thus despite the praise he may have received from the international community for his poppy ban and management of the province, few Nangarharis have good things to say about Shirzai, even as they often tremble at the mention of his name.[16]

The vast majority of my Nangarhari interlocutors—maliks from different districts, businessmen, representatives of civil society in the city, and even some government officials—complained about bad governance and power abuse. They spoke at length about oligopolistic and crony economic practices, patronage, nepotism, and corruption.[17] Since provincial and district officials in Afghanistan are appointed by the president—not elected—Afghans often do not feel they have any recourse for altering the plight of their districts and provinces.

The complaint that crime was very much on the rise in the city kept coming up in Jalalabad—and indeed, throughout much of Afghanistan. With a shudder, but without elaborating, residents of Jalalabad would mention "black windows." It took me a while to comprehend that they were referring to criminal gangs supported by the area's power brokers, who would drive around the city in pickup trucks with tinted windows and with hooded men in the back of the trucks toting visible machine guns. I had been in Jalalabad less than five hours when—in broad daylight—I encountered one of those "black window" pickup trucks and its menacing men. Apparently, the provincial government had not made any attempt to disarm them.

When I asked one tribal elder who had been complaining particularly bitterly about crime in the city whether the police were trying to crack down on it, he just laughed. "The government is behind the crime; it is weak and corrupt," he insisted passionately. "The province is run by a mafia."[18] Later, while interviewing a high official at the police headquarters in Jalalabad, I asked what the key priority of the Afghan National Police in the province was. He responded that it was to win the trust of the people. When I probed further as to what the police could do to accomplish that, he replied, with a straight face, unblinkingly, that in Jalalabad the police already had the trust of the people.[19] I did not run across anyone else during my research in Nangarhar who shared that view.

My comparative research on organized crime groups, illicit economies, and alternative forms of governance around the world shows that mafias can have robust legitimacy with local populations. Criminal groups, militant groups, and warlords often derive significant political capital—legitimacy (in the nonlegalistic sense of the term) and support from local populations—by providing socioeconomic and public goods that are otherwise not available and that the state fails to deliver. The criminals do so by sponsoring various illicit economies, such as the drug trade. By protecting the illicit economy, they obtain large financial profits; but through these various efforts, they also provide many in the local population with a reliable—and frequently only—source of livelihood. In addition to the criminal groups' key function of protecting the illicit economy from government efforts to suppress it, they will sometimes also mobilize the illicit revenues to provide otherwise absent social services such as clinics, roads, schools, trash cleaning, and places of worship. Criminal gangs in Rio de Janeiro's *favelas*, Mexican drug cartels, and Indian slum gangs are some of the many nonstate actors who have done so. And so have some of Afghanistan's khans and other warlords, even if in a limited way.[20]

Moreover, as paradoxical as it may sound, both criminal groups and belligerent groups also often provide security. Although they are the source of insecurity and crime in the first place, they often regulate the level of violence and suppress street crime, such as robberies, thefts, kidnapping, and even homicides. Too much unpredictable violence harms even illegal economies. Hence the Taliban in the 1990s became widely popular with the Afghan and Pakistani trucking mafia when it brought predictability to the traffic and reduced transaction costs by removing the warlords' tolls from the roads.[21] Similarly, as demonstrated in Diego Gambetta's classic study of the Sicilian Mafia, because of the inefficiency, corruption, and absence of the state, the local population in Sicily came to embrace the presence of the Mafia. In exploring what the mafiosi offered and what allowed them to remain successful in their business, Gambetta found that the key activity of the Mafia did not lie in the provision of illegal goods, such as drugs, which for them constituted only a peripheral activity, but in their provision of protection.[22] In poorly administered regions, such as Sicily, the threat of untrustworthy and dangerous business competitors, corrupt government officials, as well as thieves and robbers was so acute that the residents of these regions required such protection. Gambetta's core argument was that "the main market for mafia services is to be found in unstable transactions in which trust is scarce and fragile," implying that the mafiosi, in providing the otherwise absent guarantees and protection, do acquire a level of legitimacy.[23] Even though these services are illegal and inherently dependent on the use of violence, they are frequently welcomed by the residents. In fact, many residents in the region studied by Gambetta considered them "extralegal" rather than illegal. Facing uninterested and inefficient, if not outright corrupt, law enforcement, many Sicilians felt that they were better off having their physical protection and the protection of their businesses, including legal businesses, assured by a well-known "man of honor." The relationship that Gambetta described was one of legitimacy—thin perhaps, but legitimacy nonetheless—which goes beyond the initial trust between the mafiosi who are selling their services and the local population.

An even deeper legitimacy can come from a mafia's repeated and reliable service as an economic regulator and enabler. Like militant groups, organized crime groups, such as the Primero Comando da Capital in Sao Paulo's shantytowns, will sometimes provide dispute resolution mechanisms and even set up unofficial courts and enforce contracts.[24]

Functioning as providers of security, public order and rules, and socioeconomic goods not only brings criminal groups important support from the community, it also facilitates their own illegal business, since illicit economies too benefit from reduced transaction costs and increased predictability.

The extent to which criminal groups do provide public goods of course varies. But the provision of regulatory services and public goods often happens regardless of whether the nonstate entities are politically motivated actors or criminal enterprises. What is important is that the more the nonstate actors, criminal or not, do provide such public goods, and especially where they can outcompete the state in these functions of governance, the more they obtain political capital and the population's allegiance—that is, legitimacy—and become de facto proto-state governing entities.

This dynamic breaks down, however, if the nonstate entities are thuggish and do not provide such regulatory services, or if they usurp public goods and funds instead of providing them. If their rule is rapacious and capricious, and their patronage networks are narrow, they are deeply resented by the population and do not acquire any political capital. And if the thuggish mafias have the protection of the state or *are* the state, then a prime opening is created for an outside militant actor, such as the Taliban or a smarter criminal group, to challenge their rule.

Afghanistan's core problem is that the mafias that emerged in the post-Taliban period have been not only highly abusive but also unpredictable and grossly deficient in providing even semipublic services. Even by the standards of mafia rule, the post-2002 Afghanistan system comes up short. The more patronage networks have become exclusionary, the less political capital the state and government-linked power brokers would have. Moreover, since the mafia-like power brokers have frequently held formal positions of power in the Afghan government—by definition, being one and the same as the government—they could not outcompete the government in the provision of even meager security and other regulatory services or private socioeconomic benefits. In the eyes of many Afghans, the state itself has become a parochial and thuggish mafia racket.

Further south from Nangarhar, Kandahar was another province of Afghanistan widely perceived by Afghan people to be run mafia style by the half-brother of President Hamid Karzai, Ahmed Wali Karzai. And his July 2011 assassination not only rocked that key center of power in Afghanistan but also sent political shockwaves throughout the country.[25] A close confidant of the president and the chairman of Kandahar's Provincial Development Council, an influential government administrative body, Wali (as he was known among the Westerners in Afghanistan) was not only widely seen as the most powerful man in southern Afghanistan but also as one of the most influential figures in the country.[26] His death, especially in so dramatic, if very Afghan, a fashion, created an enormous power vacuum in a key center of gravity for the counterinsurgency struggle and for some of Afghanistan's most lucrative—legal and illegal—economies.

A few days later, another of President Karzai's close confidants, Jan Mohammad Khan, who also hailed from the same Popolzai tribe as Karzai, was assassinated in Kabul, most likely by the Taliban. A former governor of Uruzgan, notorious for his poor and discriminatory governance, Jan Mohammad Khan had been relied upon to mediate disputes among the Karzai brothers.[27] The two men had come to epitomize the post-Taliban rule of tight, exclusionary, and ruthless patronage networks with old and new "warlords" at the apex of the wheeling and dealing, rather than an administration of functioning and equitable state institutions. Those who fell out of favor with the powerful men would be cut out of the patronage largesse and protection, even if they themselves were members of the president's extended family.[28]

Wali's assassination had great implications for President Hamid Karzai personally, compounding his sense of vulnerability. Hamid could see the world beyond the walls of the Arg Palace closing in on his power and perhaps survival.[29] The subsequent assassination of Jan Mohammad Khan only highlighted the complex threats the president faced in the power broker–dependent regime he ran and elicited the specter of a recrudescence of the 1990s' assassination waves, civil war, and Taliban rule.

For many Kandaharis as well as members of ISAF and the international community operating in southern Afghanistan, Wali's death was a moment of uncertainty, if not outright danger. Kandahar was a critical focal point of the Taliban insurgency, ISAF's counterinsurgency campaign, and, along with Helmand, the U.S. military surge. (Helmand, including its Marja district where the first surge forces were concentrated, was in fact a misplaced military focus, for strategically, Kandahar was far more important.)[30] Kandahar was President Karzai's power base as well as the heart of the Taliban insurgency. As the seat of Durrani power, Kandahar was also a most important prize in the political contest for control in Afghanistan, second only to Kabul.

Widely perceived to be at the center of a complex web of political, militia, and economic arrangements, Wali stood at the top of political power in the south. He kept the rival Barakzai tribe and the Shirzai clan surrounding Kandahar's former governor, the very same Gul Agha Shirzai, in a precarious balance of power.[31] Like a typical Afghan power broker—except with outsized influence—Wali held frequent audiences for tribal and individual suppliants where he dispensed advice, money, and access to contracts and other juicy economic deals. Even the governor of Kandahar, Tooryalai Wesa, who nominally held considerably more power than the chairman of the Provincial Development Council and was himself a man of many professional accomplishments, was no match for Ahmed Wali Karzai. In fact, many Kandaharis as well as Westerners in southern Afghanistan considered Wesa merely an appendage and acolyte of Wali.

For months after Wali's assassination, conspiracy theory–prone Kandahar was swirling with rumors of who was behind the murder—the Taliban (who at one point claimed responsibility), an alienated Karzai family member, or one of Wali's many political and economic rivals in the south.[32] Could the disgruntled police official and long-time confidant of Ahmed Wali Karzai who actually pulled the trigger, Sardar Mohammad, have acted alone? Did the Americans wish Wali dead? (Many Afghans imbue the United States with a peculiar mixture of omnipotence—if something happens, it must be because the powerful Americans wanted it to—and gullibility, of which clever Afghans can take advantage to con money and favors out of the farangis.)

Wali had been extraordinarily apt at the power broker game. He made many in the international community in Afghanistan believe that he was indispensable, supplying a variety of services for ISAF and U.S. government agencies, including the Central Intelligence Agency (CIA).[33] He rented to them various properties and, more important, provided intelligence on the Taliban and other jihadi militant groups. At the same time, however, he became one of the first power brokers in southern Afghanistan to start talking with the Taliban about a negotiated end to the conflict. In short, Wali was the go-to man for intelligence and political deals in Kandahar.

He was notorious as well for his nefarious activities and for running southern Afghanistan like an exclusionary mafia fief. For many Wali was the epitome of the country's bad governance.[34] He was widely alleged to be a key broker of southern Afghanistan's drug trade.[35] Although the drug trade allegations surrounded him, no publicly available evidence firmly proved his involvement. The McChrystal team apparently spent a substantial amount of time trying to discover some concrete evidence, and when the smoking gun was not to be found, it was ordered to back off.[36] When I would speak with Kandaharis about Wali, I would frequently be hushed up, with locals looking over their shoulders as if Wali could have informants at every dusty Kandahar corner.[37] As to the unproven allegations of his involvement in the drug trade? "If someone had the dough on Wali," I was once told, "they'd be dead."[38]

Wali was also believed to be very much behind the electoral fraud allegedly perpetrated on President Karzai's behalf during the 2009 presidential elections.[39] Thus it was ironic, bordering on sad, that the international observers' team sent to monitor the 2010 parliamentary elections in Kandahar City, of which I was part, stayed at Wali's compound in the city. When I pointed out the potential credibility problems for the monitoring team of being seen as under Wali's sponsorship, I was told that yes, that was an issue, but that Wali's compound was the safest location in Kandahar City.[40] (Wali never showed up at our section of his vast, sprawling semifortress, and no one put any pressure of any sort on our election observation team. The cloud of insecurity over the city, however, made our visits to the polling stations very difficult.)

Because Kandahar was the center of ISAF military presence in the south, it was also the center of some of the most lucrative construction, logistics, security, and intelligence contracts in Afghanistan. Many of the deals in which Wali had his fingers were alleged to be of a criminal nature—not just the drug trafficking but also extensive land grabs and various protection rackets. Perhaps not surprisingly, some of the business conflicts over lucrative contracts with foreign governments and firms became actual *wars*, with rival businessmen, such as the Popolzais and Ahmed Wali Karzai versus the Barakzais and Gul Agha Shirzai, allegedly shooting each other's men to get access to the contract money.[41] At other times, they would negotiate a spheres-of-influence deal among themselves and set up coercive monopolies to control the high-profit rents under the guise of various business associations.[42]

And for the power brokers, *in*security was *good*. It augmented the dependence of the international community on their services and reduced the chance of effective monitoring. Insecurity provided a useful cover for the hashing out of mafia rivalries and contract wars. Often there were deep and complex layers to killings in Kandahar and southern Afghanistan. An Afghan businessman who until 2011 worked as a political adviser to ISAF in Kandahar told me, "Wali and Gul Agha Shirzai often managed to persuade the internationals that the assassinations of district governors and businessmen in Kandahar were done by the Taliban. But mostly they were bumping off each other's people, and ISAF just didn't catch onto it."[43] Which is not to say that the Taliban intimidation-assassination campaign had not, in fact, been under way for the past several years. It had, and the Taliban made it a point to assassinate those who cooperated with the Afghan government or the international community. But the resulting insecurity also hid a lot of nonmilitant criminality.

Those who were left out from the narrow but highly profitable patronage network that Wali ran often hated him. They claimed it was his exclusionary and rapacious practices that drove many in southern Afghanistan to join the Taliban or at least to detest the Karzai government.[44] Yet periodically, calls for appointing Wali the official governor of Kandahar arose, not just from those who benefited from his patronage but also from those who sought to make him more accountable by coupling his great power with formal responsibility.

ISAF and the international community were often mystified by how to deal with Wali. His notoriety and grip on power in southern Afghanistan made it difficult for the international community to endorse him. But efforts to remove him from his base of power—for example, by persuading President Karzai to appoint him ambassador to the United Arab Emirates, where the Karzai family and other Afghan power brokers deposited billions of dollars—failed.[45] But often such efforts were half-hearted since Wali, even though he behaved like a mafia don, was also useful to ISAF and the CIA.

At times, the international community in Afghanistan did succeed in removing some of the most egregious power brokers from at least some positions of power where they could do most harm. The Dutch mission in Uruzgan, where its military was deployed until 2010, had been experiencing the effects of bad governance first hand: Jan Mohammad Khan's regime there was so discriminatory and riddled with corruption that it was believed to be turning entire districts and Ghilzai communities into Taliban supporters.[46] By threatening to seriously curtail their mission in Uruzgan, the Dutch finally compelled President Karzai to remove him from the governor's post in 2006, and Jan Mohammad Khan served as a member of the Afghan parliament until his July 2011 assassination. But with Wali's help, Jan Mohammad Khan still retained a lot of sway over Uruzgan without having a formal government post.

In Uruzgan, Jan Mohammad Khan had shared the limelight and clout with his son-in-law and another friend of Wali's, Matiullah Khan. A self-appointed highway police chief in the province, Matiullah too was known for his thuggish ways, including oppressing the Ghilzai minority and allegedly participating in the drug trade.[47] Yet the Dutch efforts to also get Matiullah Khan removed from the province faltered, in large measure because President Karzai was loath to challenge two of his key proxies and major power brokers in Uruzgan. Previously, Kabul tried to get him to disband his militia or at least get an official license to transform it into a registered private security company, but Matiullah refused, and the government was unable to enforce its writ. Instead, it put Matiullah on its payroll.[48] Critically, Matiullah provided intelligence on the Taliban to the American Special Operations Forces in the province and used his armed men to fight the Taliban. And he kept the highway open between Kandahar and Uruzgan's capital Tirin Khot, keeping the Taliban at bay and thus preventing insecurity from shutting it down. For that he was reputed to receive as much as $2.5 million a month from NATO, charging between $800 and $1,200 per NATO vehicle.[49] While likely exaggerating substantially, he claimed to use some of the profits to build seventy mosques in the province, put 15,000 people on his payroll, and endow scholarships in Kabul.[50]

He was also suspected of playing a double game with the Taliban, perhaps transferring to them some of the highway profits. Certain communities in Uruzgan despised him, and many trembled in front of him.[51] But the American military in the south found him useful enough. The Dutch mission was thus stuck at best with trying to moderate Matiullah Khan's excesses of abuse, such as his discrimination against the Ghilzai minority in Uruzgan. At times, the Dutch team did succeed in pressuring and cajoling him into adopting better governance practices.[52]

Another case of the international community's success in restricting the free rein and abuses of the power brokers was the removal of Sher Mohammad Akhundzada from the governorship of Helmand.[53] One of the long line of Helmand-based power brokers and also a key supporter of President Karzai, Akhundzada, like Jan Mohammad Khan until his death, was notorious for his abusive rule, land theft, discriminatory policies, and participation in the drug trade.[54] The United Kingdom, whose forces were deployed to Helmand, ultimately put heavy pressure on President Karzai to get him to sack the governor.[55] But just like Jan Mohammad Khan, Sher Mohammad Akhundzada has been able to retain great influence in Helmand, even as he competed with Mohammad Gulab Mangal, Helmand's governor 2008–12 and a man who enjoyed major support from the United States and the international community, and even as Akhundzada's networks too have become narrower and hence more brittle.[56] The northern districts of Helmand, particularly Musa Qala and Kajaki, have keenly felt Akhundzada's weight, including via the militias and hired guns he maintains. Tribal conflicts, such as among the Alizai, fester, and few, mostly just the Taliban, have dared to tread on his turf.

Although the fears of a power struggle in the wake of Wali's death were warranted, major bloody fights among the rivals for the spoils of his empire did not ultimately spill visibly onto the streets of Kandahar City or the fertile fields of the province. Nonetheless, his demise turned out to be a crucial but lost moment of opportunity for the international effort in Afghanistan. Careful handling by the United States and the international community of the ensuing political rearrangements could have enabled major improvements in governance, with greater inclusion of various tribes and communities and greater equity, transparency, and accountability for the Afghan people. It could have increased the plurality of interests involved in policymaking, thus broadening the narrow and incestuous power networks that have come to dominate Afghanistan's politics. Although it was inevitable that President Karzai would seek to refurbish his influence in Kandahar and reinforce Popolzai control in the city, the power restructuring in Kandahar could also have been a moment to widen political representation in provincial and district development councils, and to enhance the authority of district and provincial governor's offices vis-à-vis Kabul. Here was a chance for the international community to reduce its own dependence on Afghanistan's rapacious power brokers for critical services and thus diminish their influence.

But such a governance-reforming policy would have required a great deal of skill, detailed knowledge of the power arrangements and networks in the city, consistency, and persistence. The frequent rotation of U.S. and international civilian and military personnel out of Afghanistan was not conducive to developing the capacity for such well-calibrated pressure. Equally important, such a policy also would have required the willingness to put long-term stability ahead of immediate battlefield exigencies, as well as a great deal of luck.

However, who would risk running a war on luck? Better to stick with the known, even if troublesome, arrangements and manipulators of power as long as the known deliver in the short term. And one of the knowns circling in Wali's orbit and waiting in his wings was General Abdul Raziq. By the time of Wali's death, Raziq had been embraced by ISAF for routing the Taliban out of the difficult areas of Mahlajat and Arghandab. From the strategic subdistrict and district of Kandahar, respectively, the Taliban insurgency had leaked into Kandahar City and terrified the population. And Raziq was able to severely degrade the Taliban's capacity in both areas. In the fall of 2010, a high-ranking ISAF official in Kandahar enthusiastically described to me how then Colonel Abdul Raziq successfully cleared Mahlajat of the Taliban, "something even the Soviets couldn't do."[57] He also cleared the Taliban from Arghandab, which became the showcase of the improved effectiveness of the counterinsurgency effort for visiting delegations, and to which ordinary Kandaharis began returning for weekend picnics. Yes, the former border police commander from Spin Boldak had been an alleged smuggler of notorious ruthlessness and had been accused of mass murder.[58] But he could get things done for ISAF. With Raziq willing to do battle against the Taliban, the United States and ISAF did not even really try to loosen the power networks in Kandahar, expand them to include more interest groups, and perhaps even make them more accountable. Instead, as a reward, Raziq was appointed police chief of Kandahar, a position he turned to his advantage and the expansion of his own power structures.

In a throwback to the country's past and perhaps a preview of its future, Ahmed Wali Karzai's death could have triggered waves of assassinations and counterassassinations in southern Afghanistan and beyond, akin to when a kingpin goes down in an area of weak governance and nonexistent law enforcement. It didn't. But despite the appointment of Shah Wali Karzai, another one of President Karzai's brothers, to lead the Popolzai tribe, it did set off a frenzied contest over the redistribution of power in Kandahar—particularly among the remaining Karzai brothers. General Raziq emerged out of the mix as a new pivot of power, even if one not as powerful as Wali.

By the summer of 2012, the dust of the Kandahar power struggle had not yet settled, and the turf contest was continuing even if life there was more peaceful than during Wali's heyday. Despite being the governor of Kandahar for four years, Wesa was not able to increase the power his formal position accorded him, and his clout continued to be minimized by persistent speculation as to when he would finally be replaced by someone else. Thus, although some of the faces of power in Kandahar and southern Afghanistan have been changing, the basis of governance has not fundamentally shifted from personalized power broker rule to more accountable rule of formal institutions.

Throughout my research visit to Nangarhar in April 2012, my translator Reshteen (for security reasons, another alias) kept complaining vehemently and nonstop about governance in the province. A young man in his late twenties who graduated from Jalalabad University with a degree in law and political science and now running a small legal consulting firm, Rashteen railed against patronage and nepotism in the provincial government and the lack of competence and qualifications of the government officials. He lamented the private prisons, land theft, and other abuses. Still, his law business was not doing well. "Who needs a legal advice here? In Jalalabad, you need a gun to get contracts fulfilled," he would say. And throughout the period of the research, he kept requesting that I get him to the United States.

One of our last meetings was with a very high Nangarhar government official. As we were leaving the official's luxurious outer office, where scores of people were waiting for an audience, Reshteen was accosted by a friend who had been working as a close special adviser to the governor. But through connections to Abdul Rasul Sayyaf , another notorious warlord with a checkered past and now an influential member of the Afghan parliament, Reshteen's friend was now being transferred to Sayyaf's Kabul office. He told Reshteen that his advisory position with Gul Agha Shirzai was therefore available and that he would secure it for Reshteen. When we were far away from the governor's compound, I asked Reshteen if he would in fact accept the offer—after all, he had not said one good thing about the provincial (or, for that matter, national) government in which he was now being asked to serve. "Of course I will!" he exclaimed elated. "It's a government job, it's great. I can make a lot of money, and it's forever."

Obviously, even if the mafia does not provide public goods or function as an effective regulator and provider of public goods and socioeconomic handouts, even if it is thuggish and abusive, there is a way to come to love it—by managing to join it.

6

International Efforts to Fight Corruption and Improve Governance

The Afghan people may bemoan and deeply resent government corruption and widespread abuse of power, but they have not been able to mount an effective demand for the Afghan government to reform its ways. And Washington and the international community more broadly have continued to waver in their assessment of how critical it is to challenge corruption, abuse, and other poor performance by the Afghan government. While publicly calling for improving governance in Afghanistan, Washington's policies have in practice oscillated between tolerating corruption for the sake of other goals—with the justification that Afghans are used to corruption anyway—or confronting it head on, but often with little effectiveness. Immediate military battlefield exigencies have frequently trumped anticorruption efforts. Even when the Obama administration urged the Karzai government to tackle corruption, it often did so with language that exaggerated the U.S. capacity and wherewithal to follow up on its exhortations. At the same time, such a language was keenly threatening to President Karzai's system of rule and political survival, and hence was bound to generate his refusal to cooperate and attempts to subvert the efforts. When Karzai pushed back, Washington and the international community found themselves frustrated and stymied, and unwilling to expend enough of their political capital to prevail, they often essentially folded up the anticorruption campaign.

Isolation from Local Populations and Limited Understanding of Complex Politico-Economic Structures

The counterinsurgency and state-building efforts have been plagued by insufficient understanding on the part of the outsiders of the very complex and fluid political, military, and social environment in Afghanistan. The difficult questions of how much protection of the international military forces and civilians is necessary and how much interaction (and of what kind) is permissible between the international personnel and the Afghan population have tended to be resolved in the direction of greater protection requirements and a thin amount of direct exchange between the internationals and the locals. Indeed, for most of their posting in Afghanistan, many international advisers, development specialists, and military personnel were confined behind Hesco barriers at military bases or at the headquarters of the provincial reconstruction teams (PRTs). Even many of those administering economic development and relief projects rarely, if ever, got to significantly interact with the local population. This constriction of what during the Obama administration was supposed to be a population-centric counterinsurgency strategy was reflected in the fact that out of those present at the sprawling ISAF military base at Kandahar Airfield, which at one point numbered 30,000 personnel, as many as half would never leave the base.

When visiting the airfield and other military bases, I would have the feeling that I was in a medium-security prison. Frustrated just within a few days at not being able to interact with Afghans, I developed great admiration for the civilians deployed on tours to Afghanistan who had to accept living and working within the compounds for months, at times even years. It took not only great patience to put up with the confinement but also a great deal of commitment and dedication, as many would work twenty-hour days, seven days a week for months and months. To me, the lockup at the bases seemed like having to remain in Lesotho when one really wanted to be in South Africa, or like living on an island floating in the dramatic sea of Afghanistan and not being able to even dip one's toes in the water. So after just a few days of this, I would quickly become restless and desirous of donning my burqa, as clumsy and hot as the garment is, to escape from the barbed wire and the Hesco barriers and move among the people of Afghanistan.

Since 2005, of course, moving around Afghanistan unprotected, or even with armed protection, has entailed a great deal of physical risk for the international advisers. And those international researchers and development advisers who nonetheless did live for substantial periods of time outside of the compounds were subjecting themselves to very real, very large danger—far greater than I would experience when traveling around with an interpreter for a few weeks at a time. But still, Afghanistan, with all its hardship and grind and dust, has a way of getting under one's skin. For me, the richness of experience has been worth the risks.

The security-based restrictions on circulating among the population have resulted in the international community's excessive dependence on select Afghan interlocutors, such as local government officials and power brokers, for much of the understanding of the local dynamics. However, the reliability of these Afghan contacts has often been problematic. Frequently unable to comprehend or unwilling to deal with the deeper socioeconomic and political problems in the areas of their responsibility, and predominantly interested in maximizing their power and profit, they have been prone to provide skewed intelligence and an incomplete analytical picture.

Short rotation tours for both soldiers and civilians further augmented the dependence on Afghan interlocutors and reduced the international community's ability to develop a good understanding of the local area. The short stay in the country also hampered their capacity to assess the credibility of their Afghan connections. For many non-American ISAF military and civilian embassy and contractor personnel, the tours often would be only six months long, while the tours of the Americans would span nine months to over a year. Yet in Afghanistan, it often takes months just to establish trust and a dependable working relationship with the local actors—and even longer to get to the bottom of complex and layered disputes and counterclaims that may run several generations back and still influence the behavior and preferences of power brokers or villagers. Even the top layers of the international effort—at the level of generals and ambassadors—have suffered from effects of quick rotation. Overall, the short tours have limited the ability of international assistance staff to learn and adapt their strategies.

To the extent that international civilians and military forces did go among the population (such as after the McChrystal review that emphasized population protection), they often focused on gathering very narrow intelligence, such as tactical information on who the Taliban members in a village were. Acquiring a broad socioeconomic, political, and ethnic understanding of the conditions in each locality, however, is critical for devising policies to promote good governance and sustainable economic development as well as a for a host of other policies, such as the standing up of irregular paramilitary self-defense forces. As late as 2009, General Michael Flynn, one of the prominent American generals in the Afghanistan war who was in charge of intelligence, lamented the inadequate understanding of the broader sociopolitical dynamics and the intelligence picture with which ISAF and the United States operated in Afghanistan.[1] While some improvements in intelligence gathering and analysis have since occurred, by the summer of 2012, as the international part of the war was beginning to "wind down," serious deficiencies remained.

One answer to this fundamental lack of detailed understanding of the complex political and social dynamics in Afghan districts and provinces has been the development of the so-called human terrain teams. Composed of both military members and social scientists, they are tasked to provide brigade commanders with their own resource to help understand and respond to the social, ethnographic, economic, and political elements of the people among whom a force is operating.[2] Inevitably, the performance of the human terrain teams has been uneven. How accurate and adequately complex a picture they develop of local environments is a function of both the interests of the team members and instructions from the command. ISAF military commanders too often have been obsessed with mapping tribal affiliations, to the relative neglect of other important information on local insurgent, criminal, and patronage networks and on the community's land and water distribution patterns, economic activities, and connections to the outside world. Yet even when the human terrain teams have managed to develop an impressively comprehensive and nuanced local picture, such analyses have not necessarily translated into more knowledge-based policies.[3]

Persistent Indecision over Whether to Tackle Corruption and How

Perhaps it was partially the often inadequate interaction with the local Afghan population, in addition to the unresolved strategic debate in the U.S. government over whether counterterrorism policies in Afghanistan do require state building, that produced the ambivalent and sometimes erratic policies as to how to promote good governance. Was it sufficient to focus on expanding service delivery, or was it also important to combat corruption in Afghanistan? The absence of consistent answers to these questions has resulted in persistent oscillations in both the basic counterinsurgency strategy and state-building policies.

What clearly emerged, however, was that continuing reliance on corrupt and abusive warlords for intelligence, logistics, and direct military operations—whatever its counterterrorism justifications—inevitably comes with the price tag of compromised governance. At times the international community, being too isolated behind the Hesco barriers to be aware of how rapacious and discriminatory some of their key Afghan interlocutors were, did not understand whom it was hiring. At other times, it was a willful choice to ignore the warlords' record of corruption and abuse. Thus some of the most notorious power brokers, such as Ahmed Wali Karzai, Gul Agha Shirzai, and Abdul Raziq—the men "who knew how to get things done"—came to be the key facilitators of various operations of the international community in Afghanistan. As many of these strongmen obtained official positions of power in the Afghan government, the internationals often felt all the more locked into dealing with them and could not find a way to work around them.

Throughout much of the Bush administration, the U.S. and international concern about corruption in Afghanistan was mostly only smoldering. With international prodding, the Afghan government established in 2004 the General Independent Administration for Anticorruption (GIAA). The 2006 Afghanistan Compact, a document delineating the mutual responsibilities of the international community and the Afghan government, included a section on corruption, in which the Afghan government agreed to "combat corruption and ensure public transparency and accountability."[4] But quickly it became clear that the international community was unable to find either the will or mechanisms to hold the Afghan government accountable to the compact. The GIAA rapidly showed itself to be neither independent nor dedicated to fighting corruption. Its credibility was especially compromised when in 2007 Izzatullah Wasifi was appointed as its head, despite having been convicted on drug trafficking charges in the United States ten years prior.[5] Yet even before the arrival of Wasifi, the GIAA hardly took any anticorruption action. In 2008 it was dismantled and a new anticorruption body—the High Office of Oversight and Anti-Corruption—was created. But that agency too did not exhibit any greater resolve or competence in tackling corruption, and its key people were often very close advisers and confidants of President Karzai. To satisfy the demands of the international community, President Karzai created another anticorruption body—the Monitoring and Evaluation Commission—in December 2010. But he kept appointing to its leadership compromised individuals the international community considered corrupt and discredited but who were his close allies.[6] Clientelism, rather than merit, was the determining factor of appointments even in the main anticorruption bodies—or perhaps one should say *particularly* in such bodies, given the pervasiveness of corruption and patronage.[7]

Especially in the first year and a half of the Obama presidency, at least some members of the administration, notably Secretary of State Hillary Clinton and Vice President Joseph Biden, accorded greater importance to fighting corruption in Afghanistan than did the Bush administration. While still chair of the Senate Foreign Relations Committee, Biden traveled in December 2008 to Kabul where he—in an apparently very heated conversation—warned President Karzai that the incoming Obama administration would expect more from him than the Bush administration did in cracking down on corruption. He also informed Karzai that the new U.S. president would discontinue the video-calls Karzai enjoyed with Bush.[8] But one of the problems with that blustering approach in pushing better governance was that the new administration did not speak with one voice, and many of its policies and proclamations were inconsistent and internally contested.[9] Thus, even while Vice President Biden was demanding decisive and thoroughgoing anticorruption action by Karzai, other principals in the administration were speaking about minimalist goals. Biden himself added to the confusion by arguing that the goal of the mission in Afghanistan should be defined narrowly in terms of counterterrorism, not state building. The outcome of these contradictory messages was that President Karzai, while furious at being ordered around and openly criticized, also quickly learned that Washington was itself ambivalent about its threats regarding corruption.[10]

Nonetheless, as the year progressed, the Obama administration sought to build up several anticorruption structures in Kabul, including the Major Crime Task Force (MCTF) and the Special Investigations Unit (SIU). The MCTF began to be formed in May 2009 and was formally announced in November 2009.[11] Under the joint direction of the Afghan Ministry of Interior and the National Directorate of Security (NDS), staffed with over

150 officers, the MCTF was advised by the U.S. Federal Bureau of Investigation, Britain's Scotland Yard and Serious Organized Crime Agency, and Europol. Similarly, the SIU too was supported by the United States, including the Drug Enforcement Administration, and by the United Kingdom. Rather quickly, the MCTF developed some surprising competencies. But to the extent it was effective, it ran afoul of President Karzai and his inner circle. Thus, when on the basis of wiretap evidence from the MCTF and SIU the Afghan attorney general moved in July 2010 to arrest Mohammad Zia Salehi, a confidant of the Afghan president, Karzai immediately sought to subvert the investigation and released Salehi.[12] Salehi had been charged with accepting a bribe to scuttle an investigation into a *hawala* (informal Islamic money transfer system)—New Ansari—that was suspected of moving money for Afghan government officials, drug dealers, and the Taliban at a level that totaled $2.5 billion in 2009.[13] In addition to the political fallout from any public confirmation of the suspicions regarding New Ansari, Salehi's arrest was particularly sensitive for Karzai because Salehi was one of his key operatives for establishing contact with the Taliban about possible negotiations, and the arrest occurred in the context of Karzai's having fired the minister of interior, Hanif Atmar, and the head of NDS, Amrullah Saleh, just some weeks prior. The atmosphere in Kabul was one of shaky patronage networks and political tension, with Karzai rather suspicious of the heavily Tajik-dominated NDS at that time. Given the major rift that by then had developed between the Obama administration and Karzai, described in detail below, Karzai interpreted the episode as yet another attempt by Washington to discredit him, and Washington interpreted Karzai's subversion of the investigation as yet another sign of his venality.[14]

Not only did Washington and the international community fail to prioritize what corruption needed to be addressed first and thus merited the expenditure of political capital, they also often ignored President Karzai's political debts and dependencies. The outcome overall was similar to that of the Salehi investigation: Karzai would try (and many times succeed) to reverse the anticorruption efforts, including indictments of powerful corrupt officials. He would also try to subvert the development of anticorruption and anticrime institutions that the internationals were trying to build by firing officials determined to combat corruption or placing his own people in key positions of the anticorruption bodies.[15] When on occasion some officials have been fired—ostensibly as part of an anticorruption drive—such moves have frequently disguised efforts to purge institutions of rival networks and appoint one's own ethnic kin and other clients to the vacated positions.[16] For example, when Bismullah Khan Mohammadi, a prominent Tajik commander and minister of the interior from 2010 to 2012, purged many police officers from the force on corruption charges, ISAF applauded his actions as a determination to fight corruption.[17] But he also used the purges as an opportunity to appoint close Tajik allies into key police positions north of Kabul.[18]

In the fall of 2009, as the Major Crime Task Force was being created, ISAF too was, for once, keenly focusing on corruption. General McChrystal's 2009 review argued strongly that governance should be on par with security in the counterinsurgency campaign, for without a legitimate and accountable political system, the Afghan people would not buy in, and lasting stability would be elusive.[19] Such an assessment and emphasis did not necessarily mean that the international community and the United States would have to build a Western-style democracy in Afghanistan. Rather, in addition to the list of standard accountability mechanisms such as formal elections, vibrant media, and a robust civil society, it also emphasized traditional Afghan institutions such as local shuras.[20] But McChrystal pulled no punches in arguing that the promotion of good governance should not be cavalierly subordinated to military exigencies and campaign shortcuts.

One of the key tools of the military became its anticorruption task force, Shafafiyat (Transparency), headed by Brigadier General H.R. McMaster. Building on a previous ISAF task force to investigate corruption surrounding ISAF's contracting, Shafafiyat had a broad mandate to lead ISAF's investigations into all aspects of corruption in Afghanistan. But ultimately hamstrung by both political complexities in Afghanistan and the significant drop-off of ISAF's focus on corruption and governance a year later, this anticorruption body also has struggled to make more than a sporadic difference.

Given the extent of corruption in Afghanistan and the fact that complex patronage networks came to underpin the post-2002 political system, it should have been evident that the fight against corruption would require a great deal of persistence and prioritization as well as political sensitivity in Washington to the limits of its influence and to President Karzai's political entanglements. One problem that quickly emerged was that the Obama administration often demanded governance reform of an intensity and extent that ignored Afghan realities and political complexities. In a system where the highest government officials as well as the lowest ones, line ministries, banking centers, and most international contracts were pervaded by corruption and connected to powerful patrons, developing a list of implementable corruption-reform priorities was necessary but frequently not done.[21] At the same time, dramatic demands by Obama administration officials were not followed up with tough sanctions, including punishments such as cutting off some aid, a tactic for which Washington and the international community ultimately did not have the stomach (see below). For two years, then, the outcome would be that the Obama administration, like its predecessor, would secure dramatic promises from President Karzai to tackle corruption, with little actual follow-up. Such declaratory commitments would usually ramp up before major donor pledging conferences, but most would not be implemented, with little change in practice. Frustrated and exhausted by the paltry progress in reducing the venality and abuse of the Afghan government, Washington quickly lost its zeal for fighting corruption in Afghanistan. Thus, when implementable measures were actually developed, they were rarely adopted. Often they were sacrificed to battlefield exigencies in order to protect power brokers whose assistance was seen as critical in fighting the Taliban. Or they were shelved for fear that they would only further alienate Karzai.

In the fall of 2011, some effort to decide what corruption should be tackled and what would not be a priority took place at the interagency level of the U.S. government. But the attempt to distinguish among "high-level," "predatory," and "petty" corruption proved fruitless and rejuvenated neither the will nor a greater capacity to chip away at corruption in Afghanistan.[22] Such prioritization might have had a good chance of achieving some traction for anticorruption efforts in the Afghan political system (if it had managed to avoid getting bogged down in unending definitional and metrics debates).[23] However, by the time the interagency group attempted to develop such a prioritized approach, the White House and the Pentagon had long lost much of their leverage with Kabul and, once again, much of their determination to combat corruption and foster good governance in Afghanistan.

The American public had grown tired of the dragging war, and the Obama administration imposed firm timelines on the counterinsurgency effort and transition to Afghan lead. Already by the fall of 2010, the emphasis on promoting good governance began rapidly slipping. Many in the U.S. government argued that tackling corruption was a luxury the United States could no longer afford; instead, it was necessary to prioritize stability. [24] By the May 2012 NATO Summit in Chicago, the burden of responsibility for tackling corruption was clearly placed on the Afghan government, and the role of the international community became more circumscribed. The policy of transferring to the Afghan government the responsibility for delivering services further encouraged the transformation of the international civilian role in Afghanistan into "building capacity rather than fostering accountability."[25] The strong signals from the winter of 2009 onward that a predetermined scaling down of the U.S. military presence in Afghanistan was on the way, including the military surge timelines and the emphasis on transition to Afghan National Security Forces, also further reduced Washington's and the international community's leverage with Kabul regarding efforts to stimulate a serious anticorruption drive.

Downgrading the importance of fighting corruption and promoting good governance found strong supporters among those who argued for an essentially limited counterterrorism effort in Afghanistan. They often believed that focusing on corruption was not only futile but actually counterproductive. Limiting the military mission in Afghanistan mostly to remotely delivered airborne counterterrorist strikes would require working through the local warlords and power brokers, not obsessing over the means they used to acquire their power or over their criminal entanglements and discriminatory practices. Already, U.S. counterterrorism operations were extensively using the warlords even with the level of ground presence the United States still had in Afghanistan.[26]

Lacking a coherent, prioritized, and politically sensitive policy on corruption, the Obama administration and ISAF often failed to develop mechanisms and structures to work around and marginalize the problematic power brokers or at least moderate their misbehavior. To date, many of the counterinsurgency efforts continue to depend on their services. As a high-ranking ISAF official in Kandahar told me in the fall of 2010, "In the current struggle for Kandahar, our nightmare is having to take on the Taliban and Wali [Ahmed Wali Khan, alive then] at the same time. But we understand that he has alienated some people in Kandahar."[27] Similarly, despite General Raziq's reputation for serious human rights violations, major power abuse, and extensive criminal activities, ISAF relied on him to clear Kandahar City and Arghandab and embraced him in his subsequent role as the powerful police chief of Kandahar province.[28] A former high official of the U.S. Provincial Reconstruction Team in Kandahar explained that the international community found it exceedingly difficult to restrain the behavior of power brokers like Raziq. The U.S. approach was to draw "red lines" the power brokers should not cross: for instance, there was to be no undermining of provincial and district officials and no interference with the 2010 parliamentary elections or with the Peace Jirga (a body established by President Karzai to develop a broad framework for reconciliation with the Taliban). "Very quickly, however," the U.S. official said, "they [Raziq and other power brokers in Kandahar] violated all of the red lines we set for them. But they are effective in getting things done. We can't go after them at the same time as we are fighting the Taliban. When the Taliban is defeated, the Afghans will take care of the power brokers themselves."[29] But as shown in the previous chapters, the Afghan population has not shared that view. Moreover, the consequence of announcing a red line but then being unwilling or unable to enforce it has eviscerated the credibility of the international community in Afghanistan. Such weakness only encourages Afghan power brokers to believe that they could get away with murder (literally, sometimes) and could ignore the international community the next time around again. Therefore, before the United States and its allies designate a behavior as a red line, it is imperative that they have a credible plan of punitive action if that threshold is violated.

In short, the U.S. and international community's commitment to good governance and the tackling of corruption has been deeply conflicted. And as a result, the internationals' determination to promote good governance has appeared troublingly inconsistent to Afghans, many of whom have learned how to take advantage of the ambivalence for their own gain.

One of the most dramatic examples of the extent of massive corruption in Afghanistan was the collapse of the Kabul Bank. Under the guidance of its chairman, Sherkhan Farnood, and its chief executive officer, Khalid Ferozi, the bank became not only one of the biggest financial institutions in Afghanistan but also a personal piggy bank for many of Afghanistan's most influential power brokers and highest government officials, including President Karzai's brother Mahmoud Karzai, and Haseen Fahim, the brother of Mohammed Fahim, who is one of Karzai's two vice presidents and a notorious Tajik warlord. In fact, the bank's leadership ensured that power brokers from various ethnic groups and political camps would get a cut of its loot and thus guarantee their silence about the corruption and theft at the bank. The bank's leaders also extended largesse to members of parliament to buy their votes for Karzai's political campaign or legislative agenda.[30] Running essentially a ponzi scheme and lending out money to these power brokers way above its liquidity while not expecting the power brokers to repay their loans, the bank was ultimately left with over $900 million debt that had to be picked up by Afghanistan's central bank. Corruption at the Kabul Bank was investigated by the Afghan Threat Finance Cell, an entity within the U.S. Embassy in Kabul set up in 2008 to break Taliban financing, including from the drug trade. Only approximately $300 million has been recovered, with many of the loans having been diverted into untraceable shell companies or used to purchase villas in Dubai costing tens of millions of dollars. But with the crash of the real estate market in Dubai, most of that money also could not be recovered. The corruption at the bank almost brought down Afghanistan's entire banking system. The International Monetary Fund (IMF) suspended its aid to Afghanistan for over a year due to the Kabul Bank scandal. Yet it is not clear that anticorruption measures within Afghanistan's banking sector have been fundamentally strengthened since. Moreover, prosecution of even the key culprits has been elusive. It took more than a year and half before the two chief wrongdoers, Farnood and Ferozi, were finally indicted at the beginning of June 2012.[31]

Despite the IMF's temporary suspension of some international financial flows into Afghanistan, the infusion of approximately $100 billion in foreign aid since 2002 has also generated its own corruption.[32] Massive amounts of the aid money appear to have been siphoned off by clever power brokers for their personal profit.[33] The inability of donor countries and international agencies to track the funds allowed large sums to be removed from Afghanistan, often in suitcases stacked with the foreign currency and carried out through Kabul airport. Whether hiding corruption or representing legal capital flight, the amount of cash officially declared to leave Afghanistan in such a manner in 2011 was $4.6 billion, roughly the same as the annual budget of the Afghan government.[34] The level of capital flight increased by almost five times between 2007 and 2011.[35] The vast sums of foreign aid also have politically strengthened those power brokers who could get their hands on it. Many have thus developed a vested interest in preventing others and the population at large from accessing the funds.[36] The competition over access to these aid flows has also given rise to new "khans," further undermining both the traditional governing structures as well as the official government institutions that the international community has struggled to foster. Insecurity has greatly complicated monitoring and allowed Afghan coercive and oligopolistic businesses to profit from foreign aid and contracts.[37]

Under the best of circumstances, a smaller international presence after 2014 would reduce the dependence of the international community on problematic power brokers, and in turn, the power brokers' influence would be reduced as well. However, if persistent insecurity or a narrow definition of the objective of the U.S. and international presence in Afghanistan still confines the internationals to their consulates and bases, their dependence on the very same problematic power brokers could conceivably increase and the international leverage will diminish even more.

Direct Efforts to Improve Governance: Pressuring the National Government and Going Local

At those times when combating corruption in Afghanistan has been identified as an objective of the U.S. government and the international community, the international actors have deployed two principal mechanisms for pursuing the objective. The primary tool was to attempt to induce better behavior from the national government in Kabul, such as by standing up national anticorruption bodies. When this approach did not produce any progress, the U.S. government and allies instead emphasized reforms at the local level.

Going after the Arg Palace

Believing that the Bush administration had let President Karzai off the hook on corruption and government malfeasance, the Obama administration started out with a determination either to pressure Karzai into changing his behavior or to marginalize him. Following the testy December 2008 exchange between Karzai and Vice President–elect Biden, the Obama administration explored ways to distance itself from Karzai during the run-up to the Afghan presidential elections in August 2009. Although the administration did not publicly announce that it would prefer that Hamid Karzai not be reelected, it let it be known that it sought to "level the playing field."[38] High U.S. officials, for example, granted considerable audience and face time, often publicly reported, to candidates running against President Karzai, including Ashraf Ghani and Abdullah Abdullah, while minimizing meetings with Karzai. In the Afghan culture especially, face time with the powerful is an important sign of influence and favor; therefore such signals were bound to be interpreted by Karzai as a personal and political affront, and he rapidly became deeply distrustful of the new team in Washington.

But regardless of the Obama administration's wishes, Karzai was able to ensure his reelection. As had become his habit, he outmaneuvered his rivals and Washington by making deals with major power brokers.[39] He also resorted to outright, large-scale electoral fraud.[40] The Obama administration was both furious about it and embarrassed that it had failed to prevent it. Thus a few days after the Afghan elections commission announced that President Karzai had won (his main rival Abdullah Abdullah having dropped out of the run-off), the Obama administration reacted with strong language about Kabul's need to combat corruption. On November 15, 2009, for example, Secretary Clinton stated that

> I have made it clear that we're not going to be providing any civilian aid to Afghanistan unless we have the certification that if it goes into the Afghan government in any form, that we're going to have ministries that we can hold accountable. We are expecting there to be a major crimes tribunal, an anticorruption commission to be established and functioning, because there does have to be actions by the government of Afghanistan against those who have taken advantage of the money that has poured into Afghanistan in the last eight years."[41]

Such direct and threatening language notwithstanding, the Obama administration was stuck with the worst of all outcomes: Karzai still in power, still unmotivated to fight corruption, and now also intensely antagonistic toward and suspicious of the United States even as he and his regime continued to be dependent on the United States for political and physical survival.

Subsequent public criticism from the United States also failed to increase Karzai's motivation to tackle corruption and improve governance. The public spats between Washington and Kabul on the corruption issue pushed Karzai into an ever more defensive crouch. In Karzai's view, no real friend would criticize an ally in public. Such behavior indicated that his supposed friends were still trying to destroy him (after all, they abandoned him during the presidential election) and deprive him of his political base. Much of Karzai's internal political clout had been tied to support from Washington, and his political survival has been dependent on co-opting and reshuffling Afghan power brokers. Yet here was Washington insisting that Karzai adopt anticorruption policies that threatened to unravel his internal power-balancing act without giving him alternative means of political survival; and then publicly criticizing him for not taking such political risks.[42] Moreover, Karzai was operating from a fundamentally different concept of what fostering good governance means. Washington and the West defined good governance as building effective and corruption-free institutions and bureaucracies. President Karzai, however, focused on the weakness of the central state, not the pervasive lack of accountability by public officials, and defined improving governance as expanding and deepening the Kandahari Durrani power structures and his personal network while infusing those two endeavors with a national image.[43] A fundamental misunderstanding of the purpose behind the public criticism was thus developing between Washington and Kabul.

Karzai's quiver of counterstrategies included threatening actions directly contradictory to the war effort. One, for example, was Karzai's out-of-the-blue decree shutting down almost overnight private security companies on which much of the international community depended for logistics and physical protection. The private security companies were ultimately allowed to function until March 2012, by which time they were to be replaced by the Afghan Public Protection Force. But it took a large amount of time and the Westerners' political capital to dissuade Karzai from his original scheme of shutting them down within a short deadline. By March 2013, the protection force is to provide security for all ISAF bases and construction sites, as well as foreign nongovernmental organizations, development companies, and embassies.[44] Another tactic was to start blaming the West for Afghanistan's assorted problems, including corruption—for example, by accusing international observers and international members of the Electoral Complaints Commission of the fraud in the presidential elections, or by holding foreign auditors primarily responsible for the extensive siphoning off of money from Kabul Bank.[45] Karzai's outrageous proclamations—including that if he continued to be pressured on corruption, he would join the Taliban—made it very difficult to maintain support for the Afghanistan campaign within Western legislatures and among Western publics, or to avoid openly criticizing Karzai in public.[46]

His relationship with the West ruptured, Karzai became all the more beholden to various Afghan power brokers, many of whom he already owed political debts from the 2009 reelection campaign. Rather than encouraging Karzai to become a more reliable partner of the international community, the on-again, off-again pressure from Washington—much of it publicly voiced—only fueled his paranoid distrust of the United States and its Western partners and increased his reliance on a progressively smaller and smaller clique of advisers, mainly his immediate family.[47]

Internationally, Karzai reacted the same way he does domestically: by adopting a divide-and-rule strategy. Angered by Western criticism, Karzai would hop on a plane a day or two after being criticized by Washington and fly to Moscow, Tehran, or Riyadh to cultivate new friends, such as Russia, or emphasize bonds with old ones, such as Iran and Saudi Arabia.[48] His message was not subtle: if you, the West, continue pressuring me, I'll play with others. Karzai's policy to woo new international allies only intensified after the United States and its ISAF partners became more explicit and public about their plans to radically scale back the military effort in Afghanistan. Thus, after the May 2012 NATO Chicago Summit, President Karzai rushed off to an Afghanistan-focused meeting of the Shanghai Cooperation Organization to rub shoulders with Russia, China, and the countries of Central Asia.

The overt pressure not having yielded any positive results, the Obama administration decided in late spring 2010 to adopt an alternative, "softer" method. Public criticism of Karzai ceased, and carrots rather than sticks were offered to induce better Afghan government performance.[49] But the sotto voce approach did not succeed either. It did not assuage Karzai's distrust of and anger at Washington. At the same time, it gave the impression that the international community was caving in to Karzai's antics, making the administration look weak.

The pattern was becoming dysfunctional: alienated and suspicious, Karzai would respond with unpredictable tantrums as well as periodic ravings against the West.[50] Washington would then devote extensive political capital to smoothing out the relationship and reversing some of Karzai's most problematic declarations. But this "corrective" approach would allow Karzai not only to deflect Western criticism but also to wrap himself in the cloak of nationalist legitimacy.[51] And the cycle would start all over again.

The Obama administration's pressure on Karzai thus did not pay off at all. Instead of inducing Karzai to make a determined effort to combat corruption and improve governance, the dominant effect of the vociferous (yet all too obviously half-hearted and fluctuating) complaints about corruption was that the Afghan president became profoundly alienated from and suspicious of the United States.

Going Local

Frustration with Karzai and the lack of progress in pressuring Kabul to improve governance consequently resulted in the international community's embrace of a "going local" approach to governance and reducing corruption.

Instead of seeking to work through the central government, the international community chose to focus on local officials and traditional local governance mechanisms, such as the shuras (local councils). Given Afghanistan's traditionally weak center and de facto highly decentralized power arrangements, such a policy made sense.[52] Among the key mechanisms to be used for this new local emphasis approach was the Independent Directorate of Local Governance (IDLG).[53] Established in 2007, the IDLG had a very expansive mandate that included consolidating peace and stability; promoting development, equitable growth, and service delivery; and encouraging democracy. Run by a Karzai loyalist, Jelani Popal, IDLG was rapidly co-opted by Kabul. With approximately 10,000 employees, the institution became an additional patronage tool of Kabul's, exploitable for election purposes. Thus, rather than fairly representing local interests in Kabul, IDLG "became another arena for political contestation."[54]

Another tool used to build up local governance, and one rather explicitly tied to the counterinsurgency efforts, was the Afghan Social Outreach Program (ASOP). It sought to generate village-level and district-level governance, including in highly insecure areas, by paying local tribal elders to form shuras. The hope was that the ASOP structures would be a critical tool for countering instability at the local level.[55] Yet many of the ASOP shuras ended up simply intimidated by the Taliban. Moreover, many did not accurately and equitably represent local communities. Such tribal mechanisms frequently lack the capacity to address important governance problems or are dominated behind the scenes by problematic power brokers.[56] Not surprisingly, some of the shuras created under ASOP failed to perform altogether and only served as a way for local strongmen to extract money from the international community. As with district government officials, the shuras often need to be regularly supervised by the international community to ensure that they fully reflect the various factions and voices of the community. Taliban assassination of tribal elders often further undermines both the representativeness of the shuras and their capacity to govern. According to a report of the United Nations Assistance Mission in Afghanistan, 255 people allied with the Afghan government or ISAF were killed in the first six months of 2012, a 34 percent increase compared to the same period in 2011.[57]

A corollary to going local was an effort to rapidly dispatch district officials and local representatives of line ministries to areas cleared from insurgents through the military surge. Although this "government in a box" famously announced by General Stanley McChrystal often did not materialize, the presence of district governors and line ministry officials in the liberated districts did gradually increase. Persistent and diligent Western oversight produced some important improvements at the local level. Informed by complaints from the local population, the international community tried for a while to work with Afghan line ministries and Kabul to remove, not just reshuffle, particularly odious officials at the district level, sometimes even at the provincial level.[58]

Moreover, with persistent Western encouragement, in some districts, service delivery at the local level also improved, and line ministries became more available and responsible to the needs of the people. At times improvements have also taken place in some ministries in Kabul. The Ministry of Rural Rehabilitation and Development, in particular, has become the poster child of institutional reform and capacity building in Afghanistan. Thanks to the capable leadership of its first minister, Hanif Atmar, the ministry managed to escape the problems that have plagued capacity building elsewhere (fragmentation of efforts and lack of donor coordination, focus on donor-driven outputs rather than sustainability, and patronage pressures to hand out resources, with institution building ultimately transformed into substitute delivery by outside technical experts).[59] Atmar managed to develop a strategic vision for the ministry, form a core team to promote its vision, institute strong financial management procedures, and formulate policies and programs. He did so via an incremental approach that balanced the need to attain legitimacy with international donors with the needs of his staff and their political constraints, and gradually meritocracy and nondiscriminatory access principles emerged.[60] (Atmar was not able to achieve similar success, however, when he later headed the Ministry of Interior, where the political and economic stakes were higher.) Other ministries that have gradually registered some improvements in capacity include the Ministries of Education and Public Health. Yet many of the improvements have turned out to be isolated, and systemic effects have often not been achieved. Reform efforts within particular line ministries have rarely been connected with one another. In addition, improvements, when registered, have rarely reached the provinces, and particularly districts, in a robust enough manner. The Taliban's assassination of district government officials and other Afghans seen as cooperating with the government has also critically hampered government access and service delivery at the district level.

Not simply the consequence of persisting insecurity, many of the above problems are a function of Afghanistan's underdevelopment. Crucially, however, instead of intensifying and enlarging its efforts to push for better governance at least at the local level, Washington wavered in its emphasis on anticorruption as the focus shifted to the transition of full ownership to the Afghan National Security Forces and Afghan government. Under the transition process, improving local governance quickly came to mean speeding up service delivery or building up "capacity" rather than promoting accountability. Moreover, the West continued to depend on problematic power brokers and hence found it difficult to induce them to behave better.

Other deficiencies that plagued Afghanistan's local administration prior to the surge and the creation of the Independent Directorate of Local Governance have continued to trouble it.[61] Although the Afghan president has often been disparaged as "the mayor of Kabul," the presidency was actually endowed with substantial powers and extensive centralization of administration in the Arg Palace. The 2001 Bonn Agreement adopted, and the subsequent Afghan constitution codified, core provisions of the 1964 Afghan constitution, including considerable centralization of formal power in the national government in Kabul.[62] The centralization of power was designed to mitigate the historic weakness of the center versus the power of local strongmen, an imbalance only compounded by the coups of the 1970s, the Soviet occupation of the 1980s, and the civil war of the 1990s. As a result, in the post-2001 period, the Afghan president has controlled the appointments of all government officials, from national level ministers down to district police chiefs and line ministry representatives. Kabul also controls all provincial and district-level budgets.[63]

The dependence on funds disbursed from Kabul undermined efforts to strengthen local administrations. The international community, for example, encouraged provincial planning based on supposed consultation with local communities and expressed in the Provincial Development Plans. Often just a wish list of all desirables, the plans were mostly created without a concurrent budget plan in Kabul, and thus provincial officials would have no capacity to implement their programs unless they could extract funds from Kabul and cajole local representatives of line ministries to provide resources. Mostly, local officials would just pass the buck to line ministry officials. The mere formulation of the plans and their many versions would be defined by the officials, and also by Kabul and the international community at times, as an indicator of good performance, even if little of what was in such plans was ever implemented.[64]

Moreover, since local officials are appointed by Kabul, the local population has a very limited capacity to demand accountability. Local officials—be they exiles who have been "parachuted back" into Afghanistan or local Afghans—often have minimal knowledge of local conditions, little willingness to spend time in the violent districts, and limited acceptability to local communities or power brokers.[65] The experience of Kandahar's governor Tooryalai Wesa is just one of many examples: Wesa was brought back to Kandahar from Canada, but Kandahar's power brokers, including Ahmed Wali Karzai, continued to maintain authority and ran circles around the governor.

Other local officials, even while liked by the international community, subsequently turned out to be deeply corrupt. One prominent example is the case of Abdul Jabar, Arghandab's district governor in 2010 before he was killed. He was embraced by ISAF as a committed and effective official, yet later turned out to be involved in criminal activities, such as skimming large sums of money from foreign aid, as well as being in cahoots with the Taliban.[66] That local government officials and power brokers would use anti-Taliban activities, including cooperation with ISAF and ANSF, to promote their own agenda—including expanding access to economic rents—was inevitable. Purging a local subdistrict in Helmand or Kandahar of the Taliban would often put the local power broker-cum-district official in the perfect position to take over various criminal enterprises in the area, such as the drug trade. ISAF and the international community would often not have the capacity to prevent such side activities. But what has been particularly troubling about such compromises have been the instances when the internationals were not even aware of the nefarious activities of their supposed allies because of inadequate intelligence, and worse yet, when they would extol the virtues of such power brokers in public. Even if driven simply by a lack of knowledge on the part of the international community, Afghans would perceive such pronouncements as a mockery of its claim to want to improve local governance.[67] Although the international community may not have had the capacity to remove or even just work around many such power brokers, it should have been far more circumspect about publicly embracing them and thus indicating— even if inadvertently—its support for their bad behavior.

Even local leaders who have performed well have faced great challenges. The international community has attempted to reward such well-performing local leaders by channeling money and influence through them. But as the tensions between President Karzai and the international community escalated during the Obama administration, such direct international endorsement has at times become a kiss of death for the local officials. The more the West embraces them, the more President Karzai tends to see them as a threat and has attempted to marginalize them or remove them from office.[68] Although maneuvering around Kabul by focusing on the local level may have seemed the only option left after efforts to induce better governance from Kabul failed, the going-local efforts were inevitably bound to be limited in their effectiveness. Given that patronage structures run the breadth and depth of Afghanistan and that corruption and favoritism are highly integrated vertically, attempts to improve governance at the local level would inescapably be constrained by deficiencies and vested interests at the top. However important the improvements at the local level, they could not sufficiently redress the corruption and poor governance emanating from the national level.

Then, too, there is the weakness of the national parliament, which has been largely relegated to the sidelines, although both Afghans and the international community have periodically called for strengthening its capacity and formal powers. The 2004 Afghan constitution designed the parliament to be weak.[69] And the weakness of political parties, strongly disliked by Karzai, further undermined the parliament's ability to challenge the Arg Palace. The absence of even parliamentary blocs and the largely atomized membership that Afghanistan's electoral system produces have compounded the difficulties of parliament mounting effective challenges to President Karzai's decisions.[70] Occasionally, the parliament has been able to block particular ministerial appointments or to organize protests. But President Karzai has continued trying to undermine it, by opposing reform of the single nontransferable- vote electoral system and creation of stronger political parties, and by embracing other bodies, such as the *loya jirga* (grand assembly of influential elders and leaders), to confer legitimacy on himself. It is thus ironic that the instance when the Afghan parliament seemingly took the boldest action was in the impeachment of Minister of the Interior Mohammadi and Minister of Defense Abdul Rahim Wardak, both praised by ISAF for their effectiveness in building the Afghan National Security Forces. The parliament justified these dismissals as an anticorruption effort as well as punishment for the ministers' failure to protect some of Afghanistan's border areas from artillery shelling from Pakistan.[71] But ISAF, although stating that it would work with whomever the new appointees were, saw the dismissals as destabilizing its military transition efforts.[72]

It appears that the Afghan parliament actually dismissed the officials at the instigation of the Arg Palace, with Karzai seeking to increase control over the Ministry of Interior and Afghan police, whom he had come to see as too beholden to northern Tajik political interests.[73] To appease the northerners, Karzai moved Mohammadi over to head the Ministry of Defense, although when Mohammadi was the chief of staff of the Afghan Army (2002–10), he was widely perceived as building highly personalistic and ethnically based patronage networks within the army, instead of seeking to create a unified national force.[74] Although the Afghan parliament voted no confidence in Mohammadi as interior minister in August 2012, it confirmed him for the post of the chief of defense in September 2012. As minister of interior, one of the most corrupt and dysfunctional institutions in Afghanistan, Karzai appointed a long-time police official, Gen. Ghulam Mujtaba Patang, a Pashtun without deep patronage networks of his own, and hence far more controllable by Karzai than Mohammadi, but seen as a competent official. Karzai's choice for director of the National Directorate of Security (NDS)—Asadullah Khalid—was by far most problematic and indicated once again that Karzai continued to place little emphasis on good governance and was more interested in shoring up his personal power. A Pashtun from Ghazni province and a former minister of border and tribal affairs, Khalid became particularly close with Karzai after Wali's assassination when Karzai came to rely on Khalid to preserve the Karzais' power in Kandahar. Seeking to increase control over the NDS, an institution for many years after 2002 dominated by the Tajiks and increasingly distrusted by Karzai for its Tajik orientation and a too-close relationship with the United States, Karzai had picked a highly trusted personal ally and a Pashtun. Once again, Karzai chose to ignore the widespread allegations about Khalid's major abuses of power during his tenure as governor of Kandahar (2005–08), such as murder of those who got in his way— even U.N. workers—torture of prisoners, and drug trafficking.[75] And once again, the United States and the international community did not try hard to dissuade Karzai from appointing Khalid, with some international officials commenting that whatever his accountability deficiencies, Khalid had a proven record of being tough on the Taliban.[76] In short, the new appointments mostly showed once again that despite his declarations in the 2012 summer, Karzai was more concerned about his power base, while the international forces gave priority to battlefield exigencies, and both were sacrificing a chance to improve governance in Afghanistan.

Perhaps the most successful model of local governance in Afghanistan has been the so-called community development councils (CDCs) established under the auspices of the National Solidarity Program. Inspired by a similar program in Indonesia, the CDCs were instituted in Afghanistan in 2003 by then minister of finance Ashraf Ghani. Designed to distribute small grants to village-level communities, the program has required participation of the entire target community in decisions regarding development projects and their execution as well as on the local community's contribution of its own resources.[77]

Yet the CDCs, too, have faced challenges and limitations. One of the reasons they escaped the corruption and rent-seeking problems that have frustrated larger aid programs and contracts has been that the sums delivered via the CDCs have been relatively small. Consequently, many power brokers have not bothered to muscle into the projects. If such administrative and policy designs were to be scaled up, they might well lose some of their representativeness, oversight, and joint community responsibility, and could attract detrimental attention from rapacious power brokers.

Nor do the CDCs necessarily redress inequitable access to economic resources at the village level or the concentration of discriminatory power in the hands of particular individuals or subcommunities. The preexisting political and power context in the village, before the CDCs are established, often critically determines their shape, effectiveness, and ability to promote good governance at the local level. As has been the case with other institutional innovations at the local level of governmental administration, new institutions often merely overlay and are mediated via preexisting power and institutional arrangements, rather than fundamentally reforming the preexisting arrangements.[78] When CDCs are built on preexisting norms of social solidarity and equitable access, they enhance public goods distribution and create synergy between formal state and customary institutions. But when a power broker or a narrow elite dominates the village, such actors frequently have the capacity to subvert the CDCs for their own purposes and increase their resource flows.[79] Under the latter scenario, the situation of marginalized communities and individuals is not necessarily improved.[80]

Insecurity also has jeopardized some of the CDCs, with the Taliban demanding a cut from CDC funds to support projects in areas with strong Taliban presence, such as the Ghazni province. These "taxes" paid to the Taliban shrank some of the resources to the point that the CDC programs could not be implemented. When approached for supplemental funds, the central government has mostly insisted that the local community expel the Taliban or provide intelligence on it or dip into its own pockets to take care of the financial shortfall. The CDC representatives have refused to undertake the anti-Taliban measures and have maintained that since it is the responsibility of the government to defeat the Taliban and provide security, Kabul should pay for the Taliban tax.[81] The opportunity for economic assistance has often not proven sufficient to motivate a community to rise up against the Taliban, other insurgents, and problematic power brokers.

Moreover, many of the governance and economic development problems, such as regional water management or electrification, require decisionmaking and coordination at cross-provincial levels and cannot simply be addressed locally. Thus, although the focus on local governance is appropriate because it is organic to Afghanistan's traditional political arrangements and is the way most Afghans experience the government, it is not sufficient. It can only supplement national governance, not cover the center's deficiencies. And all too often, even at the local level, governance has not improved, and abuse and corruption by government officials continue to destabilize even areas cleared of insurgents.

At the July 2012 Tokyo Conference on Afghanistan, international donors once again strongly called on the government of Hamid Karzai to undertake serious efforts to improve governance and combat corruption.[82] And this time, they conditioned 20 percent of international aid on the Afghan government fulfilling its promises. In response, at the end of July, President Karzai issued a new broad administrative reform decree.[83] The twenty-three-page list of actions to be undertaken by various Afghan ministries, the attorney general's office, and the country's supreme court essentially amounted to a grab bag of policies, some of which were provisions at least nominally focused on combating corruption. Among them were orders to senior government officials to "avoid intervening in the recruitment for the civil service, judiciary, and universities," a potentially powerful measure to combat corruption and nepotism and promote merit-based appointments. Other provisions were more rhetorical, such as an order to the Ministry of Women's Affairs to undertake a public relations campaign discouraging violence against women. Whether any of the prescribed measures will actually be undertaken remains to be seen. Given the level of corruption and nepotism in Afghanistan, including in and around the Arg Palace, the general and abstract character of the directives does not give much confidence that implementation will be possible—or was in fact seriously intended. Other provisions send blatantly double or contradictory signals or are open to widely different interpretations of their intent and likely outcomes. One decree, for example, called on the Afghan supreme court to complete all ongoing investigations related to corruption, land grabs, and serial assassinations within six months. Another provision tasked the supreme court "to simplify the legal procedures for suspects and convicts within the given timetable."[84] But would these measures indeed strengthen the rule of law and enable swifter delivery of justice, or would they be used as mechanisms to obfuscate investigations of crimes and abuses of power? The previous record of the government of Hamid Karzai and the pervasive system of corruption and nepotism in Afghanistan give little reason for optimism. The same can be said for the international community's record of holding Kabul accountable to its commitments. Yet without significant improvements in governance, it is hard to see how even a successful military transition—far from a given—could prevent major instability after 2014.

7

Logistics and Politics
in Northern Afghanistan

The pristine white snow on the Hindu Kush Mountains sparkled against the clear blue sky of a gorgeous crisp morning. At 5 a.m., my driver Habibullah, interpreter Mahmoud, and I had just left Kabul to drive to Baghlan. (Habibullah and Mahmoud are not their real names. Being known to work with Westerners can be brutally costly for Afghans—it makes them favorite targets of the Taliban.) The journey started off with a foreboding—or perhaps auspicious—augur: barely on the outskirts of Kabul, our old, beat-up Toyota Corolla would not start after being tanked up for the journey. The most common automobile in Afghanistan, a Corolla is great for keeping a low profile; and the more beat-up the better, since it is less likely to alert potential kidnappers or the Taliban that it is carrying a female foreigner. But despite my fondness for a means of transportation that disappears anonymously into the (stalling) flow of Afghan traffic, the car's struggle to start up right after being fed gasoline raised some doubts in my mind about its ability to climb to the Salang tunnel, which cuts through the Hindu Kush Mountains at the height of about 11,000 feet. Nonetheless, after some minutes of fiddling with the engine and locals helping to push the car, the Corolla did kick back to life, and off we went, north to the mountains. I was heading to Baghlan to interview Afghan residents there about the Afghan Local Police (ALP) and other militias in the area who have a critical effect on security and governance.

Northern Afghanistan

The Bumpy Climb: Tensions North of Kabul

The provinces of Baghlan and Kunduz in northern Afghanistan have become strategically important to ISAF because one of its main logistical supply routes to Afghanistan—the so-called Northern Distribution Network (NDN)—passes through them. Although the north has some of the most peaceful parts of Afghanistan, it also has some very troubled ones—and they include these two provinces. Long neglected by ISAF and Afghan security forces and left to the rule of the former Northern Alliance power brokers, parts of Afghanistan's north have become a powder keg of ethnic tensions and an important mobilization area for the Taliban and Hezb-i-Islami. For decades the area has been riddled with conflicts over land and water, ethnic rivalries, and tribal divisions.[1] Many Taliban members there and also, more broadly, many Pashtuns—a minority in the north living in enclaves among the Tajiks and other ethnic groups— suffered atrocities during the conflict with the Northern Alliance in the 1990s and also after 2002. Conversely, many Tajiks, Uzbeks, and Hazaras in the area fear violent Pashtun retribution. But at the same time, Baghlan and Kunduz are also areas where the Taliban has managed to recruit not just Pashtuns but also Uzbeks, and even some Tajiks, from those who feel disenfranchised by the post-2002 political dispensation in the area.[2] The Taliban thus has scored mobilization successes in the north despite the fact that it considers the north less vital than other parts of the country and therefore regularly assigns that region to less experienced commanders who receive less funding and fewer replacements than those in other areas.[3]

Though they may call themselves the Taliban, not all of the many alienated groups or criminal bands in the north necessarily align firmly with the Quetta Shura or closely follow Gulbudin Hekmatyar's maneuvering. In most of Badakhshan, for example, criminal gangs are a far more serious problem than the Taliban. As in southern Afghanistan, for many the Taliban label is a flag of convenience and their alignment is fleeting and loose, hiding varied resentments and ambitions.

Nonetheless, insecurity can be locally intense. So intense, in fact, that along the strategic supply road through Baghlan and Kunduz, there were daily attacks in 2010 and 2011. An increase in U.S., ISAF, and Afghan National Security Forces reduced the level of insecurity and Taliban activity by the summer of 2012. ISAF's military pressure, including the killing or capturing of Taliban commanders and shadow governors, has hampered the Taliban's operations and facilitated efforts to flip Taliban commanders.[4] But often many of the security improvements have been registered only in central parts of the provinces and mostly along the main road.

The instability there can also be seen as a portent of the ethnic fighting that could break out after 2014 between the dominant Tajiks and the groups that feel marginalized in the north. This prospect of civil war and ethnic infighting after 2014 was foremost on the mind of all Afghans with whom I spoke in the north in April 2012, palpably more so than during my previous trip to the area in the fall of 2010. "The moment the foreign forces leave, there will be civil war. The next day. All the big men are getting ready," a civil society organizer in Pul-e-Khourmi, the capital of Baghlan, told me.[5] With the exception of some government officials in the area, most local people—from across the various ethnic groups—echoed that view. Most were deeply afraid of the future and skeptical that the Afghan National Security Forces would be able to fill the security void created by the drawing down of ISAF forces and their far smaller and circumscribed presence after 2014.

The ANSF still have two years to train and become battle tested. Furthermore, the Afghan National Army and also some units of the Afghan National Police have registered important improvements.[6] The fact that Afghans, such as my interlocutor in the north, do not trust them today does not mean that ANSF will not improve and inspire the people's confidence in the future. Nor will instability in Afghanistan be uniform and—should a civil war indeed break out—necessarily involve battles among armed groups everywhere in Afghanistan.[7] In some parts of the country, stability or insecurity may not look very different from what it does today. But large parts of Baghlan and Kunduz are a tinderbox of pent-up resentments and militias in the waiting.

The Long and Winding Road: Logistics North of Kabul

The important Northern Distribution Network cuts right through Baghlan and Kunduz on its way to Central Asia. Following a deadly November 2011 firefight between Pakistani and ISAF soldiers and Pakistan's closing of the Afghanistan-Pakistan border to NATO trucks in retaliation, the importance of that logistical route only increased.[8] Until then, about 5,000 trucks a month would plough their way on the dusty roads across Baluchistan's plains and the Chaman border crossing or along the perilous Taliban-infested switchbacks of the Khyber Pass to reach Bagram, Kandahar, and other NATO logistical hubs in Afghanistan. After Pakistan closed the border, NATO had to reroute about 60 percent of its shipments through the Northern Distribution Network, transporting the rest by air. Air transportation costs about ten times as much as going by land via Pakistan.[9]

Even since Pakistan reopened the border in July 2012, NATO counts on using the Salang road for removing its supplies from Afghanistan in conjunction with the transition to Afghan security.[10] The road is not the only route connecting Kabul with the north of the country and ultimately Central Asia, but as of summer 2012, it was the only usable road. Others, such as one over the Shibar Pass, are in much worse condition: single-lane muddy trails over the mountains at even higher altitudes. The level of insecurity surrounding them is also much higher—from the Taliban and highway banditry. Vehicles that try to travel on them are often looted.[11] Making these roads usable would require not only fresh leveling and paving but also clearing surrounding areas of insurgents and criminals. Any trucks that would use them in the future may need the same armed escort provided by the Afghan National Army and Police that trucks in southern Afghanistan have.

For a decade, private security outfits, such as the one owned by Matiullah Khan in Uruzgan (described in chapter 5), also provided security for the NATO supply trucks and other travelers, raking in hundreds of millions in payoffs, even if they had to pass some on to the Taliban. An investigation by U.S. congressman John Tierney in 2010 revealed that the Taliban frequently collected about $200 per truck from the private security outfits.[12] The U.S. military estimated that approximately $360 million of U.S. tax dollars were diverted to Afghan criminals, power brokers, and the Taliban in 2011—with the Taliban supposedly receiving only a small percentage—and asserted that it was taking further steps to minimize the flow of funds to the insurgents, such as by contracting with other supply companies.[13] The Taliban itself has identified the "taxation" of the trucking and security companies as an important source of its income to pay fighters and procure supplies.[14] The private security companies are now officially prohibited from operating in Afghanistan, but that does not necessarily mean that all of the companies will stop collecting security fees along the roads. The Taliban certainly counts on continuing to extort fees or steal the supplies if the truckers do not pay or are not sufficiently protected by some legal—or illegal—force. When the border with Pakistan was shut, Taliban commanders complained that their earnings dropped badly, hampering the operational capacity of the insurgency.[15]

Even after Pakistan reopened its border to NATO supply trucks, having blocked it for eight months, the Salang road has remained an important logistical lifeline out of the war in Afghanistan. Should Pakistan once again shut the border and the Salang road again become the only available land route, NATO officials point out that to remove ISAF military equipment from Afghanistan in conjunction with the military drawdown schedule by 2014, a container would have to leave Afghanistan every seven minutes, twenty-four hours a day, seven days a week from April 2012 until 2015, or for about 33 months, if it wants to remove all of its containers by the 2014 transition deadline.[16] Overall, whatever the available routes, NATO will need to withdraw about 100,000 shipping containers and 50,000 vehicles from Afghanistan.[17]

ISAF's use of the Northern Distribution Network does not come cheaply. When the border with Pakistan was shut down and all trucks had to go through the north, U.S. Secretary of Defense Leon Panetta estimated that this routing added $100 million a month to the Afghanistan war tab.[18] What used to cost $250 per truck coming from Pakistan, cost $1,200 per truck going through Central Asia.[19] Before Pakistan reopened its border, the Pentagon had requested that Congress reallocate an additional $2.1 billion to cover the costs of the greater reliance on the Northern Distribution Network.[20] Even after Pakistan resumed cooperation, the Pentagon did not anticipate reducing the requested reallocation.[21]

Following a previous deal with Russia, the United States and ISAF signed new, two-way transshipment agreements with Uzbekistan, Kazakhstan, and Kyrgyzstan in 2012, permitting tens of thousands of vehicles carrying ISAF military equipment to be moved directly by land routes through Central Asia and Russia to Europe or to air bases from which they are flown back to the United States. In addition, all three countries now allow transport planes carrying NATO soldiers to enter their airspace. Negotiations still continue, however, on a host of unresolved issues, such as expanded access to airspace and airports, fees, alternate routes, and the removal of restrictions on what type of military cargo can be transported through Central Asia.[22] Meanwhile, NATO is also locked into talks with Russia about similar issues, such as the establishment of an air hub for Europe-bound cargo planes. Like its Central Asian neighbors, Russia previously agreed to allow nonlethal equipment to be transported through its territory into Afghanistan, but NATO would like to see the agreement expanded.

In return, the Central Asian countries have demanded, and received, large payoffs. ISAF has not released details of its most recent, June 2012, accords with them. But previously, each truck traveling through their territories had cost about five times what Pakistan had charged. And Uzbekistan, for example, has sought a 50 percent surcharge on the use of its major rail link to Afghanistan.[23] Meanwhile, each of the three Central Asian countries has complained that the others get a better deal from NATO. Reliance on the Northern Distribution Network also augments the leverage of Russia's frosty and prickly president Vladimir Putin in his uneasy relationship with the United States.[24] Russia's cooperation helped facilitate the opening and expanding of the Nothern Distribution Network, a significant accomplishment of the Obama administration's diplomacy with that country. But the NDN was a low-hanging fruit, and U.S.-Russian relations have been deteriorating since then.[25]

Although the Salang road is logistically vital for ISAF, it is in terrible shape. Much of its asphalt is gone, and especially on the northern side of the Salang Pass, the road is a few-hundred-kilometer-long obstacle course after rains of enormous puddles, mud traps, and dirt "gorges" from which a car cannot climb out. Although the road was constructed with one lane in each direction, Afghan drivers recklessly drive on it as if it were a four-lane freeway, madly passing each other on all sides and jousting with big supply trucks for the right of way on the cliffs of the Hindu Kush. If a truck breaks down or collides with another, the whole road can be absolutely paralyzed, with all movement stopped for days. Not surprisingly, the road and cliffs are littered with the corpses of trucks and cars: in some stretches, every 100 meters or so there are remnants of a vehicle that drove off the mountain or toppled over on the side of the road. Many of the wrecks are fresh. Others go back to the 1980s when the mujahideen loved to attack the road and blow up the oil supply trucks, which then— just as now—crawled their way between Central Asia and Kabul.

The Salang tunnel itself verges on being a death trap. The tunnel ventilators are out of order, leading to very high concentrations of carbon monoxide in what can resemble a gas chamber if one is stuck there for several hours. The 1964 tunnel was built by the Soviets to handle 1,000 vehicles a day; but after the closure of the Afghanistan-Pakistan border, it had to accommodate up to 10,000 vehicles a day jostling their way through it. Traffic in the tunnel regularly gets stalled for days, with kilometers-long lines of vehicles that have ground to a halt.[26] If one of the tightly packed fuel trucks exploded in or near the tunnel, others could easily ignite as well, and hundreds of people could burn and asphyxiate to death. In 1982, 900 Russians and Afghans reportedly died in one such accident.

In 2005 the road, including the Salang tunnel, was paved using funds from the Turkish government. But by the winter of 2010, the road had disintegrated once again. The tunnel was repaved anew. Yet neither the ceiling of the pre-tunnel overhangs nor the tunnel walls have ever been repaired (or, for that matter, completed); as a result, water leaks in all the time. Since the road is subject to snow and freezing temperatures in the winter, sun and heat in the summer, and intense rain and snowmelt in the spring, the asphalt laid in 2010 was gone within two years. But because the road carries about four times the weight a normal highway is supposed to withstand, repaving it is a Sisyphean undertaking. Yet given its logistical significance, ISAF decided to repave some parts again at the cost of tens of millions of dollars, with at least $20 million appropriated by the United States in the summer of 2012.

A Tough Slog for Women: Two Steps Forward, One Step Backward

I can only hope—though I expect to be disappointed—that some of the money will be allocated to building a few washrooms for women along the road. Although there are restrooms available to women at the foothills of the mountains (not to be entered by the faint hearted or those who cannot switch off their sensory organs), once the road starts climbing through the spectacular sharp peaks and gorges, there are no more washrooms and no privacy of any sort whatever. For the Afghan men, that is not a problem as they simply relieve themselves along the road. But that option is socially unacceptable for women who, in Afghanistan as throughout South Asia, suffer from serious toilet facilities discrimination.[27] Despite the risk of dehydration and altitude sickness at the Salang Pass, I earlier learned not to drink before setting off on the road. When I was crossing the Salang in the fall of 2010, I was stuck in the tunnel for about five hours and almost caused heart attacks in both my Afghan driver and interpreter when, after being on the road for more than eight hours, I finally broke down and had to go on the side of the road while wearing my burqa. Although I had violated a social taboo, the aggressive reaction from enraged Afghan men that my driver and interpreter had feared did not materialize, and neither I nor our party was attacked for my misbehavior. Perhaps the lucky outcome was because the tough-looking posture of my companion during that trip, an intrepid male U.S. journalist dressed in local clothes, scared off any potential taboo-enforcing vigilantes. But the Afghan drivers along the road were certainly mesmerized by the sight of a woman having to relieve herself there, even if the burqa hid everything. In turn, I was amazed that during the entire five hours on the Salang, I was apparently the only woman who heeded nature's call, even though many Afghan women were scrunched in the backs and trunks of the Corollas, along with their children and goats. Not one woman, as far as I could tell, had left her car during the entire time. Being an Afghan woman requires being tough.

The toilet issue notwithstanding, the condition of women in Afghanistan has considerably improved since the Taliban era—in the north and indeed throughout Afghanistan. Access to health care, education, and employment has much expanded in large parts of the country. Women now hold positions in the parliament and even occasionally in the security services. Women have become journalists, government officials, and lawyers.[28] Nonetheless, much of this progress remains restricted to women from elite urban families, while most women in rural areas continue to be ground down by restrictive social mores and poverty.[29] Insecurity in particular continues to threaten women in a variety of domains, including by motivating male relatives to restrict a women's movement outside of the household.[30] Although visible public violence against women has been much reduced since the times when the Taliban flogged women in the streets and stoned them to death in stadiums, it still remains high; and sexual violence in particular—not just rape, but also abductions and forced marriage—continues to be a major threat, and one that is rarely prosecuted.[31]

Even for elite women, family remains the sine qua non: acceptance into a family through marriage and raising a family are crucial for survival, progress, and social acceptance. The absence of support from immediate and extended family can still fundamentally jeopardize the ability of an Afghan woman to survive—economically or socially.[32] It is also male relatives who for the most part determine a woman's access to education, health, and ability to seek a job outside of the household. Thus many of the women who serve in Afghanistan's parliament through the reserved seat system function as proxies for their male relatives. On their own, few women achieve positions of formal or informal power or are able to cultivate influential patronage networks. Much worse, fathers still continue to sell or give away their daughters as a payment for debt or settlement of a dispute, and the in-law family tends to have almost absolute control over the girl.[33]

Much of the impetus for women's advancement still comes largely from Western pressure, even if the issue has been increasingly and adroitly embraced by indigenous Afghan nongovernmental organizations (NGOs) focused on women's rights. But often the Afghan NGOs are torn between satisfying conditions for donors' goodwill and operating within acceptable social dictates. As President Karzai's popularity has dwindled, he has supported very conservative *ulema* (religious clergy) to legitimize his rule, and as a result, he has sought to restrict a variety of improvements in women's status, such as the availability of shelters for women abused in the household and the production of TV shows by and for women, as well as women's participation in other media.[34]

Concepts of women's rights continue to be deeply divisive and strongly contested in Afghan society, and progress remains fragile. Although the Taliban has sought to display some moderation of its positions on depriving women of basic rights and opportunities (see chapter 3), it remains opposed to much of the progress women have been able to achieve since 2002. The Taliban still seeks to remove women from the public sphere and restrict their access to economic opportunities outside of the household; and it continues to proclaim that Western-style women's rights will lead to a degradation of society—a message that resonates with many Afghan men.[35]

Stuck in the Mud:
The Travails of Governance in Northern Afghanistan

Whatever the bumpy Salang road lacks in comfort, it makes up for in stunning imagery. You may lose your kidneys and life on the road, but your soul will be inspired by the snow-capped peaks, the brown mountainsides coated with fresh grass and wildflowers in the spring, the fertile valley along a river that supports wheat and vegetable fields, local men on donkeys, and women in burqas.

The picturesque high view from the mountain road gives way to sharper details in the valley. The state of the road does not improve as one approaches Pul-e-Khourmi, the provincial capital of Baghlan. Many of the burqa-clad women are beggars. Even by Afghan standards, Pul-e-Khourmi looks more like a neglected Afghan village rather than a provincial capital. Indeed, the issues of poor governance and mismanagement by local officials and abuse by power brokers dominated my conversations with Afghans in the province, both in September 2010 and in April 2012. Just as in Nangarhar and many other parts of Afghanistan, people complained about nepotism in the awarding of government positions and contracts, the incompetence of government officials, the private prisons of power brokers, pervasive impunity, and land theft. And just like many other Afghans, Baghlanis feel that they have no way to make their voices heard other than by transforming themselves into supplicants to the powerful ones. The mechanisms of accountability are few, in fact, because people cannot elect their local officials, all of whom are appointed from Kabul.

But unlike in Nangarhar or Kandahar, for example, the complaints about poor governance and nepotism in Baghlan are overlaid with charges of ethnic discrimination. In the Pashtun areas of the country's south and east, there are also major communal rifts—within the Pashtun tribes and subtribes—and the Taliban adroitly exploits them. But in Afghanistan's north where Tajiks, Uzbeks, Pashtuns, and Hazaras mix, and where the former Northern Alliance dominates, the complaints about communal discrimination often seem particularly vitriolic: "In the Pashtun districts in Baghlan," a Pashtun businessman in Pul-e-Khourmi told me, "the district government, the ANP do not exist. Poverty is bad: people do not have even tea and sugar. They eat meat only once a week. The Andarabis take everything."[36] The Pashtuns also complain that government positions, especially in the security forces, are dominated by the former Northern Alliance, and that Pashtuns do not have fair representation. The majority of the police in Baghlan, for example, are indeed Andarabi Tajiks. Even those Pashtuns who are in governing positions in the north are viewed with suspicion and dissatisfaction by many Afghans, especially their fellow Pashtuns, and seen as being approved by and subservient to

Field Marshal Mohammad Fahim, the first vice president of Afghanistan and one of the most prominent northern power brokers. In turn, many of the Tajiks feel that the Pashtuns are getting their just comeuppance and that the Tajiks now deserve a large share of the resource pie after all the brutality they suffered during the Taliban era and the sacrifices they made in fighting the Taliban. "The Andarabis were the first people to fight the Taliban. They are heroes, they deserve to be rewarded. The Taliban are just thieves. There is no discrimination here."[37] The competing narratives notwithstanding, the divisions between the communities in central Baghlan are visceral: the Pashtuns live west of the river, mainly in less fertile rain-fed areas, and the Tajiks and Uzbeks live east of the river, in the more fertile, river-irrigated lands.

However, just as elsewhere in Afghanistan, the realities are complex, and many different trends are in evidence at the same time, hardly all of them negative. The abusive and incompetent governance that prevails in Afghanistan is the Achilles' heel of the stabilization effort. But even if governed in an unaccountable manner, not all of the north is equally unstable. In Balkh, for example, Governor Atta Mohammad Noor, although yet another power broker with a long record of abuses, has built up enough "legitimacy" to create a rather stable regime in the province. He may rule with an iron hand, but he also distributes proceeds from rents, such as foreign aid, broadly enough to deliver at least some improvements in services.[38] Yes, he has been taking a cut on most of the economic transactions and rents in the north and allegedly has been behind land dispossession, extortion, and other serious abuses of power.[39] But he has been able to keep his client networks expansive enough to create wider access to patronage handouts and rents and even elicit support for his style of governance, at least in comparison with other areas of Afghanistan. He also has managed to develop good relations with Russia. The Afghans in Balkh may still characterize his governance as mafia rule, but it is mafia rule with ample political capital.[40] If Afghanistan does implode in civil war, Governor Atta's seat is likely to be among the last to shake, and indeed, Balkh is likely to remain far more stable than, for example, Baghlan and Kunduz.

There is another factor operating in the north, as well as in urban centers throughout Afghanistan: a younger, educated generation is coming up, one that often exhibits a willingness to rise above ethnic factionalism and communal patronage. One of the people I interviewed in Pul-e-Khourmi was a young female lawyer. Dressed in jeans, a black blazer, and fancy headscarf, she was articulate, full of energy and determination to help her country. In good English, she told me about a recent success she and her colleagues had in Baghlan. For a long time, the local arm of the National Directorate of Security (NDS), the Tajik-dominated intelligence agency of Afghanistan, kept people in Baghlan in detention incommunicado, often indefinitely. She led an effort to persuade the local NDS office to allow defense attorneys, such as herself, access to the detainees. Not only did she succeed and hence significantly improve human rights in the province, she managed to do so without alienating the NDS officers there. Since detentions by the NDS allegedly were often highly skewed to target Pashtuns—the main recruiting pool of the Taliban and Hezb-i-Islami—her intervention also helped ease some of the ethnic tensions in Baghlan.

And the resourceful female lawyer is just one of many impressive and inspiring young Afghans I have met during my trips, such as leaders of the Women for Afghan Women organization and officers of Afghanistan's Independent Human Rights Commission. They are part of an urban, educated, and energetic generation. Many expatriates who returned to Afghanistan, frequently after decades abroad, are also often tirelessly dedicated to helping their country. Of course, many other Afghan expatriates have returned to reap vast financial profits from corrupt, nepotistic deals, crony capitalism, and Afghanistan's war economy.[41]

And there is another kind of young generation, too: the sons of the power brokers and warlords, such as Batur Dostum, the son of the northern Uzbek general Abdul Rashid Dostum; Adib Fahim, the son of Marshal Fahim; Salahuddin Rabbani, the son of Burhanuddin Rabbani, Afghanistan's former president; and Kalimullah Naqib, the son of a deceased, powerful, southern power broker, Haji Mullah Naqib.[42] Mostly in their twenties, they have often been educated in the West, but they are expected to take up the mantles and politics of their fathers. (The power brokers have daughters, too, but it is mainly the sons who are groomed to follow in their footsteps of politics and power.) Will they be able to use their inherited influence for the betterment of Afghanistan, or will they fall into the patronage and coercion ways of their fathers?

The broader question—as yet unanswered—is whether the security situation in the country can be stabilized enough so that those who rise above narrow communal patronage can achieve positions of influence, and whether the current narrow, exclusionary governance system can be opened up enough to allow the reformers' voices to have a prominent impact on policies. If they do come into positions of influence, will they be able to resist narrow, self-regarding power and profit maximization, or the deeply ingrained familial pressures to provide patronage to their relatives or otherwise face dishonor and rejection by their families? The reformers' path is as winding, steep, and difficult as the drive up the Salang: advocating accountability, justice, meritocracy, and human rights in Afghanistan easily gets one fired—or fired at.[43]

Tea in the Midst of Poppy and Bandits: The Complexities of Local Security

On a Friday morning in Baghlan, when I did not have any interviews scheduled because Friday morning is time for prayer and the day for family and relaxation, I decided just for the fun of it to drive to the neighboring province of Samangan. I was planning to have a picnic at Takht-e-Rostam, an unusual Buddhist stupa and cave monastery and one of Afghanistan's most important pre-Islamic sites. Its name—Throne of Rostam—refers to a legendary Persian king, Rostam, whom Firdowsi, the Persian equivalent of Homer, immortalized in a tragic epic poem, the *Shah-nama*. When I shared the plan with a risk management officer for a development organization in Pul-e-Khourmi, one of the few Westerners I encountered in Baghlan in April 2012, he looked at me gently, with an expression that silently said, "Well, the Koran teaches that Muslims should be kind to the mentally ill," and stated aloud: "You know, this is Afghanistan. People don't come here for fun."

But, of course, as pithy as that statement is, it is also not entirely true. Historically, many Westerners did come to Afghanistan for fun— whether to trek on yaks in the Wakhan or to get high on Afghanistan's famous hashish. (Many Afghans continue to fondly indulge in the habit to escape the ravages and stress of war and grinding poverty, seeing it as a far less harmful vice than smoking tobacco. However, there is ground for concern in the face of the troubling increase in addiction rates.)[44] Even today, international soldiers and civilians come to Afghanistan "for the fun of it"—they sign up not just because of patriotism or the financial and career opportunities that such a deployment brings, but also because of the adrenaline rush of being in a war zone.

On that sunny Friday morning, the Takht-e-Rostam hill seemed far removed from a war zone. It was bright with wild poppy and other meadow flowers. There was music in the air from a live band that played traditional Afghan songs and from boom boxes to which Afghan men danced. Many families were having a picnic on top of the hill and sur-rounding meadows. Some women even ventured out to picnic without a burqa. Their kids would get a huge kick out of seeing a female farangi in Afghan clothes sitting on the grass, sipping tea, and munching on wal-nuts, *sheer pera* (a Mazari sweet with pistachios), and wild sour rhubarb that locals collect in the mountains and sell along the road. The scene was rather idyllic, so full of promise of what Afghanistan could be if security were improved and sustained.

But even during those idyllic moments on top of the hill, I could not quite fully drop my guard and kept carefully watching the young men on motorcycles who, in turn, were watching me with a great deal of interest. Energetic local youth enticed by a Western woman breaking the social burqa rule? Or lookouts for the Taliban or bandits?

I had been warned that there were bandits along the road and that their activity would pick up on Fridays when the ANP presence at check-points thins out. The police, too, would decide that Friday was a time for prayer and rest rather than dull endless waiting at a checkpoint, only occasionally punctuated by a life-threatening firefight or suicide bomber. But though we got somewhat lost on the way back from the hill amongst the alleyways of Afghan villages and field tracks away from the main road, we ran into no danger. The mood was light, and my Afghan inter-preter, driver, and I were singing along to a blaring soundtrack of Afghan pop we played in our Corolla.

During an interview later in the day, I learned that in the villages of Western Baghlan, some of which we had been driving through, the Taliban still prohibits music. The locals continue to be so afraid of the insurgents that they respect the order, eschewing playing music even dur-ing weddings, one of the most important events in their lives, on which no expense would normally be spared. Nevertheless, I was told, apart from such annoyances, security in Baghlan was much better now than in 2011. "We can't play music today; but last year, before ISAF came and ANSF were increased here, there were firefights and security incidents here almost every day. Now the insecurity is pushed away from the main roads, there are fewer kidnappings too. Central Baghlan last year looked like northern Baghlan and Kunduz still do today."[45]

And it was exactly further north, past Baghlan Jadid, in an area where insecurity palpably picks up, that we headed for my afternoon appointments to interview members of the Afghan Local Police. A local power broker had promised to facilitate such access for me. Before the ALP interviews, however, it was time to procure some lunch. The choice was between eating in a restaurant in Pul-e-Khourmi, a safer area but one where I, a Western woman and a tempting kidnapping target, had already been seen, or in Baghlan Jadid, an area far less safe but one where the local miscreants were not anticipating the presence of a Western woman. Previously, when, accompanied by my driver and interpreter, I ate in a Pul-e-Khourmi restaurant overlooking a mosque and a market, I had attracted considerable attention, at times bordering on consternation. Afghan restaurants usually are not frequented by women, though some establishments have a closed-off family section. So after much discussion weighing the risks, my interpreter and I finally settled on going to the more dangerous town to minimize my exposure in any one place.

Unfortunately, the restaurant lunch plan did not pan out. The power broker failed to meet us as promised, and the time spent waiting for him generated far more exposure for me than was safe—for lunch or just for hanging around. However, with typical Afghan generosity and hospitality, one of my interlocutors from the previous day came to the rescue, not only by inviting us to have a meal in his home but also by making a series of phone calls that ultimately set me up with members of the Afghan Local Police and the Taliban to interview. Hint, hint: in Baghlan and elsewhere in Afghanistan, the ALP and the Taliban are often one and the same, as the next chapter explains.

Release from the Mountain: A Better Future?

The drive back to Kabul turned out to be far worse than the drive north. What had taken us about seven hours going north almost doubled on the return. It had been raining for several days, and the normal road puddles had enlarged into miniature highway lakes. Transformed into instant amphibious vehicles, the Corollas would have to cross them at a fifty-degree tilt, desperately grabbing on the firmer edge of the road with at least one wheel, even as water reached midway up the door on the other side. Local boys and men sat along the road in the rain, entertained by watching the cars struggle to plod by. Within minutes of our departure from Pul-e-Khourmi, the rear window of our car was so covered with mud that absolutely nothing could be seen through it. But it did not matter. Habibullah, normally a truck driver who as a matter of course would cross the Salang with a six-wheeler, did not feel the need to look into the rearview mirror once during the fourteen hours back. Nor did he seem particularly concerned that the nonfunctioning air conditioning in the car did not permit him to clear the front window of fog: a Jedi knight in his own right, he somehow managed to sense the vestiges of the road enough not to drive us into the abyss. As we climbed higher, clearing the front window became irrelevant anyway since it was snowing and so foggy up in the mountains that the normal Afghan game of chicken on the road became a game of chicken of the blind. The road had narrowed down to essentially one and a quarter lanes, where swerving out of the way of oncoming downhill traffic with less than a car length left to avoid a crash became a matter of split-second decisions.

Anticipating that we may be stuck closer to the peak for hours, we stopped at a roadside shack to stock up on water and biscuits. During that ten-minute break, we witnessed a house, one of many precariously clinging to the mountain's steep slopes, being swept away by the rain and resulting mud slide down the side of the mountain. I do not know if any people had been in the house during the brief moment when nature destroyed it or how many died or were injured. It was just one micro-misery in the sea of pain that Afghanistan can be.

The higher we climbed, the slower and more precarious the going got. The road became lined for kilometer after kilometer with parked trucks, many of which, we were told, had not moved an inch for five days. In the final stretches before the pass, we also would be stalled in a traffic jam for an hour before moving a car length forward. With a real possibility that we may be stuck on the mountain for the night or even longer—despite the fact that we had set off before sunrise—and thin on supplies, running down our gasoline, bored and frustrated, and, in my case, also unable to get out of the car for security reasons so as to not draw attention, we began conjuring up images of a Taliban attack. After all, these grounded NATO supply trucks full of gasoline would, if hit, make a splendid fireball.[46] Alternatively, I thought, it would be really easy for kidnappers to pull me out of the car and march me off somewhere. Much better to think about other mountain activities, such as the fact that some of the expats in Kabul come to the Salang in the winter to ski.

But unlike in September 2010, when I had taken the Salang road and also had been stuck on the mountain for many hours, the police at the pass were doing a much better job of handling the stalled traffic. They were diligent about chasing back into line the trucks and cars that tried to cut in front, hitting their drivers with sticks when words of warning did not suffice. They were efficient in stopping the crawling traffic in one direction to let the other side go through for a while. And during all the long hours on the mountain, I did not see one of the police officers ask for a bribe. Unfortunately, such improvements in the Afghan National Police continue to be more sporadic than systematic, and they have not been robust enough to persuade most Afghans that the police are trustworthy. Instead, many Afghans continue to see the ANP as a source of crime and troubles for them.

When the mountain finally released us on the other side, the road descended from the shrouded peaks of snow and bare rocks into a beautiful sunny valley of aspens and blooming redbuds and cherries along an azure stream. This was the Jabal Saraj area where picturesque mud and stone houses are terraced on the slopes, but they look neither as poor nor as precarious as the shacks on the other side. Jabal Saraj would make a brilliant trekking area, though it is true that one would have to avoid the minefields demarcated on the sides of the road and up the hills.

As we wound our way down the switchbacks toward Kabul, hundreds of kids just out of school moseyed up the road. Boys started playing soccer on the side of the brook. Six preteen girls separated from the throngs of others, crossed a wooden bridge spanning the mountain stream, sat down under the blooming cherries, and pulled out their schoolbooks to read. This particular Afghan community had come very far from the days of the 1990s civil war and the Taliban's brutal order.

I wondered whether the progress would last beyond 2014. In other parts of Afghanistan, the Taliban insurgency was shutting down schools opened during the 2000s decade.[47] In some places, schools are nominally open but lack teachers, either because they have never been provided for the school facilities erected over the past decade or because the teachers have been scared off by the Taliban.[48]

I mused uneasily about the nation's future. If the country does plunge into another phase of civil war as so many of my Afghan interlocutors feared, some parts of the north that I saw, such as Balkh, would likely remain stable. They might escape the insecurity leaking in from the south, even if the north did not formally separate. But the chance that other parts of the north would explode in complex violence is substantial. As of the summer of 2012, the Taliban insurgency was well and alive in northern Afghanistan. But even in its absence, in places like Baghlan and Kunduz, the ethnic tensions and pent-up frustrations are running high. Such areas are likely to be hotly contested in the post-2014 order. How violent that contestation will be depends to a great degree on whether governance in those areas improves and becomes more ethnically equitable. It will also depend on how the Afghan National Security Forces and other armed actors renegotiate balances of power in local areas. The Afghan Local Police will be a critical player, either promoting local stability or generating serious insecurity.

8

The Afghan Local Police
and Other Militias

One complex aspect of the strategy in Afghanistan with especially problematic implications for governance is the effort to create local self-defense forces around the country. These Afghan "militias" are primarily supposed to increase security in areas where Afghan National Army, Afghan National Police, and ISAF presence is highly limited. At times, the objectives of this attempt "to stabilize Afghan villages" have also included extending the writ of the legitimate Afghan state. Nonetheless, the primary goal of the most extensive and visible iteration of such efforts as of the summer of 2012—the Afghan Local Police (ALP)—has been to weaken the Taliban military capacity in rural areas and thus "increase security." But the outcomes around the country have been highly uneven. Under opportune circumstances, such as in areas of homogenous communities threatened by non-local Taliban, the results have at times been positive, with security increased and the local population welcoming the programs. In heterogeneous communities torn by various rifts and divisions, however, the creation and embrace of such self-defense forces have often greatly complicated the security environment local populations face. And even in the supposed success cases, the long-term impact of this program on governance is worrisome.

ISAF has denied that the various community-based self-defense programs amount to a militia effort, calling the local units everything but militias. It has insisted that they are based on Afghan traditions, such as *arbakai* (tribal militias).[1] Although community-based self-defense is organic to Afghanistan and has a basis in previous Afghan militia versions, ISAF's embrace of this concept was also reinforced by the success of the Anbar Awakening in Iraq, in which Sunni militias, along with the U.S. military surge, were important for beating down al Qaeda in Iraq and decreasing the intensity of Iraq's civil war.[2] By September 2012, the ALP numbered 16,000, located at over sixty sites, and were slated to grow to at least 30,000 located at ninety-nine sites by the end of 2014.[3] (In August 2012, the *New York Times* reported that the ALP stood at 14,000.)[4] In comparison with the Afghan National Army and Afghan National Police, which are being established as the principal providers of security in Afghanistan before and after 2014, the relatively small numbers of the self-defense forces, including the Afghan Local Police, are highly unlikely to radically change the security situation in Afghanistan.[5] But irrespective of their relatively modest effects on security, their troublesome impact on governance in Afghanistan is potentially large.

Security and Other Objectives the ALP Are to Accomplish

The primary purpose of the Afghan Local Police is to extend at least a modicum of security to communities where the Afghan National Army and Afghan National Police are unlikely to be deployed any time soon. In those communities the ALP are relied upon to generate intelligence for ISAF and Afghan security forces and weaken the Taliban, Hezb-i-Islami, and the Haqqanis. This objective is to be accomplished by having the ALP fight the insurgents, encouraging local villagers to deny resources to the insurgents, or inducing the insurgents to join the ALP and de facto buying them off. The stated objectives of previous iterations of ISAF's efforts to raise self-defense forces—including the Afghan Public Protection Program (AP3) and Local Defense Initiative (LDI)—have also included "improving the local population's confidence in the government," "preventing insurgent attacks on key infrastructure," countering "the reasons insurgents are effective at the village level—poverty, unemployment, lack of adequate protection, lack of education," and "extending the legitimate reach of the government."[6]

U.S. military officials claim to be thrilled with the program. In their conversations with me in Afghanistan, they have invariably described it in glowing terms and portrayed it as a tremendous success.[7] They have reported that the ALP have been enthusiastically embraced by local communities and has been effective in fighting the Taliban—often characterizing the effort as a "game changer." As a U.S. Special Operations Forces officer explained to me: "All politics is local. The ALP's local, so it must be good. After all, that's what counterinsurgency theory teaches us."[8]

In contrast to the U.S. military's rosy portrait of the ALP, many Afghans tend to fear the ALP and other self-defense force programs and often have negative views of such militia efforts. Local communities have frequently experienced militias and arbakai turning on them, extorting them, stealing land and goods, and even engaging in murder, kidnapping, and brutalizing rival ethnic groups. "They come to our village and ask for food and money. And if we don't give it to them, they take it anyway," a resident of Baghlan told me. "How can we resist the men with guns?" he asked.[9] And a Kandahari businessman feared that the proliferation of such militias would usher in "the chaos and war of the 1990s. The Soviets tried it, too, when they were defeated," he argued, "and look where it brought Afghanistan. People just use the ALP as a justification to arm up their tribes. Everyone is afraid."[10] Fearing both the manipulation of the self-defense forces to locally empower his rivals and in general a further weakening of his power in the long term, even President Karzai was apparently reluctant to agree to the creation of the ALP and their other versions.[11]

Of course, historically, local communities have also been able to materially benefit from their own arbakai—using them to strengthen their capacity for self-defense or to aggressively expand their lands. Today, too, some communities have positive views of the ALP and other arbakai and even volunteer to stand them up. "Before the ALP was created in our village," a Pashtun resident in Baghlan told me, "no one could travel on the road, even in broad daylight. Even the ANA would not dare come to our village. Now it's much better."[12] Although he was personally not a member of the ALP, some of his relatives were. Indeed, often the Afghans who most enthusiastically embrace such programs are the ALP commanders themselves, or the power brokers who try to sell their unofficial militias to the ISAF and the Afghan government programs for hefty payoffs.

The Tenth Time Around, We'll Get It Right

The ALP effort and other concurrent versions of self-defense programs are nothing new: raising self-defense forces or inducing various tribes to do one's fighting has been repeated in Afghanistan's history many times.

The Soviets in the 1980s resorted to raising tribal militias when they realized that they were not winning in Afghanistan, and they used the militias as part of their exit strategy.[13] Indeed, many Afghans associate the current militia programs with the Soviets' defeat and see the U.S. embrace of them as yet another signal that the United States is preparing to leave without a stable order in place.[14]

Since 2002 various versions of the self-defense programs have been tried in order to stabilize pesky or troubled villages; these include the Afghan National Auxiliary Police, the Afghan Public Protection Program, and the Local Defense Initiative, also known in some areas as the Community Defense Initiative.[15] In some of these efforts, the self-defense forces receive a salary. In others, they are not supposed to be paid; but many of them insist on some sort of salary, so the noncompensation rule is often adjusted.

In March 2009, the Afghan Public Protection Program was created by the U.S. Special Operations Forces in the central province of Wardak where security had been difficult for at least three years. Wardak was also troubled by deep divisions and political rivalries among various ethnic groups and two political actors—Hezb-i-Islami and Harakat-i Islami-yi, a faction of the Northern Alliance. To improve local governance, the Afghanistan Social Outreach Program (ASOP) had also been established there, and the intention was that the ASOP-supported shuras would select the Afghan Public Protection Program recruits.[16] The recruits were to originate from the district; but the shura process was largely circumvented, and mostly local power brokers, such as prominent commanders, and influential maliks chose the recruits, with little vetting and Ministry of Interior supervision.[17] Although the Afghan Public Protection Program was supposed to be supervised by the provincial Afghan National Police, it ended up operating as an essentially independent force, dominated by its Harakat commander, Ghulam Mohammed Hotak, and his men. Hotak had a checkered past, changing sides many times (including having been a Taliban commander arrested by U.S. forces).[18] While the commander of the Public Protection Program in Wardak, Hotak chose not to interact with the provincial government and Afghan National Police, debunking any pretense that he conceived of his militia as an extension of the legitimate writ of the state. Despite being a rather loose cannon, having a reputation for major human rights abuses, and being extremely politically controversial in Wardak, he was regarded by the U.S. Special

Operations Forces as an effective commander since he recruited militia-men from previously hostile areas and seemed capable of delivering successes against the Taliban. He also was able to facilitate meetings between the Afghan Public Protection Program, U.S. Special Operations Forces, and insurgent leaders.[19] Yet during the existence of the Afghan Public Protection Program, security did not palpably improve in the province, and to date Wardak continues to be hotly contested.[20] Despite problems with the Afghan Public Protection Program, its personnel in at least one province was recently rebranded as Afghan Local Police by the Ministry of Interior—without the knowledge and approval of the local Afghan National Police chief, maliks, and even U.S. Special Operations Forces.[21]

Starting mid-2009, Local Defense Initiative units were organized in parts of southern and eastern Afghanistan, including Kandahar, Helmand, and Nangarhar. Once again, Afghan Social Outreach Program–sponsored shuras or community development councils (described in chapter 6) were to select, vet, and supervise the Local Defense Initiative, but in a way that was faster and cheaper than with the Afghan Public Protection Program.[22] Local Defense Initiative members were thus to bring their own weapons but still receive a salary 50 percent that of the Afghan National Police. The Local Defense Initiative effort backfired most visibly in Achin, Nangarhar, as detailed later in this chapter. It was most fully developed in Arghandab, Kandahar, where at its peak it had twenty-five paid and another fifty unpaid members and the community was rewarded for the Local Defense Initiative with several cash-for-work programs sponsored by the U.S. military and managed by International Relief and Development.[23] The U.S. Special Operations Forces also considered standing up a Local Defense Initiative unit in Daikundi province and picked a notorious commander with many crimes to his name for the job of the LDI commander. But to their credit, the Special Operations Forces backed off from the effort when local Afghan officials opposed it.[24]

Not all of the militias have been stood up under the supervision and blessing of the U.S. military. The National Directorate of Security has for years been encouraging the establishment of separate self-defense units, especially in areas where the Tajik-dominated National Directorate of Security fears the presence of too many Pashtun self-defense groups.[25] Recently, the NDS apparently also began developing its own "reintegration" program (separate from the ISAF-sponsored effort to lure insurgent fighters away from the battlefield with amnesty and other inducements) with the goal of flipping Taliban and Hezb-i-Islami combatants to fight their former comrades.[26] Some of these separate militia programs have been at times folded into the Afghan Local Police; others persist outside of the control and even access of ISAF. Particularly under the leadership of Bismullah Khan Mohammadi, the notoriously corrupt and ethnically factionalized Ministry of Interior also sought to legitimize and formalize its own favorite: non-Pashtun militias in northern Afghanistan. In fact, the former minister tried to get ISAF to legitimize these non-Pashtun militias in exchange for sponsoring and expanding the creation of Afghan Local Police units in the south and east of Afghanistan. When ISAF was reluctant to agree to the loose practices in the north, Mohammadi would halt the disbursement of ALP salaries elsewhere in the country.[27] As the various self-defense forces frequently alter or reinforce local balances of power among ethnic groups or patronage networks and insert themselves into local conflicts, the Ministry of Interior, the National Directorate of Security, and the Independent Directorate of Local Governance, as well as local government officials, have often fought intense turf battles over who controls them. Many other militias are simply self-generated or have long fought for a local power broker, and simply carry their weapons less ostentatiously since 2002.[28] The U.S. Central Intelligence Agency has also created its own separate and special paramilitary forces, known as Counterterrorism Pursuit Teams. Highly secret and relatively unknown, the 3,000-member force is tasked with generating intelligence and conducting raids and combat operations in Afghanistan against the Taliban and al Qaeda but is not supposed to engage in lethal action when crossing into Pakistan.[29] Although supposedly tasked with a more narrowly defined counterterrorism, rather than broader counterinsurgency, mission, the existence of the Counterterrorism Pursuit Teams and at times their reportedly rough behavior toward local populations do have important counterinsurgency and governance implications.[30]

In short, to the extent that institutional biases and ethnic competition and political rivalries, rather than a careful evaluation of local dynamics, drive the creation of such self-defense and paramilitary forces, supervision and control are bound to loosen significantly. Such dynamics in turn raise troubling concerns about the intensification of predatory behavior by the self-defense forces themselves.

Insufficient Control Mechanisms

When compared with the other self-defense programs, the Afghan Local Police purportedly have stronger oversight mechanisms. U.S. military officials are quick to note that the ALP program is far more sophisticated and far better than the Soviet militia program and that the program has been informed by the previous post-2002 efforts to generate self-defense forces.[31] Even so, the oversight mechanisms and controls are hardly sufficient, and indeed not that dramatically different from some of the previous iterations.

Like many of the previous programs, the ALP, too, are mostly supervised and trained by U.S. Special Operations Forces (SOF). (The original plan was that the U.S. Special Operations Forces would do all the training and programming, but as the program expanded amidst U.S. troop drawdowns, U.S. conventional forces also have been increasingly used for implementation, even though the SOFs are better suited for such a mission.)[32] The U.S. trainers are to embed with the ALP in the village or area where the ALP operate. Embedding may imply a variety of arrangements: under optimal circumstances, exemplified by the ALP program in Arghandab (an effort that built on the previous experience with the Local Defense Initiative in the district), SOF units will live in the village for six weeks, develop a deep knowledge of the community's composition and political actors, fully participate in the vetting of the recruits, and maintain close supervision of the ALP units subsequently.[33] In other cases, however, such as in parts of Kunduz, the SOF monitoring may only amount to visiting the village once a week.[34] Training mostly consists of teaching the recruits how to handle small firearms (which they either have and already know how to handle, or are issued), deliver first aid, and communicate with the SOFs.

Those recruited are to be vouched for by three maliks or a village shura or both. The maliks or shuras are relied upon to determine that the ALP recruits will not secretly work for the Taliban or other antigovernment elements, turn on their U.S. advisers, or abuse the local community. ISAF considers this control mechanism adequate since the maliks are assumed to know the men they are recommending. The problem with this malik-based control mechanism is that not infrequently a power broker controls the village elders, dictating his preferences in a way that may escape the outsiders' scrutiny. Thus in September 2012, after a spate of attacks against ISAF forces by Afghan National Security Forces personnel, including Afghan Local Police members, the United States temporarily suspended training new recruits in order to increase operational security of the U.S. trainers because the militias came to be feared as unreliable, even vis-à-vis their American sponsors.[35] At other times, the village elders have no problem vouching for the militia members as long as they only extort a rival village. Complaints lodged with human rights organizations, such as the Afghan Independent Human Rights Commission, that the ALP units and other pro-government militias recruit underage boys (and at times subject them to sexual abuse—hardly a rare phenomenon in Afghanistan and not restricted to pro-government militias) have also surfaced.[36]

Outsiders, including the small teams of the Special Operations Forces dispatched to a village to organize an ALP unit, also often have difficulties assessing the credibility of a person's claim to be a respected malik. If the SOF team actually lives in a village for a number of weeks, it may well develop a good sense of the power distribution in the locality and the level of acceptance and authority the purported elders have in the community. But when the SOF team first arrives and seeks out maliks who can identify reliable recruits for the militia, any three older men with beards and wearing turbans (or *pakuls* in Tajik communities) may present themselves as the three wise elders of the village. It is equally problematic for the SOF teams to be "shopping" for some maliks who will agree to an ALP unit in their community if other maliks there have already objected. At minimum, a lack of consistent buy-in from the community reveals profound rifts among the villagers and the potential for conflict. Such limited buy-in may also indicate that the community is afraid of the Taliban or that at least some members of the community are manipulated by either the Taliban or a power broker. In such a context, the ability to ensure legitimacy and control of the ALP unit is of course compromised.

A second control mechanism of the ALP program, as in the case of the Afghan Public Protection Program, is that the district police chief is to supervise the ALP units. The problem with this mechanism is that the post of district police chief has often been entangled in some of the worst and most consistent corruption in Afghanistan. Appointments of district police chiefs are rarely based on the high moral character and outstanding professional qualifications of the individual; even the absence of a criminal record is often asking too much (or not enough). Instead, the position is, at times, bought by those who can afford to pay for it (expecting to collect hefty "taxes" from the local population), or most frequently, the appointment is negotiated between Kabul and local power brokers, with the goal of satisfying their competing demands.[37] Consequently, the credibility and quality of the police chief's supervision of the Afghan Local Police units are often poor. In some areas, problems with the Ministry of Interior's supervision, such as its desire to cleanse ethnic rivals from the ALP, has led the SOFs to operate via other programs, such as the so-called pro-government militias in northern Afghanistan, in order to guarantee that the self-defense forces were in fact being paid and not being manipulated by the Ministry of Interior.[38] Since many district (and provincial) police chiefs appointed by Kabul are from outside the area, they simply may not know the local community enough to be able to evaluate the reliability of the ALP recruits being put forth by the maliks or the reliability of the maliks themselves, for that matter. And local power brokers in charge of ALP units may nominally be under the supervision of the Afghan National Police district chief but in practice do not obey the police chief.

Recruitment and vetting become especially problematic when the ALP and other militia recruits are former Taliban or Hezb-i-Islami members. Indeed, the ALP have functioned at times as a mechanism to provide employment for reintegrated insurgents and to keep them on a payroll.[39] Many ex-insurgent groups that have gone through the reintegration programs have asked to keep their arms and be given a checkpoint, and the ALP and other militia efforts have provided a means to satisfy their demands.[40] This fox-in-the-henhouse approach may buy reductions in violence, but it hardly guarantees that a community feels safer or is not abused by the ALP, or that the community in any way more closely embraces the Afghan government.

Furthermore, even if the ALP actually are more closely monitored and perhaps controlled than other militia programs in Afghanistan, local Afghans rarely have the ability to distinguish among the various self-defense groups and tend to just call them all arbakai. Accurately attributing abuses to a particular group may be especially difficult for the local population.[41] Members of the ALP are issued their own separate uniforms or at least armbands, but as one Afghan civil society organizer in Nangarhar told me, "If they go to houses to demand money, they take off the uniform. They're not stupid."[42] At other times, of course, various armed and criminal bands in Afghanistan do put on official uniforms—whether of the Afghan National Police or ALP—to stop cars, extort money, and perpetrate attacks.[43] ISAF points out that its Afghan Local Police units are thus frequently and unfairly blamed by the local population for abuses they did not commit. That may be so; but if the purpose of the ALP program is to improve the security of the population and establish the foundation of a legitimate government, the (mis)identification problem—however inadvertent—seriously undermines the objectives. If bad deeds are (mistakenly) attributed to the government and the ISAF counterinsurgency effort, the hearts-and-minds campaign to win the support of the population for the government and for the counterinsurgency effort obviously will not have been successful.

The greatest weakness in the ALP effort, and its many preceding and concurrent programs, is that there are no firmly established mechanisms for disarming an ALP unit that has gone rogue and extorts or otherwise abuses its own or rival communities. A formalized and diligently implemented procedure could greatly reduce the ALP's propensity toward abuse and increase the program's legitimacy. In Wardak, for example, the U.S. military took action against a particularly troublesome ALP unit, reorganizing it and sending away its out-of-district members, with the apparent outcome being a reduction of ALP predation.[44] In Baghlan, the regular police arrested twenty-two ALP members for human rights violations and extortion, and the offenders were sentenced to jail with six- or seven-year prison terms. As a result, the community perceived a decline in the level of abuses perpetrated by the ALP.[45] A possible glitch in the cleanup effort was alleged by some of the Baghlan residents I interviewed, who claimed that the Afghan National Police's clampdown on the abuses of the ALP was really a subterfuge by the local Afghan National Police contingent—heavily dominated by Tajiks—to reduce the number of its ethnic rivals—the Pashtuns—in the local police.

At the end of December 2011, upon the urging of President Karzai, ISAF moved to dismantle another little-known irregular police force under its supervision, the Critical Infrastructure Police (CIP). The outfit operated in northern Afghanistan, at least in the provinces of Balkh, Kunduz, Jowzjan, and Faryab, and perhaps also in Sar-i-Pul. Formerly unpaid, the CIP operated as an abusive militia of untrained self-armed men under the control of local power brokers, extorting money from local communities. These militia members numbering in the low thousands were then rolled into an ISAF irregular forces program and paid between $150 and $200 a month from an American discretionary fund.[46] Under the supervision of ISAF's Regional Command-North (the command structure responsible for northern Afghanistan), the CIP officially operated for at least three months before President Karzai heard about it.[47] Fearing that the effort reinforced the power of rival power brokers in the north, such as Atta Mohammad Noor, Karzai ordered the program shut down. But the disbandment efforts have been troubled, not the least because militiamen to be disarmed frequently just bury their weapons and also because their response to losing employment is often predation on local communities.

At other times, the corrective responses to problematic official militias are even more flimsy—as in, for instance, the Afghan National Police's reaction to a case of kidnapping and rape perpetrated by an ALP commander in Kunduz. Although the Afghan National Police officers supervising the ALP eventually arrested the ALP commander accused of the crime, they appointed his brother, allegedly also a participant in the kidnapping of the raped girl, to lead the ALP unit.[48] Ethnic favoritism and the cultivation of personal clientelistic networks turned out to be more important considerations than a sense of responsiveness and accountability to the local population. When the villagers complained about the appointment of the brother, the Kunduz Afghan National Police commander in charge of the decision dismissed the complaints by responding that the presence of the ALP unit was critical for preventing the village falling into the hands of the Taliban. But a brutal, unaccountable ALP may actually facilitate the Taliban's mobilization efforts among the local population.

Great Variation in Outcomes: Local Context Does Matter

The U.S. Special Operations Forces officer working with the Afghan Local Police who insisted to me that the ALP are all about local politics was, of course, correct. The problem is that the local context in Afghanistan is often very problematic. The structure, composition, history, and insider-outsider relations of a community all significantly influence how well behaved a local self-defense unit will be.

If a community is homogeneous, and particularly if it is also isolated but subject to outside Taliban extortion and abuse, it may well enthusiastically welcome the creation of the ALP and even volunteer to create it. Or its members may, on their own, rise up against the Taliban, without the umbrella of the ALP or another official self-defense program, and then later simply be anointed as ALP.[49] Under such circumstances, the ALP may significantly improve security and the quality of life within the community.

Communities abused by Taliban outsiders can generate a force on their own to fight the Taliban. And sometimes they do. The negative outcome of such self-arming, subsequently blessed with an ALP label, is described later in this discussion, in the context of an intensifying tribal conflict in Nangarhar. However, in other instances, the outcome of such self-arming may be more positive—at least in the extremely narrow sense of expelling the Taliban.

In Andar district in Ghazni province—an area riven by tensions between Hazaras and Pashtuns where the Taliban has been strong for several years—members of several villages rose against the Taliban in the summer of 2012.[50] Incensed by Afghan government corruption, people in the conservative district at first welcomed the Taliban. But as Taliban outsiders from Pakistan increasingly tried to impose an ever more restrictive rule, including shutting down a boys' school and closing several bazaars, men in one village took up arms against the Taliban. The tribal uprising quickly spread to fifty villages representing 4,000 people and fielding 250 armed men who fought some tough skirmishes against the Taliban. Yet that does not mean that the villagers were aligning themselves any closer with the Afghan government, which they continue to resent. Instead, the Ghazni communities in revolt were adamant that they wanted nothing to do with the Afghan government, even rejecting government and U.S. funding and arms, unlike most communities that decide to rise up against the Taliban and then want to be anointed ALP and receive U.S. support.[51] Yet concerns quickly emerged that the Taliban's insurgent rivals also fighting against the Afghan government—Hezb-i-Islami—were trying to take over the Ghazni rebellion, by raising funds and providing logistics for the rebellion. Hezb-i-Islami has long fought the Taliban over turf in Ghazni. Other Afghan power brokers, including Asadullah Khalid, then chief of security for southern Afghanistan, now director of the National Directorate of Security (Afghanistan's intelligence agency), who comes from Ghazni, and Faizanullah Faizan, former Hezb-i commander, Andar native, and, like Khalid, also a former governor of the province, were also actively seeking to control and take over the rebellion, such as by providing it with their own money outside of official government channels.[52] Khalid attempted to integrate the rebellion into his patronage and procurement networks and even brought outside commanders to take over the leadership of the rebellion, much to the chagrin of the local rebels.[53] As of this writing, it was not yet clear what the outcome of the uprising would be: would the Taliban prevail militarily or accommodate the villagers by loosening some of its restrictions, or would the uprising indeed be co-opted by other insurgent groups or power brokers? The verdict was still out as to whether the revolt would bring greater security to the area. Yet it is critical to note that to an important extent, the rebellion came as a result of a Taliban splintering within Andar, with local Taliban commanders who joined the rebellion seeking to expel Pakistani Taliban factions from the area. One of the rebellion's commanders, Lutfullah Kamran, apparently stated that he would direct his men to fight the United States after the rebels had taken care of the Pakistani Taliban factions in the area.[54]

Even if the Andar rebels did not want U.S. sponsorship, considering themselves as much anti-American as anti-Taliban, one important benefit of the Afghan Local Police structure overall is that it can relieve some of the logistical problems that an independently operating self-defense group may have. ALP units, for example, are given small arms and ammunition. But the logistical support is hardly perfect. In Wardak, for example, the Afghan Public Protection Program there—a predecessor of the ALP—had originally been issued one rifle and three magazines of ammunition per volunteer by the Afghan Ministry of Interior, as well as one vehicle for every twenty-five men and one radio for every ten men by the United States.[55] But when the AP3 personnel ran out of ammunition as a result of Ministry of Interior neglect and shed their uniforms to avoid being targeted by the Taliban, all the U.S. military supervisor of the program could offer was to encourage them "to put on a brave face and look like you have ammo."[56]

The ALP, by contrast, receive not only supplies but, crucially, backup from U.S. Special Operations Forces during a firefight. In many parts of Afghanistan, tribal structures in communities ravaged by war have been critically weakened, and their ability to fight against the Taliban can be very limited. A U.S. Special Operations Force backup can be a lifesaver for the self-defense forces if they come under overwhelming pressure from the Taliban. In Baghlan, for example, an ALP commander reported that the local Taliban groups dared not engage in more than minor harassment attacks because they knew the ALP would call on the

SOFs for support during a serious attack.[57] The only offensive the Taliban would undertake was to occasionally plant improvised explosive devices or shoot at the ALP checkpoint. Of course, to the extent that the deterrent effect comes predominantly from the SOF backup, the disturbing question arises as to what will happen to the improved security in the area and the capacity of the ALP to deter and resist Taliban attacks when one day the SOFs are not available for support. Already there has been at least one instance of collapse, in the Western province of Baghdis, where over eighty members of the ALP and their commander surrendered (or defected) to the local Taliban.[58] At the same time, dozens of ALP members have been killed by the Taliban in Afghanistan just in the first half of 2012. And the ALP have not been immune to logistical problems: the Afghan Ministry of Interior has routinely failed to deliver weapons and other supplies, and for reasons of political contestation and ethnic rivalries has also at times denied salaries to some ALP units.[59]

ALP presence in a community has an important *political* impact, which sometimes is positive. If the community has been systematically disfranchised from power in an area—for example, Ghilzai Pashtuns in Uruzgan do not have representation in local district government and the local police forces—establishing ALP units in such a community does empower it. This empowerment, however, can be used against the district Afghan government as much as the Taliban. In fact, this may be the primary reason why a community would welcome the "village stabilization" programs, as the self-defense efforts, including the ALP, are also known. For example, the U.S. SOFs became the heroes of Baghlan Pashtun groups from which they established ALP units when, during a firefight between the Andarabi Tajik-dominated Afghan National Police in Baghlan and the Pashtun ALP units, they took the side of the ALP. The local Afghan National Police, on the other hand, were not thrilled about the "betrayal" by the SOFs nor about how the Pashtun ALP units were challenging the Andarabis' hold on power in the province.[60] Inevitably, the ALP either reinforce or disturb local balances of power, and so the program has profound political and hence governance implications. But they are a positive element only some of the time.

Under the best of circumstances, the ALP can increase security against antigovernment forces, such as the Taliban, in communities previously left to suffer; open up roads to villages previously deemed too dangerous to travel and hence boost economic activity in the area; and even reduce local crime, extortion, and land theft. ISAF frequently points to Arghandab, a relatively homogeneous district where about 80 percent of the population belongs to the Alikozai tribe, as the exemplar of ALP effectiveness. The ALP units in this district of Kandahar province have been operating under tight supervision of the Special Operations Forces, receiving arguably some of the most intense partnering from the SOFs that ALP and other paramilitary forces have received anywhere.[61] At one point, one of the ALP units did start extorting local communities, but the SOFs were able to roll back and restrain the unit, apparently with the help of the district police chief.[62] Overall, the ALP units in Arghandab are purported to have achieved excellent results: they have proved particularly adept at and determined to fight the Taliban, and local communities have been happy with the program.[63]

The Department of Defense Office of the Inspector General, in its report on the Afghan Local Police, also noted important successes in an unspecified eastern province near the Pakistan border where a 500-men-strong ALP apparently helped to significantly turn around a security situation that was so bad that villagers were too afraid even to attend funerals. The establishment of Afghan Local Police there (and supposedly in some other areas) resulted in "significant and unexpected progress" in expelling insurgents from remote villages and districts. In the eastern province, the provincial ALP commander assessed that "you can ride a bicycle safely up and down about 80 kilometers of highway."[64]

Difficulties and complexities in many forms, however, tend to arise quickly when a community or an area is not homogeneous and when the Taliban, Hezb-i-Islami, or other antigovernment elements are not simply thuggish outsiders. The experience with militias in Nangarhar illustrates some of the complexities of such efforts and the limits to how easily they can be controlled. In 2010 the Sepoy tribe of the Achin region of Nangarhar province spontaneously decided to raise an anti-Taliban militia. Enthusiastically embraced by the U.S. Army and promised financial sponsorship, members of the tribe were incorporated into a Community Defense Initiative, yet another militia effort parallel to the ALP.[65] Quickly, however, the Sepoy militias turned on a rival tribe—the Alisherkhel.[66] Using U.S.-provided weapons and contending they had U.S. backing, they "reclaimed" land disputed between the two tribes and triggered violence in large portions of the province. After a series of negotiations and efforts to reduce hostilities, a delegation of National Directorate of Security,

Afghan Natiional Police , Afghan National Army, and U.S. Special Operations Forces was sent to the area in 2011 to persuade the two tribes to disarm. In the fighting that ensued despite this effort, eighteen Sepoy were killed; but still only the Alisherkhel conceded to disarming, incorrectly believing that the Sepoy would also hand over their weapons.[67] As of the summer of 2012, the land dispute was still not resolved, though a ceasefire was extended. The early experience of the Community Defense Initiative in the Achin district notwithstanding, the new version of the self-defense forces—Afghan Local Police units—was being organized in Nangarhar in spring and summer of 2012. By then, one ALP unit was already in existence in the Goshta district. With an astounding disregard for the disastrous experience with the CDI in Achin, as of summer 2012 plans were also under way to try to stand up ALP units in Achin—as well as in other areas of Nangarhar.

Experience with militias in northern Afghanistan reveals multiple problems and complications. Out of the original pro-governmental militias in Baghlan and Kunduz that were created four years ago, several were later converted into the Afghan Local Police. But because of limits on the ALP size in the area, some pro-government militias could not be rolled into the ALP and instead were told to hand over their weapons and go home. But they balked: keeping their arms, they went back to their checkpoints, and no one has dared attempt to disarm them. As of the summer of 2012, they were still there, running out their former pro-government militia salary and, according to Baghlanis from the area, "getting angrier and angrier for not being paid by the Afghan government and the Americans."[68] The Baghlan residents with whom I spoke overwhelmingly expected that these former pro-government militias would resort to highway robbery and extortion when their remaining money finally fully ran out.[69]

There is substantial risk that ALP and other self-defense forces will begin preying on host or neighboring communities, serious abuses of human rights will take place, and the basic security of such communities will be undermined. In Kunduz and northern Farah, for example, after the ALP expelled the Taliban from their own villages, they started extorting the communities and demanding taxes for themselves.[70] As early as 2009, then minister of interior Hanif Atmar was concerned about the abuses perpetrated by the militias: "In Kunduz, after they defeated the Taliban in their villages, they became the power and they took money

and taxes from the people. This is not legal, and this is warlordism."[71]
Many instances of abuse by the ALP have also been reported from
Takhar, where the ALP unit would label its personal enemies as Taliban
and try to get ISAF to eliminate them.[72] Nonetheless, several hundred
ALP members have been vetted in Takhar since. The fact that six hundred were validated in just one vetting session at one shura raises questions about the diligence of the malik-directed vetting process.[73] At other
times, the various ALP units, when drawn from rival communities or supported by rival warlords, have turned on each other instead of fighting
the Taliban. One notorious case of such infighting occurred in Uruzgan
in 2010, a place particularly troubled by tribal discrimination and power
broker rivalries as well as by severe underdevelopment.[74] Another bad
incident with the self-defense forces in Uruzgan took place in August
2012, when a Hazara militia commander, Shujayee, massacred at least
nine Pashtuns in a village in revenge for the deaths of two fellow Hazaras. The outraged Pashtun communities believed him to be a member
of the U.S.-sponsored local ALP—a claim denied by the United States
military as well as some Afghan officials in Uruzgan—but there seemed
to be widespread confusion among local officials and the population as to
whether Shujayee belonged to the ALP or not.[75] The Pashtun community
in response organized anti-government and anti-U.S. protests that the
Taliban was able to exploit and mobilize within the community. Far from
extending security to the community, the self-defense militias—whether
ALP or not—increased insecurity, Taliban mobilization among the Pashtuns, and ethnic tensions.

Similar negative outcomes resulted from actions of another pro-
government militia in Kunduz in September 2012. Also in revenge for
a Taliban assassination of a militiaman, the militia, led by commanders
Qaderak and Faizak, massacred eleven Pashtun boys and men. Qaderak
had previously attacked the Pashtun village at least three times because
it had refused to pay him "taxes." Once again, the Pashtun community
labeled Qaderak's and Faizak's militias as Afghan Local Police units and
organized protests to demand the dismantling of the militias, also blaming the Americans for the massacre and seeing them as responsible for
the reaction and sponsorship of the militias. At the same time, Kunduz
residents expressed grave concern about the degree to which militia-
perpetrated violence would escalate after the U.S. military and other ISAF
officials leave the area as part of the 2014 transition.[76]

Yet, at other times, such ethnic rivalries also overlap with the struggle against the Taliban, with local ALP units, drawn from different ethnic groups and tribes, unable to resist violent ethnic tit-for-tat while justifying it as the struggle against the Taliban.[77] In central Helmand, ALP units, mimicking the similar split allegiances and factionalization of the official ANP units in the area, reflect the competing interests and deep-seated rivalries of former Hezb-i-Islami and Communist fighters as well as rival drug gangs.[78] Intensive and diligent supervision by U.S. Special Operations Forces might be able to contain these rifts, but once any such supervision is reduced, there is a high potential for the inherent enmities to explode into violence, with disastrous effects on both the quality of local governance and the safety of the local population.

Sometimes the negative effect on human security and perception of safety is more subtle. The establishment of an Afghan Local Police unit may provoke the Taliban to start attacking the unit and the community, expanding the scale of insecurity. The U.S. military considers it a sign of the ALP's effectiveness that they draw Taliban fire.[79] But from the perspective of the local community, security may be considerably worse than before the creation of the local ALP outfit.

In very heterogeneous, polarized, and fractured communities, the establishment of ALP units often exacerbates the security dilemma among the communities and triggers an armament spiral. Baghlan provides a prime example. The ALP units there have been drawn predominantly from the Pashtun minority in order to "drain the swamp" of the Taliban and Hezb-i-Islami. The Pashtuns in Baghlan have felt deeply marginalized and disfranchised since 2002, especially since many government positions, including in the Afghan National Police in the area, have been dominated by former Northern Alliance members. Many Pashtun communities there have believed that their villages were being abused by the Andarabi Tajik-dominated ANP and power structures. Consequently, the Taliban and Hezb-i-Islami could easily mobilize support among the Pashtun communities. So establishing the Afghan Local Police among the same groups was seen as mechanism to reduce the Taliban's strength.[80] But, in turn, rival Tajik and Uzbek communities and power brokers felt extremely threatened by the arming of their opponents under the ALP program (often the ALP units would be recruited from local members of the Taliban and Hezb-i-Islami), and they began arming their own ethnically based militias and lobbying local Ministry of Interior officials to recognize their militias as the ALP, not those of the Pashtuns.[81] One such commander, who went by the *nom de guerre* Afghankush (which implies "Pashtun killer"), had been renowned for "fighting the Taliban" for several years before the ALP were officially in place and for securing the Baghlan-Kunduz road from attacks.[82] He demanded that his Uzbek militia be recognized as part of the ALP. When refused, he simply announced that his men already were the ALP and were just not yet being paid. Several other warlords in the north adopted that approach, often with the backing of their governors and chiefs of police.[83] Many Tajik and Uzbek communities and power brokers in the north have felt betrayed and treated unfairly as a result of the ALP program, believing that it rewarded Pashtun Taliban-supporting villages whereas those who have been fighting the Taliban for two decades were being sidelined.

While the effects of establishing Afghan Local Police units are highly contingent on local contexts, cumulatively the ALP phenomenon transcends the local context and can, through contagion, as it were, generate a widespread and complex security predicament for the whole country. Regardless of the order to ALP units not to travel or operate outside of their villages (and, of course, they violate that rule), their reputations do travel among widespread communities. What happens in one Afghan village does not stay in that Afghan village. Instead, rival communities, observing that their antagonists are being armed, seek to arm themselves as well.

Even when security improves as a result of the creation of a local ALP outfit, the robustness of that improvement may be far less than meets the eye. Sometimes security in an area improves simply because a community typically hedges its bets and pays part of its income, including what it gets through the ALP salary payments, to the Taliban. The local ALP reach a *modus vivendi* with the Taliban and the Taliban reduces its attacks.[84] Indeed, such hedging is typical of Afghan history, with local warlords, khans, and tribes siding and making peace with those they sense would prevail in a conflict, and easily breaking deals if the situation on the battlefield changes. Sometimes, as in Logar in 2010, the accommodation between the militias and the Taliban even results in temporary improvements in security in the area and the community welcomes it.[85] But the reduction in violence often exists only at the mercy of the Taliban, and the deal collapses when the Taliban chooses to renege on it or when the external payoffs dry up and can no longer be divided among the various warring parties.

In some cases, such as in Kunduz and Baghlan, creating the ALP may merely mean putting the Taliban and Hezb-i-Islami on the ISAF–Afghan government payroll and essentially paying them not to fight the government and foreign troops. Buying off one's enemies is, of course, another time-honored tradition in Afghanistan, and at times groups align themselves on the basis of whichever side can provide them more money rather than on the basis of any hardened ideological preferences or deep-seated communal rifts. But paying your enemies not to fight you can turn out to be only a short-term solution. What happens if the ALP money suddenly dries up? An ALP commander ("former" Hezb-i-Islami leader) answered the question for me: "It's all about money. Now the Afghan government pays us. If the opposition starts paying us more, we switch to them."[86]

Ominous Future

Herein lies one of the biggest problems with the Afghan Local Police. The U.S. military readily agrees that the ALP are a "temporary" solution. No one, however, knows as yet how temporary and when they will be retired. What will happen with the ALP and other militia programs after 2014 when even the regular Afghan forces of the Afghan National Army and Afghan National Police are to be reduced by as much as 130,000 because the Afghan state will not be able to afford to pay for the current size of the Afghan National Security Forces?[87] What will happen if a National Directorate of Security or Ministry of Interior strongly dominated by one ethnic group decides after 2014 to deny salaries to Afghan Local Police units composed of rival ethnic groups? If the ALP officially persist, will Afghan Special Operations Forces be able to maintain even just the existing level of supervision over the ALP, inadequate as it may already be in some areas? How likely are the ALP units to disarm if they are told to so after 2014? If the ALP units are simply told to go home, they may well offer themselves up to the highest bidder, switch to the warring party they assess will most likely prevail in an area, or simply turn to crime. Most answers to these questions raise serious concerns about the ALP and other militia programs and the likelihood that they will abuse local communities on a widespread basis and generate and perpetuate new violent conflict.

Under even the best circumstances—if after 2014 the Afghan National Army and Afghan National Police can effectively take over security in Afghanistan—the (former) Afghan Local Police will still represent a huge challenge for improving governance. Its predatory tendencies will be hard to control, and in very polarized communities, the presence of former ALP members may trigger local conflict. If they are perpetrators of local crime, the ALP units will undermine perceptions of public safety and rule of law more broadly and, paradoxically, legitimize actors such as the Taliban, who deliver "order and justice." They will be used by power brokers to augment their power, challenge their rivals, and oppose the writ of the central state. In short, even when the program is performing its function of beating down the Taliban in a particular locale at a particular time, it still leaves behind armed men who can and often do challenge the already weak central government and prey on local communities.

Under the worst circumstances, the Afghan Local Police militias will be one of the actors in a post-2014 civil war—whether as loose roaming bands or, more likely, under the sway of prominent warlords and insurgent factions. Already many prominent former commanders are digging up their weapons and refurbishing their former militias. While at the helm of the Ministry of Interior, Bismullah Khan Mohammadi was determined to make sure that as many non-Pashtun militias as possible were established or legitimatized in northern Afghanistan to ensure a favorable disposition of forces there. In any future disintegration of Afghanistan, the ALP outfits will be one of many warring "self-defense" groups and be incorporated into power brokers' armies.

If one takes this dire scenario as the most likely future of Afghanistan, one can find several reasons to proceed with and even further expand the ALP effort. One is that, yes, the militias are not a good development, but they are happening anyway, with or without ISAF's and the Afghan government's sponsorship, so why not get into the spirit of the time and exploit them to the advantage of the United States? Especially if a civil war is believed to be coming, the concerns about ALP's negative effects on governance and security in Afghanistan can be discarded, and instead the ALP can be seen as maximizing the number and strength of groups that may oppose the Taliban and hence reduce the Taliban's post-2014 power and territorial control. Putting many of the Taliban on the payroll via the ALP mechanism may also extend the time before a civil war arrives after 2014.

Yet if one believes that a civil war is not inevitable, that there is still a chance to stabilize Afghanistan sufficiently to avert a full-blown conflict and prevent extensive Taliban territorial control, then succumbing to the

ALP siren song will prove counterproductive. Whatever tactical gains the ALP may bring are likely to be offset by their potential to trigger long-term conflict as well as their negative impact on the already poor quality of governance in Afghanistan. And without progress in governance, it is hard to imagine how the current dispensation in Afghanistan can be sustained after 2014, even if sufficiently robust improvements in the ANSF materialize. Thus, if one still believes in a reasonably stable Afghanistan after 2014, then further buildup of the ALP is not the way to go.

Instead, credible and robust mechanisms should be developed immediately to roll back rogue ALP units already in existence. Now is also the time to start developing a serious plan to disarm and demobilize the ALP after 2014. Although the U.S. military has suggested that the program be made permanent, Afghan government leaders, including in the Ministry of Interior, are ambivalent, wary that such a program will threaten governance in the long run. And there is indeed a high chance that it will. Ideally, the United States and the international community would commit themselves to carry out that disarmament and to establish a credible program with procedures for diverting the decommissioned ALP from future predatory behavior and ethnic infighting.[88] Even if the United States and ISAF themselves do not undertake the actual disarmament of the ALP, they should at minimum help the Afghan government create the plans and procedures for it to do so after 2014. At least the joint planning effort needs to start now. Waiting until after 2014 may well be too late. An ALP stand-down program will be credible only if other militias, whether under the aegis of the United States or belonging to Afghan warlords, are also incorporated into a disarmament program. If they are not, the security meltdown will be triggered by them, just as it is currently being triggered by the ALP, and consequently the ALP units may shed their uniforms but not their weapons.

Should the United States and ISAF not find the wherewithal to actually disband the ALP and other militias after 2014, then the U.S. military and the Afghan government should at least consider developing credible plans to incorporate the Afghan Local Police into the Afghan National Police after 2014. Such an approach, if it is the only one for which the United States can generate any resolve, is risky and much less optimal than disbanding the ALP. For one, even if lodging the ALP units within the ANP could increase and strengthen supervisory oversight of the ALP, it could also greatly augment the intense factionalization and criminal propensity of the ANP. For Afghanistan's future security and public safety and for the quality of governance in Afghanistan, the Afghan National Police are more important than the Afghan Local Police. Thus any incorporation plans would need to be carefully evaluated: an Afghan National Police rotted by the incorporation of the ALP would be worse than a rogue ALP that the Afghan National Police have to combat.

But not planning the ALP's end and letting them go loose after 2014 is a bad policy. The United States will do Afghanistan and ultimately itself a great disservice if it rushes to create as many ALP units as possible before the end of 2014 and then hands them over to the Afghan government to worry about.

9

Counternarcotics and Economic Development Policies

Counternarcotics policies in Afghanistan have been no less complex than the efforts to stand up the Afghan Local Police and other militias, and far more controversial. No wonder, for the counternarcotics policies pressed on the post-Taliban government prior to 2009 had serious counterproductive effects not only on the Afghan economy but also on the counterinsurgency, stabilization, anticorruption, and rule of law efforts being pursued in Afghanistan by the United States and its allies. The flawed counternarcotics programs hampered both counterinsurgency and good governance efforts. In a courageous break with thirty years of U.S. counternarcotics policies around the world that featured forced eradication of illicit crops as a way to reduce the supply of drugs and bankrupt belligerents, the Obama administration wisely decided in 2009 to scale back eradication in Afghanistan and focus instead on selective interdiction of high-level—and particularly Taliban-linked—traffickers and on rural development.

But the effectiveness of the administration's well-thought-out counternarcotics strategy has been challenged by major implementation difficulties. Effective implementation ultimately depends on robust progress in improving security and governance in Afghanistan—the former very tenuous at best, the latter overwhelmingly characterized by corruption, abuse, and incompetence. Critical problems with the new counternarcotics strategy have also arisen as a result of misguided policies in the field. Interdiction has lost its selective focus on high-level, Taliban-linked traffickers and indiscriminately targets small-scale farmers. Eradication and bans on poppy cultivation still continue, once again impoverishing farmers and causing more instability and conflict—and once again defining "good governance" in ways that undermine human security and contradict conceptions of good governance acceptable to the Afghan people. In most of Afghanistan, including some of the most strategic areas, alternative livelihoods efforts have not amounted to comprehensive long-term development. Some important improvements in socioeconomic development, such as in the health sector, have been achieved. But skewed by counterinsurgency pressures, many of the chosen agricultural policies have been plagued by a myriad of problems and have not encouraged good governance practices. As part of the 2014 transition process toward full Afghan ownership of security and governance, better—more accountable and sustainable—rural economic development approaches have been at least formally agreed upon by the international community and the Afghan government. But at the same time, Afghanistan is heading toward a large post-2014 economic contraction that will rock whatever political stability and socioeconomic progress will have been registered up to that point.

Why Scaling Back Eradication Was a Good Decision

For two decades now, the opium poppy economy has constituted a large portion of Afghanistan's GDP.[1] Poppy has been deeply entwined in the socioeconomic and political fabric of the whole country, not simply in the southern province of Helmand where most of the nation's opium poppy cultivation currently takes place.[2] In 2011 poppy cultivation and opium production in Afghanistan were estimated at 131,000 hectares (ha) and 5,800 metric tons (mt). During the past decade, the lowest level of poppy cultivation hovered around 74,000 ha in 2002, following an extensive Taliban prohibition of poppy cultivation in 2000, and the highest level was 193,000 ha in 2007, with an estimated opium production of 3,400 mt and 8,200 mt, respectively.[3] Beyond the high profitability that often privileges cultivation of opium poppy over many legal crops, there are structural drivers of poppy cultivation in Afghanistan that encompass a complex set of intertwined public goods and socioeconomic deficiencies, such as inadequate security, limited access to legal markets, poor infrastructure and irrigation systems, absence of a legal microcredit system, and lack of value-added chains.[4]

The Taliban insurgents profit from the illicit drug economy, as do the Afghan police, tribal elites, and many ex-warlords cum government officials at various levels. Measuring the size of illicit economies and any derivative numbers, such as profit levels, is notoriously difficult, but estimates place Taliban profits from the drug trade somewhere between $70 million to $500 million, with about $100 million a year being the most credible estimate, and amounting to somewhere between 20 and 40 percent of the Taliban's income.[5] The United States military believes that drugs are the primary source of the Taliban's funding.[6] That may be the case, but the Taliban's funding is highly diversified and mostly involves the taxation of any economic activity in an area under its influence. Taliban detainees estimate that the insurgency requires only between $100 million and $150 million a year to operate.[7] If the detainee estimate is reasonably accurate, the insurgency seems to be operating with a significant surplus. This and the fact that the Taliban revenue portfolio is so diversified have crucial implications for counternarcotics and counterinsurgency strategies—one critical implication is that trying to bankrupt the Taliban through poppy eradication (or even opiate interdiction) is close to impossible outside of small isolated localities where wider logistical insurgent channels do not operate. This realization is especially important since eliminating the Taliban's financial base through counternarcotics efforts was long considered a crucial element of the counterinsurgency strategy, even as some in the U.S. and allied militaries feared that a program of extensive eradication would complicate counterinsurgency efforts.[8] Unfortunately, the latter concern was well founded: eradication did complicate counterinsurgency efforts, without delivering the promised results.

Aggressive interdiction and eradication were undertaken in Afghanistan between 2004 and 2009, after three years of essentially laissez-faire policy toward poppy cultivation.[9] Interdiction was supposed to target large traffickers and processing laboratories. However, the effort was immediately manipulated by local Afghan power brokers to eliminate drug competition, particularly drug trade operations belonging to their rivals. Instead of targeting top echelons of the drug economy, many of whom had considerable political clout, interdiction operations were largely conducted against small, vulnerable traders who could neither sufficiently bribe nor adequately intimidate the interdiction teams and their supervisors within the Afghan government.[10] The result was a significant vertical integration of the drug industry in Afghanistan and an intensification of small traders' dependence on powerful patrons.[11] A second negative impact of the way interdiction was carried out was that it allowed the Taliban to integrate itself back into the Afghan drug trade.[12] Having recouped in Pakistan, the Taliban was once again needed to provide protection to traffickers targeted by interdiction.

Eradication efforts, adopted with progressively greater intensity since 2004, were supposed to bankrupt and hence physically weaken the Taliban, and also reduce the level of poppy cultivation and drug trafficking in Afghanistan. Instead, by 2009 when the Obama administration was to take over Afghanistan counterinsurgency and counternarcotics policies, eradication had had the following—overwhelmingly negative—effects. First, it did not bankrupt the Taliban. In fact, the Taliban reconstituted itself in Pakistan between 2002 and 2004 without access to large profits from drugs, rebuilding its material base largely with donations from Pakistan and the Middle East and with profits from another illicit economy: the illegal traffic with licit goods between Pakistan and Afghanistan.[13] Second, rather than weakening the insurgency, eradication strengthened it by driving economic refugees into the Taliban's hands. Eradication also alienated the local population from the national government as well as from those local tribal elites who agreed to eradication, thus creating a key opening for Taliban mobilization.[14] Moreover, the local eradicators themselves were in a position to profit best from counternarcotics policies by being able to eliminate rival drug businessmen and power brokers by labeling them Taliban, as well as by altering market concentration and prices, at least in the short term and within their region of operations.

Eradication was thus complicating counterinsurgency and stabilization efforts in Afghanistan, and the Obama administration's decision to focus instead on interdiction and rural development was the right decision.

Selective Interdiction Has Become Indiscriminate

The Obama administration decided to gear the interdiction policy primarily toward Taliban-linked traffickers. Going after these particular traffickers became the sole counternarcotics mandate of ISAF forces, though other international and Afghan counternarcotics units, with U.S. Drug Enforcement Administration assistance, could target other traffickers as well. ISAF's interdiction efforts have sought to reduce the flows of weapons, money, drugs, precursor agents, and improvised explosive device (IED) components to the Taliban, with the goal of degrading the Taliban's finances and physical resources and dismantling its logistical networks. Although hundreds of interdiction raids have now been conducted, especially in southern Afghanistan, and large quantities of opium and IEDs have been seized in these operations, it is questionable whether the impact on the Taliban's resource flows has been more than local.

On the other hand, large-scale military operations to clear the Taliban from particular areas, such as Marja, Helmand, have had more pronounced effects on the insurgents' funding capacity and resource flows in those particular areas.[15] One reason this is the case is that even when local Taliban funding sources are not disrupted, local level Taliban commanders require additional money from their higher-up commanders in Pakistan to purchase more significant equipment, such as vehicles and heavy machine guns—often a point of contention between local commanders and their bosses in Pakistan.[16] Preventing the Taliban from accessing established funding streams thus complicates the operational capacity of lower-level Taliban commanders, who find it easier to replace personnel than equipment. But so far, the cumulative effects of the narcotics interdiction effort to suppress *financial* flows do not appear to interfere with Taliban activities at the strategic level. This is because the Taliban fundraising policy has long been to tax any economic activities in the areas where the insurgents operate—be it sheep herding in the north, illegal logging in the east, or National Solidarity Program projects in the center.

The strongest effect of focusing interdiction on Taliban-linked traffickers appears to be the disruption, at least temporarily, of its logistical chains, since many of its logistical operatives move IED materials as well as drugs. In combination with ISAF's targeting of mid-level commanders, the shift in the counternarcotics-interdiction focus is probably palpably complicating the Taliban's operations in Afghanistan's south, where both the military surge and interdiction have been prioritized.

But in the zeal to disrupt the Taliban's logistical chains and weaken its command structures, especially at the operational middle level, where the Taliban insurgency appears to be highly vulnerable to repeated strikes, the ISAF interdiction policy has strayed from the selectivity carefully crafted into the design of the Obama administration counternarcotics strategy.[17] ISAF units often do not have an easy way to ascertain whether someone is a middle-level commander or not. What does it take to be a middle-level commander—being in charge of three, ten, or one hundred Taliban? What does it take to be a Taliban supporter?[18] The dual focus of night raids and house searches on capturing "high-value" (whatever that actually means) targets *and* searching for drugs and explosives has blurred the distinction between farmers and high-value drug or Taliban operatives. Does the fact that a household has opium make the household members Taliban supporters? Obviously not, since many rural Afghans do not hold their assets as cash in a bank but rather as opium stocks at home. ISAF house searches that seize or destroy any found opium, perhaps under the belief that they are destroying Taliban stockpiles, can in fact wipe out the entire savings of a household. Thus, in areas that have been subject to intense interdiction raids, such as the Marja or Nad Ali districts of Helmand, the effects of supposedly selective and hearts-and-minds-oriented interdiction can resemble blanket eradication.[19] Indeed, their impact on the economic well-being of a household is often more detrimental than that of eradication because after eradication a family still can have a chance to replant, but interdiction forays can wipe out all of the long-term assets of a household. And the effects on stability and the counterinsurgency campaign are the same as from eradication: intense alienation of the affected population from the Afghan government and ISAF forces and susceptibility to Taliban mobilization.

Although the implementation of the interdiction policy has frequently lost its selectivity in distinguishing between small and high-level traders, its selectivity regarding the Taliban connection has also generated problematic side-effects. One is the signal to Afghan power brokers that the best way to conduct the drug business in Afghanistan is to undermine Taliban competitors by providing counterinsurgency services, such as intelligence, militias, and real estate property to ISAF, or to align oneself with the Afghan government. The very hard choice of pursuing only a certain type of trafficker—namely, those linked to the Taliban—may well be necessary and appropriate under conditions of an insurgency and a very extensive drug economy featuring all types of actors, including government officials. But coupling such hard choices with indiscriminate seizure of opium stocks at the level of households (frequently poor households) further alienates the population from the government and defines good policy as favoring the powerful ones, thus contradicting public claims of accountable governance.

Eradication Still in Fashion

Even worse, counterproductive eradication operations still continue. The Obama administration has encountered withering criticism from Russia for its counternarcotics policy in Afghanistan. Suffering from twin epidemics of drug use, including heroin originating in Afghanistan, and infectious diseases linked to intravenous drug use as well as a broader demographic crisis of low birth rates and high population morbidity, Russia has complained that its drug and related public health crisis are caused by the large supply of heroin from Afghanistan. If there were not this massive supply of cheap heroin from Afghanistan, Russian officials claim, Russia's drug use and related disease spread would be far lower. Rejecting overwhelming evidence from forty years of counternarcotics efforts that actions on the supply side tend to have minimal effects on drug-use trends, and unwilling to invest in appropriate drug prevention and treatment facilities, Russia has demanded aggressive eradication in Afghanistan.[20] It also provides counternarcotics training to Afghanistan and Pakistan.

But despite Russia's vociferous complaints that the United States is not eradicating poppy in Afghanistan, poppy eradication in Afghanistan actually is continuing. The Obama administration defunded only the centrally led, U.S.-trained Afghan eradication unit operating from Kabul. Eradication efforts led by the Afghan Ministry of Counternarcotics and provincial governors are still ongoing. Discounting the occasional major eradication drive or poppy cultivation ban, such as in Nangarhar in 2008 (described below), eradication has consistently hovered between 2,500 and 4,000 hectares a year, both before and after the Obama administration's counternarcotics policy in Afghanistan was adopted.[21]

The current Afghan-led eradication program continues to be associated with the same problems that plagued the previous, centrally led process, including undermining good governance practices and weakening the legitimacy of the Afghan government. Powerful elites are able to bribe or coerce their way out of having their opium poppy fields destroyed, or they direct eradication against their political opponents. The poorest farmers, most vulnerable to Taliban mobilization, bear the brunt of eradication.[22] Alienated farmers often join with the Taliban to oppose eradication and entire regions are destabilized as a result. The violent protests against eradication and attacks on the eradication teams in Nangarhar's

Khogyani, Shinwar, and Achin areas in the spring of 2012 provide a vivid example. Eradication targets are frequently set without regard for the effects on the economic conditions of the farmers, local conflict dynamics, and counterinsurgency efforts. Officials from Kabul tend to arrive in a provincial capital, round up governors and police chiefs, and order them to destroy a predetermined number of hectares of poppy. In the western province of Herat, overall one of the most stable parts of Afghanistan and a major locus of drug smuggling routes, the Ministry of Counternarcotics decided in April 2012 that eradication should take place in the Shindand district, where insecurity and Taliban presence have been strong, just as ISAF and the ANSF were planning to undertake clearing operations there.[23] Any hearts-and-minds efforts were bound to be ruined by the eradication drive, and intelligence about the Taliban from the population was likely to dry up.

Given the potential for serious side-effects, it is ironic that the scale of eradication is miniscule when compared with what is necessary to significantly suppress poppy cultivation in Afghanistan. Eradication levels hover in the low thousands of hectares per year, but with yearly cultivation levels of significantly over 100,000 ha, such a level of eradication cannot change more than very local market dynamics. Experience from Colombia, Burma, Peru, Thailand, and China suggests that for eradication to significantly affect the drug market, it would have to reach well over three-quarters of the land cultivated with illicit crops—that is, in the case of Afghanistan, over 100,000 ha a year—and be sustained for a number of years. Such suppression could only be achieved through sheer brute force in Afghanistan, since alternative livelihoods cannot be developed quickly. Of course, such an effort would destroy the larger stabilization prospects for Afghanistan. And even at such levels of eradication, success could be elusive because farmers and traffickers have a variety of adaptive strategies at their disposal and because such levels of eradication tend to be politically unsustainable. Critically, for eradication—whether through a mailed fist approach or through a more gentle strategy emphasizing alternative livelihoods and accountability—to significantly reduce cultivation in a country or a particular locale, conflict must have already ended or have been very significantly reduced.[24]

Without a significant reduction in global demand, suppression of poppy cultivation in one place will merely drive it to another. Therefore, aside from undermining counterinsurgency efforts and attempts to stabilize the national government in Kabul, an intensive eradication drive, if actually effective in suppressing poppy cultivation, would merely push opium poppy cultivation into one of Afghanistan's neighboring countries. Quite likely that neighbor would be Pakistan, where extensive poppy cultivation would be even more detrimental to U.S. interests than it is in Afghanistan.[25]

Not all poppy suppression efforts in Afghanistan are implemented by bulldozing the poppy plants. In Helmand, the province with the most intense poppy cultivation, where Governor Mohammad Gulab Mangal, governor of the province between 2008 and 2012, was held up as the paragon of good governance, poppy has been suppressed by destroying farmers' water pumps, especially in the poor, insecure, recently liberated poppy-growing areas north of the Helmand River.[26] That approach, which requires that poppy crops live purely on rain water, may reduce the amount that survives, but it also kills legal crops and destroys the farmers' means of procuring water for consumption and other household use. Not surprisingly, this lack of concern for the farmers' well-being has effectively played into the Taliban's mobilization efforts. And once again, good governance is being defined in terms of the number of poppy hectares reduced even though meeting that criterion entails compromising human security and alienating the population from the government.

Bans on poppy cultivation can have as devastating an economic impact on the rural population as eradication. Although hailed as hallmarks of great governance—for instance, in Nangarhar or Balkh—they are ultimately as politically and economically unsustainable as premature eradication before alternative livelihoods are in place. Nor are they consistent with how the population views good governance. In Nangarhar, for example, Governor Gul Agha Shirzai has managed to keep poppy cultivation negligible or limited—driving it down from a 2007 peak of 18,739 hectares to zero for the following several years.[27] He achieved this "success" through a combination of buyoffs of influential maliks, promises of alternative livelihoods, threats of eradication of the poppy crops, and imprisonment of violators.

But the promises of alternative livelihoods have mostly failed to materialize. While farmers close to the provincial capital Jalalabad have often managed to cope by switching to vegetable crops, increasing dairy production, and working in construction in cash-for-work programs, farmers away from the provincial center, in districts such as Achin,

Khogyani, and Shinwar, have suffered great economic deprivation.[28] As their incomes have crashed (often by 80 percent) and few (sometimes no) alternative livelihoods programs have been made available to them, their political restlessness has grown steadily.[29]

Those areas have seen great levels of instability. There, tribal conflicts over land, water, and access to resource handouts from the international community have often intensified—in large part as a result of greater economic deprivation. Rebellions of young men against local maliks supporting eradication have occurred.[30] So have physical attacks on eradication teams, intense Taliban mobilization, and increased flows of militants into and through the province from Pakistan. This year Nangarhar has experienced the flare-up of significant, violent resistance and protests against eradication.[31] Meanwhile, the area under poppy cultivation has crept up to nearly 2,000 ha.[32] Many farmers, especially those farther away from Jalalabad, have few means of making a living under the poppy ban. Having depleted their assets during the years the opium ban has been in place (since 2007), many have had to fall back on poppy cultivation to secure a basic livelihood for their families. Maliks have complained that the government defines "starving the poor people" as a good policy.[33]

In Afghanistan's north, the devastating effect of the ban on poppy cultivation has been intensified by prolonged and repeated droughts. The cumulative effects have been a liquidation of long-term savings and productive assets in order to cope with acute short-term economic distress. As economic development programs, often mostly focused on infrastructure building, have not generated enough jobs—always the toughest goal of economic development and often the last aspect of development to take off—the economic insecurity of ordinary Afghans amid conditions of extensive poverty has only increased.[34] Social cohesion also weakens as a result of economic decline, giving rise to increasing crime, more exclusionary patronage networks, and reductions in charitable funds.[35]

Several, at times perverse, motivations and incentives encourage poppy eradication by Afghan governors and officials of the Ministry of Counternarcotics, despite the fact that this policy is instigating instability and hampering counterinsurgency efforts. First of all, some Afghan government officials, especially those with a communist background, genuinely believe that poppy cultivation is bad for Afghanistan and that its suppression is important, no matter what costs for the country such suppression generates. Afghan government officials who believe in aggressive eradication have frequently asserted that since the Afghan constitution prohibits poppy cultivation, it is their duty to destroy it, regardless of any side-effects.[36] Others believe that pushing ahead with eradication will secure the favor of the international community—whether in Washington or in Moscow. Such considerations are particularly important to those officials in Afghanistan who entertain presidential ambitions or need to curry favor with Moscow, such as Governor Gul Agha Shirzai in Nangarhar, Governor Mohammad Gulab Mangal in Helmand, and Governor Atta Mohammad in Balkh. Even though, as a result of eradication and poppy cultivation bans, local populations are alienated from these governors and the positive links between them are severed, the international community often still hails their performance as a model of good governance to be emulated elsewhere in Afghanistan.

This equating of good governance with poppy suppression, regardless of its legitimacy and long-term effectiveness, has been institutionalized in an Afghan government program called the Good Performance Initiative (GPI). Funded primarily by the United States, the initiative aims to deliver high-impact development assistance to those provinces that have eliminated or significantly reduced poppy cultivation, or demonstrated other effective counternarcotics achievements. Its objective is poppy elimination and maintenance of poppy-free provinces through the provision of financial support for priority development projects.

The program is readily embraced by governors who qualify for the rewards—usually between several hundred thousand and one million dollars a year—because governors do not have any taxation capacity and depend on Kabul for all provincial funds. Rarely, however, do the Good Performance Initiative funds result in systematic alternative livelihoods programs. This is partially a function of the level of funding, which is often too small to have a chance to address the structural drivers of poppy cultivation beyond a small locality. Instead, the allocations frequently allow well-positioned provincial government officials and their friends, such as in Nangarhar, to obtain profits by hiring their companies to carry out any chosen projects or otherwise hijacking provided resources.[37] The sponsored projects themselves often amount to one isolated undertaking here and there, at best, rather than any robust and synergistic rural development. A very high-level provincial official in Nangarhar, for example, could not tell me what happened with all of the GPI funds that the province received over the past several years, beyond highlighting that one generator was delivered to a district (he was not sure which one) and a university dormitory and several other unspecified buildings were built in Jalalabad.[38]

Promises of systematic rural development and viable alternative livelihoods made to poppy farmers are thus mostly unfulfilled. Whatever level of poppy suppression has been achieved has come mainly from threats and coercion rather than from the establishment of robust and sustainable legal livelihoods. The outcomes are consequently both fragile and often an additional stimulus to the insurgency and instability in Afghanistan.

After the 2014 transition, poppy cultivation in Afghanistan is likely to increase to some extent. The global opiate market has been saturated by Afghanistan's production over the past decade. But when not driven by a decrease in global opiate prices, downward fluctuations in Afghanistan's poppy cultivation have been achieved principally through unsustainable economic handout policies (described below), governors' coercion, or the deterrent effect of ISAF's presence in some of the key poppy-producing areas. A thinning down of U.S. troops will diminish this deterrent effect. Thus some upswing in production after 2014—primarily in areas squeezed by bans and eradication drives—is likely. But that should be expected and not bemoaned. Instead of being seduced by the false promise and quick gratification of eradication, policymakers should focus on sustainable rural development. Unfortunately, despite the investment of large amounts of money, especially in Kandahar and Helmand, few sustainable rural development programs have been successfully implemented so far.

Ineffectively Designed Rural Development: Seeking to Buy Love and Failing to Address Root Causes

Throughout most of the 2002–09 period, alternative livelihoods programs were slow to reach the vast majority of the Afghan population. They also largely failed to address the structural drivers of opium poppy cultivation.[39] The lack of security and increasing insurgency in the south halted many of the alternative livelihoods projects. A legal microcredit system, as well as any kind of formal rural credit, continued to be nonexistent in most of Afghanistan. Traditional sources, such as family and moneylenders, provided the vast majority of credit, while NGO-led microfinance initiatives under the Microfinance Investment Support

Facility for Afghanistan had been taking off slowly.[40] Infrastructure deficiencies, such as poorly maintained road networks and the lack of electrification, inadequate market facilities, a lack of processing centers and value-added chains, inefficient use of resources, and low productivity all hampered rural development.[41] Afghanistan's agricultural sector, the economic engine of the country until the 1970s, was underdeveloped even then (never having experienced the green revolution) and was subsequently decimated by the Soviet scorched-earth counterinsurgency policy of the 1980s and then by the civil war and Taliban neglect of the 1990s.

Although in the post-2002 period some areas, such as Helmand, received a fair amount of aid for agricultural development, much of it failed to reach ordinary farmers. Projects such as the Kajaki Dam, the centerpiece of efforts by the United States Agency for International Development (USAID) in the south of Afghanistan for much of the decade, could not be completed because of insecurity.[42] At the same time, economic development programs in more secure areas, such as in northern Afghanistan, often simply did not materialize, even though bans on poppy cultivation were achieved through promises of alternative livelihoods.

The Obama administration set out to redress this glaring hole in the counternarcotics and stabilization policy in Afghanistan by emphasizing rural development and allocating about a quarter billion dollars a year to the effort. Two principal alternative livelihoods programs to support cultivation of licit crops were created: the Incentives Driving Economic Alternatives for the North, East, and West, with $150 million funding and budgeted to run through 2014 in the less violent areas, and Afghanistan Vouchers for Increased Production in Agriculture (AVIPA-Plus) for Helmand and Kandahar, which had an original budget of $60 million that was expanded to $474 million. Originally scheduled to operate through 2011, AVIPA was then to be transitioned to a more sustainable USAID program, the Southern Region Agricultural Development Program. But because of persistent insecurity, counterinsurgency imperatives, and other problems, the redesign did not occur by the planned date, and AVIPA was extended.[43] The program provides vouchers for wheat seed, fertilizer, and tools as well as cash-for-work programs and small grants to cooperatives. In the north, the reported outputs of the rural development efforts have included improving irrigation for 23,000 ha of land, creating approximately 42,000 employment opportunities in farm communities since 2010, and facilitating $4 million in off-farm sales in fiscal year 2011.[44] In the south, the reported results of AVIPA and other rural development efforts have included the training and employment of over 4,000 laborers in planting more than 1 million fruit tree saplings, creating over 100,000 other labor opportunities, and distributing seeds and fertilizer to several thousand farmers.[45] Other small success stories have included increasing Afghan exports of a high-quality pomegranate juice called Anar to Dubai and elsewhere, and raisins to the United Kingdom.[46] Overall, during the fiscal years 2009 and 2010, approximately 77 percent—or about $1.65 billion—of USAID's total Afghanistan budget was spent in the insurgency-plagued south and east. In fiscal year 2011, the funding for the two regions was about 81 percent of the total budget, or about $872 million.[47]

In actuality, however, the programs delivered much less than the reported output numbers suggest. In particular, many of the projects have not proved sustainable. Especially in southern Afghanistan, where counterinsurgency has been strong, the economic development programs were plagued by vacillation between two competing understandings of the purpose of economic development projects: either to buy off the population and wean it from the insurgents, or to produce long-term sustainable development.

The buy-off concept, embedded in AVIPA-Plus in particular, built upon the so-called Quick-Impact Projects first implemented via the provincial reconstruction teams in 2003 and funded by U.S. Department of Defense money from the Commander's Emergency Response Program (CERP).[48] These projects were later to be transitioned to more sustainable economic programs, but because of continuing insecurity, counterinsurgency imperatives, and bureaucratic inertia, they were perpetuated in their original form for the remainder of the Bush administration. During the Obama administration, in conjunction with the expanded counterinsurgency effort, the Quick-Impact Projects were elevated in scale to so-called economic stabilization projects. But once again, they were designed to start with temporary economic injections, often short-term cash-for-work programs, to last weeks or at best months, and only later were to be switched to more sustainable efforts. Their goals have been to keep Afghan males employed so that economic necessities do not drive them to join the Taliban, and to secure the allegiance of the population who, ideally, would provide intelligence on the insurgents. Under these goals, U.S. economic development efforts have prioritized the most violent areas. In

2010 alone, for example, USAID allocated $250 million for Kandahar and Helmand. [49] And in Helmand's Nawa district, USAID spent upwards of $30 million within nine months in what some dubbed "[the] carpet bombing of Nawa with cash."[50] With Nawa's 75,000 people, such aid amounted to $400 per person. (Afghanistan's per capita income is only $300 a year.)

Although U.S. government officials emphasize that these stabilization programs have generated tens of thousands of jobs in Afghanistan's south, many of the efforts have been unsustainable short-lived projects such as canal cleaning, grain storage, and road building, or small grants for the purchase of agricultural supplies such as seeds and fertilizers. Characteristically, they would collapse as soon as the money ran out, often in the span of several weeks.[51] Moreover, they tended to be available only to households with sufficient male labor.[52] Adequate consideration often was not given to the development of assured markets; consequently, much of the produce cultivated under the USAID-contracted programs would possibly not find buyers and rot. And there is no robust and systematic evidence that the stabilization programs have secured the allegiance of the population to either the Afghan government or ISAF forces, nor have they resulted in increased intelligence on the Taliban from the population.[53] Moreover, since the vast majority of low-level Taliban fighters are not paid by the Taliban and have to maintain employment to sustain themselves and their families anyway, the premise that Afghan men on the ISAF-sponsored cash-for-work programs will have no incentive to join the insurgency does not hold water.[54] Whether or not they are on the ISAF payroll, Taliban fighters would have to work during at least a part of the year. In fact, it is quite possible that many of the men who benefit from the cash-for-work program some of the time also fight for the Taliban during other times.

Nor have these programs yet addressed the structural deficiencies of the rural economy in Afghanistan, including those that drive poppy cultivation, such as the lack of legal microcredit, inadequate rural infrastructure, and no processing facilities for legal crops to make them more profitable.[55] In particular, CERP-funded and PRT-implemented programs have tended mostly to replace government capacity rather than to increase it.[56]

Via the so-called District Delivery Program and District Stabilization Framework, the U.S. military, USAID (the implementer), and other government agencies sought to streamline the economic stabilization programs into Afghan planning and execution processes. Premised on the widely accepted notion that local ownership is critical for the efficacy and sustainability of development projects, the goal of these initiatives was to involve not just local provincial officials but also line ministries.[57] But these programs often perpetuated off-budget, unbalanced, and unsustainable expenditures and compounded confusion about the responsibilities of line ministries and provincial and district officials.[58] PRT-delivered projects also have tended to be far more expensive than projects delivered through other means, and have often been captured and distorted by local power brokers. One study, for example, estimated that the Afghan National Solidarity Program could construct a school with a $30,000 budget, whereas it cost the United Nations Children's Fund, in conjunction with Afghan ministries, $50,000, and the PRTs in southeast Afghanistan upwards of $150,000.[59] This is not to say that the military officers and civilians working in the PRT projects have not been highly dedicated. But the framework within which the PRTs operate and the incentives they, the CERP funding, and the economic stabilization programs provide have been prone to market distortions and a lack of sustainability. Thus fast and loose spending has warped local labor markets and channeled investments into systems that Afghans do not always necessarily want. For example, although many Afghans accepted wheat seeds via an internationally sponsored program—why would they pass up cheap handouts?—many in fact indicated that seed distribution was not their priority because they could acquire seeds elsewhere, and they would have preferred to receive extension services instead.[60]

In fact, many of the stabilization efforts, such as the wheat seed distribution program, directly undermine long-term measures for addressing the structural market deficiencies, such as the development of microcredit or the establishment of local Afghan seed banks and seed markets, rural enterprise, and value-added chains. Similarly, free (or very cheap) and rapid handouts by outside donors can kill a sustainable market an international NGO has been developing with local buy-in for several years. In Helmand, for example, Mercy Corps ran a veterinary program for several years, getting farmers over time to pay for the cost of the animal medications and thus establishing a sustainable local market for the medications and incentives for enterprising Afghans to establish veterinary businesses. But a sudden delivery of cheap veterinary medications by USAID prematurely wiped out the Mercy Corps project. The flood of nearly free medications from USAID also encouraged poor, uninformed farmers, lacking proper medical care, to use the animal meds themselves, with often serious repercussions to their health.[61]

There is a delicate three-way balance among long-term development, the need to generate support among the population and alleviate economic deprivation in the short term, and state building. A counternarcotics "alternative livelihoods" program in Afghanistan provides a telling example. Aware of the deeply destabilizing effects of poppy suppression in the absence of alternative livelihoods but under pressure to reduce poppy cultivation, Helmand governor Mangal, widely acclaimed as a competent and committed governor, launched a wheat seed distribution project during the 2008–09 growing season. Farmers were handed free wheat seeds to encourage them to grow wheat instead of poppy. Many Helmandis took the wheat seed, and the program was emulated throughout Afghanistan. Poppy cultivation did decrease in Helmand in 2009, and many enthusiastically attributed the results to the wheat distribution program rather than low opium prices. And yet from the beginning, there were good reasons to be skeptical about the effectiveness of the program, at least with respect to development and even governance. For many reasons, wheat was a highly problematic crop. Land density in Afghanistan often does not favor the cultivation of wheat, particularly in areas where families hold small plots or power brokers control large swaths of land. Wheat prices tend to fluctuate a lot—often driven by external market conditions in Pakistan, Kazakhstan, and worldwide—from which Afghan farmers cannot isolate themselves. Thus wheat often has a far more unfavorable price ratio to opium than horticultural goods. (Although most development economists consider high-value, highly labor-intensive horticultural goods to be better replacement crops in Afghanistan than wheat, fruit trees often need several years to mature before they can be harvested.)[62] And poor milling facilities and inadequate market access further hamper a sustainable switch to wheat cultivation. Furthermore, wheat cultivation is far less labor intensive than poppy cultivation, generating only 12 percent of the employment that opium poppy can.[63] Indeed, wheat turned out to be a singularly inappropriate replacement crop.[64] Unsurprisingly, much of the wheat seed ended up being sold in markets rather than sown.

Due to the insecurity prevailing in Helmand at the time, the program was undertaken without any field assessment of what drives poppy cultivation in particular areas of Helmand and in Afghanistan more broadly.[65] During periods of acute insecurity and under intense pressures from the military to stand up programs to counter the insurgency, U.S. government agencies rarely have the patience to accept a long period of study to assess a problem and devise a tailored response, however appropriate such assessment and planning would be. And when such hastily adopted programs turn out to be inadequate and deficient, political considerations and budget pressures make it difficult to acknowledge mistakes and to step back, reassess, and develop new, better policies. Thus too often Washington's tendency is to maintain even ineffective policies. With the acknowledgement of failure seen as extremely costly and experimentation regarded as risky, innovative ideas have to struggle to get adopted.[66]

In the case of the wheat distribution effort, Afghan domestic political pressures also helped perpetuate it. Although the program was deficient from a development perspective, it was popular with Afghan government officials and power brokers, such as Governor Mangal, who could use it to enhance their power and legitimacy. Since it brought political benefits to officials who sponsored it, including President Hamid Karzai, who at that time was seeking reelection, the program was emulated in other parts of Afghanistan as well.[67] Good governance was thus equated with immediate handouts and their political payoff, without regard for long-term economic development, sustainability, best practices lessons, or optimal decisionmaking processes.[68]

The economic "stabilization" programs often created expectations in the population of cheap handouts from the central government and international community, without the programs being economically viable and sustainable in the long run and without requiring commitments from the local community. Many of the CERP and stabilization programs also have encouraged Afghans to expect payoffs from the international community for activities that they would have (or should have) performed without compensation. For example, the commander of the U.S. PRT in Zabul told me in the spring of 2009 that during a patrol, his team came across one clean village and one village littered with trash. Since the Taliban was often coming into the second—dirty—village, he decided to hire local boys to clean it up so as to provide them with employment, reduce their susceptibility to Taliban mobilization, and win over hearts and minds. But the outcome, he acknowledged, was not less Taliban activity in the village. Instead, when his patrol visited a month later, the village that used to be clean "was now littered with trash all over." Village maliks approached him to establish a trash collection fund, like the one he had authorized in the other village.[69] This particular PRT commander became highly attuned to how the CERP quick-impact programs generated moral hazard and distorted incentives and thereafter endeavored to fund only sustainable, even if often only small-scale, projects. Typically, however, such lessons have not been learned. In many an Afghan village, ISAF military forces seeking to establish positive relations with the Afghan population delivered an electric generator, to the cheers of the community. And as a result, many villagers bought electrical appliances. However, once the fuel provided by the military ran out, electricity production in the village ended, much to the frustration and at times fury of the locals.[70]

U.S. efforts to improve electricity generation and distribution in Afghanistan, overall, have been highly troubled. Because of insecurity, the Kajaki hydropower plant is still not running, despite a U.S. investment of more than $100 million.[71] The United States is also funding repairs on the Dahla dam outside of Kandahar City, at the cost of $200 million.[72] Contracting problems and Pakistan's closure of its border to NATO trucks during the first half of 2012 (discussed in detail in the following chapter) further delayed work on Kajaki and power grids in southern Afghanistan for at least a year.[73] Moreover, since insecurity frequently abounds beyond the actual dam, in areas that the power lines traverse, Taliban forces have the option to attack electric transmission towers whenever it serves their purposes and thus cut off power distribution. Since access to electricity is highly welcomed by the population, the insurgents often do not try to disrupt it but instead tend to collect fees for electricity distribution themselves.[74]

In frustration with the slow refurbishment of the Kajaki dam, ISAF resorted to buying massive diesel generators for Kandahar, on the premise that electrification would be enthusiastically welcomed by the Kandaharis and reduce the Taliban's mobilization effectiveness in the city. Despite vehement objections from USAID and the U.S. Embassy in Kabul that the power generators would be extremely expensive, could operate only as long as the United States was footing the bill for the fuel, and would ultimately be redundant once Kajaki came fully back on line, it was still a U.S. military "must do" for 2010.[75]

The two 10-megawatt generators require a U.S. budget of about $50 million to pay for the diesel fuel and cannot function without it. Since the diesel budget is expected to run out by the middle of 2013, Kandaharis will likely have to significantly cut down on their energy consumption.[76]

Overall, between 2010 and August 2012, Congress has authorized $800 million for infrastructure building in Afghanistan via the Afghan Infrastructure Fund and the Department of State has allocated another $1 billion for such efforts.[77] Because of the complexity and opacity of Afghanistan's political, economic, and contracting scene, many of these international programs have continued to flow to problematic, discriminatory, and corrupt power brokers, generating further resentment among the population and adding to Afghanistan's rampant corruption and lack of accountability.

At times, the influx of foreign aid has spurred new tribal rivalries and community tensions.[78] Economic development shortcuts, seeking to buy love through economic handouts, are indicative of the mode of minimal short-term payoffs (but substantial medium-term costs) in which many international programs have operated in Afghanistan. The result is persistent, deep market deficiencies and compromised rule of law. Overall, the vision of economic transformation of Afghanistan through the growth and diversification of agriculture has produced few tangible outcomes over the decade, with over a third of the population still at extreme poverty levels and another third only slightly above poverty levels. No doubt, reducing poverty takes a long time.[79]

Moreover, continuing insecurity also threatens the short-term "stabilization" programs. In 2011, for example, even in high-profile areas such as Marja and Arghandab, the Taliban strongly intensified a campaign to assassinate Afghan government officials, contractors, and NGO personnel who cooperated with ISAF and the Afghan government. Both the implementers and Afghan beneficiaries of the economic programs were killed. This intimidation campaign scared off some Afghans from participating in the programs. Since insecurity has prevented even the provincial reconstruction teams from accessing contested rural areas, most PRT projects have tended to be concentrated in provincial capitals and often consist of building construction.[80]

U.S. and ISAF officials emphasize that in cleared areas in the south, shops have reopened on the streets and bazaars seem livelier. Those are important indicators of progress. Yet Afghan shopkeepers often say that they are trying to make as much money as possible during a short window of opportunity because they expect security to deteriorate again after 2014, and then they may lose all business opportunities.[81] Thus, even for these stabilization programs, as for any economic development efforts, security is a critical prerequisite.

Apart from the ongoing insecurity, programmatic uncertainties surrounding the Afghanistan transition have also hampered the expected transformation of projects into sustainable long-term economic development programs. Despite the success of the July 2012 Tokyo Conference in eliciting a commitment of international funds for Afghanistan for the next several years, and despite the Obama administration's request for $2.5 billion for civilian assistance in Afghanistan for 2013 (up from the $2.2 billion approved for 2012), USAID officials have become increasingly concerned that the expected money for such long-term development efforts may not be available.[82] A reduction in unsustainable funding that cannot be properly monitored may actually be to the good by putting a premium on sustainable programs and reducing corruption, crime, and conflict. But massive, unexpected drops in funding also critically disrupt programs.

None of this is to say that no economic programs have worked in Afghanistan or that every single project has been a failure. Hardly. Many projects have been very effective. Sometimes, such effective projects have been simple and small, such as teaching Afghan farmers how to grow grapes on a rope instead of on the ground or to provide veterinary care for their sheep and cattle to reduce mortality and overgrazing.[83] Other positive achievements have been on a much larger scale, such as in health programs and education. Continuing massive problems and deficiencies notwithstanding, the number of health facilities (regardless of how extensive they are) in Afghanistan has grown from an estimated 498 in 2002 to 2,136 in the spring of 2012, expanding access to basic health services for millions of Afghans.[84] In 2002 only about 9 percent of the population had such access; in 2008 the number reached an estimated 85 percent.[85] The Basic Package of Health Services, delivered by the Afghan Ministry of Public Health, has helped to reduce the infant mortality rate during the 2001–08 period from 172 to 77 deaths per 1,000 live births, and the mortality rate for children under age five from 257 to 97 deaths per 1,000. The maternal mortality rate also declined significantly, from 1,600 to 327 per 100,000 births.[86] Still, one in ten Afghan children dies before the age of five, and one Afghan women dies every two hours due to pregnancy-related causes.[87] The number of children enrolled in schools (mostly at the primary level) comes to 8 million—more than ten times the number of children enrolled in 2002.[88] Between 2002 and 2010, the United States provided close to $800 million in health assistance to Afghanistan and close to $680 million in education assistance.[89] Efforts to improve the administrative capacity of line ministries have also registered some notable accomplishments, such as those within the Ministry of Rural Rehabilitation and Development.[90] And in some districts under intense Western supervision, service delivery has improved.

Afghanistan's macroeconomic performance in 2012 (if not its economic outlook for after 2014) is far better than it was in 2002. The economic and social opportunities for the vast majority of Afghans have improved significantly. Well-positioned Afghans have been able to reap large profits from Afghanistan's economy over the past decade. (No doubt, many have been cronies of government officials and major power brokers, and their effect on the rule of law in Afghanistan has been predominantly negative.)

Yet many of the policies that have been adopted have been deeply flawed and not based on lessons learned and best practices. Many U.S. and international officials implementing the economic development policies have been well-known and respected experts on Afghanistan and development. But as the war heated up, the military placed intense pressure on these development experts to spend vast amounts of money fast to win hearts and minds. That pressure only increased when Special Representative for Afghanistan and Pakistan Richard Holbrooke unveiled the so-called "whole-of-government" approach in 2009. Nominally, the whole-of-government approach was to integrate war planning with development, coordinate input from all government agencies, and mobilize for action all of the various U.S. government agencies. In practice, the Department of Defense frequently dominated the interagency process, prevailing upon USAID to adopt economic policies the agency did not prefer, such as the economic stabilization programs. Moreover, under any circumstances, effectively executing such cross-government integration and moving large bureaucracies to a different policy from a set course is very difficult.[91]

This challenge increases if one or two individuals deployed to a locality need to supervise the disbursement of millions of dollars so as to demonstrate a fast burn rate. In 2010, for example, USAID still had only one contracting officer's technical representative overseeing a $92 million contract with Deloitte to provide technical assistance to the Central Bank of Afghanistan.[92] Supervisory and burn-rate pressures on field officers outside of Kabul have often been even greater. This was the case even though, as part of its civilian surge, the Department of State increased its civilian employees from 531 in January 2009 to 1,300 in February 2010, with approximately 920 in Kabul and 380 elsewhere in Afghanistan.[93] Inevitably, contractors' ability to get away with poor program execution was significant, and U.S government oversight capacity limited. The Government Accountability Office has found oversight "inadequate at times, raising questions about the agencies' ability to ensure accountability for multibillion dollar investments."[94]

Economic Development and the 2014 Transition

In line with the 2014 transition, the United States Agency for International Development as well as other Western donors have—once again—committed themselves to phase out the economic stabilization initiatives and short-term cash-for-work programs, and switch to economic development programs that focus on long-term capacity building and sustainability based on careful assessments of local context and conditions.[95] The Afghan government has also embraced such a policy shift. This kind of fundamental change in the orientation of the development assistance programs is highly desirable. But the forthcoming reduction of the U.S. and ISAF's presence in Afghanistan and the anticipated smaller budgets after the 2014 transition have diverted much of USAID's and other international organizations' attention and energies from field implementation of the programs to programmatic restructuring of their assistance efforts. One large question yet to be resolved is what entities—international or Afghan—will replace the provincial reconstruction teams, which are to be retired in 2014. Despite how ill-suited they were for the task and how problematic their implementation was, the PRTs have been the principal providers of economic assistance in some of the most isolated and insecure areas of Afghanistan. Although regular development agencies have the potential to execute better-designed policies more effectively, it is not a given that either they or Afghan line ministries will fill the PRT void, no matter how much the Afghans are promised that the 2014 transition will result in beefed-up economic development efforts. Much will depend on the state of Western donors' economies, as well as the security situation and rule of law in Afghanistan. Moreover, the transfer of policies to entities that operate under completely different guiding principles is not easy. Even with the transition priorities and commitments, immediate (battle) field imperatives often continue to drive desires for readily visible, even if unsustainable, results.

By the summer of 2012, particularly in the run-up to the Tokyo Conference on the economic development and future of Afghanistan, the talk once again was about deemphasizing the short-term economic stabilization programs and focusing instead on long-term sustainable development. Indeed, such a shift would considerably help to align donors' economic activities with Afghan priorities, including infrastructure, administrative capacity, financial mechanisms, and human capital development. The international community has recognized that such a transformation of economic assistance policies in Afghanistan is a critical part of the transition process and very highly desirable.[96] But how diligently and effectively such a radical, if crucial, shift in policy will be executed remains to be seen. And Afghanistan has been a difficult place to implement policies well.[97]

Also in line with the 2014 transition is a plan to channel international aid mostly through the Afghan government, or "on budget" as the process is known, as opposed to bypassing the government in Kabul and providing money directly from the international community to "the Afghan people." Throughout much of the post-2001 period, there have been constant challenges and dilemmas concerning how to channel the money. Channeling outside financial aid through the national government is appropriate since it increases the fiscal capacity of the state and links the population more closely to the state, building accountability.[98] Yet, because the international community found the Afghan government at its various levels too corrupt to process the money (at least what was left of it after the international community's "overhead" deductions), it considered it necessary to spend its aid off budget. At the same time, bypassing the national government and channeling funds directly to the localities or through NGOs sometimes delivered the money to the ground faster, but not always or necessarily in a less corrupt manner. The direct-to-project approach, however, did undermine the government's authority and capacity and often strengthened local power brokers. At the July

2010 donor conference in Kabul, President Karzai won a pledge from the international community that at least 50 percent of all economic assistance would be channeled through the Afghan government within two years, while the United States announced it believed it had developed a certification process to determine which Afghan ministries were qualified to receive U.S. assistance directly.[99] But the switch to on-budget expenditures has been plagued by numerous problems, including the continuing lack of transparency and accountability and pervasive corruption within the Afghan government. Thus in 2011 only about 38 percent of USAID funding was on budget.[100] The Kabul Bank fiasco highlighted once again the extent of corruption in Afghanistan and the lack of unreliability of oversight mechanisms, and for months it halted the disbursement of funds for Afghanistan from the International Monetary Fund.[101] Therefore, although the so-called Kabul process and subsequent conferences in Bonn in 2011 and Tokyo in 2012 kept reiterating the need and promise to bring international assistance on budget, the switchover has been slow going.[102] Indeed, even with the conditions placed on the Kabul government in Tokyo, there continues to be a high likelihood that large sums channeled through the Afghan government may end up being stolen. The international community has not been very successful in implementing diligent controls. Moreover, internationally sponsored projects continue to be highly fragmented and rarely coordinated across even major stakeholders.

Still, there have been some important successes in channeling money on budget, notably, the Afghanistan Reconstruction Trust Fund. Although at $573 million as of August 2012 (of which the United States has provided $371) the Reconstruction Trust Fund constitutes only a small portion of total aid—the United States alone has spent almost $90 billion on reconstruction in Afghanistan over the past decade—its Incentive Program initiatives have been particularly well designed.[103] They have been based on broad international lessons and supported reform constituencies seeking to improve governance in the Afghan government.[104]

The Coming Economic Crisis in Afghanistan

Even if robust security holds after 2014 and better donor policies are in fact adopted, Afghanistan is heading toward dire straits economically—for at least several years after 2014. Much of the money coming into Afghanistan has been associated with the large presence of foreign military forces. That money will inevitable shrink dramatically as a result of foreign troop reductions. And so will the entire economy of Afghanistan—at least in the short term.[105]

The World Bank estimates that even under favorable assumptions, Afghanistan's real GDP growth may fall from the 9 percent a year over the past decade to an estimated 5–6 percent during 2011–18.[106] The total annual international aid (estimated at $15.7 billion in 2010) approximately equals Afghanistan's GDP and cannot be sustained. Yet it has been foreign aid that has funded the delivery of essential services such as education, health, and infrastructure as well as government administration. Afghanistan's fiscal capacity will be particularly badly hit: the World Bank projects a 25 percent GDP financial gap in Afghanistan by 2021–22, or about a $7 billion annual deficit.[107] Closing the gap requires that foreign donors deliver about $7 billion annually for several years: about $4 billion for Afghan National Security Forces and another $3 billion for the nonmilitary budget. At the Tokyo Conference in July 2012, donors did indeed pledge $16 billion in nonmilitary assistance for 2013–16. But how much of the money will actually be disbursed to Afghanistan will depend on two factors. First is the level of security in Afghanistan: with more insecurity, Afghanistan's budget deficit will grow much more than the $7 billion projected under favorable conditions, and foreign funds are likely to contract further. The second factor that could affect disbursement is the socioeconomic situation in donor countries: Western donors could initiate cutbacks in response to domestic economic crises and austerity measures, as well as their publics' weariness with the war, exacerbated by perceptions of extensive corruption in Afghanistan. If Afghanistan can manage to reduce some of the revenue loss from untaxed imports and illicit mining it has been experiencing over the past decade (and before), it may be able to trim down its budget deficit by a billion or two and perhaps double its GDP.[108] But the prospects for any speedy recovery of such assets and a resulting increase in the government's taxation capacity any time soon are minimal, especially if insecurity increases after 2014.

Employment will also be badly affected. Tens of thousands of Afghans currently work as interpreters and drivers and also as "secondary civil service" for international companies on contract with the foreign militaries. Many of these jobs are going to disappear. Construction and logistics businesses in particular depend heavily on the military and aid economy. Already, unemployment and underemployment are running high, at an estimated annual rate of 8 percent and 48, respectively.[109] Both affect not only poor, uneducated rural populations but also university graduates in cities. Not surprisingly, the flow of Afghans out of the country has increased substantially since 2005. According to United Nations data, more than 30,000 Afghans applied for asylum in industrial countries in 2011, the highest level in ten years and four times the number seeking asylum in 2005.[110] And the number of those officially registering for asylum is likely much lower than the number of Afghans trying to arrive abroad illegally, estimated at over 50,000 in 2011.[111] Fearing insecurity after 2014 and a further contraction of economic and educational opportunities in Afghanistan, fewer Afghans are also voluntarily returning home.[112]

Insecurity after 2014 is also very much on the minds of foreign and Afghan businesses. The only Western bank in Afghanistan, Standard Chartered, has announced that it will sell its Afghan operations. One of Afghanistan's four major cell phone companies, among the businesses that grew most in the post-2002 decade, announced similar plans to take money out of the country.[113] According to the Afghanistan Investment Support Agency, capital spending by foreign companies newly registered in 2011 was at the lowest rate in seven years, about one-eighth the rate's peak in 2006.[114] Some foreign businesses catering to the expats in Afghanistan have already registered a 40 percent decrease in profits.[115] Many ordinary Afghans also are trying to liquefy their assets and thinking about exit strategies. Those who seem most optimistic about staying in Afghanistan and deny that they would want to leave tend to be young, educated, and accomplished Kabulis.[116]

If security can be maintained and improved, Afghanistan's mineral riches can start generating vast revenues in years to come—on the order of tens of billions of dollars annually.[117] Under optimistic assumptions, the investments and projects could rise from bringing in $105 million in 2009 to almost $3.8 billion in 2026.[118] The wise expansion of this sector, if the revenues are invested in infrastructure, human capital, and local community development and not usurped by the privileged few, can be a tremendous boost for Afghanistan's development. But so far, the activity of many foreign multinationals that normally pant to begin exploiting such mineral riches has been primarily limited to a cautious exploration of possibilities.[119] Until the fall of 2012, Exxon-Mobil has been the only fully private company to even consider bidding in Afghanistan—at least before the new Afghan mining legislation became stalled in the Afghan government.[120] So far, most firms that have won (or bid for) mining contracts in Afghanistan have been at least partially state-owned companies— from countries like India, Brazil, Turkey, and Pakistan—that have the greatest capacity to ride out risks and losses.[121] Even the normally active and risk-taking Chinese firms have satisfied themselves mainly with establishing a presence (so as not to yield the field to India) and signing contracts, such as for exploration for copper, iron ore, and oil, rather than actually beginning to extract resources. (The fact that Chinese companies have been burned in some of their investments abroad over the past decade is also a factor in their cautious approach to the Afghan market.)[122]

To effectively exploit the mineral resources, multinationals or the Afghan government need to invest massively in infrastructure development. But that is a long-term investment that can easily be lost if intense insecurity prevails again. Of equal importance is the lack of established judicial processes and dispute resolution mechanisms. In their absence, foreign investors continue to be deterred. Chinese firms, typically not particularly concerned about corruption, also have expressed misgivings about the lack of rule of law in Afghanistan and its implications for foreign investment.

Apart from extracting minerals and expanding agricultural production, transforming Afghanistan into a regional trading and transportation hub is also being explored as an economic engine for the country. After all, Afghanistan lies at an East-West/North-South crossroads, and much of its history is one of outsiders competing on its territory for access and influence. Why not turn the crossroads location into an advantage, such as by reviving ideas of a "New Silk Road," with Afghanistan at the center?[123] India's strategic interests in Afghanistan are clearly motivated by its desire to expand access to Central Asia. Russia, China, and Iran similarly want to expand geostrategic access and business opportunities.

But to have such a New Silk Road materialize, the deep and intense rivalries that characterize Afghanistan's neighborhood will have to be overcome first, an issue explored in detail in the following chapter.[124] The more instability there will be in Afghanistan after 2014, the harder it will be to achieve a cooperative regional framework.

10

Pakistan and the Region

Not just the "New Silk Road" but Afghanistan's peaceful future depends to a great extent on an auspicious regional environment. Yet Afghanistan's location at the crossroads of the Middle East, Central Asia, and South Asia has for centuries made the emergence of a friendly neighborhood elusive, and the vision of Afghanistan's neighbors embracing nonintervention in Afghanistan and regional cooperation remains largely unrealized. Instead, although escaping colonization, Afghanistan has for millennia paid a heavy price for being the buffer state between regional powers and the battleground for their ambitions, with the armies of Alexander the Great; the Mughals; the Persian, Czarist Russian, and British empires; and Soviet Russia all seeking to control it or at least influence it by maintaining a friendly government in power.[1] During the cold war, Afghanistan became a battleground in the global conflict between the Soviet Union and United States, with Pakistan as a key U.S. ally supporting the anti-Soviet mujahideen.[2] Today, after the bloody Soviet occupation of the 1980s, the civil war and Taliban rule of the 1990s, and the U.S. counterinsurgency efforts of the past decade, most of Afghanistan's neighbors are still competing with one another and persist in interfering in Afghan affairs. In particular Pakistan, whose own past and future are deeply intertwined with Afghanistan, continues to be a difficult and disruptive neighbor, seeking strategic depth on the Afghan side of its border, even as its government officially denies it, and cultivating radical groups there as proxies. Despite a decade of U.S. attempts to bring Islamabad and Rawalpindi (the seats of Pakistan's

Afghanistan and the Region

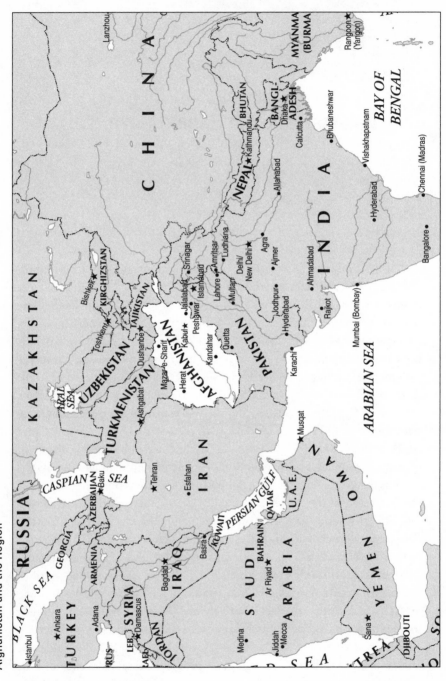

government and military establishment, respectively) on board with its efforts in Afghanistan, Pakistan continues to be ensnared in—while also augmenting—Afghanistan's instability.

Pakistan's Tunnel Vision

For decades, relations between Afghanistan and Pakistan have been characterized by mutual suspicion and deep-seated animosities. The two countries share a long, rugged, and porous border—the Durand Line (named after the late nineteenth-century foreign secretary of British India, Henry Mortimer Durand)—that Afghanistan has refused to recognize and that inhabitants on both sides cross with ease and regularity.[3] Pakistan and Afghanistan also share a population of ethnic Pashtuns that Kabul has at times sought to mobilize as tool against Pakistan. Kabul has also periodically resorted to deriving domestic political capital from Pashtun irredentism and claims of "Greater Afghanistan."[4] In turn, Pakistan has attempted to manipulate Afghan refugees in Pakistan against Kabul, sending them back to an uncertain fate in Afghanistan and overwhelming Afghan authorities.[5]

Since the British colonial era, Pakistani Pashtuns have been a troubled people, isolated from and neglected by the rest of Pakistan. Even today, the Federally Administered Tribal Areas (FATA), the home of many of Pakistan's Pashtuns, are stuck in an inherited colonial design: appointed "political agents" who rule over the territories and the Pashtun people via tribal maliks; a draconian Frontier Crime Regulations system based on collective punishment; and no accountable political representation in Islamabad. The government of Pakistan under President Asif Zardari eliminated some of the harshest elements of the Frontier Crime Regulations code and permitted the formation of and campaigning by political parties in the FATA. But the systematic reforms required to equalize the status of the FATA with the rest of Pakistan have not been undertaken.[6] The tribal areas continue to be economically and socially underdeveloped and backward, deprived of basic legal and human rights, and hence politically restless.[7]

Assassinations and military coups have plagued Pakistan since the early years of independence, leaving behind a weak political system unable to effectively deliver elementary public goods and respond to the fundamental needs of the struggling Pakistani people. Pakistan's foreign

Northern Region of the Afghanistan–Pakistan Border

Central Region of the Afghanistan–Pakistan Border

and security policies have for decades been controlled by the country's military-intelligence establishment, even during times when a civilian government has nominally been in power. The dominant lens through which the military-intelligence establishment continues to look at Afghanistan is Pakistan's long-standing, existential rivalry with India. Since 1947, when Britain granted both states independence, Pakistan has fought four wars with India: three over the status of Kashmir and the so-called Line of Control that separates the Pakistani part of Kashmir from India's, and one over the transformation of East Pakistan into the independent state of Bangladesh. More than a decade after 9-11, Pakistan's military-intelligence establishment remains preoccupied with India's ascendance at a time of Pakistan's own stagnation and atrophy.[8]

Pakistan also continues to be deeply suspicious of India's ambitions in Afghanistan. Afghanistan has repeatedly been a prime theater for Indian and Pakistani rivalries. As early as the 1950s, India offered itself to Afghanistan as a counterbalance to Pakistan, via military and economic assistance and major cultural exchanges. Many Afghan elites, including President Karzai himself, have been educated in India and lived there in exile.[9] During the 1980s, while Pakistan and the United States supported the mujahideen, India backed the pro-Soviet regime of President Mohammad Najibullah. During the 1990s, when Pakistan supported the Taliban, India provided assistance to the Northern Alliance. Since 2001 India has pledged approximately $2 billion toward Afghanistan's reconstruction, including infrastructure, hospitals, and other highly visible projects, such as a new Afghan parliament building.[10] President Karzai's embrace of India has been a major irritant to Islamabad.[11] Thus Indian consulates in Afghanistan have been regarded by Pakistan as spying outfits and sources of aid to the separatist movement in Pakistan's province of Baluchistan; and Indian aid in dam construction in the Afghan province of Kunar was interpreted by Islamabad as a way to divert water resources from Pakistan. Pakistan also considers Karzai to be deeply influenced by the West and Iran—hence, yet another threat to Pakistan's interests.

Pakistan's paranoia about being encircled and possibly carved up between Afghanistan and India was tragically manifest in the attack on the Indian Embassy in Kabul in July 2008. Although the attack was conducted by the Haqqani network, U.S. and Afghan intelligence sources showed that elements in the Inter-Services Intelligence (ISI, Pakistan's intelligence agency) provided support.[12] Indeed, some of the other

dramatic terrorist attacks in Afghanistan, such as against the Intercontinental Hotel in Kabul, and the April 15, 2012, attack against the Afghan
parliament and the Kabul Star Hotel, while perpetrated by the Haqqanis,
have been consistently linked by U.S. intelligence officers to Pakistan's
ISI.[13] Notably, the former chairman of the Joint Chiefs of Staff, Admiral
Michael Mullen, felt compelled before retiring to call the Haqqanis "a
veritable arm of the ISI," even though he had sought for years to build up
a positive relationship between the United States and Pakistan.[14]

Clearly the Pakistani government (or at least parts of it) has been
coddling the Afghan Taliban, Hekmatyar's groups, and the Haqqanis.
Its relationship with the Haqqani network has been particularly tight.
More than merely allowing the groups to enjoy safe havens in the FATA,
Khyber-Pakhtunkhwa, Baluchistan, and Karachi and fundraise in Pakistan, the ISI has also provided logistical support, armaments, and technical and planning advice to the insurgents.[15] At the same time, the ISI
has actively sought to exploit its provision of these resources and safe
havens to the militant groups to influence their strategic decisionmaking
as well as tactical operations. ISI observers have participated in meetings of the Quetta Shura and used coercion, such as selectively arresting
and releasing key Afghan militant leaders and de facto holding hostage
their families in Pakistan, to manipulate their decisions regarding military
operations in Afghanistan or negotiations with Kabul or Washington.[16]
Interrogations of Taliban and Haqqani militants have revealed that in
ISI meetings with the insurgents, ISI officers are regularly hostile to the
United States, ISAF, and the Afghan government, calling for continued
jihad and for expelling "foreign invaders" from Afghanistan, a message
that strongly resonates with Taliban members.[17] However, the relationship between the ISI and Afghan militants is also fraught with tensions,
and both the Taliban and the Haqqanis resent the degree of influence and
control the ISI is trying to exercise over them.[18] Quetta Shura Taliban
members especially complain about being under the thumb of the ISI
and argue that the interests of the intelligence agency and Pakistan more
broadly are often not consistent with the interests of Afghanistan.[19]

To be sure, poor governance and an initially under-resourced counterinsurgency effort have been the principal reasons why since 2001 the
Taliban has been able to regain traction among portions of the Afghan
population and sustain bases of operation within the country. But there
can be no doubt that the external safe havens in Pakistan also greatly

hamper the counterinsurgency and stabilization efforts in Afghanistan. The meekness and duplicity in Pakistan's efforts against the militants have critically enhanced the latter's ability to regroup, resupply, train, recruit, and fundraise in Pakistan, thus contributing to the already serious level of violence within Afghanistan's borders. In a rare and isolated moment of candor in August 2007, President Pervez Musharraf admitted that "there is no doubt that Afghan militants are supported from Pakistan soil. The problem you have in your region is because support is provided from our side."[20]

To the extent that Pakistan has undertaken any actions, however fickle and lukewarm, against the Afghanistan-oriented militants, they have been the result of intense political pressure from the United States and hefty aid payoffs. The Pakistani reluctance to suppress the Taliban and Haqqani networks and sanctuaries in Pakistan reflects the persistent view of the Pakistani military-intelligence establishment that the jihadi groups are critical assets in preventing threats on Pakistan's western flank from an India-friendly regime in Kabul and in securing access to Central Asia's trade routes.[21] The Pakistani military has never stopped viewing Afghanistan as a source of needed strategic depth during any future military confrontations with India. Given India's conventional military superiority and Pakistan's inherent difficulties in defending the narrow territory that separates the border with India from Islamabad and Peshawar, the Pakistani military has considered it imperative to be able to redeploy back into Afghanistan, recoup forces there, and launch a counterattack against India. Above all, according to Rawalpindi, encirclement by hostile powers in Afghanistan and India must be avoided.[22]

So instead of cracking down on the Afghan Taliban, Haqqani, and Hekmayar networks, Rawalpindi has sought to cultivate the various mujahideen and jihadi groups in order to prosecute its asymmetric war against India and prevent the latter's dominance in Afghanistan. Beyond fostering the Afghanistan-oriented groups, it has similarly built up anti-Indian militant groups, such as Lashkar-i-Taiba, Laskhar-i-Jhangvi, and Sipah-i-Sahaba, and has been equally reluctant to crack down on them, despite extensive pressure from the United States.[23]

But in creating or supporting these many jihadi militant groups, Pakistan has created its own Frankenstein monster. The offspring from and mutations of the externally oriented jihadi groups that the ISI has coddled for security and foreign policy purposes have turned against Pakistan itself, as explained in more detail below. But instead of adopting the view that support for all terrorist networks is dangerously wrong-headed and threatening to Pakistan itself, Rawalpindi has sought to divide militants into the "good" ones—those who are externally oriented and subject to Pakistan's manipulation—and the "bad" ones—those who are internally oriented and therefore need to be suppressed.[24] Thus, apart from the objective of securing a friendly Afghanistan and countering India's influence there, Pakistan's reluctance to go after the Afghanistan-oriented militants in Pakistan has also been motivated by a determination not to provoke them into reorienting their deadly and destructive energies against the Pakistani state. Moreover, the ISI has also used the Afghan militants—namely, the Haqqanis, who are well connected in North Waziristan—as a back channel to other militant groups operating there. The Pakistan intelligence service has been rather successful in splitting off middle-level commanders of a dangerous anti-Pakistan militant group, Tehrik-i-Taliban Pakistan, and redirecting their militancy against Afghanistan's government and ISAF forces and toward supporting the Quetta Shura and Haqqanis.[25] Yet despite ISI machinations to curry favor and thus manipulate the Quetta Shura, the Taliban leadership council has apparently established its own networks in Baluchistan, often through coercion, extortion, and provision of "security" for neighborhoods, and investment in hospitals and real estate, thereby potentially creating influence independent of Rawalpindi.[26]

Despite the evidence and Musharraf's rare candor, the Pakistani government vehemently denies that it tolerates and cultivates Afghanistan-focused militants. Instead, Rawalpindi claims that it is Kabul's toleration of safe havens for Baluchi separatists and Washington's ineffectiveness in suppressing anti-Pakistan militants, such as the Tehrik-i-Taliban Pakistan, in eastern Afghanistan that generate cross-border tensions and destabilize Pakistan.[27] Pakistan's minister of interior has also alleged that elements of the Afghan government likely support Maulana Fazlullah, the leader of the reinvigorated Tehreek-e-Nafaz-e-Shariat-e-Mohammadi (TNSM).[28] The TNSM is one of the anti-Pakistan groups about which Rawalpindi and Islamabad have been deeply concerned and that had previously managed to take control of fairly large territories close to Pakistan's capital, such as the Swat and Malakand administrative areas, before the Pakistani military dispersed and suppressed the group. Since then, Pakistan's military alleges, the group has developed some operating bases in Afghanistan. At times, Afghan politicians have been rather vocal that Kabul should indeed exploit the fact that Pakistani militants do cross into Afghan territory, thus serving Pakistan some of its own medicine.[29] The cross-border incursions have resulted in Pakistan periodically shelling Afghanistan's border territory—a policy often resulting in civilian casualties and intensifying anti-Pakistan rhetoric among Afghan politicians—as well in border clashes between Pakistan's and Afghanistan's military.[30] For its part, Afghanistan has been steadfast in its refusal to recognize the Durand Line as a legitimate and permanent border. Despite Pakistan's counter-accusations about the United States willfully tolerating anti-Pakistan groups operating out of Afghanistan's territory, the reality is that the United States and NATO have never had the requisite military resources in eastern and southern Afghanistan to seal off the border with Pakistan. The U.S. brigades deployed there have never succeeded in stopping the flows of militants across the border into Afghanistan, even as they fought some of the bloodiest battles in Afghanistan in the eastern mountains and valleys. And there is little prospect that the Afghan security forces will be able to do any better after 2014.

The Strategic Trust Deficit

After four years of the Obama administration, Pakistan's officials and citizenry are more anti-American than ever, being deeply distrustful of U.S. motives and priorities in the region. A 2012 Pew Research Center poll showed that 74 percent of Pakistani respondents considered the United States an enemy, compared with 69 percent in 2011 and 64 percent in 2010.[31] Although much intensified by the U.S. raid into Pakistan to kill bin Laden in May 2011, this distrust long preceded that event. Islamabad sees the United States as an unreliable and selfish ally that periodically abandons Pakistan.[32] Pakistan's national security strategists regard the country's vital interests as fundamentally at odds with the emergent grand strategy of the United States, including the U.S. Asia-Pacific "pivot," which they see as increasingly anti-China and pro-India. They are also fearful of a U.S. plot to snatch or disable Pakistan's nuclear weapons, which they consider essential to their ability to deter power plays and military attack from a conventionally superior India. Moreover, Pakistan doubts the ability of the United States to establish a secure government in Afghanistan, especially one that will not be hostile to

Pakistan. So it pursues a strategy of cultivating its own allies in Afghanistan—be they anti-Kabul jihadists or rivals of the United States, such as China—as a protection policy.

The lack of trust on the part of Pakistani military, political leaders, and people in Washington's resolve to see its stated policies in Afghanistan through and to remain a reliable ally of Pakistan has long and deep roots. Several times since Pakistan's independence, the United States lavished attention and resources on Pakistan, only then to switch its policies and, as Pakistan has defined it, abandon the country.[33] In the 1950s, the United States embraced an unpopular military dictator in Pakistan as part of its anti-communist strategy in South Asia, declaring Pakistan an essential strategic ally. Yet to Pakistan's great dismay, Washington did not support Pakistan in its 1965 war with India, and did so only half-heartedly in the 1971 war over Bangladesh. The United States also ostracized the democratic government of Zulfikar Ali Bhutto because of its pursuit of nuclear weapons to match India's bomb. But in the 1980s, once again spurred on by its renewed, post-détente, cold war imperative of opposing the Soviets (in large part generated by the Soviet invasion of Afghanistan), the United States resurrected its alliance with Pakistan and embraced its military dictator Mohammad Zia ul-Haq. In order to legitimize his coup d'état and to divert attention from his failure to address Pakistan's pressing socioeconomic needs, Zia adopted an official policy of Islamization, decreeing a variety of Islam-promoting laws to be applied to the public sphere and supporting religious leaders in the private sphere. It was Zia's Islamization drive in the 1980s that not only planted the seeds but also provided the climate for the emergence and growth of many different jihadi groups. It also set off the radicalization of the Pakistani military. Washington and Zia's government closely collaborated in supporting the anti-Soviet mujahideen in Afghanistan, exploiting jihadi networks to funnel large amounts of financial assistance to them, providing them with logistical help, and having ISI agents advise them on tactics and operations. Yet after the Soviets were defeated in Afghanistan, Washington once again turned its attention from the region. It discontinued aid to both Pakistan and Afghanistan, failed to support democratic civilian governments in Pakistan, and publicly reprimanded and ultimately imposed economic sanctions on Pakistan for its 1998 nuclear tests.[34]

U.S. policy toward Pakistan has thus oscillated between lavish aid and close cooperation when it momentarily served U.S. interests and profound neglect and sanctions when other U.S. interests diverted Washington's attention or trumped cooperation. And when interests demanded it, the United States did not hesitate to embrace illegitimate and unaccountable Pakistani leaders. In many ways resembling the foibles of U.S. policy in Afghanistan, U.S. policy toward Pakistan has thus systematically privileged short-term interests and cosseted problematic leaders who could not deliver effective governance to its people but who promised to bolster U.S. strategic and military objectives. As Bruce Riedel writes: "For good reasons and bad, successive U.S. presidents from both parties have pursued narrow short-term interests in Pakistan that have contributed to its instability and radicalization, and thereby created fertile ground for global jihad."[35]

Pakistan's civilian leaders, like its military dictators, have hardly been paragons of virtue and effective governance. Rather, they too have often been venal and self-interested. Stuck in feudal ways, they have lacked both the capability and motivation to devise policies for releasing Pakistani people from the bonds of poverty, extreme inequality, and disempowerment. Pakistan's politics have not centered on the selection of best policies but rather on the contestation of ossified patronage networks, such as the Pakistan People's Party of the Bhutto family and the Pakistan Muslim League of the Nawaz family, for state resources to be usurped for personal profit and power.[36]

After 9-11, driven by counterterrorism imperatives, Washington once again cast its lot with a progressively more unpopular military dictator in Pakistan, General Pervez Musharraf. Under intense U.S. pressure, Musharraf promised to cooperate with Washington in dismantling the al Qaeda network. Yet, as detailed above, Rawalpindi frequently wavered in its professed commitment: it not only continued to cultivate the Afghan Taliban and its jihadi affiliates but also exhibited great unreliability in targeting al Qaeda. In 2006, when the Bush administration signed the U.S.-India nuclear deal, granting India exceptions from the normal rules of the Nuclear Suppliers Group, Pakistan became newly alienated from Washington, feeling once again betrayed. The agreement allowed the United States and other nuclear suppliers to export materials and technologies for civilian nuclear power to India, despite the fact that it was not a party to the Non-Proliferation Treaty and continued to increase the robustness of its nuclear arsenal.[37] Although the rate of Pakistan's buildup of its nuclear arsenal greatly surpasses the rate of India's, and Pakistan, via the A.Q. Khan network, has had a deeply troubling history of nuclear proliferation, Islamabad was angry and resentful that Washington did not offer it a similar deal.[38]

The Obama Administration's Efforts to Patch Things Up

As in the case of Afghanistan, the Obama administration inherited a deteriorated security situation in Pakistan. The country's structural problems had also deepened, its polity was fractured, and after decades of mismanagement the state's fiscal and institutional capacities had been hollowed out. And the strategic trust deficit plagued the bilateral relationship. But in Pakistan U.S. leverage was considerably more limited than it was in Afghanistan.

President-elect Barack Obama and his foreign policy advisers had hoped to launch a new initiative to embed the Afghanistan effort in a regional security framework that included Pakistan and India. But on November 26, 2008, Lashkar-i-Taiba militants, linked to the ISI, dramatically attacked several civilian targets in Mumbai, India, brutally killing hundreds of people. Thus what was supposed to have been the centerpiece of the incoming administration's policy toward the region was suddenly undermined. The initiative had been designed to give priority to inducing Pakistan and India to reach an accommodation over Kashmir and reduce tensions along their border.[39] Resolution of the Kashmir dispute would eliminate a major trigger of Pakistan-India conflict and allow Pakistan to genuinely pursue military efforts against jihadists on its western front abutting Afghanistan.[40] (In 2001–02 the deployment of the Pakistani military on its eastern border with India during a military crisis between the two countries critically contributed to al Qaeda's ability to slip out of Afghanistan into Pakistan. The military standoff was precipitated by a terrorist attack on the Indian parliament, perpetrated by Lashkar-i-Taiba and Jaish- i-Mohammed—yet another militant Kashmiri group with deep connections to Pakistani intelligence services.) The incoming Obama administration also considered reducing tensions between India and Pakistan as an essential piece of a larger regional process and framework to mitigate the power rivalries that for centuries had destabilized Afghanistan.

Although a major military confrontation between India and Pakistan was avoided following the 2008 Mumbai terrorist attacks—in substantial measure due to intense and diligent U.S. diplomacy—the shock of the attacks did sap the political will in India (and Pakistan) to participate in any such conflict resolution efforts. Moreover, New Delhi made it very clear that it would consider it intolerable for the Obama administration to treat India as a part of a joint Afghanistan-Pakistan-India portfolio.[41] It insisted instead that the mandate of Richard Holbrooke, the newly appointed U.S. special representative for Afghanistan and Pakistan, be just that—Afghanistan and Pakistan—and not include India. A rising great power, India demanded that it continue to be treated on its own terms, decoupled from Pakistan.[42]

Over the subsequent four years, India-Pakistan reconciliation efforts repeatedly started and withered. India's weak Congress Party government was unable to secure sufficient domestic political support for overtures of rapprochement with Pakistan, even though India's strategic establishment became increasingly fixated on China, not Pakistan, as the country's greatest strategic threat and competitor and hence the appropriate focus of its military and foreign policy.[43] In Pakistan, the civilian government of Asif Ali Zardari, which assumed power after a dramatic lawyers' protest movement toppled Musharraf's military dictatorship in 2008, has struggled to remain in power. And just like its other civilian government predecessors, it has been unable to wrest authority and control over Pakistan's foreign and military policy away from the military-intelligence establishment, especially for dealing with archrival India.

The Obama administration continued the unsuccessful struggle to persuade Pakistan to undertake serious and visible actions against dangerous international terrorist groups in its part of Kashmir, such as Lashkar-i-Taiba and Jaish-i-Mohammed. It equally failed to persuade the Pakistanis that it was in their interest to target the Afghanistan-oriented militants, such as the Haqqanis and the Afghan Taliban. Although for a while trilateral initiatives among Afghanistan, Pakistan, and the United States—such as tactical coordination meetings and cross-border combined troika planning—appeared to be flourishing, they produced few tangible results.[44] Recognizing Islamabad's concerns, however, Washington sought to restrain India from adopting policies in Afghanistan that could be interpreted as provocative by Pakistan and from expanding its activities there. At the same time, the White House and State Department endeavored to maintain a robust, intensive, and direct engagement with Indian officials on non-Pakistan issues; but that in and of itself was grating enough to Pakistan, intensifying its fear of India's strength and increasing its resentment toward the new U.S. focus on India.

The Obama administration did succeed in helping the Pakistani military and civilian leadership develop the will and capacity to confront the ever-more dangerous Pakistani jihadists, particularly those operating in areas close to Islamabad, such as the TNSM in Swat. But even there, after bloody operations by the Pakistani military and massive displacement of people from the area, economic reconstruction and the resurrection of civilian administration have been painfully slow.[45] Just as during the Bush years, Washington occasionally persuaded the Pakistani military to conduct anti–al Qaeda operations. But even Pakistan's anti–al Qaeda efforts were not robust and convincing enough to allow the White House to trust their Pakistani counterparts sufficiently to inform them of the raid on Osama bin Laden's compound in Abbottabad in May 2011.[46] Indeed, the location of bin Laden's compound—so close to Pakistan's military and intelligence installations in the heart of Pakistan—only raised further suspicions in Washington that Pakistan's duplicity extended to issues of the utmost and uncompromisable U.S. interest and priority—namely, its hunt for al Qaeda and bin Laden.

Nor was the Obama administration successful in persuading the Pakistani leadership that the United States wanted to be a genuine long-term partner of Pakistan. During the Bush years, the U.S.-Pakistan relationship acquired a blatant transactional character, with the United States buying and forcing Pakistan's assistance with generous military aid and a hefty dose of hard-nosed cajoling and pressure. Seeking to transform what was becoming a dysfunctional relationship into a long-term strategic partnership, President Obama declared in December 2009 that "we are committed to a partnership [with Pakistan] that is built on a foundation of mutual interest, mutual respect, and mutual trust."[47]

The new strategy toward Pakistan sought to reduce U.S. dependence on the Pakistani military in an attempt to break with the historic U.S. tendency to privilege short-term goals and thus perpetuate Pakistan's unhealthy pattern of civilian-military relations. It was the Obama administration's hope to build up Pakistan's civilian governing capacity and, via an enlarged program of development aid, improve the country's struggling economy and reduce its extensive poverty. One key motivating concern behind this effort to reinforce Pakistan's notoriously underperforming civilian leadership was that the Pakistani military was not only an unreliable ally but also perhaps had a deep interest in perpetuating external insecurity to justify the military's large budget, its domination of the Pakistani economy, its frequent military coups, and its overall privileged position in society.[48]

The new U.S. approach was embodied in the Kerry-Lugar-Berman Bill, formally the Enhanced Partnership with Pakistan Act of 2009, which authorized $1.5 billion a year in U.S. aid to Pakistan over five years. But instead of providing the foundation for the highly touted new strategic partnership, the conditions the legislation stipulated for disbursing the aid were widely interpreted in Pakistan as an intolerable encroachment on Pakistani sovereignty. Despite an enormous personal investment of time and energy from high U.S. officials, including Admiral Mullen, to cultivate relations with Pakistan's military and ease its distrust of the United States, plus the large transfer of weapon systems to improve Pakistan's military balance vis-à-vis India, the Pakistani military, like the Pakistani public, continued to sour on the United States.[49] Given Pakistan's highly corrupt and patronage-based political environment, poor administrative structure, and profound economic problems and underdevelopment, economic aid from Washington was inevitably slow and hampered in reaching Pakistan's people and producing visible improvements in their lives.[50] Overall, after a decade of some $21 billion spent on defense assistance and reimbursements and on economic aid, whether defined as a transactional payment or the undergirding of a strategic partnership, the United States received little systematic and committed cooperation from Pakistan in return, even on key issues.[51]

Thus, in dealing with the Pakistan-based al Qaeda and other anti-American militants in the Afghanistan war, the Obama administration was basically left with the option of intensifying its drone strikes across the Afghanistan-Pakistan border. Although purportedly highly effective in decimating al Qaeda's leadership structure, the policy also came with the cost of further alienating the Pakistani leadership and public from the United States.[52]

A GLOC(k) at the Durand Line:
Pakistan Pulls Out Another Weapon

In November 2011, a U.S. military cross-border raid at Salala, Pakistan, resulted in the death of twenty-six Pakistani soldiers and plunged the already poor U.S.-Pakistan relationship into a morass. For Pakistan, the killings were the last straw in a year of tense U.S.-Pakistani crises, which included the killing of two Pakistani men in Lahore by a likely CIA contractor, Raymond Davis; retaliatory compromising of CIA agents in Pakistan by Pakistani officials; and the raid on Osama bin Laden's Abbottabad compound, which the United States undertook without informing Pakistan in advance.

Furious about the Salala incident, Pakistan responded by brandishing probably the strongest weapon it thought it could pull without provoking a total rupture of the relationship: it shut down the Afghanistan-Pakistan border for NATO supply trucks. Although Afghan and Pakistani traffic was allowed to continue, NATO supply vehicles could not cross the border, and thousands were stranded on the Pakistani side.

It took seven months of tough bargaining with Islamabad for the United States to get Pakistan to reopen its border for NATO. Two main stumbling blocks prolonged the difficult negotiations. First, Pakistan demanded that the fee ISAF had to pay per truck crossing its territory be raised from $250 to a whopping $5,000.[53] The Pakistanis also wanted to be legally absolved of any responsibility for any damages that may happen to NATO trucks as they pass through Pakistan's territory—from looting and theft by Karachi's many mafias to being torched by the Pakistani Taliban. Second, Pakistan insisted that the United States issue a formal apology for the November 2011 Salala raid. Incensed by Pakistan's sponsorship of anti-American militants in Afghanistan, including possibly during the fateful November 2011 firefight, Washington for months refused to do so.

On the truck fee issue, Pakistan largely backed down, settling for the original price of $250 per truck. But the United States had to promise to improve 210 kilometers of roads that NATO trucks would transverse between Karachi and the Afghan border.[54] Also Pakistan extracted a promise that NATO subcontractors would be the ones to pay a $6,000 per truck compensation fee to Pakistani truck owners who suffered economic losses during the border closure.[55] Pakistan did agree to beef up security at an important crossing, Torkham, where trucks would regularly get attacked by militants and criminals.[56] But presumably to make its continuing displeasure known, Pakistan also insisted that it would x-ray every ISAF container to make certain that, as per the deal, it did not contain any lethal equipment. Before November 2011, the Pakistani guards usually only verified a few random containers. The check would, of course, delay the transport and increase non-fee costs for the United States.

On the second demand—an apology from the United States—the United States stood firm through the winter of 2011 and spring 2012. It repeatedly expressed its unwillingness to apologize, and it froze the $1.1 billion in the U.S. Coalition Support Fund that had been earmarked to reimburse Pakistan for its cooperation in counterinsurgency operations. It was not until July 2012 that, as described below, the impasse was brought to an end with Secretary Clinton's telephoned apology.

Before November 2011, few analysts had believed that Pakistan would find the wherewithal to keep the ground lines of communications (GLOC) shut down for this long. Yes, Pakistan had periodically used the GLOC like the weapon with a similar-sounding name, to point in anger at the United States in response to U.S. actions it found most objectionable, such as the bin Laden raid or the controversial drone attacks. The border would be shut down for days, the Taliban would be allowed to burn some (at times tens) of NATO's trucks, and then, presumably, Pakistan's economic and strategic interests would prevail. The scope of U.S.-Pakistan cooperation might be narrower and narrower and the overlap of their interests smaller and smaller, but some mutually advantageous policies could be maintained.[57]

Moreover, Pakistan's trucking industry—with some justification popularly referred to as the "trucking mafia," as it is pervaded by patronage, oligopolistic tendencies, and violent contract wars—is very well connected in Islamabad and Rawalpindi. The closure of the border cost it a lot of money, on which Pakistan's elites have been getting ever richer over the past decade. It is also the primary source of employment in some of Pakistan's poorest and most militancy-prone areas, such as the Federally Administered Tribal Areas, Khyber-Pakhtunkhwa, and Baluchistan.

By the summer of 2012, the tab for Washington's Northern Distribution Network (described in detail in chapter 7) reached several hundred million dollars beyond what the transportation costs through Pakistan would run. Moreover, ISAF became increasingly pressed by its own deadline to hand over security responsibility to the Afghan National Security Forces by the end of 2014 and its determination that ISAF military equipment be removed from Afghanistan by then as well. (How many troops and what equipment would remain in Afghanistan after 2014 was not yet determined as of the fall of 2012.) Thus, in July 2012, the United States ultimately caved in, and Secretary Clinton communicated an apology to her Pakistani counterpart over the phone. In response, Pakistan reopened the border, and the United States then released the withheld money from the Coalition Support Fund.

For years, the dependence on the logistical networks through Pakistan was one important factor limiting how tough Washington could get with Islamabad in pressuring it to go after the Haqqani network in Northern Waziristan, the Quetta Shura in Baluchistan, and al Qaeda throughout the country. But when the border was closed, Washington was unable to turn its greater reliance on the Northern Distribution Network into strengthening its hand vis-à-vis Pakistan. With the border shut, Washington arguably could have been freer in increasing the pressure on Islamabad regarding the Haqqanis and the Quetta Shura and Pakistan's other double-dealings in Afghanistan. Instead, Washington ended up dividing (and thereby diluting) its pressure between getting Pakistan to stop providing safe havens to Afghan militants and reopening the border. Once again, Pakistan managed to manufacture a crisis that interfered with an effective prosecution of the war in Afghanistan, resurrecting its strategy of obtaining leverage from weakness.

Indeed, Pakistan's trump card in dealing with Washington has been its own internal frailty. The Pakistan People's Party government headed by President Zardari has not been able to pass many meaningful reforms, and its popularity barely hovers above 10 percent. The only reason it has managed to survive formally in power for four years (even as Pakistan's military continued to control foreign and security policies) was that neither the opposition party of Nawaz Sharif, the Pakistan Muslim League, nor the Pakistan military wanted to be left holding the governance bag. Pakistan's economy is in shambles, the country suffers from massive electricity blackouts, and severe poverty and unemployment are widespread. Secessionist and jihadi militancy, including in southern Punjab, may have been somewhat suppressed, but it has not been tamed.[58] For several years, Karachi, the major business hub of Pakistan and one of its key economic engines, has been like a civil war battleground for Pakistan's political parties, criminal mafia, businessmen militias, and land-grabbing militants—all at various times sponsored by the Pakistani military and intelligence services and ignored by the hamstrung and corrupt Pakistani police.[59] The country also faces many acute and long-term challenges of energy and water deficiencies, large population growth, and limited employment opportunities.

The fissiparous and fraying tendencies within Pakistan are intensifying along this multitude of dimensions, and its institutions are mere shells. Pakistan's civil government has been unable to govern even in the economic sphere and has abdicated the responsibility for decisionmaking in many other domains. A tug of war over power arrangements among Pakistan's many contending centers of power—the military establishment, the political parties and their near-feudal leadership, the activist and aggressive judiciary, militants, and local strongmen—continues to divert energies away from tackling the country's many and intense domestic crises.

With good reason Washington is deeply concerned that its actions could push Pakistan over the edge into collapse, which would truly be a nightmare for the United States and the region given the potential this has for loosening the control of its nuclear weapons and for extremists provoking a major military (even nuclear) confrontation between Pakistan and India. And Islamabad plays such Washington fears for all they are worth—the effective leverage of the weak.

At stake, however, are not just U.S. interests but also Pakistan's own strategic interests in Afghanistan. Pakistan does not want to be bypassed as the United States and NATO reshape or wrap up their roles in Afghanistan after 2014. It fears being left out of any potential deal between the Taliban, the Unites States, and Kabul. (Ironically, Kabul is equally terrified of being left out of a Taliban-U.S. deal brokered by Pakistan.) Ultimately, although Pakistan is highly likely to continue cultivating vicious allies in Afghanistan like the Haqqanis, an unstable Afghanistan, especially if again plunged into a civil war after 2014, will be like an ulcer bleeding into Pakistan, destabilizing that country, too. India will then feel much less restrained in supporting Pakistan's enemies in Afghanistan, such as a reconstituted Northern Alliance, and Pakistan's paranoid fears of encirclement will be more than ever based in reality. Other Afghan neighbors and regional powers will once again compete over their spheres of influence in Afghanistan, with their gloves off. Some cooperation with the United States to do all that is still possible to ensure that Afghanistan does not explode into a full-blown civil war after 2014 is in Pakistan's own interest.

Regional Cooperation despite Pakistan?

Stuck with an intransigent Pakistan, the Obama administration still labored to develop some regional—even impartial—framework facilitating a stable Afghanistan. Its efforts culminated in organizing the November 2011 Istanbul conference where participating countries were to pledge noninterference in Afghanistan's affairs and commit to developing the New Silk Road to bolster Afghanistan's economy. Like many other conferences on Afghanistan, the effort produced only vague platitudes without any concrete commitments. It became apparent that most countries were maneuvering to position themselves advantageously after 2014 rather than being interested in multilateral cooperation.[60]

Indeed, the region continues to be plagued by enduring animosities and contestations that go beyond the India-Pakistan rivalry and Pakistan's belief in the primacy of its interests in Afghanistan. Iran views U.S. involvement in Afghanistan with increasing suspicion, but its actions there have been far less destabilizing than those of Pakistan. Iran has provided some weapons to the Taliban, particularly in Herat and Badghis provinces of Afghanistan, to cultivate the insurgent cadres there in case the Taliban ever controls substantial territory in Afghanistan.[61] Iran also seeks to demonstrate to the United States that it can significantly complicate its life in the event of an Iranian-U.S. military confrontation.[62] The rulers in Tehran enjoy seeing the United States bleed, and they are afraid of any U.S. bases remaining in Afghanistan after 2014 that could be used against Iran.

But at the same time, the Iranians are afraid of the reemergence of a radical Sunni, Pakistan- and Saudi Arabia–dominated government in Kabul, such as the one under the Taliban. During the 1990s, they assiduously opposed the Taliban and provided extensive support to the Shia Hazaras and other members of the Northern Alliance.[63] And they have other interests in a stable Afghanistan: their neighbor is a large and growing export market for Iranian goods. Tehran also wants to limit the flows of drugs from Afghanistan to Iran's large addict population. (At the same time, smuggling of U.S. dollars from Afghanistan to Iran has become an important source of hard currency for Iran, which as a result of U.S. and European sanctions for Tehran's nuclear program has faced dramatic declines in hard currency reserves.)[64] Thus it has diligently cultivated a variety of political, religious, and civil society actors in Afghanistan, spreading cash in the Arg Palace and among Afghan journalists and politicians.[65]

Turkey, economically growing and politically ambitious, wants to use Afghanistan as an opportunity to demonstrate its new clout and active foreign policy. It has helped to organize several multilateral forums on Afghanistan, including the 2011 Istanbul conference, and it has attempted to stimulate negotiations with the Taliban.

Like Turkey, Saudi Arabia is anxious to be included in a regional dialogue, but for different reasons. Saudi Arabia primarily wants to counter Iran's efforts in Afghanistan, having invested for years in spreading Wahhabi religious beliefs in Afghanistan and Pakistan. During the 1990s, it was one of only three countries, along with Pakistan and the United Arab Emirates, that recognized the Taliban government.

Russia's attitudes toward developments in Afghanistan resemble those of Iran. The Russian military cannot help but enjoy the United Stated getting bruised in Afghanistan, relieving some of the humiliation the Soviets suffered there, thanks to the United States, in the 1980s.[66] President Vladimir Putin and his coterie of current and former officials of the Soviet and post-Soviet Russian intelligence service, who are powerful voices in Russia's security and foreign policy, continue to be preoccupied with and hostile toward the United States.[67] The Obama administration "reset" of the U.S.-Russian bilateral relationship, as the policy came to be known, delivered some important, if low-hanging, fruit: the signing of the New START treaty on U.S.-Russian nuclear arsenals, the end of Russian arms sales to Iran, and—crucially for NATO's Afghanistan policy—the opening of the Northern Distribution Network.[68] However, Russia has sought to position itself as a crucial broker on the issue, not allowing the United States to bypass it in its negotiations with the Central Asian countries. Russia also strongly objects to any long-term U.S. presence in Afghanistan, seeing it as a threat to its position in Central Asia. And, as described in the previous chapter, it is very concerned about the Afghan poppy and drug trade.

But, just like Tehran, Moscow also deeply fears jihadi terrorists enjoying safe havens in Afghanistan and their activities leaking all the way to Russia, thus giving a boost to anti-Russian terrorists in Chechnya, Dagestan, and elsewhere. Hence Russia has voiced its support for the United States persevering in Afghanistan after 2014, even if it does not want to see the United States establish permanent bases there. The most important objective for Russia in Afghanistan is that a jihadi government—whether Taliban or other—does not return to power in Kabul. During the 1990s civil war in Afghanistan, Russia, along with India, was a major supporter of Afghan Uzbeks and Tajiks, while Iran supplied the Hazaras. Russia also has 6,000 troops stationed in Tajikistan to stop any jihadi contagion spreading from Afghanistan into Central Asia.

Tajikistan is a chronically weak country that never quite recovered from its 1990s civil war. Uzbekistan, too, fears any Afghanistan-based support for anti-Uzbekistan jihadists, such as the Islamic Movement of Uzbekistan (IMU). The Taliban allowed the IMU to operate out of Afghanistan's territory in the 1990s, and IMU forces still remain there, although having taken serious hits from NATO.[69] Since 2001 IMU has also established a presence in the FATA. Enduring animosities complicate Uzbekistan's relationship with Tajikistan.[70] The former Soviet Central Asia countries—Tajikistan, Uzbekistan, and Kyrgyzstan, in particular—have their own deep internal challenges of legitimate rule, Islamist mobilization, center-periphery tensions, underdevelopment, and intense geostrategic competition.[71]

Kyrgyzstan is the only country in the world that hosts both Russian and U.S. military bases. For that privilege—namely the lease of the Manas base—Washington has paid $150 million a year. It also awarded a Kyrgyz-Russian fuel company a lucrative contract to supply 50 percent of aviation fuel to the U.S. military at Manas, which brings about $4.5 million to the company every month.[72] That amount is likely to grow as ISAF draws down its presence in Afghanistan and increases the use of Manas for the withdrawal of its troops and equipment from Afghanistan. None of the Central Asian countries want to see Afghanistan destabilized through civil war or once again dominated by a jihadi government. Tajikistan and Uzbekistan, along with Turkmenistan, hope for the development of a reliable energy corridor through Afghanistan to potentially lucrative customers like India. Such a corridor would also allow them to reduce their dependence on Russia for energy transport.

China's increasing economic interests in Central and South Asia have made it a more active player in Afghanistan as well. It is anxious to protect its economic investments, such as in the Aynak copper mine, and it does not want to be excluded from the potentially massive resource extraction in Afghanistan. But for that, as explained in the previous chapter, it needs both stability in Afghanistan and an Afghan legal system robust enough to enable at least predictable dispute resolution processes (or predictable corruption) for its businesses. China, too, is concerned about any possible safe havens in Afghanistan for its own Islamist militants, the East Turkestan Islamic Movement of ethnic Uighurs, who continue to suffer marginalization in China. But even as China has shown a more visible interest in Afghanistan's security, it continues to reject any possibility of providing military or police support in Afghanistan. And for all the fanfare of the June 2012 Shanghai Cooperation Organization summit on Afghanistan, China made only a small aid commitment of $23 million to Afghanistan.[73] Moreover, the same intense rivalries over Central Asia and over their relative global power that haunt the Russia-China relationship also limit the ability of the Shanghai Cooperation Organization to cooperate on Afghanistan. China also has long cultivated its relationship with Pakistan, presenting itself as a more reliable ally than the United States.[74] Thus, to some extent, it needs bear in mind Pakistan's moves when calibrating its Afghanistan policy.

Paradoxically, all of Afghanistan's neighbors and regional actors would benefit to one degree or another from a stable Afghanistan. Even Pakistan, while defining a pro-India Kabul as the worst possible outcome, would prefer a neutral, nonaligned, stable Afghanistan to one torn by an outright civil war or destabilized by extensive militancy. But with a NATO failure to stabilize the Afghan government not unlikely, all of the countries in the region continue to cultivate their ethnically based proxies and stimulate each other's insecurity. If Afghanistan does in fact collapse into intense turmoil, even if not a full-blown civil war, all of the countries in the region will only expand their money and weapons flows to their particular Afghan allies. Such flows across Afghanistan's western and eastern borders have long been in existence, and already rumors abound in Afghanistan of weapons pouring in across its northern border.[75]

Military Transition and Negotiations with the Taliban

The lynchpin of the U.S. and international strategy in Afghanistan and its most developed element is the gradual transfer from ISAF to the Afghan National Security Forces of the responsibility for maintaining Afghanistan's security and fighting the still-entrenched Taliban. Yet even this core aspect of the strategy cannot be separated from political trends and governance patterns in Afghanistan. Moreover, in handing over the responsibility to the Afghans, the United States and ISAF are handing over a stalemated war.

The McChrystal plan was endorsed by the White House in December 2009, albeit with far fewer resources than the general had recommended and, over the objections from the military, with timelines stipulated for the withdrawal of U.S. forces. The plan assumed that by the time of the transfer ISAF would have secured large parts of Afghanistan. Three years later, some real progress had been achieved, such as in central Helmand and Kandahar, both of which had been either intense battle zones or strongly under the Taliban's sway.

But as this book goes to press, the territory cleared of insurgent forces that is being handed over to the Afghans is much smaller than had been assumed. From the perspective of Afghan citizens, the spring and summer of 2012 have been particularly violent, with insurgent attacks and high-casualty incidents significantly up in May through August, compared to the same period in 2011.[1] Progress in central parts of the south is real, but how robust it is remains to be seen. Because of interservice rivalry within the U.S. armed forces and standard operating procedures of the U.S. Marine Corps—specifically, its unwillingness to deploy without its own air support—much of the U.S. military surge within the south was directed to the less strategically vital Helmand, while it was Kandahar that has been the center of gravity of the insurgency. This was a decision that potentially weakened the punch the surge could deliver to the Taliban.[2] Moreover, many parts of the south beyond the central areas did not see an increase in U.S. or Afghan National Security Forces, and strong Taliban influence there often persists. Although those are often far less populated areas (70 percent of the population lives in the big central cities, such as Kandahar and Lashkar Gah), they can nonetheless be sources of insecurity leaking into the areas where the Taliban has been weakened.

The east continues to be intensely contested, and ISAF and the ANSF are essentially in a stalemate there with the insurgents. There is also persisting and possibly intensifying insecurity in important central provinces—Wardak, Parwan, Logar, and even the long-peaceful Bamian—from which threats can leak into Kabul and affect critical access to Kabul. Large parts of Afghanistan's west are among the most stable and peaceful areas in Afghanistan. But even there, such as in Herat, attacks appear to be growing in intensity, even if they remain more sporadic than elsewhere. Like the west, northern Afghanistan has some of the most stable areas, but even that region is hardly free from insurgency problems. The increase of ISAF and ANSF units improved security in a corridor along the major roads in Kunduz and Baghlan, two provinces where rising threats to security had been particularly noticeable. But ethnic tensions are simmering and poor governance feeds the rivalry and conflict.

Indeed, poor governance continues to stimulate and provide fuel for conflict throughout much of the country. And threats from crime, which in Afghanistan often critically undermines human security and triggers and exacerbates violent disputes within and among communities, have gone unmitigated. The U.S. and international ambivalence toward remaining robustly engaged in Afghanistan after 2014 only encourages criminality, poor governance, and violent conflict as well as reinforces the resolve of the insurgencies.

The White House may be speaking about "winding down" the war, but at this point, the only component of the war that is in fact winding down is the U.S. and international participation in it.[3]

The Military Transition and Its Challenges

Aside from the increase in Afghan Local Police units (which arguably is *not* a healthy development), the growth of the Afghan National Security Forces—particularly the Afghan National Army—has been one of the brightest spots in the transition process of creating Afghan capabilities. The size of the ANSF has been expanding rapidly, and the quality of their military skills has also been growing. As of the summer of 2012, even before the ISAF's revised rules of engagement were announced in September 2012, Afghan soldiers or police were participating, in some way, in at least 90 percent of all operations and were leading some 40 percent of operations, although these were mostly the less complex ones.[4] The Afghan National Army Special Forces are the most capable component of the ANSF and are closest to operating on their own without extensive international support. With much of the pre-2014 transition being about the gradual shift in ISAF's mission from "combat to support," the growth of the ANSF is very important. But much about their capabilities remains as yet unknown.

Afghan National Army

The target strength to which the ANSF was scheduled to be expanded by November 2012 was 352,000: 195,000 Afghan National Army troops and 157,000 Afghan National Police. That target size reflects a manyfold increase over the early post-2002 estimates of the appropriate strength of the ANSF, a development driven by the intensifying Taliban and affiliate insurgencies since 2006.[5] With up to 90 percent of the recruited force being illiterate, finding suitable candidates for the officer corps in particular has at times been a challenge. Competent tactical officers have often been former mujahideen, while capable logistics and management officers at more senior posts would have been trained by the Soviets and fought in the pro-communist 1980s Afghan army—with frictions between them at times emerging.[6] Although ISAF training and partnering over the years have improved morale to a considerable extent, such tensions are yet another manifestation of the problematic patronage networks within the Afghan National Army (see below).

Other aspects of the Afghan National Army capacity also raise concerns. The ANA still suffers at least a 20 percent desertion rate, and according to some accounts, a typical ANA unit is only at about 50 percent authorized strength at any given time, often because Afghan soldiers refuse to serve far from home.[7] There are also significant shortages in as much as 40 percent of equipment items because of deficiencies in Afghan planning and logistics capacity and theft by ANA members and commanders.[8] Such theft is driven both by corruption and by hedging on the part of ANSF members who, fearing the reductions in ISAF presence, seek to buy off the Taliban with weapons and intelligence transfers (see below). Weapons bazaars in Miram Shah, the capital of North Waziristan, have become well supplied with ISAF-issued arms; Taliban personnel ride throughout Afghanistan in Afghan Army pickup trucks.[9]

Moreover, at the cost of several billion dollars a year, the Afghan government will not be able to afford the current size of the ANSF for many years. In 2011 ISAF spent approximately $10 billion on building the Afghan National Security Forces, almost all of which was U.S. funded, including $3 billion for infrastructure, $3 billion for equipment, $1 billion for training, and $3 billion for salaries, food, and related costs.[10] In 2012 the United States will have spent $11.2 billion on the ANSF, with only about half that much requested for 2013.[11] Even that reduced expense is nowhere close to what the Afghan government can afford since that number is roughly twice the size of Afghanistan's GDP of approximately $2 billion a year.[12] Thus, in addition to agreeing to continue footing the ANSF bill, participants at the 2012 NATO Chicago Summit agreed to maintain the 352,000 strong ANSF until 2017 and then undertake a "gradual managed force reduction . . . to a sustainable level," with a working target of 228,500, estimated to cost about $4.1 billion a year.[13]

This anticipated force reduction has implications beyond the ANSF's military capabilities against the insurgent networks. The ANSF are one of the largest sources of employment in Afghanistan. Even if the 130,000 ANSF force reduction is gradual, the downsizing may still leave a lot of young men, recently trained and issued weapons, without a job. Afghanistan's unemployment is already running high, and it is precisely the salary that induced many to sign up for the ANSF. The more military men will be laid off without being able to find alternative unemployment, the greater the chances for political disquiet, criminality, and violent conflict. Peacefully integrating those young men into Afghanistan's society will be no less a challenge than effectively integrating demobilized Taliban fighters. It is of course possible that the ANSF cutback will be accomplished simply as a result of the existing high attrition rate, expiring enlistments, and reductions in recruitment, which together would be the most benign form of ANSF reduction.

But if the Afghan government seeks to compensate for insufficient funding by reducing the quality of equipment, training, and benefits in order to keep more men on the roster with fewer financial resources, that too would have negative implications for the fighting capacity of the force. Afghan soldiers need not live in air-conditioned barracks (they don't in their homes); but it would be a serious problem if they were issued faulty arms and lacked ammunition (as has periodically happened with the various auxiliary paramilitary forces.)[14]

With respect to the impact of a smaller force on the nation's security, much will depend on whether the ANSF reductions are driven merely by affordability or are merited by a corresponding diminution in the strength of the insurgents.

The quality of the Afghan National Army has undeniably grown as a result of beefed-up ISAF training between 2009 and 2012. Increasingly, ANA units are able to conduct entire operations independently and respond to Afghan-set priorities. But how durable such improvements are is not yet clear. Furthermore, transition will weaken NATO's training and supervisory capacity. Between 2003 and 2008, Afghan *kandaks* (essentially a battalion and the main unit of the Afghan military) were mentored by an ISAF team. The 2009 McChrystal review particularly stressed "unit partnering" between U.S. and Afghan military units, considerably intensifying and lengthening the in-(battle)field training of the Afghan units. The effect has been positive according to a U.S. Department of Defense April 2012 quarterly report: there has been a major increase in the number of ANA kandaks able to operate "independent[ly] with advisors," that is, with a much diminished ISAF embedded partnering presence.[15]

While accurate to some extent, such an assessment is likely also driven by necessity. Because of set timelines dictating U.S. and coalition troop reductions, including the end of the surge, ISAF has had to cut back on partnering, and at least since the beginning of 2012 it has not initiated any new partnering with Afghan units. Of course, weaning the kandaks and Afghan command structures off their international mentors necessitates cutting back on partnering and transitioning the units to standing on their own. But much of the speed of the cutbacks in unit partnering is driven by U.S. and ISAF withdrawal timelines, not necessarily the readiness of the Afghan units. The surge and other drawdown schedules are already reducing the number of available trainers, with the outcome that a smaller number of trainers will increasingly have to float among several Afghan units rather than being embedded within one. During the previous one-on-one embedded phase, Afghan soldiers and police were instructed in elementary skills they would not have been taught in basic training, such as map reading, handling different weapons, and organizing a patrol or an ambush.[16] But the remaining ISAF support teams that will now have to circulate among and advise multiple Afghan units are not fully fungible. The support teams were developed for a specific task: for example, an ISAF support team for the Afghan Border Police cannot be easily switched to support an Afghan infantry kandak.

Instead of partnering, the new support role emerging for U.S. and international forces is one of advising Afghan units, such as via the so-called Security Force Assistance Advisory Teams (SFAATs). Because their role is significantly narrower than the scope of tasks assigned to ISAF units fully partnered with ANSF contingents, the SFAATs require many fewer personnel. But if the troop drawdowns are too rapid, and too few international troops remain in Afghanistan after 2014, even the advisory capacity of ISAF may be compromised. This will be especially the case if the SFAATs and other advisory units will have to delegate much of their personnel to their own force protection and if their access to the battlefield is constricted.

The 2012 spate of the so-called insider attacks generated further pressures to limit partnering and restrict interactions between ISAF and the Afghan National Security Forces as well as between international civilian advisors and Afghan government officials. Previously known as green-on-blue attacks, they are security incidents in which members of the ANSF turn on their international partners. In the first nine months of 2012, over fifty international troops were killed that way in more than thirty attacks, a sizeable increase over such insider killings prior to 2012.[17] Altogether, between 2007 and September 2012, 105 international troops were killed by rogue Afghan forces, with almost half the incidents occurring in the first nine months of 2012.[18] Although NATO has stressed that many of these attacks have been conducted by disgruntled ANSF recruits with personal grudges rather than by Taliban infiltrators, the Taliban has been keen to appropriate the attacks as a purposeful component of its insurgency strategy. Indeed, Afghan officials detained or fired hundreds of ANA soldiers for links with insurgents to prevent further insider attacks, and in September 2012 ISAF suspended training new Afghan Local Police recruits in order to develop better vetting procedures to prevent insider attacks from those forces.[19] Regardless of the validity of the Taliban's claims of responsibility for the insider attacks, such incidents undermine domestic support within the international coalition for the mission in Afghanistan and the perpetuation of extensive military and civilian interactions with their Afghan counterparts after 2014. Reducing the frequency of insider attacks indeed requires tighter vetting—not easy to square with the drive to expand forces, including the Afghan Local Police, or with the availability and nature of information for background checks—as well as detailed criminal investigations and psychological studies, which require time. Meanwhile, every further attack erodes support abroad. Initial ISAF responses included having ISAF forces carry their weapons loaded with live ordnance every time they interact with Afghan forces and having so-called guardian angels—specially designated ISAF soldiers—monitoring their Afghan interlocutors all the time so as to be ready to fire on Afghan forces if they try to kill NATO soldiers.[20]

Then, in September 2012, ISAF announced dramatic changes to the ISAF-ANSF interactions, restricting partnering and unit interactions below the battalion level unless ISAF officers obtained special permission from a two-star regional command ISAF general.[21] As this book went to press, much yet remained unclear about the new guidelines. But depending on their permanence and extent, they could potentially affect the entire military effort—from training and supervising the ANSF and the Afghan Local Police to routine counterinsurgency operations, such as night raids, to ISAF military advising via the SFAATs and even to specialty enabler support. After international reporting on the changes sent a shock wave throughout Afghanistan's military forces and the international community, NATO subsequently insisted that the new policy did not represent a change in its military strategy and transition plans and would not reduce the effectiveness of its campaign in Afghanistan, and that it was only a temporary security measure in light of the violent reactions evoked by a video made in the United States that mocked Prophet Mohammad.[22] ISAF also clarified that even the temporary measure would not affect ISAF specialty enablers, such as medevac, embedded with or supporting Afghan units.

NATO's pronouncements not withstanding, if the new force protection measures and rules of engagement are not, in fact, temporary, it is hard to see how they would not seriously reduce the effectiveness of the military campaign, including the training of the ANSF. It is precisely below the battalion level where the vast majority of counterinsurgency operations—from patrolling in villages to supervising the Afghan Local Police to conducting counterinsurgency operations—take place. If from September 2012 onward Afghan forces are left to take on the Taliban on their own during most counterinsurgency operations, they will have to do so without being fully prepared and trained. Inevitably, their effectiveness will be reduced and their morale undermined, while the Taliban will gain a major psychological boost.

Despite ISAF's announcement that special support operations, such as medevac, would not be affected by the new rules of engagement, the restrictions could in fact hamper such ISAF support. Yet for many years to come, certainly well beyond 2014, the ANSF will continue to be deficient in several critical domains. These include command, control, and intelligence; air support; medical evacuation; logistics and maintenance; contractor management; battle space integration; and other specialty enablers. Currently, the Afghan National Security Forces frequently know how to fight and win battles at the tactical level, but they have yet to learn how to fight and win campaigns. The latter requires the development of logistical systems, ability to combine arms, and strengthened command and control at the strategic level.

The lack of specialty enablers is not a failure of the effort; ISAF chose to prioritize growing the combat forces first and did not begin building enablers until 2011. There are still two years to grow these ANSF capacities, and the expectation is that the international community will continue providing such critical assets after 2014 until indigenous Afghan specialty enablers are ready. However, the extent and robustness of specialty enabler delivery will depend on how the role of U.S. and coalition forces after 2014 is defined: if the U.S. mission is defined in terms of narrowly implemented counterterrorism and training operations, such as on-base training, or if the September 2012 force protection measures and rules of engagement stay in place, the United States may be severely constrained in providing crucial resources to the ANSF. For example, without on-the-ground, in-combat embedded units, the U.S. military will be highly unlikely to provide air support or even medevac.

Similarly, many IEDs are located by ISAF signal intelligence; therefore a great reduction of such ISAF assets after 2014 will likely increase the lethality of IED attacks and possibly undermine the morale of the ANSF, including their willingness to patrol among the population. The ANSF dependence on externally delivered specialty enablers thus creates a third mission beyond training and counterterrorism: filling the gaps in combat support until indigenous specialty enabler capacities have been developed in Afghanistan. Compromising on assisting with such capability would critically undermine the effectiveness of the ANSF.

The Afghan National Army and the Afghan National Police are becoming increasingly battle tested, but their effectiveness and capacity to stand primarily on their own are yet to be proven. The NATO Lisbon Summit in November 2010 established that the ANSF would be gradually placed in charge of security in Afghanistan, area by area, in a series of five periods and geographic segments covering Afghanistan's territory, referred to as "tranches." In a tranche handed over to the Afghans, the ANSF are to be the dominant security provider and ISAF is to be only in the background, deployed only when called upon by the Afghan forces. So far, out of the five-tranche transition, two tranches have been completed, and a third began in May 2012. As of fall 2012, 122 districts and all provincial capitals have been transferred to the ANSF.

How the ANSF handle especially the third and fourth tranches will be an important test of their capacities, since the previous two tranches consisted mainly of stable or secured areas. There have been some tough places among them, such as the Marja, Nawa-i-Barakzayi, and Nad-e-Ali districts of the Helmand province and its capital, Lashkar Gah, which, although cleared by ISAF before and registering major security improvements, are nonetheless areas where the Taliban has been entrenched and that historically have been difficult security environments. Interrogation of Taliban detainees reveals that often Taliban governance persists in supposedly cleared areas, such as Marja.[23] However, it was only in the third tranche that the ANSF were to take over areas still violently contested and with poor governance.[24] Especially in 2013, some difficult fighting lies ahead for the security forces. How the ANSF perform during the third and fourth tranches will be the most telling indicator thus far of their likely performance after 2014.

Particularly in eastern Afghanistan, which did not receive the same level of ISAF "surge" reinforcements as Afghanistan's south and was still mostly left for tranches 4 and 5, the fighting can get very tough. And even the significant security improvements in the south are fragile. The Taliban will have every incentive to bloody the nose of the ANSF there to show that the transition process is not working and that the ANSF cannot effectively fight them once the international community's presence is reduced. If the ANSF can respond robustly to an intense Taliban military campaign in the south, that will be an important sign that they can hold their own after 2014.

At the same time, a small number or limited scope of Taliban attacks in the south or east does not necessarily mean that the Taliban there has been greatly weakened. The insurgents may be just waiting it out until after 2014 before expending significant effort and resources to resurrect their control and intimidate the government and population into submission. In fact, although the late spring and summer of 2012 were very bloody in Afghanistan, and the number of Taliban-initiated incidents and civilian casualties greatly increased compared to 2011, there are some indications that the Taliban has been holding back. Its offensive in the east, such as in Kunar province, in the summer of 2012 has consisted mainly of rocket-propelled grenades and mortar attacks and the planting of IEDs.[25] ISAF frequently points out that it prevails in every single battle against the insurgents and that increasingly the Afghan National Security Forces are achieving similar results. Yet winning a battle may not be the goal of the insurgents, however much they would welcome such an occurrence. Simply causing extensive mayhem and conducting high-profile attacks may well be sufficient for them to scare the population and persuade it that the Afghan government will not be able to maintain even existing levels of security after 2014.

One of the major deficiencies of the military component of the transition is its one-way direction. The NATO Lisbon Summit established that the transition process was to be conditions based—and to an extent it is. ISAF's recommendations of which districts are selected for handover to Afghan responsibility are based on a rather comprehensive—if not necessarily always robust—assessment of the security situation, quality of governance, and strategic significance of the areas.[26] But ultimately, the transfer decisions lie with President Hamid Karzai and his principal advisor for the transition, Ashraf Ghani. Complex political considerations, including those of ethnic balancing and satisfying local power brokers, will at times influence the transfer decisions, despite ISAF's advice.[27] Furthermore, ISAF may miss critical political trends in a district that should inform handover decisions.

More worrisome, in the handover process, there is very little scope for NATO forces to return in force to an area that was handed over to the Afghans if the original assessment of handover readiness proves incorrect or if ANSF perform poorly. Under an ideal scenario, the shift from "unit partnering" to an ISAF advisory role on the ground would be gradual rather than like an on-and-off switch, with ISAF having the ability to "let Afghan units fail" to some extent and retain a sufficient capacity to come back with combat forces to "pick up the pieces."[28] However, squeezed by the timelines set by the international community, such as the U.S. military drawdown schedule, the transition process has become essentially a one-way street: once handed over to the Afghans, the territory belongs to the Afghans, and there is close to no prospect of the international community returning there with any strong military presence. Neither the foreign capitals nor Afghan government officials have an appetite for anything but scaling back the international military presence. The September 2012 restrictions on partnering below the battalion level rapidly shifted the process from a gradual dial-down to close to a flip of the switch.

Some problems were emerging even before the new rules of engagement were announced, even if assessing their pervasiveness has been difficult. Although particular episodes may highlight likely problems, they may not necessarily be indicators of broader trends. Nonetheless, they illustrate some of the challenges that lie ahead for the security transition process. For example, when two ISAF bases in Wardak were handed over to ANSF in 2011 and ISAF troops departed, both bases rapidly fell into disrepair.[29] The ANSF abandoned one of them quickly because they found it too dangerous, and the Taliban took over the base. At the second base, the Afghan forces faced major equipment and supply problems: lack of night vision goggles compromised their ability to suppress the Taliban's nightly harassment; the unit quickly ran out of fuel; the Afghan soldiers were not able to repair their equipment, such as Humvees previously repaired by ISAF contractors, who had also left. The ANSF unit's mobility and capacity to patrol among the local population were thus severely reduced. And even when the Afghan soldiers could patrol, they were unable to establish a positive rapport with the population. Believing that support for the Taliban among the population had increased, as had Taliban activity and morale, the ANSF's own morale was undermined. And critically, with the departure of the American support unit, the Afghan unit had also lost air support and medevac service. Again, it remains to be seen whether what happened at these Wardak bases constitutes two isolated incidents or whether they are a portent of serious ANSF problems and deeper security deterioration during the military transition and after 2014. The Wardak episode also leaves important questions unanswered: Did the ANSF leadership learn of the problems at the bases and through what channels? Did it take any action to redress the problems? Did it learn lessons from the problems there that it applied to other bases to be transitioned? Answers to such questions have a critical bearing on how durable the transition outcome will be or whether or not security will indeed be seriously compromised and perhaps unsustainable in many areas after 2014.

Alarmingly, there are indications that the pervasive hedging that dominates the behavior of much of the Afghan population is also affecting the Afghan National Security Forces. As interrogations of Taliban detainees revealed, low-level ANSF commanders and Afghan government officials regularly reach out to the Taliban to establish informal ceasefires. In many parts of Afghanistan, such informal ceasefires between the local ANSF and the insurgents are reportedly becoming a norm.[30] Captured insurgents even disclosed the existence of officially signed ceasefires and loyalty agreements. To curry favor with the Taliban, ANSF personnel leak ISAF intelligence on operations and impending arrests and guarantee safe passage to the Taliban, even providing it with ISAF-issued equipment and assisting in the release of captured insurgents, without the customary bribes.[31] There is a sense that in areas where ISAF has withdrawn, Taliban influence has increased, though by how much and how permanently is still a question.[32] And many captured Taliban fighters are confident that once ISAF is no longer a factor—however they define that—they will prevail over the ANSF.[33]

Speeding up the withdrawal of ISAF forces thus does not bode well for stabilizing the Afghan government. Yet the May 2012 NATO Summit in Chicago added a new milestone to the transition process—namely, that all parts of Afghanistan would begin the military transition process and that the Afghans would be in the lead everywhere by mid-2013.[34] Still, what "lead" means is also not yet fully defined.[35] However, U.S. senior military officials have stressed that at least until 2014, U.S. forces would remain "combat-capable."[36]

Nor is the level and type of U.S. and ISAF military support for the ANSF after 2014 exactly determined as yet. Decisions still have to be made as to the number of U.S. and other international troops and the character of their mission. At the signing of the U.S.-Afghanistan Strategic Partnership Agreement, President Barack Obama spoke of "steady military reductions" in U.S. troop levels in Afghanistan after the end of 2012.[37] That phrasing seems to suggest that the United States will not maintain the 68,000 troops in Afghanistan in 2013 that the U.S. military would prefer. Yet too fast a reduction in U.S. forces will critically undermine the military transition in Afghanistan, inhibit the growth and much-needed improvement of the ANSF, and risk undoing whatever military successes have been achieved since the surge of U.S. troops in 2009. The president also stated that the U.S. military forces remaining in Afghanistan after 2014, pending the signing of a U.S.-Afghanistan Bilateral Security Agreement, would focus on only "two narrow security missions": counterterrorism and training of the ANSF.[38]

But if the post-2014 mission of international (including U.S.) troops is defined very narrowly as only counterterrorism, that is, anti–al Qaeda and anti–global jihad operations—any remaining mentoring capacity will be severely weakened, as will likely be the overall ANSF capacity.[39] As explained above, it will be particularly bad if ISAF advisory teams do not thoroughly embed within Afghan units, and if the provision of air support, medical evacuation assets, and other specialty enabler services is compromised. Nor will the Afghans be reassured overall or continue to welcome a foreign military presence restricted to bombing al Qaeda or other counterterrorism targets, for that will expose the Afghan people to the risk of terrorist retaliation while doing little to satisfy their need for much more broadly defined security and improved governance.

Moreover, while ISAF forces are thinning out, they will become ever more dependent on the ANSF for ground-level intelligence. Already U.S. and ISAF forces face challenges in collecting intelligence and generating the requisite analysis, the lack of which compromises not only antiterrorism operations but also the capacity to develop the kind of sophisticated political and socioeconomic understanding that the ANSF need if they are to wrest and secure areas from Taliban influence. For example, ISAF's access to and participation in the processes of interrogating and locally reintegrating insurgents who want to come out of the cold must at times be negotiated with the local Afghan National Police commander and National Directorate of Security officials. Such cooperation is not always forthcoming. Similarly, the Afghan Ministry of Interior has sometimes sought to limit ISAF's access to non-ALP militias.[40] Such trends are likely to intensify the further along transition is. Afghan interlocutors, for example, may try to manipulate intelligence in order to eliminate rivals by labeling them as Haqqanis. The subtle interactions between poor governance in a district and Taliban mobilization may go undetected. Such detrimental developments will worsen if the widely alleged conflict between Afghan intelligence and security services goes beyond the inter-agency rivalry that characterizes most countries and shows itself to be a symptom of the broader ethnic rifts afflicting the ANSF.[41]

Similarly, if the government of Afghanistan decides to relegate the international military forces to their bases and rarely calls them out for assistance, such as for night raids, or if the September 2012 restrictions on ISAF-ANSF engagement remain in place, the effectiveness of any continuing international military training will be further undermined. In short, the faster ISAF forces depart before 2014 and the more limited in size and scope their missions are after 2014, the more likely it is that any improvements in Afghan military and police capacities will be jeopardized and chances for stability in the country will be undermined.

A big, disturbing unknown is whether the Afghan National Army will be able to withstand the ethnic factionalization that is already fracturing the institution. The NATO Training Mission in Afghanistan (NTM-A) has worked hard to bring the ethnic balance among the Afghan officer corps closer to what is believed to be the ethnic composition of the overall population. Apparently, until 2008, 70 percent of Afghan kandak commanders were Tajiks, a situation that was resented by Pashtuns.[42] In 2012 ethnic distribution within all senior positions—kandak commanders through generals (ISAF does not separate out kandak commanders in its latest records)—was 42 percent Pashtun, 29 percent Tajik, 13 percent Hazara, 8 percent Uzbek, and 8 percent others.[43] The NTM-A also has been striving to make the entire force ethnically balanced. And while overall that is indeed the case, the ANA still manages to recruit disproportionately low numbers of southern Pashtuns, despite working hard to boost recruitment among this important segment of the population where Taliban presence and mobilization are the strongest. Still, most Pashtuns recruited for the ANA come from central and northern Afghanistan.[44]

The factionalization problems within the Afghan force, however, are more serious than merely the ethnic balance. Deep ethnic fissures and patronage networks run through the Afghan military, with segments of the force loyal to particular top-level commanders rather than to the institution overall or—more important—the government in Kabul.[45] Until mid-2010 the two chief power brokers within the Afghan Ministry of Defense were Minister Abdul Rahim Wardak (a Pashtun) and Chief of Staff of the Army Bismullah Khan Mohammadi (a Tajik and a former lieutenant of the famous northern commander Ahmad Shah Massoud). Mohammadi's network was particularly strong. When Mohammadi became minister of interior in mid-2010, the new chief of staff, General Sher Mohammad Karami (a Pashtun) sought to purge at least some of Mohammadi's networks, such as by quickly replacing corps commanders.[46] The dismissal of both Mohammadi from the Ministry of Interior and Wardak from the Ministry of Defense in August 2012 aroused concern that the new appointees would bring in their own men and get rid of at least some officers associated with the previous power brokers, generating uncertainty within the Afghan National Security Forces. In September 2012, Mohammadi was appointed as the new defense chief, and he will likely seek to reestablish and expand his patronage networks within the Afghan Army.

Not surprisingly, power and loyalty in Afghanistan continue to be attached to individuals rather than institutions. Institutionalization inevitably takes time, and after a decade of international state-building efforts, it remains disappointingly low, partly because the international community often chose to embrace power brokers at the cost of undermining institutional growth. The fragmentation within the Afghan National Army, of course, reflects similar patronage networks and power arrangements within the Afghan political system.

The more fragmented, ethnically riven, and pervaded by patronage networks the political system is and the more conflict escalates among the various factions, the harder it is to insulate the Afghan National Security Forces from a similar intensification of such factionalization. Corruption—both generalized and patronage driven—is also increasingly weakening the Afghan Army. This development is not new, but it may be on the rise.[47] ISAF's adoption of biometric systems, such as iris scanning, has helped to reduce Afghan commanders stealing soldiers' salary and has improved morale. But other problems persist. In some of the best kandaks, excellent soldiers are not being promoted because they do not have influential friends. Conversely, many extra positions, at the level of colonel, for example, are being created so that commanders can give payoffs to their loyal supporters. Soldiers from marginalized groups, without powerful patrons, or simply those who cannot afford to pay a bribe are being repeatedly posted to tough environments whereas their better-positioned compatriots get cushier postings.[48] Clamping down on such corruption is as important as increasing the Afghan National Army numbers.

Diligent efforts are needed to roll back and keep a lid on such factionalization as much as possible. For example, commanders who operate even-handedly across the ethnic groups within the ANA and do not seek to cultivate a circle of ethnic friends should be rewarded and supported by the international community. If they are not, the odds will greatly increase that the Afghan National Security Forces will splinter along ethnic lines after 2014, heightening the likelihood of civil war.

Indeed, it is precisely the reconstitution of the Northern Alliance, capitalizing on Tajik, Uzbek, and Hazara patronage networks within the Afghan National Security Forces, that is the greatest fear of the Taliban. During interrogations, Taliban detainees expressed a general belief that the Taliban cannot win as long as ISAF remains in Afghanistan, but they were also convinced that ISAF would not stay forever. Thus they were very optimistic about defeating the ANSF, in Pashtun areas at minimum. Their principal fear was a bloody protracted war with the Northern Alliance over the control of Northern Afghanistan.[49] Many northern power brokers, commanders, and government officials are of course doing their best to prepare for and reinforce their positions before any such civil war.

Afghan National Police

The Afghan National Police have been notorious both for just such intense ethnic factionalization and patronage fragmentation and for general corruption.[50] Their retention problems and rates of illiteracy, drug use, and desertion are much higher than within the Afghan Army.[51] This also holds true for the theft of equipment. Even though the ANP are increasingly being provided with heavy weapons and now have approximately 5,000 vehicles countrywide, they often suffer from equipment deficiencies.[52] Logistical problems remain acute, especially among Afghan Uniformed Police, which numbered over 85,000 as of March 2012; they are the largest component of the overall police forces and are tasked with delivering on-the-streets security.[53] Often under the sway of local power brokers, many ANP units continue to function essentially as militias. In the worst cases, they exhibit an unwillingness to work with the Afghan government and even the Afghan National Army. Increasingly, ANP commanders, especially at the local level, are prone to reach out to the Taliban in their areas to establish ceasefires and hedge their bets. In at least one instance, a police commander in Farah province defected with eleven of his men to the Taliban. He was recruited precisely because of his connections to the Taliban, with the hope that he would bring some Taliban to the government.[54] As with the Afghan army, many of these problems will be compounded and the overall effort to establish the Afghan Police will be compromised if robust cooperation between the ANP and ISAF forces can no longer take place before and after 2014.

The problems of the Afghan National Police should not be surprising. Historically, Afghanistan has lacked a strong central police force. A national police force existed only briefly during the 1960s and 1970s. The Soviets created some police forces during the 1970s and 1980s, but their purpose was to arrest and interrogate political prisoners, provide internal intelligence, and subvert tribes, not to protect the population.[55] During the 1990s, the vestiges of the police force completely disintegrated.

The post-2002 efforts to create an Afghan police force had a slow start. Between 2002 and 2007, Germany was the lead nation for Afghan police development. But the German effort produced only 2,600 non-commissioned officers and 870 commissioned officers in the first three years.[56] In 2006 the United States took over responsibility for the Afghan Ministry of Interior and for police training. Between 2007 and 2011, the principal training mechanism for the police became the Focused District Development (FDD). In that program, district police forces of the Afghan Uniform Police were taken out of a district, retrained in a regional training facility for between six and eight weeks, and then mentored by ISAF for another two to three months upon return to their district. During the period when the Afghan Uniformed Police were taken out of a district, the Afghan National Civil Order Police (ANCOP)—the gendarmerie—would assume their duties in the district. With more rigorous vetting, a longer training course of twelve to sixteen weeks, and the highest level of international partnering, ANCOP has been a far more competent force. It has been trained to deploy in support of large-scale civil order operations as well as counterinsurgency operations and to be the principal Afghan police interface with the military. As of March 2012, ANCOP numbered close to 17,500 personnel.[57] However, many ANCOP officers are currently being used for lower-level functions, such as staffing new checkpoints, rather than being deployed to more problematic areas.[58]

The Focused District Development program suffered from many challenges. The recruiting and training standards were low. In the United States, for example, more than 90 percent of applicants for the police forces are rejected—that is how selective the police departments can afford to be—and the basic police training is at least six months. Obviously, such standards were impossible to replicate in Afghanistan, nor are they the norm in the rest of Central and South Asia, including India. In the region as whole, the training and overall quality of police forces tend to be abysmal, and the police are often implicated in crime. As a result populations usually do not have positive relations with their police forces. But the abuse by the Afghan police is particularly high and the population's dislike of the police intense, even by South Asia measures.

The FDD program originally envisioned an integrated approach where police reform in a district would be combined with other efforts to improve governance in the district, such as in the justice sector, development projects, and public works. But since the other activities take much longer to implement and gain traction than the six to eight weeks allocated to the FDD, the effort soon became almost entirely focused on police training.[59] ISAF's selection of the districts to receive the FDD police retraining became predominantly driven by counterinsurgency imperatives, such as the need to secure districts along major roads, and few considerations were given to how much capacity the district had to improve in other governance and development areas; nor were the politics, factionalization, and power arrangements factored into the district selection process. Such flawed selection criteria undermined the effectiveness of efforts to considerably reduce the vices infecting the police force.

On the positive side, the Afghan National Police's antiterrorism capacity, such as their ability to detect bombs and respond to spectacular Taliban and Haqqani attacks, has increased dramatically. The performance of the police special forces in responding to the April 2012 attack on the Afghan parliament and the June 2012 attack on the Spozhmai Hotel near Kabul was considerably better than their response to the attack on the Intercontinental Hotel in Kabul in June 2011.[60] In the more recent incidents, the ANP and other ANSF units were able to handle the situation largely on their own, both in terms of the tactical operations and command and control, with essentially limited ISAF backup. In the 2011 incident, the terrorists remained in control of the target site until ISAF joined in. When the ANSF, including the ANP, perform well, their legitimacy with Afghans grows. Thus the successful response of the Afghan commandos to the April 15 Kabul attack stimulated a spontaneous support-your-troops campaign throughout Afghanistan. Public appreciation, in turn, motivates the troops to risk their lives and reduce abusive behavior toward the citizenry. It is also in the realm of counterterrorism that the population most trusts the Afghan police, even if overall trust in the institution is very limited.[61]

But critically, the Afghan National Police continue to lack an adequate anticrime capacity, and the anticrime training they receive is minimal, bordering on nonexistent. Instead, the ANP are more of a light counterinsurgency and SWAT-like counterterrorism force. There are several reasons for the lack of focus on anticrime capacity. First, anticrime training takes time, and the United States and ISAF lack expeditionary police trainers. If soldiers train policemen—as has been the case in Afghanistan—they produce paramilitary units. Moreover, the lack of literacy among ANP recruits compromises their ability to record information, investigate a crime, and build evidence for prosecution, which makes training for civilian policing and anticrime purposes difficult. Giving a paramilitary emphasis to the Afghan police has been justified by the need to fight the insurgency, as well as by the misguided notion that policemen will start performing anticrime functions after the insurgency has ended.[62]

Yet crime—murders, robberies, and extortion—is the bane of many Afghans' daily existence, a fact that the Taliban is happy to harp on. The inability of the Afghan government to respond to crime (as well as its own participation in crime, of course) thus allows the Taliban to impose its own brutal forms of order and develop a foothold in Afghan communities. Operating on different evidentiary standards, the Taliban is not constrained by illiteracy in meting out justice. Meanwhile, most Afghan police are not familiar with the Afghan laws they are supposed to enforce.[63] Nonetheless, they are aware that kidnapping, extortion, bribery, and land theft are both formally illegal and inconsistent with traditional customs. But the bigger problem is that Afghan police have been and remain notorious for perpetrating many crimes.

The Afghan Border Police are Afghanistan's law enforcement arm responsible for safeguarding the Afghan border and providing security for a corridor of up to fifty kilometers inside Afghanistan's territory.

Notoriously corrupt and pervaded by smuggling and power patronage networks, the institution has demonstrated little capacity to accomplish either of its tasks.[64] The difficult and extensive border is and for a long time will remain completely porous. With an overall strength of about 25,000 men, lacking noncommissioned officers and having received the least training and partnering, the Afghan Border Police often function primarily to regulate cross-border smuggling and extort the Afghan population in the border areas.[65]

Nonetheless, given the high likelihood that Haqqani and Taliban safe havens in Pakistan will not be shut down before or soon after 2014, the Afghan Border Police can have a vital role in reducing terrorist and insurgent infiltration. At least that component of the agency's training should be intensified as much as possible. Some progress had been achieved: by the summer of 2012, the amount of cargo screened at the important border crossing at Torkham increased from less than 1 percent to 24 percent in a span of two years.[66] But achieving 100 percent screening at a border post is almost never possible, and smugglers simply divert their routes away from a heavily screened post anyway.

As discussed in chapter 9, achieving reductions in custom losses at the border would help boost Afghanistan's GDP and offset some of the economic difficulties on the horizon after 2014. In that too, the border police can play a critical role. But reforming border police forces, reducing custom revenue losses, improving the caliber of border guards, and tightening the border are among the most difficult tasks within the always enormously challenging process of police reform. Even countries with overall highly effective police forces still struggle with border control. The most realistic priority for the Afghan Border Police thus may be to focus on developing good intelligence networks on terrorist and insurgent infiltration.

It is important that the international community continue to demand credible progress against ethnic factionalization and general corruption within the Afghan National Police overall. Careful assessment will be required to determine whether personnel shifts and dismissals are indeed designed to reduce corruption or merely mask ethnic and patronage rifts and the targeted removal of ethnic opponents and members of rival networks. It is equally imperative that the international community make a far more concerted effort to create some anticrime capacity within the police, although such efforts will inevitably be constrained by rifts, tensions, and power and patronage arrangements in the broader political system. A focus on achieving progress in one location—such as a major city—would be an appropriate start. Whichever the city chosen, Kabul's cooperation would be essential, and for the international community to obtain it would likely require a long period of negotiations since Kabul would have to be willing to go after the city's government and criminal power brokers. If crime reduction in a major city could be achieved, it would send a powerful signal to the Afghan population than some progress in suppressing crime can be made by the government, and not just by the Taliban, and that the government is finally becoming at least somewhat responsive to the needs and concerns of the people.

For some of these serious challenges that plague the Afghan National Security Forces there are no easy solutions. But one thing is clear: the faster the international community leaves Afghanistan and the more it reduces its presence, particularly its military presence, the more the negative dynamics in the still very problematical Afghan security environment will be intensified, and the fewer means and reduced leverage the international community will have to combat them.

Negotiations with the Taliban: Still a Question Mark

The long-term U.S.-Afghanistan Strategic Partnership Agreement notwithstanding, a U.S. and ISAF rush out of Afghanistan will also hamper negotiations with the Taliban. Driven by a determination to avoid negotiating from a position of weakness and waiting until Taliban capacity on the battlefield was degraded first, the United States hesitated a long time before reluctantly agreeing to begin them.[67] But the ensuing talks with the Taliban—and reportedly also at least feelers with the Haqqanis (before the United States designated them as a terrorist group in September 2012, thus significantly complicating any possibility of including them in further negotiations)—have mainly amounted to talking about talking.[68] Despite repeated contact with various factions of the Taliban, talks have been no more than initial explorations of what confidence-building measures could look like.[69] And even these initial overtures have stalled.

The Taliban's willingness to seriously negotiate has also been lukewarm and conflicted. The group has repeatedly called for quick implementation of confidence-building measures. The United States agreed to allow the Taliban set up a negotiating office in Qatar, and the Taliban backed off its demand that all of its members be removed from the UN blacklist (which prohibited their international travel and banking and other activities) before negotiations could proceed further.[70] An agreement was also apparently reached on the release of Taliban prisoners by the United States in exchange for releasing the one American soldier the Taliban holds.[71] But in March 2012, supposedly in frustration over the slow release of prisoners from Guantanamo, the Taliban suspended negotiations.[72] Then in August 2012, an active senior Taliban commander, Mullah Agha Jan Motasim, publicly called for restarting the talks, "welcoming important preliminary steps."[73] If genuine, this Taliban move might have been in response to a reported U.S. concession to transfer five senior Taliban commanders incarcerated in Guantanamo to a facility in Qatar, to be supervised by the Qatari government—even though the Taliban had yet to release the captured U.S. soldier, Sergeant Bowe Bergdahl.[74] But the Taliban did not respond and continued with the suspension of the talks.

For the United States, a Taliban prisoner release is legally complicated and politically sensitive for the White House, as it would likely be opposed and exploited by the Republicans on grounds that the released Taliban commanders could return to active fighting.[75] And the Afghan government would prefer that any Taliban detainees released from Guantanamo, in particular any senior commanders, be sent to Afghanistan, where the Kabul government could negotiate with them more directly and have greater control over them.[76]

However, as of this writing (fall 2012), two issues have thus far proved to be far more difficult sticking points in the negotiations than the prisoner release: how to include the Karzai government in the negotiations and whether the Taliban will publicly break with al Qaeda.

The United States has insisted all along that the Karzai government be part of the negotiations. Fully understanding that much of the Karzai government's strength comes from the U.S. and international support, the Taliban has refused to talk with Kabul before it reaches its own separate agreement with the United States. The group thus talks about first solving the "external dimension of the Afghanistan conflict"—what it calls the "U.S. occupation" of Afghanistan—before dealing with the "internal dimension of the conflict"—namely, a new political settlement within Afghanistan.[77] Such a sequential approach would, of course, enormously strengthen the Taliban's hand in any future internal Afghan negotiations. Understanding the large threat such a negotiating sequence would pose to the survival of the Kabul regime and perhaps to most of the U.S. and international efforts in Afghanistan, the United States thus far has balked at that approach.

Equally frustrating for the United States has been the Taliban's unwillingness to publicly break with al Qaeda. Elements of the Kandahari Taliban, in particular, may well have learned that their association with al Qaeda ultimately cost them their power. Indeed, different sets of interviews with Taliban members present powerful evidence that the Taliban has become disenchanted with al Qaeda. A Taliban commander interviewed by the scholar and former British and UN diplomat Michael Semple suggested that at least 70 percent of the Taliban were angry at al Qaeda and considered it a "plague."[78] Taliban detainees interviewed by ISAF exhibited similar attitudes: they indicated that in most regions of Afghanistan—Nuristan and Kunar provinces in eastern Afghanistan being exceptions—the Taliban has no interest in associating with al Qaeda because it exposes Taliban members to intensified ISAF targeting and because al Qaeda personnel are no longer adept fighters.[79] The Taliban detainees also indicated that any outside groups, such as al Qaeda or the Islamic Movement of Uzbekistan, can only operate in Kabul with the Taliban's permission.[80] The death of bin Laden further weakened the Taliban–al Qaeda connections.

But so far, the Taliban leadership has refused to issue a declaration denouncing al Qaeda. The group has also suggested that no such declaration is necessary because no al Qaeda is present in Afghanistan today, citing U.S. officials to back up that claim; it has hinted, however, that it might make such a declaration later in the process in exchange for some form of political recognition.[81] In addition, the Taliban has publicly stated that it wants to have peaceful relations with other countries: "We said we will not allow anyone to use the soil of Afghanistan against any country, that we need cooperation of the international community in order to economically advance our country in all fields—cultural, education, and other fields, technical."[82] Of course, the fact that, in the same TV interview, the Taliban denied ever permitting al Qaeda to operate out of Afghanistan did little to enhance the credibility of its other declarations.[83]

Even if the Taliban has actually determined that association with al Qaeda will continue to prove extremely costly and risky, even if it has indeed soured on al Qaeda, it nonetheless may want to avoid a complete break with al Qaeda, for fear that reneging on its debts to its global jihadi brothers will isolate the movement too much, no matter how locally oriented the Taliban's southern and northern elements are. Indeed, the Taliban commander interviewed by Semple disclosed that while the Taliban did not need al Qaeda in Afghanistan and Pakistan to reinforce its military resources, the Taliban leadership did not want to openly renounce al Qaeda for fear that such a move "might alienate some Islamist constituencies."[84]

Apart from these difficult and fundamental negotiating positions, the Taliban's ambivalence toward negotiations has likely also been driven by internal factors. The Taliban may well fear that overt negotiations would alienate its middle-level commanders and make them unruly— an outcome that ISAF would love to see, believing it would fracture the operational capacity of the movement.[85] (But such fracturing would also decrease the prospect that *any* negotiated agreement could hold.) The Taliban's March 2012 decision to suspend the talks, for example, could also have been a maneuver to pacify disquieted young, radical, middle-level commanders who do not support negotiations. And from a strategic perspective, of course, the Taliban leadership may simply be running down the clock to the 2014 transition by dragging out the negotiations.[86]

The Afghan polity is equally conflicted about negotiations with the Taliban, with some segments deeply opposed. The May 2010 Peace Jirga set up by President Karzai to generate public support for negotiations failed to accomplish its stated purpose. Instead, it turned out to be more a political cover rather than a meaningful process to integrate the voices of various sectors and groups of Afghan society into the negotiations and reconciliation process. Similarly, the High Peace Council created to facilitate negotiations with the Taliban has failed to gain any real traction and momentum. Although exchanges between the Karzai government and the High Peace Council have taken place, the Taliban thus far has maintained its principal negotiating position of talking first exclusively with the United States and deferring any potential negotiations with the Karzai government until after a deal is struck with the United States.

Not surprisingly, despite U.S. insistence that it will only negotiate with the Kabul government present at the negotiating table, both Kabul and Islamabad have been paranoid about the possibility that they will be bypassed. President Karzai has felt extremely threatened by the Taliban preference to negotiate bilaterally with the United States. Despite Washington's extensive efforts to bring Kabul to the table and assuage the suspicions of the Arg Palace, President Karzai does not trust Washington to refrain from signing a separate deal with the Taliban that will leave him high and dry. Although Washington continues to insist that any negotiated deal must be Afghan led and that the U.S. role is only one of a facilitator, Kabul has not been persuaded.

Islamabad similarly fears being left out of any negotiated deal. As discussed in chapters 3 and 10, given its connections to and influence over the various Afghan insurgent groups, Pakistan remains a key spoiler in any negotiations. Always wary of India, Pakistan is primarily determined to ensure the establishment of a friendly government in Kabul and to promote that outcome through insurgent proxies under its sway.

Thus both Afghanistan and Pakistan have attempted to assert greater control over negotiations. Accordingly, Pakistan has arrested Taliban interlocutors like Mullah Abdul Ghani Baradar under the guise of counterterrorism and has been reluctant to grant Afghan negotiators from the High Peace Council access to him.[87] Kabul, for its part, leaked the identity of a U.S.-Taliban interlocutor, Tayyab Agha, to indicate its determination that all negotiations and access go through the Arg Palace.[88]

Furthermore, international actors, including Turkey, Saudi Arabia, the United Arab Emirates, and Germany, have all tried to play a prominent role in the negotiations at various times. The result has been many different processes and initiatives happening at the same time, making an already opaque negotiating situation even murkier.

Nor has the High Peace Council managed to assuage the misgivings and fears of many Afghan groups that a negotiated outcome would be detrimental to their interests and jeopardize their security. Foremost among the concerned have been the non-Pashtun groups, such as Tajiks and Uzbeks in the north and the Hazaras, who have strong memories of Taliban oppression and who achieved unprecedented political, economic, and military power in post-Taliban Afghanistan. Key northern leaders may prefer a war to a deal that they expect could compromise their security and power. Many in the north are actively arming themselves and resurrecting their patronage networks and militias.[89] Those fears did not lessen after the Taliban, most likely the Haqqani network, assassinated the leader of the High Peace Council, Burhanuddin Rabbani, a prominent northerner and the former president of Afghanistan, in September 2011. Given Rabbani's role in the civil war in the 1990s and the bloody persecution many Pashtuns suffered at his hands in the tit-for-tat brutality of the civil war, the

Taliban considered his appointment an affront.[90] The appointment of his son Salahuddin Rabbani to replace the murdered leader once again catered to the interests of the northern groups but did not please the Taliban.

Similarly, women's groups are deeply afraid that a negotiated deal will sell their rights short once again.[91] Many other civil society groups equally lament being left out of the process.[92] Afraid too are Kandahari Durrani elites, who during the 1990s suffered the Taliban's wrath for centuries-old oppression of the Ghilzai. Thus few are satisfied with the performance of the High Peace Council that President Karzai designated to integrate the various Afghan voices into the negotiations and to promote a broad-based societal reconciliation.

Given these reactions, serious negotiations with the Taliban, if they do take place, may require a very long time—most likely years—before they can bring about any sort of a settlement beyond a mere fig leaf for the West's departure from Afghanistan.

The more limited the international community's presence is, the more limited its leverage in such negotiations will be. The Taliban's negotiation strategy thus may be to engage in preliminary talks without giving up anything, while waiting for any serious negotiations until after 2014. The signing of the U.S.-Afghanistan Strategic Partnership Agreement was therefore an important signal to the Taliban that simply waiting it out may not work since the international community and its militaries may yet find the will to stay robustly present in Afghanistan after 2014. Before January 2012, many of the interrogated Taliban detainees believed that their control of at least southern Afghanistan was inevitable and impending.[93] However, after the signing of the Strategic Partnership Agreement in May 2012, at least one senior Taliban commander subsequently interviewed by Semple admitted that the Taliban remained far from achieving its objectives of winning in Afghanistan as long as ISAF troops remained in the country. Victory, he averred, would require divine intervention, and the Taliban's recapture of Kabul was a distant prospect.[94]

Ultimately, the shape and content of any negotiations will be linked to what happens on the military battlefield and on each side's assessments of its military strength and prospects for achieving a better deal through military means. The Taliban thus does not need to rush to conclude negotiations or commit to substantially relinquishing its power, such as by disarming, before 2014. Moreover, if the U.S. presence after 2014 is essentially limited to narrowly defined counterterrorism missions, such as against al Qaeda and perhaps also the Haqqani network, the ability of the continuing international presence to change the calculus of the Taliban and force it to the negotiating table will be limited.

Not much is known at this point about what the Taliban might settle for. Certainly, it will be loath to give up any influence it already has in large parts of the country. The Taliban commander interviewed by Semple stated that it was difficult to predict what the Taliban could agree to, but rejected "what has been offered many times—surrender and slavish bowing to the authority of their enemies."[95] Taliban detainees interrogated by ISAF were more specific, indicating that the Taliban, in addition to insisting on the departure of all foreign forces, demanded changes to the Afghan constitution, dramatic changes in the leadership of the Afghan government, and an end to the corruption of the Afghan government.[96] At other times, Taliban negotiators have made more opaque (and vacuous) statements, suggesting, for example, that the Taliban's principal goal is "independence of Afghanistan and formation of a government on the basis of the will of the people so they have a government in the framework of their national values, religious values and they live as free people like other people of the world live."[97]

The Taliban may be leery of simply accepting to be allowed to participate in elections, especially if only at the local level, although the interviewed Taliban commander indicated that if the Taliban falls short of taking national power through military means, it may have to settle for functioning as an organized party within the country.[98] At other times, when asked about participating in elections, Taliban negotiators have avoided answering the question, responding only that after the Taliban has reached a deal with the United States, "All Afghans [would] come together to consult each other about the formation of [an] Afghan inclusive and Islamic government in Afghanistan which is based on the aspirations and will of the people of Afghanistan so all the people will feel their participation in the government."[99] Although such proclamations in principle resonate with the Afghan people, many are skeptical of such statements coming from the Taliban. Moreover, the Taliban's strengths often lie far more in being a spoiler rather than in being able to offer a forward-looking political, economic, and social agenda.[100] However, it can capitalize on memories of the security it provided in the 1990s and its current ability to outperform the Afghan government in imposing order and justice, albeit brutally.

The Taliban would also face some tough dilemmas in agreeing to a compromise with Kabul—for example, accepting the Afghan constitution or agreeing to a power-sharing deal.[101] Such a promise and political bargain with Kabul might discredit the Taliban leadership in the eyes of many of its fighters as well as in the eyes of the broader population, to whom it has castigated Kabul's venal, predatory, and unjust behavior. This may explain the Taliban's proclamation that the Afghan government must end corruption before a deal can be struck, even if such a posture is simply a public relations tactic.[102] Similarly, whether the Taliban will be able to abide by the international community's red lines, including breaking with al Qaeda, remains a question. During the negotiation process and in any deal, the Taliban can agree to many things, but will it honor those commitments? The smaller and more narrowly defined the presence of the international community in Afghanistan after 2014, the smaller will be its capacity to roll back any Taliban violations of a peace deal. And such violations do not have to be blatant takeovers of territory; after 2014, as now, the Taliban can exercise a lot of influence through far more subtle forms of intimidation and gradually accrete more power while chipping away at the authority of the Afghan government.

Notwithstanding the difficulties and inadequacies of the process so far, negotiating with the Taliban could provide an opportunity for improving governance. But that will be the case only if the deliberations on the future of Afghanistan (as distinct from the negotiations on the disposition of the military forces) are designed as an inclusive process that brings in multiple political stakeholders, including non-Pashtun ethnic groups and civil society representatives. Such groups would also have to include not just women's and Western-style nongovernmental organizations but also representatives of marginalized tribes and Islamist movements. To the extent that Washington and the international community or Kabul seek to strike a deal with the Taliban at all costs and the negotiations become close-to-the-vest bargaining among the United States, Afghan power brokers, Pakistan's intelligence services, and key Taliban factions, they will merely reward the Taliban's military tenacity and produce neither improvements in governance nor peace and stability.

Structuring negotiations in a way that broadens political representation in Afghanistan will be very difficult, however. The negotiating process can be easily subverted by a myriad of spoilers—from factions within the Taliban, to the country's ethnic factions, to a mistrusting Arg Palace, to tribal factions and power cliques within the non-Taliban Pashtuns, to neighbors—Pakistan in particular. Genuine reconciliation and progress toward improving conditions in war-torn Afghanistan will require extraordinarily skillful diplomacy and coordination among multiple actors and on multiple levels. And fundamentally, it will require that promoting good governance is elevated to a level comparable to that of military considerations.

What a Collapse Could Look Like

If the current political order and security arrangements cannot be sustained and civil war does break out, the odds are low that the ensuing conflict will approximate a neatly delineated war between clearly defined groups along clearly defined lines on the map.[103] Unlike in the mid- and late 1990s, when the Taliban was steadily pushing its way from the south, there is unlikely to be an easily recognizable zone of battle moving north past the Shomali Plain and across the Hindu Kush. Nor will the conflict quickly escalate to the level of killing that Afghanistan experienced from the late 1970s through the 1990s. In 1978 an estimated 40,000 Afghans were killed, followed by 80,000 in 1979. By 1987 between 1 million and 1.5 million Afghans, or about 9 percent of the population, had died in the war.[104] Deaths due to disease and starvation were also high among Afghan refugees. In comparison, between several thousand and 20,000 Afghans are believed to have died in 2001 as a result of the U.S. intervention.[105]

In a post-2014 civil war, the fighting can be expected to be highly localized and complex. Some locations, including perhaps in the surge areas of the south, may well remain isolated security pockets as a result of strong ANSF presence and perhaps sufficiently effective governance. Other places, such as the province of Balkh and most of the province Herat, also have a chance of remaining rather stable and experiencing little fighting since key local government officials or power brokers have these areas firmly in their grip. Elsewhere, such as in parts of Kandahar and in Nangarhar, the contest may be as much between the Taliban and the Afghan National Security Forces as among various Durrani Pashtun power brokers linked to the Afghan government. There may also be fighting among the "new warlords" and power brokers who have emerged in that region over the past decade by providing services to the international community. Parts of the north, including Kunduz and Baghlan, have a high chance of blowing up into vicious ethnic conflicts. Kabul would likely be among the last places to succumb to any future civil war; but if it does, the bloodbath is less likely to come from the capital being shelled from the outside, like during the 1990s, but rather from fierce street fighting. Rightly or not, many Pashtuns in Kabul feel that they were dispossessed of their land there by the influx of Tajiks after 2002, and many are poised to settle the score. A splintering of the ANSF would rapidly fan such civil war fires, with the Afghan National Police, Afghan Local Police, and other militias being the first to fall apart and start supporting rival power brokers.

One big question is, can whatever pockets of security, micro-deals, and micro-accommodations that might exist in such a future scenario remain sufficiently insulated from external fighting and contestation elsewhere in the country? At least some locales will be highly vulnerable to security problems leaking in from the outside. Since many patronage networks run throughout the country, there may well be only a few communities and areas in Afghanistan able to avoid being drawn into surrounding conflicts. Much will depend not only on the quality and robustness of the security forces in the areas—whether the ANSF, the ALP, or warlords' militias—but also on the quality and robustness of local governance.

Of course, the increasing instability will also leak beyond Afghanistan's borders. Conflicts and outright civil war will make it irresistible for outside actors, including Pakistan, Iran, India, Russia, the Central Asian countries, and China, to once again cultivate their favored proxies to prosecute at least their minimal objectives in Afghanistan and the region. Because of its counterterrorism and other concerns, the United States is also unlikely to refrain from sponsoring and supporting its own favored groups among the warring Afghans. Whether direct or indirect, U.S. involvement on the Afghan battlefield will intensify the conflict dynamics in some areas and perhaps reinforce some of the pockets of security elsewhere. And in turn, the outsiders' rivalries in Afghanistan will spill beyond that country and intensify their competition in other territories and functional domains as well.

But there is also the possibility of a military coup after 2014, not a rare phenomenon in South Asia. Even with all its outstanding problems, the Afghan National Army will be the most trained institution in

Afghanistan. One coup scenario could feature a revolt by the increasingly professional mid-level commanders whose promotions are frustrated by their politicized bosses. Another possibility is that Afghan National Army commanders, or at least commanders of a particular ethnic faction within it, may well consider military rule preferable to a civil war. Given how extremely dissatisfied with the current political system many Afghans are, overwhelmingly seeing it as an exclusionary mafia rule, they may even welcome a coup. Already, calls for a strongman rule are not infrequent in Afghanistan.[106] But the different groups at odds with each other—Ghilzai Pashtuns, Durrani Pashtuns, Tajiks, Uzbeks, and Hazaras—and the many subgroups under these broad categories are hardly likely to agree on who that strongman should be.

President Karzai is no doubt conscious of the coup specter. For a long time his relationship with the Afghan National Security Forces was at arm's length at best, despite the fact that at other times he has fired various ANSF leaders in order to break up their patronage networks and has appointed new leaders more likely to be loyal to him, or at least without the same level of independent power. The summer 2012 reshuffle of key cabinet security and intelligence posts was yet another example of his approach to controlling the ANSF. Rather than trying to develop his own strong and direct control over the Afghan National Security Forces, he has—typically—preferred to operate by dividing and co-opting his potential political rivals within the ANSF.

So what the battlefield would look like in 2015 and after remains very much undetermined. The disposition of international forces throughout the country at the time is likely to be highly dependent on the political and governance situation in Kabul and the public support it stimulates or discourages in the Western capitals. Clearly, Western presence will be much reduced, and the mission of U.S. and Western soldiers will be much more circumscribed in scope—but exactly how has not yet been resolved. Such military decisions will have an important impact on further security and political dynamics in Afghanistan. The military situation may also be affected by any serious negotiations with the Taliban that might get under way between now and then. But of course such political variables are themselves part of the feedback process wherein what has happened on the battlefield is highly determinative of who wins the political power plays, who sits at the negotiating table, and who prevails. Indeed, it is the iron grip of these feedback loops on events that makes the analysis here of the prospects for transition from mostly U.S. control to Afghan control also central to the overall assessment of U.S. policy.

One thing, however, is clear. The faster ISAF forces reduce their presence before 2014 and the more limited in size and scope their missions are after 2014, the more any improvements in Afghan military and police capacities will be jeopardized and any chances for stability in the country will be undermined. But equally, without major improvements in governance, it is difficult to see how lasting stability after 2014 could be achieved, whatever the balance of remaining military forces on the ground.

12

What, If Anything, Can Still Be Done?

The year 2014 will mark a critical juncture in Afghanistan's odyssey. After more than a decade of arduous fighting and political involvement, the U.S. and international presence there will be significantly reduced and circumscribed. Although the international community has committed itself not to abandon Afghanistan as it did in the 1990s, the onus will be on the Afghan government to provide for the security of the country, its economic development, and governance that attempts to meet the needs of the Afghan people. Difficult challenges, major unresolved questions, and worrisome trends surround all three sets of processes. The biggest hole in the U.S. strategy and international efforts to stabilize the country is the failure to adequately address the country's fractured and brittle political system and very poor governance.

The fundamental deficiency is not that Afghan governing practices fail to match those of the West. Nor is the need to improve governance in Afghanistan about imposing Western values and processes. The fundamental problem is that the post-2002 governance in Afghanistan has become so predatory, capricious, and rapacious that the Afghan people find the current system profoundly illegitimate. The current political dispensation in Afghanistan deeply offends them, crushes their aspirations, and thus stimulates intense desires for a different political order.

Afghans are thirsty for sovereignty. Many, especially those living in highly contested areas, are tired of the foreigners' presence. At the same time, however, Afghans are also deeply afraid of the post-2014 future. A disintegration of the country into yet another civil war is on everyone's mind. Indeed, various preparations for a possible civil war are under way. Ethnic tensions are at the highest level in ten years, with the alignments and antagonisms being exploited by powerful patrons who are resurrecting local militias. In this context of great uncertainty, the dominant tendency is to operate on the basis of short time horizons and seek to maximize power and profit before it all comes down.

Indeed, serious questions remain about the capacity and coherence of the Afghan National Security Forces and the likelihood that they will fracture along ethnic lines and patronage networks after 2014. The economic condition of Afghanistan also will be precarious for years to come. Its mineral riches and visions of a potential New Silk Road notwithstanding, Afghanistan is almost certain to experience a severe economic shock after 2014 as a result of the contraction of international resources flowing into the country.

The destabilizing political processes in the country—from ethnic mobilization to the increasingly narrow and exclusionary nature of patronage networks—and overwhelmingly poor governance are even more disconcerting. Afghans are deeply alienated from a government and power structures they see as abusive and unaccountable. Many speak of living under mafia rule.

In contested localities and in communities deeply divided along patronage, tribal, or ethnic lines, poor governance easily undermines any security improvements and allows for—even creates—new instability. Corrupt and incompetent government officials are rarely fired or punished for their misbehavior; mostly they are just posted to another area.

The Afghans with whom I talked during my trips to Afghanistan over the years despise the impunity and abusiveness that have characterized the political dispensation of the past decade. They are outraged by the nepotism and clientelism that prevail, even if they are at times susceptible to such practices themselves. They crave accountability and justice. Afghans may be currently stuck with the new and old warlords, many empowered by the international community and appointed by Kabul, but they are also fed up with them. And their dissatisfaction with the current political order provides fertile ground for the Taliban to mobilize and remain entrenched.

Most Afghans overwhelmingly long for peace and security. They also hunger for justice, a say in how they are ruled, and accountability from those who rule them. But during times of intense conflict and great uncertainty, they hedge their bets on all sides, whether with the Taliban or with local power brokers—even as they dislike them. In a highly contested and volatile environment, people frequently desire less uncertainty, even if the price of reduced uncertainty is repression—as long as that repression is stable and predictable. Thus, in large areas of Afghanistan, many find the capricious and unpredictable brutality of the power brokers they have experienced since 2002 even more difficult to adjust to than the stable and predictable, if severe, brutality of the Taliban of the 1990s. But of course, what Afghans really and ideally want is not just predictability and stability but also accountability and fairness.

Unfortunately, the legacy of governance that the international community hands over to the Afghans is the weakest among all the elements of the transition and the overall stabilization strategy in Afghanistan. The international community's position on governance has been ambivalent and has failed to embrace and energize the aspirations of the Afghan people. Its strategy has thus oscillated between tolerating corruption for the sake of other goals, battlefield shortcuts, and exigencies—with the justification that Afghans are used to corruption anyway—or confronting it head on but with little effectiveness. Even when the international community has periodically mustered the will to focus on governance, it has found its task hard going and often has quickly given up. Due to frustration, the sheer enormity of the undertaking, and continuing conflicts with short-term expedients, Washington, ISAF, and the international community have often chosen to ignore corruption and justify that decision as prioritizing stability. Increasingly, with the 2014 handover approaching, goals for improving governance in Afghanistan and reducing corruption have been repeatedly lowered and deemphasized. But since corruption and the lack of rule of law are major sources of Afghans' anger with their government, and therefore key to the Taliban's ability to mobilize support, it is extremely doubtful that additional insurgent gains or a full-scale civil war after 2014 can be avoided without addressing at least the most egregious forms of corruption.

Many of these negative trends are compounded by Afghanistan's meddlesome neighbors. Pakistan in particular remains a deeply problematic factor in efforts to stabilize the country's future. Even though Afghans from all walks of life and all ethnic groups demand and expect the United States to stop Pakistan's interfering in Afghanistan's affairs once and for all, the United States and the international community are unlikely to develop such a capacity between now and 2014. Uncertainties about Afghanistan's future are only likely to further harden Pakistan's determination to cultivate proxies in Afghanistan and subvert processes it cannot control or sees as inconsistent with its interests. Pakistan has thus far proven cleverly resistant to pressure from Washington. While engaging with Pakistan—persuading and rewarding it for good behavior as well as cajoling and pressuring it—clearly needs to be a key priority for U.S. engagement in the region before 2014 and well beyond, it is unlikely to suddenly start producing vastly different outcomes. Yet if Afghanistan can get its own house in order and significantly improve its governance, it will be far less vulnerable to troubles stirred up by Pakistan. Indeed, in the likely continuing absence of robust cooperation from Pakistan, it is all the more imperative that Afghanistan become more internally resilient—by improving its governance and thus increasing the legitimacy of central and local rule with the Afghan people.

A complete post-2014 crash is not inevitable. Afghans are afraid of a civil war. They are also weary of it. The past decade for many Afghans, despite the battles with the Taliban insurgents, featured considerable improvement in the lives of many, expanding their social and economic opportunities. Even those poor Afghans whose lives have involved only eking out a bare existence as back-and-forth fighting and Taliban intimidation continued to ravage their homes do not want to see their hardships augmented by a full-blown civil war.

Many in the educated and energetic generation that has come of age over the decade exhibit the capacity to rise above ethnic factionalization and narrow, self-interested profit maximization. Many of these young people, mostly living in major Afghan cities, particularly Kabul, speak of willingness to take on the massive challenges in their country, of suppressing ethnic tensions, improving governance and the delivery of public goods, and strengthening accountability. The ideas they put forth include devolving power from Kabul to the provinces and districts, such as allowing for local taxation and elections for lower-level government officials. They propose reforms to end the current, distortive, single nontransferable vote system to allow the formation of political parties and to reduce electoral corruption. With passion they also call for ending the current culture of impunity and bringing to justice warlords, power brokers, and criminals—including those at the highest levels of the government and with the greatest power—by subjecting them to the rule of law and removing them from government positions. Many of these young Afghans are very impressive and inspiring.

Obviously, however, should the young reformers ever be in a position to implement their aspirations, they will constitute a huge threat to those power brokers and businessmen who benefit enormously from the current system. Will the voices of the young reformers have a near-term impact on policy? How many will be co-opted into the system and succumb to family pressures to deliver patronage handouts to relatives or pursue other self-regarding power and profit rewards? How many will be intimidated by the power brokers or the Taliban? And how many will stay in Afghanistan instead of seeking a better future abroad? Often the international community in Afghanistan inadvertently undermines the potential reformers by embracing their antithesis: both the old and young power brokers. The international community proclaims the power brokers to be their good friends, requests that they take care of things, and rewards them with resources, attention, and highly visible regard.

Afghanistan's future is not predetermined, and the international community's policy of building up the Afghan National Security Forces as much as possible before the 2014 handover and continuing to engage with Afghanistan militarily, diplomatically, and economically after 2014 still remains a plausible path to a stable Afghanistan. The exact scope and shape of the post-2014 engagement are yet to be determined, and they will have an important impact on the stability of Afghanistan. The United States and the international community continue to have very important interests in Afghanistan and the region. These include continuing counterterrorism operations, maintaining the credibility of the United States and international community, and protecting the basic welfare of the Afghan people, given that the United States has so radically interfered in their lives. Critically, those interests also include fostering stability in Pakistan. A strategy that in effect would abandon stability and state-building objectives for Afghanistan also ignores the serious and highly likely risk that an unstable Afghanistan will be like a dangerous ulcer leaking threats into Pakistan and diverting the attention of its leaders from Pakistan's massive internal problems. An unstable Afghanistan will thus further destabilize Pakistan and, as a result, the entire Central and South Asian region. The current international strategy can still work, and there are really no alternatives to stabilizing Afghanistan and thus protecting U.S. and international interests, thereby vindicating the large investments of blood and treasure made by the international community and the Afghan people.

The international community needs to make the transition process as judicious, orderly, and unrushed as possible. This includes continuing to support Afghan security forces with training, critical specialty enablers, and embedded U.S. and international forces to provide them a sufficiently robust advisory capacity on the battlefield after 2014. Maintaining restrictions on ISAF-ANSF interactions below the battalion level will not be conducive to effective counterinsurgency or to training and standing up Afghan National Security Forces. And critically, the international community needs to urge and demand, with more resolve and commitment than before, improvements in governance in Afghanistan. Up till now, the international community's insistence on better governance from its Afghan interlocutors has been meek and fickle at best: the risks of forcing confrontations with Afghan power brokers have always seemed too great to U.S. and international policymakers. But in the absence of considerable improvements to governance in Afghanistan, it is hard to see how the stabilization and state-building efforts there will not fall apart after 2014, unless the new order in Afghanistan comes merely from the barrel of a gun—either that of a local warlord or a coup's commanding general.

Finding the wherewithal to address these imperatives will be hard. The sacrifices have been great, and Western publics are understandably tired of seeing their sons and daughters, brothers and sisters, and friends die in a faraway land with progress looking so elusive and uncertain. But the faster the United States draws down militarily, the more it restricts its mission to narrowly defined counterterrorism efforts to target al Qaeda, and the more it reduces its support to the Afghan National Security Forces to a very limited scope of training, the more it will deprive itself of the tools to stimulate the needed improvements in governance. And without such reforms, any security gains in Afghanistan will be extremely fragile and hard to sustain after 2014. Advocating a sustained commitment to Afghanistan, particularly a sustained military commitment, is an excruciatingly hard decision. If one believes that Afghanistan is beyond salvage, then sacrificing any more international blood and treasure would be futile. But it is too early to conclude that Afghanistan has reached that stage. There have been some improvements, particularly in the growth of the Afghan National Army. And much remains unknown. As long as there are some indications that instability can be reduced and the chance of another civil war minimized, the stakes are important enough to merit doing what is yet possible—even with restricted means and within the transition process—to avert a major collapse after 2014.

Governance Reforms: Necessary, but How Likely?

Unfortunately, the international community's strategy toward governance in Afghanistan continues to exhibit the same ambivalence that has characterized it until now. On the one hand, there has been of late some enhanced focus on governance and demands for greater accountability from the Afghan government. The July 2012 Tokyo Conference, for the first time, conditioned some aid on better Afghan government performance. The declining willingness of Western publics and governments to simply continue committing resources with little performance improvement on the part of the Afghan government could perhaps lead to sharpened international scrutiny of the funds flowing into Afghanistan and more stringent standards for good governance. In fact, some international officials are speaking about moving toward a transactional relationship with Afghanistan, in which only good governance performance will be rewarded with development (and perhaps even military) funding.[1]

But just a few weeks earlier, the May 2012 NATO Chicago Summit couched talk of improving governance in Afghanistan in language that strongly indicated that this was something the Afghans would now do for themselves. And although the Tokyo Conference indicated that 20 percent of international aid would be conditional, the international community has had a poor record of acting on its declarations and imposing sanctions—of any form—on Afghan officials and institutions that egregiously violate their commitments. Overall, the United States has strongly signaled that its own expectations, objectives, and requirements for improving governance in Afghanistan are highly limited at this point.

Moreover, the continuing embrace of problematic warlords for political deals and military action in Afghanistan and the standing up of militias, such as the Afghan Local Police, all push against improvements in governance. The warlords may possibly get things done for the international community and, under some circumstances, even facilitate better service delivery to their client groups, but they have no intention of subjecting themselves to the rule of law. Rather, their inclination is to portray themselves as indispensible for helping the international community deal with the coming instability. The more the international community remains dependent on working through them, the more it undercuts any signals to other Afghan government officials that this time it is determined to follow through with its anticorruption and good governance demands.

Moreover, the level of scrutiny, monitoring, and leverage is inescapably a function of the level of U.S. and international presence and the prospects for continuing that presence. The more the Unites States and the international community are seen as leaving—reducing the number of troops they are retaining in Afghanistan, narrowing the mission of the troops to counterterrorism training from bases, and scaling back their economic development and institution-building efforts—the less leverage they will have.

Restricted and conditional international assistance may in fact be for the good. For years, the international community had substantial leverage and chose not to exercise it. Fewer financial flows with far greater scrutiny and accountability will do far more good for governance and stability in Afghanistan than extensive but untraceable, usurped, and stolen funding, which just encourages conflict, instability, power abuse, and criminality. But inevitably there will be a palpable diminishment of some international leverage as a result of reduced presence and resources. To the extent that international leverage had been exercised at the local level, it came from the international presence on the ground—in the provinces, districts, and local communities. If after 2014 the international community will no longer be present in such a manner, it will lose the tool of in-person persuasion, cajoling, and instruction that it has used with local Afghan National Security Forces, Afghan Local Police commanders, warlords, and district officials until now, albeit often half-heartedly, inconsistently, and not very effectively.

And even if a transactional relationship that conditioned disbursement of foreign aid on better government performance and greater rule of law were in fact strictly implemented, it could still be subverted: Pakistan, for example, has become a master at getting maximum payoffs from Washington and the international community for delivering the minimum in return. Kabul, too, could be tempted to play Islamabad's game by claiming that an Afghan meltdown would be so dangerous—the country becoming once again a haven for terrorism, for example—that the international community simply could not afford to demand too much of the country's leaders or impose strongly punitive measures. After all, Kabul

can ask, do you want to jeopardize all the massive international investments made in Afghanistan?

A bad decision would be to set up vague conditionality—or, alternatively, specific and stringent conditions that the international community
does not have the will to uphold. Such mistakes in defining or implementing good governance initiatives would teach the Afghan mafia types that
the international community still remains ignorant enough that money
can be conned and muscled out of it. A strict prioritizing of what is most
important for the United States and the international community will
enable international stakeholders to better coordinate their policies and
thereby minimize vague and unenforceable conditions.

The 2014 Afghan Presidential Elections

The same rule—that one should not announce as intolerable that which
one is in fact going to be stuck with or which one does not truly have the
will and capacity to prevent—also applies to the international community's handling of the 2014 elections.

The presidential elections scheduled for 2014 (or 2013, should they
be advanced as President Karzai has suggested) provide an opportunity
for some governance reforms.[2] For many months now, the elections
have been on the minds of many Afghans. For some, the elections offer
a beacon of hope for improved governance, with the Karzai era ending
and the possibility of new opportunities for greater service delivery and
accountability emerging. For others, they provide a tempting opportunity
to expand patronage networks and capture previously inaccessible economic oligopolies. Yet, although President Karzai stated repeatedly that
he would not run again for president, many Afghans also doubt that the
elections will be held—either because Karzai will use lack of security as
an excuse to delay the elections and declare emergency rule or because
he will seek to legitimize the extension of his rule via a captive loya jirga.
Violence could be set off by the cancellation of elections as well as by
perceptions that the elections were once again fraudulent, or even, should
they be considered clean, by those losers who are no longer willing to
participate in a political system they can no longer manipulate. Already
during the 2010 parliamentary elections, many of those who lost claimed
that it was due to fraud or a lack of security that prevented their supporters from reaching the polling places.[3]

In many ways the elections could trigger major political power plays and infighting, whether or not President Karzai seeks to remain in office. The fight over the remaining rents of the ending political dispensation and the need to consolidate one's support coalition in anticipation of the shaky future—and hence to deliver spoils to them in order to ensure their allegiance—will not be conducive to consensus decisionmaking and broad-based good governance.

Given how brittle and fractured the political landscape in Afghanistan has become, even a clean and safe process does not guarantee peaceful outcomes from the elections. But that should not be an excuse not to try to make the process as legitimate as possible. It will entail early assistance to the Afghan National Security Forces for planning security for the elections as well as provision of appropriate funding and training for the election commission staff. The international community should also devote maximum leverage to motivating President Karzai and other key Afghan political leaders to keep the elections free of fraud. And to the extent that any meaningful traction on electoral reform develops, such as efforts to reform the single nontransferable voting system or to move toward proportional representation, the international community should encourage it. But the United States and the international community should not give the impression that *they* can deliver clean and legitimate elections to the Afghans. Afghan politicians and civil society will need to push for and implement such reforms and processes. The international community no longer retains the leverage to do it for them, and the worst outcome would be to promise and then fail to ensure success. Getting across the message of necessary restraint on the part of the international community will not be easy. Many Afghans continue to believe that the United States in particular has far greater influence on political processes in Afghanistan than it actually enjoys and therefore will doubt that the United States cannot in fact bring about such changes to the electoral law or guarantee free and fair elections. And they will likely interpret the message that they are the ones who need to push for reforms as an expression of covert support for Karzai or his anointed successor. Thus the point that the country's future, including reforms to its electoral system, is now *principally,* not exclusively, in their hands will have to be consistently repeated to Afghan politicians and civil society leaders at all levels.

Nor should the international community pick winners and start designating which candidates it prefers and which are unacceptable. The fiasco of the 2009 elections and Washington's attempt to "level the playing field" (described in chapter 6) should serve as a caution about the enormous difficulties and serious consequences entailed in committing to such a course of action and then failing to see it through. Indicating publicly that certain leaders are unacceptable requires being ready to forcibly remove them if all else fails. There is little reason to believe that the international community will develop the resolve for such a course of action. And quietly telling certain politicians that they would not be acceptable—such as, for example, insisting that President Karzai cannot remain in power after 2014—has a high chance of leaking out. But even if it did not, it might still require forcible action by the international community against those who would still choose to run—and again, the likelihood that the international community would actually follow through is minimal. The worst outcome would be to declare that a certain election result was unacceptable and then not only look weak when one has to accept it but also must deal with a hostile leader. And frankly, Washington has not had a good track record for picking effective and accountable leaders abroad.[4]

What Else Can Still Be Done?

Although the international community and the United States are clearly on their way out of Afghanistan, and although few strategic options are left and many trends in Afghanistan are distressing (some are even dismal), there are still tactical and operational level policy options and decisions to be made. Of course, even cumulatively, they cannot guarantee success in the form of a stable government, but they can encourage or discourage stability. One way or another, such options and decisions will have an impact on the security, political life, and economic conditions of Afghanistan, even if many of the larger and deeper trends there may well be outside the control and beyond the leverage of the international community at this point.

A set of recommendations is offered below. Not just a good strategic design but on-the-ground implementation will be key to the success of most. Their effectiveness depends on comprehensive knowledge of the local environment. The policies proposed entail the application of astute judgment, tough-minded selectivity, careful calibration, judicious pacing, and a willingness to absorb short-term costs and risks. Not all of the policies can be implemented at the same time in equal scope.

And they require coordination—between the top U.S. military commander in Afghanistan and the U.S. ambassador and with as many international donors and partners as possible. Such coordination and agreement on the basic policies is important because selectivity requires not just diligently promoting an issue one selects but also making choices as to what aspects and levels of a problem will *not* be tackled, at least not at a particular time. The basic outlines of the priorities need to be communicated throughout the involved bureaucracies because in large institutions with perpetually shifting individuals, a need to constantly and freshly decide what will and will not be done is likely to eviscerate selectivity. In turn, achieving some badly needed consistency necessitates longer assignments for U.S. and international major civilian and military leaders in Afghanistan—until 2014, but also from 2015 on—so that policies are not all the time reshaped by new arrivals. Just as the short time horizons of Afghans weaken the effectiveness of our policies, America's own constant shifts in approaches undermine Afghan buy-in.

Critically, the policies require the expansion of the U.S. and international community's own time horizons in Afghanistan. Important U.S. interests in the country and region will not evaporate at the end of 2014. They will continue to evolve. So policies cannot be designed on the basis of the 2014 or even the projected 2015 situation. Promoting U.S. interests over the long term—a decade and more—requires that the United States and the international community be willing to adaptively absorb some short-term risks, uncertainties, and costs. All too often inadequate and flawed policies are perpetuated because military and civilian leaders do not dare risk temporarily destabilizing a security situation or a political order, even though such policies are unsustainable, corrosive, and often outright combustible in the long term. Adopting the policies described below may well result in short-term costs and difficult trade-offs, but they increase the prospects for sustainable long-term gains. As long as the United States and the international community lack the determination and fortitude to break the habit of operating on the basis of short-term exigencies, they will not be able to correct course in Afghanistan sufficiently to help stabilize the country and region.

Emphasizing U.S. and International Engagement with Afghanistan from 2015 Onward

Much of Afghans' hedging behavior stems from the enormous uncertainties of what the post-2014 political, economic, and security (dis)order will look like, including whether and how the United States and the international community remain involved in Afghanistan. Both have stated that they will maintain their engagement, but many Afghans doubt these proclamations.

The form of the engagement will be a critical determinant of effectiveness. It will also be an important driver of Afghan behavior. And many contours and shades of that engagement are yet to be determined.

But the first step of inducing the Afghans to break with self-regarding, short-term maximization of power and profit is to emphasize the international engagement from 2015 onward. The more the rhetoric in the United States and the international community fixates on 2014, the more it creates the impression that everything will crumble as the international community reduces its presence at the end of that year. And the more Afghans believe that, the less they will be responsive to international pressure or advice. The effectiveness of every U.S. and international policy adopted in Afghanistan will be severely compromised if the Afghans believe that the international community's departure and disengagement are imminent or that their commitment is minimal and pro forma. Instead of highlighting 2014, the rhetoric of the international community should underscore 2015 and beyond.

Maintaining International Military Presence and Robust Training and Advisory Capacity until 2014 and Beyond

Within the 2014 drawdown guidelines and—equally important—from 2015 onward, the United States and the international community need to maintain a sufficiently robust and capable force posture in Afghanistan to provide the Afghan forces with embedded advisory teams, training support, and critical specialty enablers. Reducing U.S. military forces too quickly will be highly detrimental. So will be severely restricting, as per the September 2012 ISAF rules of engagement, the interaction between ISAF and the Afghan National Security Forces, particularly below the battalion level where most counterinsurgency operations take place. Both risk jeopardizing whatever military accomplishments have been achieved, in turn allowing the Taliban and its affiliated insurgencies to recoup their physical losses and whatever weakening of resolve they have suffered. Limiting whatever U.S. and ISAF advisory and assistance forces that remain after 2014 to training on bases only and to a very narrow anti-al Qaeda mission would equally undermine the stabilization effort in Afghanistan and also weaken hedges against Taliban resurgence, violation of any negotiated agreements, or both.

The advisory teams that remain in Afghanistan after 2014 thus need to be sufficiently robust and have enough reachback capacity to participate with Afghan National Security Forces in action in the field. They will be the umbilical cord that connects Afghan security forces to ISAF air support and medical evacuation, both of which require ISAF presence on the ground and intense interactions with Afghan forces. Nor should the ANSF be denied the critical support of international specialty enablers such as air support, medevac, logistics and maintenance, contractor management, battle space integration, and command, control, and intelligence assets. The ANSF cannot function effectively without them and are nowhere near being able to generate such capacities internally. Building up such Afghan capacities is important, but it is a process that will take several years beyond 2014 to complete. Until then, ISAF should commit to providing them.

Effective international training of the Afghan National Security Forces requires a shared vision with the Afghans of what the priorities are and, more broadly, of how security and public safety will be provided from 2015 onward. Developing such a framework in turn requires a realistic assessment of (and commitment to) what international funding over a decade, not just two or three years, will really look like. Effective training by ISAF is also predicated on continuing trust between the international forces and their Afghan counterparts. Without a speedy development of measures to counter the growth of the so-called insider attacks by Afghan security forces personnel against international forces, such trust will break down, and donor countries will lose the will to sustain military deployments limited even to just training.

ISAF's reporting on the quality of the Afghan National Security Forces, particularly the Afghan National Army, needs to become more rigorous, consistent, and transparent. In the absence of such information, available to policymakers principally but also to outside experts, it will be immensely difficult to detect critical weaknesses in the transition process and develop any countervailing strategies that may still be feasible in the context of the transition timelines and the reduction of the international presence in Afghanistan. Moreover, ISAF urgently needs to strengthen its internal monitoring of patronage networks within the Afghan National Security Forces. Such monitoring needs to go beyond counting the overall ethnic balance within the ANSF and trying to match the national ethnic distribution estimates. It must include developing detailed intelligence on how commanders are creating their own personal forces within the national force and remaining vigilant in countering such tendencies, which will threaten to fragment the ANSF after 2014 and intensify pressures toward a civil war. The United States and ISAF should also exercise strong oversight in the promotion of combat commanders to ensure that those who are ineffective on the battlefield, corrosive to the institutional integrity of the Afghan forces, or highly abusive to local communities do not occupy positions of authority—even if they have powerful sponsors. Some corruption among combat commanders will have to be stomached, but ineffectiveness and highly malign influence should not be.

Anticrime training needs to become an urgent focus for the police forces. Obviously, such an undertaking starts with reducing the level of criminal and predatory behavior perpetrated by the police themselves. Since the baseline is so low, achieving some improvement may not be hard; but making truly meaningful progress on reducing police participation in criminality and improving their anticrime capacity will be much harder, all the more so because the United States and the international community lack the appropriate police-training capability. Furthermore, police development is arguably the most difficult form of institution building and reform a country can undertake, and the record around the world—both for internal domestic efforts and externally assisted ones—is poor.

Nonetheless, reducing crime in one or two major cities, such as Kabul, Kandahar, or Jalalabad, by concentrating resources and focus on that one area would vastly improve the legitimacy and standing of the Afghan government. Of course, any such progress even in one city is predicated on the willingness of Kabul and the international community to break their dependence on the city's and region's power brokers. Without such a renegotiation of the local political compacts, little progress is likely to be accomplished by anticrime measures because crime and politics in Afghanistan are so deeply intertwined.

A lengthy period of negotiations between the international community and the Afghan president will likely be required to bring Kabul on board with both the overall undertaking and its specifics, for the Afghan president will fear the short-term cost such an effort will entail. Emphasizing to the Arg Palace the long-term boost to Kabul's legitimacy and an opportunity to weaken some power brokers will be important, as it will be to indicate that the international community is prepared to give Kabul something it values. Selecting a city for such a demonstration effect involves multiple considerations. Picking a city where there is one tight network may facilitate implementation because it is easier to think through strategies and counterstrategies when dealing with one large criminal organization. But this approach will also require greater expenditures of political capital by Kabul and the international community. Picking a city where there are multiple mafia–power broker networks allows the international community and Kabul to pit one against the other and may be cheaper in terms of political capital; but controlling the potential escalation of violence within these criminal markets could become exceedingly difficult. Either way there will need to be reasonably well-disciplined police to work within that area—even if they are not fully free of corruption.

The Afghan Border Police are in bad shape in terms of both their capacity and their participation in crime. Building up the Afghan Border Police has been a higher priority for the international community than developing the National Police's anticrime capacity, but still the efforts have been inadequate. Reforming border police forces, reducing custom revenue losses, improving the quality of border guards, and tightening the border are among the most difficult tasks within the already enormously challenging undertaking of police reform. Nonetheless, given the high likelihood that Haqqani and Taliban safe havens in Pakistan will not be shut down before or soon after 2014, the Afghan Border Police have a vital role to play in reducing terrorist and insurgent infiltration. At least that component of its training should be intensified as much as possible.

Reducing Corruption and Improving Governance

The international community's long-term goals in Afghanistan over the next decade should include strengthening checks and balances within the Afghan political system, reducing patronage, clientelism, and corruption, and enhancing government service delivery.[5] The steps toward accomplishing these goals include promoting electoral reform, strengthening political parties, and assisting the Afghan parliament and line ministries in developing technical capacity.

Some of these policies have already been attempted, often with little meaningful progress. Efforts to reduce corruption and improve governance have been difficult to undertake effectively since the international community frequently lacks the knowledge, influence, and resolve to push for such initiatives. Such good governance efforts will not become any easier, and the international community's knowledge and influence are likely to diminish more and more as the transition progresses and also beyond 2014.

This does not mean that nothing can be usefully attempted or accomplished within a year or two. The political and governance system in Afghanistan is so pervasively corrupt and so deeply and intricately linked to key structures of power and networks of influence that some prioritization of anticorruption focus is required. After 2014 the international community will likely continue to lack the capacity to fully break with all problematic power brokers. Nonetheless, Washington and the international community can try to urgently mitigate at least the most egregious abuses of power and types of corruption that are most detrimental to long-term stability in Afghanistan.

Anticorruption efforts should focus on limiting tribal or ethnic discrimination in access to jobs, especially in the Afghan National Army and Afghan National Police, and on expanding access to markets and contracts. A corollary to limiting ethnic discrimination within the security services is to make sure that particular ethnic groups or people from particular regions who do not have access to influential power brokers in the higher-level commands are not selectively posted to very violent areas for too long without being rotated out; that command levels are not dominated by a particular ethnic group, such as the Tajiks; and that salaries and leaves are equally distributed by superiors. None of these reforms is easy to implement, but there have been periodic successes, mainly at the district level and occasionally also on the provincial level. But even such achievements have frequently been undermined by inconsistent U.S. focus and international effort.

Sometimes the above criteria will be in conflict, and difficult choices will have to be made—for instance, promotion of some deserving Tajik commanders may have to be held back in order to ethnically balance the command levels of the force. Thus case-by-case determinations will at times be necessary to establish which trade-off is least harmful to the institutional development of the Afghan forces and Afghan stability. Since the Afghan National Police are even more politicized and bound up in Afghanistan's conflictual politics than the National Army, achieving merit-based promotion, weeding out favoritism, and cleaning up the senior officer corps will be far more difficult in that institution and take much longer to accomplish than in the Army (where these have hardly been easy tasks). That does not mean that no progress can be achieved within the ANP; but it does mean that diligence and persistence on the part of the international community are essential.

In addition, it is critical to focus on the corruption that seriously undermines the emergence of the already fragile markets in Afghanistan. Such severely detrimental corruption includes the proliferation of unofficial checkpoints and the ever-escalating bribes to be paid at those checkpoints, major corruption in the banking sector that could bring down Afghanistan's financial system (as almost happened during the Kabul Bank crisis), and corruption in line ministries that paralyzes service delivery rather than facilitating it.

Countries in South and Central Asia (as well as in other parts of the world) tend to have high corruption rates yet do not necessarily face imminent collapse. Predictable corruption connected to the delivery of services can be seen as another form of taxation: yes, it is highly suboptimal, but it need not make the political system combustible. Highly politically explosive problems do arise, however, when corruption leads to paralysis within government offices, when money or property are typically stolen without any service being provided, and when the unofficial taxation reaches such heights or is so unpredictable that the vast majority of revenues from an economic activity is lost. Combating these types of corruption should be a priority of the United States and the international community.

Anticorruption efforts tailored to each kind of malfeasance operate on different timelines and involve different U.S. and international actors. Combating proliferating illegal checkpoints and their ever-escalating bribes is, of course, a very different undertaking than limiting the corruption of the Afghan banking sector. For the latter, the objective should be to reduce the level of corruption and theft sufficiently to ensure that the financial system does not go under or defraud thousands of Afghans, even if the financial integrity of the Afghan banking sector will not be pristine. Washington should seek to leverage the influence of the International Monetary Fund—rather than undermine it, as ultimately happened in the case of the Kabul Bank—and of other multilateral partners, such as the World Bank.

Making major progress on checkpoints should be feasible as the Afghan government increasingly fields ANSF units throughout its territory. It is an anticorruption measure that can be rolled out immediately and accomplished in the short term. Apart from Taliban-controlled territory, if the Afghan government cannot shut down illegal checkpoints in an area where it operates, it can do little else there. It is thus a measure by which the Afghan government can quickly demonstrate greater responsiveness and a resolve to be more accountable to the Afghan people. (Recall that the Taliban's own successes against such illegal checkpoints have boosted that group's legitimacy.) Such an effort will, of course, require that the Afghan government gradually takes on at least one aspect of the power brokers' malign behavior in particular areas. But such enforcement would also serve to chip away at their power.

Finally, attempts to undermine effective local officials should be countered as much as possible. And with whatever limited leverage and choices are left to the international community, it should encourage merit-based appointments in the government; it can at least seek to influence the process by interacting with, encouraging, and rewarding well-performing government officials. Often, pushing for meritocratic appointments may not be successful: Afghan government officials have mostly been resistant to such efforts because often their only mechanism of influence is patronage.[6] But even with clientelistic networks, not all potential appointees are equally incompetent or abusive. Even if the choice is only between bad and less bad, the international community should weigh in on behalf of those who are less grating to local populations. Moreover, there may well be opportunities to move against corrupt and incompetent officials who fall out of favor with their patrons. Of course, it is vital to make sure that any anticorruption efforts are not merely a ruse for appointing one's ethnic kin—a subterfuge that is only likely to further aggravate ethnic tensions.

Again, there will be some tough trade-offs. The appointment of a competent official who on merit deserves the position may threaten the local or institutional dominance of a particular ethnic group or other holders of power. Case-by-case assessments—often difficult—will have to be made regarding which problem—power imbalance or a lesser competency—will need to be prioritized in particular instances. Meritocratic appointments may not be free of patronage or corruption. The most important criterion is that the government officials are as broadly and deeply acceptable to their constituents—local Afghans or institutional interest groups—as possible. And when many Afghans find a government official too grating and predatory, the international community should make an effort to back them up to change his behavior or have him removed. The officials who will be most aggravating to local populations will be those who are not competent and do not deliver services even after bribes are paid, who are rapacious and capricious in their bribery, and who are part of a highly exclusionary patronage network.

A strict prioritization of anticorruption efforts may well be necessary. The international community should save its greatest political leverage—such as refusing to work with some appointees—for persuading the Afghans to dismiss officials or blackball applicants who are most egregious, such as those who turn whole communities against the government and thrust them into the hands of the Taliban. The more frequently the international community asks for the removal of problematic appointees, the fewer they are likely to get. But if an official is deemed so corrupt and ineffective that the international community asks for his removal, it needs the will to back up that demand with punitive action, having determined that it actually has some punitive action at the ready. Often there are sanctions that can be imposed, such as denying visas to the corrupt Afghan officials and their families, stopping international payments to their favorite programs, or just limiting interactions with them.

But equally, the international community should seek to develop as much of the prioritization as possible in consultation with the Afghans. There will be disagreements on some moves—such as reining in those power brokers on whom the Arg Palace has become dependent—but there may well be a Kabul buy-in on some important initiatives, such as targeting abuses that push whole communities into the hands of the Taliban or that undermine the military effort. Agreement will often not be easily forthcoming, and it may require a great deal of persistence backed up by strong evidence to bring Kabul on board.

There is a real cost, however, to prioritizing the anticorruption campaign as opposed to attacking corruption of any sort in a blanket way, since prioritization, which may mean going easy on some offenders, can subject the international community to charges of inconsistency, hypocrisy, and timidity. But with a continuing need to depend on problematic interlocutors, such a prioritized focus is perhaps the maximum that can currently be accomplished. Even so, the United States and international community need to maintain as robust analytical capabilities as they can, including on-the-ground analysts with as unrestricted access to broad segments of the Afghan population as possible, and not merely signals intelligence platforms. Indeed, such a prioritized anticorruption strategy requires a detailed, comprehensive, and complex understanding of local conditions and evolving dynamics, and hence is highly dependent on accurate intelligence and sophisticated analysis.

Trying to prevent all corruption equally will likely run up against the political dependencies of the current Afghan government and motivate it to do nothing on corruption to avoid rocking the boat.[7] But equally, giving up on corruption spells failure for the stabilization effort.

Paradoxically, the chance to push through any governance reforms will be enhanced if the international community finds a way to work with President Karzai rather than against him. The Obama administration's early confrontation with Karzai over corruption left him deeply suspicious of and antagonistic toward Washington without motivating him to improve governance or tackle corruption. Many aspects of the stabilization strategy will be hampered if the relationship between Kabul and Washington deteriorates further. Karzai has remained resistant to focusing on corruption. However, the international community needs to continue stressing to him, and to his successor after 2014 (if in fact Karzai does not remain in power), that he is likely to lose much more political and economic power and physical security from a collapse of governing authority in Afghanistan than he will by gradually transforming his co-opt-and-close-your-eyes system into one of greater accountability and lesser impunity.

To start with, achieving visible progress in one key locality, such as Kandahar, Nangarhar, or Baghlan, can create a powerful demonstration effect. It would send an important signal and could be a beacon of hope for the Afghan people as well as a guiding example for Afghan policymakers, while boosting the legitimacy and sustainability of the country's political order.

Reining in the Warlords

The United States and the international community have shown little willingness to break with problematic warlords; instead, they have embraced many warlords for reasons of short-term effectiveness on the battlefield. In the case of others, the international community simply could not figure out how to have them removed or neutralized or how to restrain their highly pernicious behavior. The smaller the international presence in Afghanistan, the less resources and capacity the international community will have to finally sever its dependence on the power brokers and effectively encourage their removal from official and unofficial positions of power. It may be true that the damage such power brokers can inflict on the international community's efforts may well necessitate "having them in the tent rather than trying to pull the stakes off the tent on the outside," as one U.S. official put it.[8] But if the power brokers bring down the tent from the inside by their rapacious behavior, the state-building effort will be equally ineffective. The shrinking international presence in some areas may in fact permit greater pressure on Kabul to hold them accountable (despite the reduced leverage to force such a removal).

However, even as its presence is reduced, the international community will retain some means of influencing the behavior of the power brokers. The decline of its leverage does not mean that the international community should not seek opportunities to weaken at least the most pernicious power brokers and modify the behavior of others by creating incentive structures that discourage at least egregious abuse. As with broader anti-corruption efforts, prioritizing the focus on the most malign actors—such as power brokers who create and fuel conflict among communities, systematically marginalize particular groups, or perpetrate major human rights abuses—will be necessary. There will be short-term costs and risks in taking them on. But without U.S. and international willingness to absorb at least some of such costs, the prospects of protecting U.S. and international interests will be severely undermined, as will any remaining chance to ensure a reasonably stable Afghanistan that can provide for its own security and the elemental needs of its people, and thus acquire the legitimacy that any political system needs to survive.

International influence may not always be able to effect the removal or even weakening of such power brokers. However, the leverage may be sufficient to alter the behavior of the power brokers enough so that they become more acceptable to local communities. The international suasion may, for example, include merely encouraging local power brokers to expand and broaden their patronage networks so that more people and more communities have access to some of the privately sponsored goods. But the international community should demand that the Afghans institute accountability measures and appropriately severe punishment for serious crimes perpetrated by the power brokers, such as major land theft, rape, kidnapping, and murder. By the same token, the international community itself should use problematic power brokers as little as possible and only as a last resort.

There is no guarantee that if a highly pernicious power broker is removed, a good official will then be appointed. The choices will often have to be between bad and awful. The post-2014 environment of reduced international monetary flows will intensify competition among the power brokers. That will have some negative outcomes and may become a source of conflict; thus this risk will have to be carefully monitored and managed. But such competition will also provide opportunities to shape the behavior of the power brokers.

Even if the international community cannot get the noxious power brokers removed and has to engage with them, it should limit any visible public embrace of them and not publicly declare them great commanders and friends. The international community should take care to engage with the critics of the power brokers, civil society actors, and reformers who do not yet have formal or informal power. Even just praising them can boost their influence. And quietly, even if it cannot accomplish the removal of the problematic power brokers, the international community can impose other sanctions on them, such as denying them and their families visas. Portfolios of corruption and evidence of abuse should be assembled, which can be used if the political context becomes more permissive. The mere existence of such a folder of evidence—if quietly communicated to the power broker—may well increase leverage.

Washington and the international community should not be beguiled by the argument that the more security in Afghanistan disintegrates, the more they will need to depend on the warlords, and therefore they should not be antagonized in advance. Such an argument assumes—incorrectly—that the warlords, perhaps in conjunction with the tribes and the Afghan Local Police, will be necessary agents of security and stability across the country. At best, they may be able to maintain pockets of security in particular areas. But if the situation in Afghanistan does become more atomized after 2014, there will be opportunities then to selectively resurrect relationships with some of these warlords. After 2014 the warlords will not be loyal to the U.S. effort anyway, especially if it is just a narrow anti–al Qaeda mission: they will simply cooperate with anyone who pays them more or increases their power—be it the Taliban or the international community. Given their enmity toward the Taliban, the Northern Alliance commanders will be far less likely to ever be co-opted by that insurgent group, but they too will ultimately seek to cultivate as many internal and international friends as they can and play them off against one another. However, until such dire necessity of making deals with warlords truly arises in a post-2014 meltdown, the international community should seek to weaken problematic power brokers or restrain their behavior as much as possible.

Whatever red lines the United States and the international community set for the power brokers, they need to be prepared to uphold. They need to have plans and resolve to take punitive actions if the power brokers and the Afghan government violate the red lines. Thus conditionality should not be vague, and the red lines should only be those that Washington and the international community have the will and capacity to enforce. A consistent failure to act against behavior designated as intolerable only undermines the reputation and effectiveness of the international community.

Reining in the Afghan Local Police and Other Militias

ISAF needs to resist the siren song of a shortcut to "security" in Afghanistan via the Afghan Local Police. With rare exceptions—mainly in homogeneous communities threatened by outside Taliban—the ALP do not significantly improve security. Short-term security gains often come from the groups' accommodation with the Taliban rather than effective resistance and are exceedingly fragile. Instead, the development of the ALP and other militias often actually triggers multiple forms of conflict, in the short term even undermining human security. And in the long term, such militia efforts pose serious threats to security, public safety, and governance in Afghanistan.

If the vetting process becomes more rushed and even less reliable than it already is, serious human rights abuses, security dilemmas, ethnic tensions, and other local conflicts will only grow. Ideally, the program would be scaled down. At minimum, any initiation or expansion of the program in a locality needs to be based on a comprehensive and credible assessment of local conditions, with long-term (over the next decade, not just two or three years) governance ramifications factored in as strongly as short-term battlefield exigencies. In highly heterogeneous areas with preexisting conflicts among communities or with discriminatory governance, the ALP and other militias should not be stood up.

Credible and robust mechanisms should be developed immediately to roll back rogue Afghan Local Police units already in existence. The current arrangements are not adequate. Stronger accountability measures need to be implemented, and accusations of crime, abuse, and ethnic and tribal discrimination need to be investigated and prosecuted far more diligently and effectively than they have been. ISAF needs to commit itself to and involve itself in such accountability procedures and not simply wait for the Afghan Ministries of Interior and of Justice to undertake them— else it may have to wait forever in many cases.

Developing comprehensive assessments of the suitability of particular areas for the creation of ALP units, monitoring the behavior of the units, discouraging and countering abuse perpetrated by them, and having the capacity to roll back those that have gone rogue requires sufficient on-the-ground personnel resources that are well suited for such oversight. If the United States is not willing to continue fielding such personnel resources, it should not be expanding the program further.

Now is also the time to start developing a serious program to disarm and demobilize the ALP after 2014. Although the U.S. military has suggested that the program be made permanent, Afghan government leaders, including in the Ministry of Interior, are ambivalent, wary that such a program will threaten governance in the long run—and with good reason. The United States and the international community should commit themselves to undertake that disarmament and to establish a credible program with procedures for diverting the decommissioned ALP from future predatory behavior and ethnic infighting. Such a stand-down program will be credible only if other militias, whether under the aegis of the United States or belonging to Afghan warlords, are also included in it. For if they are not, the various militia units, even if they do shed their uniforms, are unlikely to give up their weapons or to feel particularly constrained in their behavior.

If the Afghan Local Police and other militias cannot be disbanded after 2014, the United States military and the Afghan government should at least consider developing credible plans to incorporate the Afghan Local Police into the Afghan National Police. Such an approach, if it is the only one for which the United States can generate any resolve, is highly problematic and much less optimal than disbanding the ALP. For one, even if lodging the ALP units within the Afghan National Police can increase and strengthen supervision over the ALP, it can also greatly augment the already intense factionalization and criminal propensity of the Afghan National Police. For Afghanistan's future security and public safety and for the quality of governance in Afghanistan, the Afghan National Police are more important than the Afghan Local Police. Thus any incorporation plans would need to be carefully evaluated, for an Afghan National Police completely rotted by the incorporation of the ALP would be worse than a loose rogue ALP that the Afghan National Police have to combat. Nonetheless, integrating better performing and less abusive ALP units into the Afghan National Police may well be possible in some areas where the ALP are not highly predatory, and where relations between the National Police and the Local Police are positive and there already is good cooperation and interface. But such case-by-case assessments need to be conducted within a larger comprehensive framework for security delivery in Afghanistan in the future. At the absolute minimum, the United States and the international community must start working now with the Afghan government to develop some credible, depoliticized (as much as that is feasible within the context of the Afghan political and institutional system) Afghan oversight and rollback capacity for the Afghan Local Police—such as through Afghan Special Operations Forces.

Good Governance and Counternarcotics Efforts

The international community must rapidly wean itself from measures of "good governance" that are misleading. One salient example is the extent of poppy eradication: it is not only a bad measure of counternarcotics effectiveness but also a bad measure of good governance. Yet this standard has often been used by the international community to measure and define both.

Instead, it should define good governance in ways that are consistent with the views of the Afghan population: not just the delivery of services but also, critically, physical security, food security, the provision of justice, and a reduction in impunity for egregious corruption and extensive crime. A good measure of the quality of governance is one that is derived from a comprehensive concept of human security—that is, security from physical abuse, whether from insurgents, criminals, warlords, local militias, or the local government, and security from great economic want, as well as access to justice and accountability mechanisms.

The faster the international community leaves Afghanistan, the more the counternarcotics efforts in Afghanistan will be undermined or stalled, even reversed. This will especially be the case if sustainable comprehensive rural development programs are not in place by then—and in the vast majority of Afghan communities they will not be. Greater insecurity will also increase poppy cultivation and intensify the drug trade and other illegal economies in Afghanistan. The worst policy under such circumstances or in advance of the 2014 transition would be to insist on more aggressive eradication, such as by providing more funding for the so-called Good Performance Initiative. Instead of encouraging sustainable development and accountable governance, the initiative actually distorts the meaning of good governance. Eradication and bans on poppy cultivation without alternative livelihoods being in place only thrust vulnerable populations—much of the rural population of Afghanistan in fact—into the hands of the Taliban.

Interdiction of the drug traffickers, including by ISAF forces, needs to become far more selective than it has been for the past four years. Opium seizures should be limited to truly large stockpiles and not target household opium holdings. Because many Afghan households do not keep cash in a bank but rather hold their assets in the form of nonperishable opium, which can be easily converted into cash, the seizure of a household's opium holdings may completely wipe out the years-long savings of a family, thus acutely and chronically impoverishing it. Just like the highly detrimental crop eradication program, a blanket interdiction policy can undermine even the basic food security of rural Afghans.

Counternarcotics efforts are a key component of stabilization and development policies in Afghanistan. However, premature—that is, without alternative livelihoods in place—and inappropriate efforts to suppress the drug economy greatly complicate counterterrorism, counterinsurgency, and stabilization objectives. And thus they ultimately also jeopardize economic reconstruction, political consolidation, and the rule of law.

Prioritizing Economic Sustainability and Capacity Building

For Afghanistan's dire post-2014 economic outlook, there are also no silver bullets. The legal economy will not magically expand, and mineral resource extraction and the New Silk Road are a long way off. Both will depend on the security situation in Afghanistan and the level of political tensions or cooperation among countries in the region. Economic flows from donor countries will also depend on their own fiscal conditions and public support for further engagement with Afghanistan.

But whatever money is available can be spent in a much better way than has often been the case. The so-called economic stabilization programs should be terminated as soon as possible; they are not sustainable, they distort legal economies, and in fact can be the source of local conflict. Showering communities with money and being obsessed with burn rates buys neither love nor economic growth. Instead, economic development policies should focus on comprehensive, sustainable, ground-assessment-based development that prioritizes food security; long-term, sustainable job creation (not just jobs lasting three months); human capital growth; infrastructure expansion; and capacity building. In particular, policies need to take into account and frequently prioritize food security for marginalized communities.

The United States and the international community need to find the will to undertake detailed, if occasionally time-consuming, studies of local conditions before economic projects are rolled out. Such assessments need to include an analysis of the preexisting political structures, social cohesiveness, and (in)equality in access to resources with which economic interventions will interact. Rather than a one-shoe-fits-all approach, donor policy designs need to thoroughly account for local contexts and be based on consultation with local stakeholders. Donor programming and financial commitments should become multiyear; but they need to retain enough flexibility in their structure so that implementers can adjust ineffective policy design and restructure programs that allow narrow, exclusionary networks to capture program resources, to the exclusion of the wider community.

Such an approach will take years—not the two-year time frame to 2014—to produce visible results. But switching to such an approach is essential, since the short-term measures, which were supposed to bring about economic stabilization, have in fact destabilized both local security and hindered the prospects for long-term growth.

With proper monitoring and punitive measures to discourage serious corruption, as much money as possible should be channeled through the Afghan government. Developing mechanisms for monitoring and oversight is a major challenge. Yet channeling outside financial aid through the national government is highly desirable since it increases the fiscal capacity of the state and links the population more closely to the state, building accountability. But—as already noted—the international community should be ready to reduce this money if it detects serious fraud by the Afghan government. Where monitoring is not possible, money should not be spent, except on projects essential for humanitarian relief. And even in those cases, while some illegal money diversion may need to be accepted, monitoring and accountability should be maximized. That does not mean that all projects should be terminated simply because some of the money is leaking to the Taliban or being pocketed by a local government official or warlords. Preventing the starvation of a community should trump other considerations. Nevertheless, all possible steps should be taken to minimize such leakage and to penalize money usurpation by actors over whom the international community has some leverage, such as local power brokers and Afghan government officials.

Tying the level of funding sent through the Afghan government to accurate assessments of the absorptive capacity of a locality and to the Afghan government's capacity to disburse the money is equally important. If even honest Afghan government officials cannot figure out how to spend and allocate funds or distribute them to the subnational level, services will still not be delivered and faith in the Afghan government will continue to plummet.

Encouraging better governance requires resolve and consistency—on the part of Afghan officials and on the part of the international community. But while such efforts require expenditures of political capital, they do not necessarily require greater financial expenditures. In fact, substantially turning off the spigot of money flowing to Afghanistan and disbursing only funds that can be monitored and spent sustainably would on its own improve governance and reduce corruption.

Using Negotiations with the Taliban to Improve Governance

As of this writing, negotiations with the Taliban have mostly amounted to talking about talking. They have produced more fear than confidence among various Afghan constituencies, including the non-Pashtun and civil society groups. If the Taliban believes that ISAF forces will leave or dramatically reduce their presence, it can simply hope to use protracted negotiations to run down the clock. Inevitably, the shape and content of any negotiations will be linked to what happens on the military battlefield and each side's assessments of its military strength and prospects for achieving a better deal through military means. Given the stalemated war and the likelihood of a significant reduction in international, including military, presence, the Taliban feels in no rush to compromise. Moreover, to the extent that Washington and the international community or Kabul seek to strike a deal with the Taliban at all costs and the ensuing negotiations are close-to-the-vest bargaining among the United States, Afghan power brokers, Pakistan's intelligence services, and key Taliban factions, they will merely reward the Taliban's military tenacity and produce neither improvements in governance nor peace and stability.

Negotiations with the Taliban can however provide an opportunity for improving governance if they can be structured as an inclusive process involving the country's multiple political stakeholders. Those provided a voice would have to include non-Pashtun communities, marginalized tribes, and Islamic movements as well as women's and Western-style organizations and representatives of civil society.

But structuring negotiations in a way that broadens political representation in Afghanistan will be very difficult. The process can be easily exploited and spoiled by factions within the Taliban and other self-seeking ethnic and tribal groups as well as by the Arg Palace, let alone by Pakistan and Afghanistan's other neighbors. Therefore, any progress toward improving conditions in war-torn Afghanistan and achieving a genuine reconciliation among its feuding peoples will require coordination among multiple actors on multiple levels as well as skillful diplomacy. Most important, it will require that the good governance objectives be emphasized as much as winning military engagements.

If improved governance in Afghanistan is accorded the same level of importance as security, or nearly so, the United States and the international community could still devote resources to helping the Afghan people reinvigorate legitimate political processes and establish the rule of law. The time horizons for achieving major progress in improving security versus promoting good governance will be different. But the resolve and focus should not be, even if strict prioritization of the efforts to foster good governance is required. The international community still has a chance—however small at this point—to embrace and energize the aspirations of the Afghan people.

Ultimately, however, even with far better policies in place than have been adopted so far, the United States and the international community only assist the Afghan people; they cannot inoculate the society against corruption and dispense good governance and the rule of law from abroad. The Afghans need to achieve such improvements through their own political struggles, social mobilization, and enlightened rule. If they do not take responsibility for this process, it has little chance. There are Afghans, including many in the next generation of leadership, who are determined and committed. They face enormous obstacles, entrenched power structures, and a substantial likelihood of great insecurity after 2014, including civil war. The international community, including the United States, should do all it can, with whatever restricted means available, to help Afghans realize their aspirations. And the notion that inadequate governance is "good enough for the Afghans" should not be accepted.[9]

The challenges that Afghanistan faces are daunting. Even if the recommendations proposed here were adopted and reasonably well implemented, there is no guarantee of success in fully stabilizing Afghanistan. At this point, the chances are moderate at best. But given the U.S. interests and international stakes in Afghanistan, it is imperative that the United States and the international community do their best with whatever influence they have to promote better practices. Because even if efforts to stabilize Afghanistan do not succeed, U.S. interests in Afghanistan and the region will persist. The United States will still need to attempt to maximize these efforts with whatever restricted means available at that point. Thus, if the current political and security order in Afghanistan does collapse and all that is left for the United States is to muddle through the aftermath, there will still be a need to make the muddling through as consistent as possible with U.S. and international interests and the aspirations of the Afghan people. And there will still be the need to make difficult policy choices.

Western Arrogance or Afghan Government Corruption?

During one of my last days in Kabul, I invited Mahmoud, one of the translators with whom I had worked in Afghanistan, to dinner to thank him for his help and to say goodbye—for a few months anyway. I was first to arrive at the restaurant, a place frequented by international advisors. In the evening, the ever-present Afghan dust scattered the shorter wavelengths of the sun, which now appeared intense orange as it descended toward the horizon. There were warblers in the garden, looking for the last meal of the day, stocking up on fuel before setting out on their spring migration to Europe. All of a sudden there was a commotion, and then a furious Mahmoud stomped in. The guards at the entrance would not let him in because he was an Afghan, and they ultimately resorted to calling the Western owner of the restaurant to issue the dispensation for Mahmoud to enter.

Disturbed by the treatment Mahmoud received for being an Afghan and not an international, I at first attributed the behavior of the Afghan guards to an increased sense of danger that prevailed in Kabul just a few weeks after the April 15 Taliban attacks and the launch of the Taliban's yearly spring offensive. It was a harsh reality, I thought, that after a decade of Western efforts in Afghanistan and on the verge of the mission transition to Afghan ownership, Westerners in Afghanistan would feel so insecure in interacting with the local population that they would exhibit an ever greater need to lock themselves up at the compounds where they stay, despite the fact that such a policy generated great resentment among the Afghans. I felt quite awful: Mahmoud and I had a good number of adventures together, and by working as a Westerner's interpreter, he was putting himself in danger. Many a Taliban would find that more than a sufficient justification to kill him, and many a militiaman and local criminal would find him a prime target for extortion or robbery.

Mahmoud was rightly outraged. A Pashtun man, he carried himself with a great sense of honor and dignity. Having lived for almost two decades in Canada, he was imbued with notions of rights and equality. And having worked with the ISAF command in southern Afghanistan for many years, he considered himself an important man. Fuming, he had the owner called to our table, shouting angrily: "How arrogant you Westerners think you can be?! This is our land, my land. You are here at my invitation, not I at yours! You think you are running the Raj again?" The owner remained calm and, apologizing, explained that the reason for controlling Afghan visitors' access to the restaurant was that they were trying to come there to buy or sneak in alcohol, which Afghan law prohibits being sold to Afghan nationals, and the Koran prohibits Muslims from drinking. Mahmoud was not pacified and insisted that he and others did not need to resort to such a subterfuge because he could easily (if clandestinely) buy liquor in many a Kabul bazaar.

While granting that it was indeed very easy to come by spirits elsewhere in the city, the owner insisted that, nonetheless, Afghans constantly did try to sneak liquor into the restaurant in a variety of disguises or have their Western friends buy it there for them. As a result, the restaurant was subject to raids by inspectors and the police. A few months ago, a pregnant Afghan staff member was arrested, although she had nothing to do with the liquor that an Afghan sneaked in, and it took the owner months to get her out of jail. Mahmoud was not moved, and the argument went on for quite a long time, until the owner finally exclaimed: "You know what, man, this is not about the Koran. It's not about the liquor or the laws. This is about your government's corruption. The police and the inspectors set up raids to extort us. Every time I need a new license, every time they come here, they ask for bribes. We refuse to pay, and as a result they harass us as much as they can."

Mahmoud finally agreed.

Acknowledgments

I would like to thank first and foremost my many Afghan friends and interlocutors. This is a book about their country, their aspirations, and their disappointments with their political leaders as well as with the international community's well-meaning, but often ineffective and at times misguided, efforts to improve conditions in Afghanistan. Unfortunately, with few exceptions, in order to protect these interlocutors and their families from retaliation, I cannot identify them by name. In my accounts of conversations with them I usually employ aliases or do not use any names. This bargain with them is adhered to throughout this effort: to give them voice without compromising their security. A special note of appreciation particularly goes to the Afghan drivers and interpreters I have worked with on my trips to Afghanistan who often exposed themselves to great danger in accompanying a lone female American throughout the country. I can, however, identify a few fellow Afghan analysts and members of Afghan nongovernmental or human rights organizations who have been inspiring in their dedication to bringing about a better Afghanistan, such as Shahmahmood Miakhel, Nader Naderi, Omar Sharifi, Assadullah Fareedzai, and Zaid Siddiq.

My appreciation of the dilemmas faced by the Afghan, U.S., and other governments in Afghanistan has been aided immeasurably by the many consultations I have been generously granted by current and former officials—civilian and military—responsible for formulating and implementing Afghanistan policies. Most of these have been on background and not for attribution. Nonetheless, among such officials, I am delighted to be able to acknowledge General John "Mick" Nicholson, Ashraf Ghani, General Jon Vance, William Crosbie, Jack Twiss-Quarles van Ufford, Simon Shercliff, Richard O'Hara, and Marcin Piotrowski. I am also grateful to members of the United Nations Assistance Mission for Afghanistan and international NGOs operating in Afghanistan with whom I have interacted over the years, whose substantive insights and practical advice have been invaluable for both fieldwork and analysis. Because of their need for safety in continuing to operate in Afghanistan, most of them have also been interviewed on the condition of no attribution, though they have included, for example, representatives of Mercy Corps and the Afghanistan NGO Safety Office.

Among the numerous scholars who have provided me with important analytical and practical insights for conducting my fieldwork in Afghanistan, and whose own analyses have greatly informed and enriched mine, are Alex Strick van Linschoten, Felix Kuehn, Gerard Russell, Danae Bougas, David Mansfield, Candace Rondeaux, Brian Grzelkowski, and Thomas Ruttig. For years, being able to catch up with Alex, Felix, Brian, Danae, or Candace in Afghanistan has been one of the highlights of visiting the country again. In the United States, my regular, and no less valued, interlocutors, whose insights have strongly stimulated my thinking, include Alex Their, Ali Jalali, Mark Schneider, Scott Worden, Andrew Wilder, Paul Fishstein, William Byrd, Michael Semple, John Dempsey, Erica Gaston, Rachel Reid, Caroline Wadhams, Lisa Curtis, Peter Bergen, T. Kumar, Rick Inderfurth, Daoud Yaqub, Chris Fair, Daniel Markey, Dave DeAtley, Thomas Johnson, Chris Mason, John Nagl, Stephen Biddle, and Larry Goodson. Their excellent written reports and the extensive conversations I have had with them have been key assets in this investigation and the body of my Afghanistan work. Over the years, I have benefited from many other Afghan and international experts—too numerous to be listed here—but I am deeply appreciative of their insights.

I must also particularly highlight the wonderful companionship and very stimulating intellectual exchanges with colleagues during the NATO-sponsored part of my spring 2012 trip to Afghanistan, with which this book opens. Daniele Riggio worked extremely hard to ensure that the trip ran as smoothly as is possible in a war zone and was highly informative. Germano Dottori, Olivier Guillard, Clive Williams, and Philippe Rotmann ensured that no matter what was happening around us, the discussions were not just extremely productive, but also fun. Philippe stayed deeply engaged in the investigation and writing of the book after the NATO portion of the trip ended and, throughout the process, sent daily texts to me in the Hindu Kush and Pashtun plains to make sure I was still alive and to provide crucial input for various of the book's arguments. I am deeply grateful for his insights and his friendship.

Yet another traveling companion and comrade in many Afghanistan adventures needs to be specially acknowledged—Jon Landay, a long-time observer of Afghanistan's wars and struggle for peace and an intrepid journalist. Jon and I have bounced many ideas off each other, often as we were being bounced about in a Corolla on Afghanistan's potholed roads. There are very few people with whom I would share the joys and risks of traveling in Afghanistan and doing fieldwork there as gladly as with Jon.

My work owes a great deal—in its analytical and prescriptive aspects— to two very distinguished U.S. public servants: Bruce Riedel and Ronald Neumann. Bruce, former official of the Central Intelligence Agency and the National Security Council and now a colleague of mine at Brookings, has provided invaluable insights into the Afghanistan policy process during the Bush and Obama administrations as well as broad perspectives on the evolution and drivers of U.S. policy in the region over the decades. He has also been an inspiration in his determination to find innovative policy solutions to seemingly intractable foreign policy problems and in his exemplary determination to promote a discussion of different viewpoints and stimulate broad debate about U.S. policy in Afghanistan.

Former U.S. ambassador to several countries, including Afghanistan, Ronald Neumann has been an extremely generous interlocutor on how to comprehend decisionmaking within the Afghan government and how to improve U.S. foreign policy. His extremely illuminating insights about not just the policy process in Kabul and Washington, but also the criticality of policy implementation have guided my work throughout. Most important, in his writings and exchanges with me about U.S. aims and lost opportunities in Afghanistan, he has provided a model of what it means to be a realist without illusions when it comes to evaluating and recommending policies for effecting changes in countries and how not to become prematurely discouraged because of unanticipated difficulties.

Wendy Chamberlain, the former U.S. ambassador to Pakistan and yet another prominent and highly accomplished U.S. public official, has been a great source of advice on how to deal with one of the most difficult U.S. foreign policy issue areas—the U.S.-Pakistan relationship. Another authority on Afghanistan and Pakistan whose insights have strongly influenced my work is Marvin Weinbaum. His deep understanding and conceptualization of the feedback relationships between the domestic and international factors affecting conditions within these countries and the problems of implementing U.S. and ISAF strategies have done much to shape my analysis. From the first years I started working on Afghanistan policy, Marvin has been a highly valued colleague in sharing his wealth of knowledge and introducing me to the Afghanistan expert community. For the same reasons, I am also strongly indebted to Barnett Rubin of New York University. Barney's writings have greatly informed mine, and I have benefited enormously from his insights and help over the years.

This book would not have existed without Ken Williams of the Marine Corps University. A senior editor there, Ken strongly encouraged me to write a book bringing together the thinking and policy advice I had previously sketched or alluded to in my various articles on Afghanistan. Indeed, Ken managed to talk me into undertaking this project while I was in the middle of fieldwork in Nepal conducting completely different research, sending me persuasive daily emails in the high Himalayas and the scorching Terai, until I caved in and agreed to do the book. Ken subsequently became a wonderful sounding board for many of the arguments offered here. My very special thanks to him.

Catherine Dale of the Congressional Research Service and Michael Casey of the House Armed Services Committee also merit special recognition and equally special thanks. They too have been invaluable interlocutors and great friends, lending generous support, encouragement, and wit throughout the years of my fieldwork in Afghanistan and the book-writing process. Both have worked on Afghanistan policy in various capacities for many years, and both have shared with me their wealth of advice and insights on the various aspects of the policy process. I have learned much from their keen identification of the variables determining and causing difficulties for U.S. strategies in Afghanistan and of ways to move U.S. policy forward.

I am also very appreciative of the multiple contributions of my resourceful research assistants, Erasmo Sanchez and Bradley Porter. Not only did they provide excellent substantive research assistance for the book, they often had to hold the fort while I was off in Afghanistan or somewhere else in the world. They managed not just what was happening at work in Washington, but also promptly responded to urgent requests while I was in the middle of a firefight in Afghanistan or kept up with Afghanistan developments and sent me updates while I was making my way through Borneo's rainforest.

Absolutely crucial to this effort has been the stimulus and support received from the Brookings Institution and its president, Strobe Talbott, and its vice president for foreign policy, Martin Indyk. I am deeply grateful for Martin's attentive encouragement and intellectual engagement; without his inspirational leadership of the Foreign Policy division and multifaceted support for my Afghanistan work, many of my Afghan endeavors would not have taken place and my analysis would be intellectually much poorer. Michael O'Hanlon, director of research in Foreign Policy, deserves special recognition for deftly shepherding the manuscript through Brookings's rigorous review process and for his own substantive as well as editorial input. Many other colleagues at Brookings have been invaluable interlocutors over the years—whether as experts on the region or as keen outside observers of U.S. efforts. Among those who most directly contributed to the work reflected in the book are Stephen Cohen, Charles Ebinger, Teresita Schaffer, Fiona Hill, Richard Bush, Steven Pifer, Carlos Pascual, Ted Piccone, and Charlotte Baldwin. My special thanks also go to the anonymous reviewers who provided very detailed and pertinent reactions and advice.

A note of special appreciation for the great job of the Brookings Institution Press editorial and production team, Starr Belsky, Larry Converse, Janet Walker, and Susan Woollen, and the design firm they worked with on the cover, as well as the press's marketing staff, Chris Kelaher and Melissa McConnell, and Foreign Policy's Gail Chalef in ensuring that what I wanted to communicate about the often very intricate relationships in the Afghanistan situation did come through clearly, without dilution of my main arguments.

On behalf of Brookings, I acknowledge with immense gratitude the government of Norway and individuals who shall remain anonymous for their generous financial support of this project.

There is yet another group of friends and colleagues who, though not experts on Afghanistan, have been of great help during my Afghanistan fieldwork over the years and the writing of the book. They are experts on Latin America, Africa, Southeast Asia, terrorism, and drug and crime policy—areas I also work on. Their highly stimulating engagement with me on issues in areas of their focus while I was away in Afghanistan and their generous willingness to share their analyses of developments and updates after my return have ensured that the difficult task of doing comparative work and following several geographic areas simultaneously does not become completely impossible. They include Alfredo Corchado, Dianne Solis, Eric Olson, Andrew Selee, Clare Selkee, David Holiday, Sandra Dunsmore, Mauricio Romero, Maria Victoria Llorente, Camino Kavanagh, James Cockayne, Cyndi Arnson, Chappell Lawson, Desmond Arias, Adam Isacson, John Walsh, Peter Reuter, Mark Kleiman, Jon Caulkins, Phil Heymann, Brooke Stearns Lawson, and Lex Rieffel.

To my mother, Jelena Felbabova, and to dear friends like Amy Wagenfeld, Elliot Feldman and Lily Gardner-Feldman, Elaine Neumann, Manny Superville, Vera Regulova, Rod Hills, and others on whom I have inflicted many days and nights of worry as to my safety while in the war zone, I must confess that knowing of your touching concern did keep me from crossing the line between being adventuresome and being reckless.

Finally, a principal sounding board for me on this project, as on so many others, has been one of my favorite scholars and strategic analysts, my best friend and my husband, Seyom Brown. Whether over breakfast, over a campfire deep in Africa's bush, on the Internet, or on the phone late at night when I would call from Afghanistan—his being there 24/7 for intellectual and emotional ballast has been indispensible.

Notes

Chapter 1

1. Although touting the emergence of Afghanistan's young but lively media as a major accomplishment of his government, President Hamid Karzai proposed in July 2012 a new media law that would severely restrict the freedom of journalists and subject them to greater government control. Already the government has exploited the existing clause that reporting must observe "the principles of Islam" to muzzle critics and detain journalists. See Amie Ferris-Rotman, "New Afghan Law Ignites Fear over Shrinking Press Freedoms," Reuters, July 1, 2012.

2. Media outlets funded by the Afghan government and regional actors, such as Iran, are likely to have a much easier time. I am grateful to Erica Gaston of the U.S. Institute of Peace for sharing with me her insights on the state and likely future of Afghan media.

3. The U.S. Geological Survey made that estimate in 2010. For details, see James Risen, "U.S. Identified Vast Mineral Riches in Afghanistan," *New York Times*, June 13, 2010.

4. Ministry of Mines, Government of Afghanistan, "Sustaining Afghanistan's Economy after the Transition," PowerPoint presentation, Center for American Progress, Washington, February 2011.

5. Corruption rating from Transparency International, "Corruption Perceptions Index 2011," http://cpi.transparency.org/cpi2011/results/.

6. Matthew Rosenberg, "Afghan Cabinet Raises Concern about Mining Legislation, to West's Unease," *New York Times*, July 23, 2012.

7. "Afghan Forces Kill 5 Insurgents over Attack Plan," Associated Press, August 2, 2012.

8. Interviews with Afghan politicians, analysts, and civil society organizers, Kabul, April 2012.

9. For details, see Habib Zahori, Rod Nordland, and Alissa Rubin, "Witnesses Describe Brazen Attack on Resort Hotel near Kabul," *New York Times*, June 22, 2012.

10. Matthew Rosenberg, "Coalition Sharply Reduces Joint Operations with Afghan Troops," *New York Times*, September 18, 2012.

11. "ISAF Officials: Reports on Partnering Change 'Not Accurate,'" American Forces Press Service, September 18, 2012; David Stringer and Slobodan Lekic, "NATO: Change in Afghanistan Ops Won't Hurt Strategy," Associated Press, September 18, 2012.

12. Interviews with ISAF officials, Kabul, April 2012, and with U.S. officials, Washington, March and April 2012. For a more optimistic outlook on Afghanistan than presented in this volume, one that recognizes Afghanistan's challenges but is still consistent with NATO's own more positive assessments, see Michael O'Hanlon, "Life after Karzai," *ForeignPolicy.com*, June 13, 2012, www.foreign policy.com/articles/2012/06/13/life_after_karzai.

13. Deb Riechmann, "AP Interview: Afghan Civil War Unlikely, U.S. Says," Associated Press, July 12, 2012.

14. For similar findings, see Dexter Filkins, "After America: Will Civil War Hit Afghanistan When the U.S. Leaves?" *New Yorker*, July 9, 2012, www.newyorker.com/reporting/2012/07/09/120709fa_fact_filkins.

15. To protect their safety and allow them to speak openly, I have conducted all interviews for nonattribution. My non-Afghan interlocutors included officers and political advisors of ISAF, officials of various foreign embassies and development agencies in Afghanistan, representatives of foreign NGOs, employees of foreign security companies, civilian contractors, foreign business owners operating in Afghanistan, and foreign correspondents, as well as foreign analysts living in Afghanistan.

16. Interviews with Afghans from all walks of life in Kabul and in eastern, southern, and northern Afghanistan during fall 2010 and spring 2012. See also "Afghans Fear Future after Foreign Troops Leave, Even after Donor Nations Pledge Ongoing Support," Associated Press, August 2, 2012.

17. Interview with a tribal elder, Baghlan, April 2012.

18. For the debate, see Bruce Riedel, *The Search for al Qaeda: Its Leadership, Ideology, and Future* (Brookings, 2010); Alex van Linschoten and Felix Kuehn, *An Enemy We Created: The Myth of the Taliban/al Qaeda Merger in Afghanistan, 1970–2010* (London: C. Hurst, 2011).

19. TV interview with three senior members of the Taliban negotiating team, NHK World TV, "Today's Close Up," www3.nhk.or.jp/nhkworld/english/tv/todayscloseup/index20120911.html; Michael Semple, "'Al Qaeda Is a Plague': A Remarkable Insight into the Mind of a Senior Member of the Afghan Taliban Movement," *New Statesman*, July 16, 2012, pp. 32–35.

20. On al Qaeda strategic planning, see Bruce Riedel, "The al Qaeda Document Release: What They Tell Us about Bin Laden and His Supporters,"

May 3, 2012, www.brookings.edu/blogs/up-front/posts/2012/05/03-alqaeda-documents-riedel; and Daniel Byman, "The History of Al-Qaida," *Slate*, September 1, 2011, www.slate.com/articles/news_and_politics/foreigners/2011/08/the_history_of_alqaida.html. On al Qaeda in Yemen, see, for example, Bruce Riedel, "Al Qaeda's 'Final Trap' in Yemen: Costly Demise Planned for U.S.," *Daily Beast*, May 27, 2012, www.thedailybeast.com/articles/2012/05/27/al-qaeda-s-final-trap-in-yemen-costly-demise-planned-for-u-s.html.

21. On al Qaeda in West Africa and Nigeria, see Vanda Felbab-Brown and James Forest, "Nigeria's Boko Haram Attacks Are Misunderstood as a Regional Islamist Threat," *Christian Science Monitor*, January 12, 2012; and Vanda Felbab-Brown and James Forest, "Political Violence and the Illicit Economies of West Africa," *Journal of Terrorism and Conflict* (Winter 2012, forthcoming). On al Qaeda in the Horn of Africa, see International Crisis Group, "Somalia: An Opportunity That Should Not Be Missed," Africa Briefing 87, February 22, 2012, www.crisisgroup.org/en/regions/africa/horn-of-africa/somalia/B087-somalia-an-opportunity-that-should-not-be-missed.aspx; and Ken Menkhaus and Jacob Shapiro, "Non-State Actors and Failed States: Al Qa'ida's Experience in the Horn of Africa," in *Ungoverned Spaces: Alternatives to State Authority in an Era of Softened Sovereignty*, edited by Harold Trinkunas and Anne Clunnan (Stanford University Press, 2010), pp. 77–94.

22. See, for example, Stephen Cohen, *The Idea of Pakistan* (Brookings, 2004); and Anatol Lieven, *Pakistan: A Hard Country* (New York: Public Affairs, 2012).

23. Bob Woodward, *Plan of Attack* (London: Simon and Schuster, 2004), p. 150.

24. The term Valhalla was used by Secretary of Defense Robert Gates—not in the original Norse sense as the hall where heroes killed in battle would feast for eternity with the supreme god Odin, but to designate overly ambitious, paradise-like goals that were not really appropriate for the United States to be pursuing in Afghanistan. See Ann Scott Tyson, "Gates Predicts 'Slog' in Afghanistan," *Washington Post*, January 28, 2009, www.washingtonpost.com/wp-dyn/content/article/2009/01/27/AR2009012700472.html.

25. I refrain from using the more common term nation building, which implies the construction of an identity as a nation, that is, a people associated with a particular territory that is sufficiently conscious of its unity to seek a government of its own. Construction of such a consciousness has never been the purpose of the United States in Afghanistan or, for that matter, in many other places around the world. Instead, the United States and the international community have sought to assist in the construction of the apparatus of a state, including its key institutions and laws. Hence nation building is a misnomer, and state building is a far more appropriate term.

26. See, for example, Afghanistan Study Group, *A New Way Forward: Rethinking U.S. Strategy in Afghanistan*, September 2010, www.afghanistanstudygroup.org/read-the-report. For a recent prominent call for emphasizing governance

in Afghanistan, see Stephen Hadley and John Podesta, "The Right Way out of Afghanistan," *Foreign Affairs* 91, no. 4 (2012): 41–53.

27. For details of the conceptual framework, see Vanda Felbab-Brown, *Shooting Up: Counterinsurgency and the War on Drugs* (Brookings, 2010), chapter 2; and Vanda Felbab-Brown, *Human Security and Crime in Latin America: The Political Capital and Political Impact of Criminal Groups and Belligerents Involved in Illicit Economies* (Florida International University, Western Hemisphere Security Analysis Center, September 2011).

28. White House, Office of the Press Secretary, "Remarks by President Obama in Address to the Nation from Afghanistan," May 1, 2012, www.whitehouse. gov/the-press-office/2012/05/01/remarks-president-address-nation-afghanistan.

29. Javed Hamim Kakar, "Some Governors Reshuffled, Others Sacked," Pahjwok Afghan News, September 19, 2012, www.pajhwok.com/en/2012/09/19/ some-governors-reshuffled-others-sacked.

Chapter 2

1. For excellent discussions of the limited resources, increasing ambitions, and mounting challenges during the Bush years, see Dov Zakheim, *A Vulcan's Tale: How the Bush Administration Mismanaged the Reconstruction of Afghanistan* (Brookings, 2011); Ronald Neumann, *The Other War: Winning and Losing in Afghanistan* (Washington: Potomac Books, 2009). See also Bob Woodward, *Bush at War* (New York: Simon and Schuster, 2002); James Dobbins, *After Taliban: Nation-Building in Afghanistan* (Washington: Potomac Books, 2008).

2. Neumann, *The Other War*; Seth Jones, *In the Graveyard of Empires* (New York: Norton, 2009).

3. Kathy Gannon, "Afghanistan Unbound," *Foreign Affairs* 83. no. 3 (2004): 35–47.

4. Barnett Rubin, "Saving Afghanistan," *Foreign Affairs* 86, no. 1 (2007): 57–78.

5. For the increase in international military casualties, Afghan civilian casualties, and the number of insurgent attacks from 2001 through 2008, see icasualties.org. See also Ian Livingston and Michael O'Hanlon, *Afghanistan Index*, July 31, 2012, www.brookings.edu/~/media/Programs/foreign%20policy/afghanistan%20index/index20120731.pdf.

6. For the administration's internal debates and deep continuing rifts regarding Afghanistan policy, see Bob Woodward, *Obama's Wars* (New York: Simon and Schuster, 2010); Rajiv Chandrasekaran, *Little America: The War within the War for Afghanistan* (New York: Knopf, 2012); Michael Hastings, "The Runaway General," *Rolling Stones*, June 22, 2010.

7. For details, see "Transcript: Obama Announces New Afghanistan, Pakistan Strategies," *Washington Post*, March 27, 2009, www.washingtonpost.com/ wp-dyn/content/article/2009/03/27/AR2009032700891.html.

8. See, for example, Jon Boone, "Hillary Clinton Vows to Defend Rights of Afghan Women," *The Guardian*, July 20, 2010; Rajiv Chandrasekaran, "Clinton: U.S. Will Keep Helping Afghan Women," *Washington Post*, March 11, 2011.

9. Cited in Helene Cooper and Thom Shanker, "Aides Say Obama's Afghan Aims Elevate War," *New York Times*, January 28, 2009.

10. Ibid.

11. White House, "White Paper of the Interagency Policy Group's Report on U.S. Policy toward Afghanistan and Pakistan," March 2008, www.whitehouse.gov/assets/documents/afghanistan_pakistan_white_paper_final.pdf.

12. Interviews with Obama administration officials involved in the review, Washington, spring 2009.

13. For details, see "Obama Announces New Afghanistan, Pakistan Strategies."

14. I am grateful to Bruce Riedel for these insights on the effects of the 2009 elections on decisionmaking in the White House.

15. Rajiv Chandrasekaran, "'Little America': Infighting on Obama Team Squandered Chance for Peace in Afghanistan," *Washington Post*, June 24, 2012.

16. Interviews with officials of the United States Agency for International Development and the Department of Agriculture and with the staff of the special representative, Kabul, fall 2010, and Washington, winter 2010 and spring 2011.

17. I am grateful to Bruce Riedel for these insights.

18. Interviews with Afghans across different ethnic groups and many walks of life, Kandahar, Kabul, and Baghlan, September 2010.

19. General Stanley McChrystal, *Commander's Initial Assessment*, unclassified version, August 30, 2009, http://media.washingtonpost.com/wp-srv/politics/documents/Assessment_Redacted_092109.pdf?sid=ST2009092003140.

20. Richard Holbrooke, "The Obama Administration's Challenges in Afghanistan and Pakistan," Keynote speech, Brookings Institution, January 7, 2010, www.brookings.edu/~/media/events/2010/1/07%20afghanistan/20100107_afghanistan.pdf.

21. Peter Baker and Helene Cooper, "All Afghan War Options by Obama Aides Said to Call for More Troops," *New York Times,* November 7, 2009; Peter Baker, "Inside the Situation Room: How a War Plan Evolved," *New York Times,* December 6, 2009. On the divisions in the Obama administration and the debate about the surge numbers, see also David Sanger, *Confront and Conceal: Obama's Secret Wars and Surprising Use of American Power* (New York: Crown Publishers, 2012), pp. 28–34; James Mann, *The Obamians: The Struggle Inside the White House to Redefine American Power* (New York: Viking, 2012), pp. 134–40.

22. Ambassador Karl Eikenberry, "COIN Strategy: Civilian Concerns," Memorandum, November 9, 2009, http://documents.nytimes.com/eikenberry-s-memos-on-the-strategy-in-afghanistan. See also Gregg Jaffe, Scott Wilson, and Karen DeYoung, "U.S. Envoy Resists Troop Increase, Cites Karzai as a Problem," *Washington Post*, November 19, 2009; Eric Schmitt, "U.S. Cables Show Worries on Afghan Plans," *New York Times*, January 25, 2010.

23. White House, Office of the Press Secretary, "Remarks by the President in Address to the Nation on the Way Forward in Afghanistan and Pakistan," December 1, 2009, www.whitehouse.gov/the-press-office/remarks-president-address-nation-way-forward-afghanistan-and-pakistan.

24. For the comments on timelines and winding down the war, see White House, Office of the Press Secretary, "Remarks by President Obama in Address to the Nation from Afghanistan," May 1, 2012, www.whitehouse.gov/the-press-office/2012/05/01/remarks-president-address-nation-afghanistan. For a more positive assessment of the Obama administration's Afghanistan policy, see Martin Indyk, Kenneth Lieberthal, and Michael O'Hanlon, *Bending History: Barack Obama's Foreign Policy* (Brookings, 2012), chapter 3.

25. See, for example, Sherard Cowper-Coles, *Cables from Kabul: The Inside Story of the West's Afghanistan Campaign* (New York: Harper Collins, 2012).

26. Carlotta Gall, "As U.S. Weighs Taliban Negotiations, Afghans Are Already Talking," *New York Times*, March 11, 2009.

27. For details on the Musa Qala deal, see Neumann, *The Other War*, pp. 128–29; Ahmed Rashid, *Descent to Chaos: The United States and the Failure of Nation Building in Pakistan, Afghanistan, and Central Asia* (New York: Penguin, 2008), pp. 272, 274–78, and 369.

28. For details of the North Waziristan ceasefire that became most damaging to U.S. objectives in Afghanistan, see, for example, Ismail Khan and Carlotta Gall, "Pakistan Lets Tribal Chiefs Keep Control along Border," *New York Times*, September 6, 2006; Arthur Bright, "Pakistan Signs Peace Deal with Pro-Taliban Militants," *Christian Science Monitor*, September 6, 2006.

29. See chapter 10 in this volume. See also Bruce Riedel, *Deadly Embrace: Pakistan, America, and the Future of Global Jihad* (Brookings, 2011).

30. For strong statements calling for prompt negotiations with the Taliban, see Lakhdar Brahimi and Thomas Pickering, co-chairs, *Afghanistan: Negotiating Peace,* Report of the Century Foundation International Task Force on Afghanistan in Its Regional and Multilateral Dimensions, 2011, http://tcf.org/publications/pdfs/afghanistan-negotiating-peace/AfghanTCFTaskForceBookSummaryOfRecommendations.pdf; Michael Semple and Fotini Christia, "Flipping the Taliban: How to Win in Afghanistan," *Foreign Affairs* 88, no. 4 (2009): 34–45; Alex Strick van Linschoten and Felix Kuehn, "A Pointless Blacklisting," *New York Times*, September 11, 2012.

31. For a comprehensive analysis of previous reconciliation efforts as well as the current strategy to lure individual insurgents away with economic incentives, see Matt Waldman, "Golden Surrender: The Risks, Challenges, and Implications of Reintegration in Afghanistan," Afghanistan Analyst Network, March 2010, http://aan-afghanistan.com/uploads/2010_AAN_Golden_Surrender.pdf. See also Thomas Ruttig, "The Other Side: Causes, Actors, and Approaches to Talks," Afghanistan Analyst Network, January 2009, http://aan-afghanistan.com/uploads/200907%20AAN%20Report%20Ruttig%20-%20The%20Other%20

Side.pdf; Elisabeth Bumiller, "U.S. Tries to Reintegrate Taliban Soldiers," *New York Times*, May 23, 2010.

32. For an overview of some of the key questions, challenges, and dilemmas involved in dealing with the Taliban, see Vanda Felbab-Brown, "Negotiations and Reconciliation with the Taliban: Key Policy Issues and Dilemmas," Brief (Brookings, January 2010), www.brookings.edu/articles/2010/0128_taliban_felbabbrown.aspx.

33. Cited in Karen DeYoung, "Afghan President Plans Meeting on Reintegrating, Reconciling with Insurgents," *Washington Post*, January 2010.

34. Chandrasekaran, "'Little America': Infighting."

35. See chapter 11 in this volume.

36. White House, Office of the Press Secretary, "Remarks by the President on the Way Forward in Afghanistan," June 22, 2011, http://london.usembassy.gov/obama190.html. See also Catherine Dale, "In Brief: Next Steps in the War in Afghanistan? Issues for Congress," Report R42137 (Congressional Research Service, Library of Congress, June 15, 2012).

37. See the leaked report from TF 3-10 Bagram, Afghanistan, *State of the Taliban: Detainee Perspectives*, January 6, 2012, http://s3.documentcloud.org/documents/296489/taliban-report.pdf.

38. Earlier, similar restrictions were agreed to by General McChrystal. See "ISAF Issues Guidance on Night Raids in Afghanistan," ISAF, March 5, 2010, www.isaf.nato.int/article/isaf-releases/isaf-issues-guidance-on-night-raids-in-afghanistan.html. But under the successive leadership of General David Petraeus and General John Allen, who followed McChrystal as commander of U.S. forces and ISAF in Afghanistan, the restriction loosened and the frequency of night raids increased. Furthermore, the directive by McChrystal was at the discretion of the ISAF commander and not codified in a treaty, as President Karzai sought.

39. On one dramatic escape of hundreds of prisoners from the Kandahar City jail, see Taimoor Shah and Alissa Rubin, "Taliban Help Hundreds Tunnel out of Prison's Political Wing," *New York Times*, April 25, 2011.

40. See, for example, Matthew Rosenberg, "Karzai's Ultimatum Complicates U.S. Exit Strategy," January 8, 2012; Afghanistan Independent Human Rights Commission and the Open Society Foundations, *Torture, Transfers, and Denial of Due Process: The Treatment of Conflict-Related Detainees in Afghanistan*, March 17, 2012, www.aihrc.org.af/media/files/AIHRC%20OSF%20Detentions%20Report%20English%20Final%2017-3-2012.pdf.

41. Graham Bowley, "U.S. Puts Transfer of Detainees to Afghans on Hold," *New York Times*, September 9, 2012. For the implementation challenges of transferring authority for detentions to Afghan authorities, see also Open Society Foundations, *Remaking Bagram: The Creation of an Afghan Internment Regime and the Divide over U.S. Detention Power*, Regional Policy Initiative (New York, September 6, 2012), www.soros.org/sites/default/files/BagramReportEnglish.pdf.

42. Paul Miller, "Promises, Promises: The U.S.-Afghan Strategic Partnership," *Foreign Policy.com*, May 21, 2012, http://afpak.foreignpolicy.com/posts/2012/05/21/promises_promises_the_us_afghan_strategic_partnership.

43. "Enduring Strategic Partnership between the United States of America and the Islamic Republic of Afghanistan," May 2, 2012, www.whitehouse.gov/sites/default/files/2012.06.01u.s.-afghanistanspasignedtext.pdf.

44. Interviews with Afghans from all walks of life about their attitudes toward the possible signing of the SPA, Afghanistan, April 2012, and personal communications with retired ambassador Ronald Neumann about the reactions of his interlocutors (mainly educated Kabul elites) during his May 2012 research trip in Afghanistan.

45. Personal communication with Ronald Neumann.

46. See "Afghans Fear Future after Foreign Troops Leave Even after Donor Nations Pledge Ongoing Support," Associated Press, August 2, 2012; Miriam Arghandiwal, "Entrepreneurs Serving Afghan Expats See Good Times Ending," Reuters, August 6, 2012.

47. White House, "Address to the Nation from Afghanistan."

48. Interviews with ISAF military officers and civilian political advisers from various allied countries, Afghanistan, April 2012.

49. White House, "Address to the Nation from Afghanistan."

50. Missy Ryan and Hamid Shalizi, "Troop Immunity Likely to Be Focus of U.S. Afghanistan Deal," Reuters, June 29, 2012.

51. Ibid.

52. See Ernesto Londoño and Greg Jaffe, "Karzai Demands U.S. Troops Leave Village Outposts; Taliban Suspends Peace Talks," *Washington Post*, March 15, 2012.

53. See chapter 11 for a detailed discussion.

54. I am grateful to Ambassador Ronald Neumann for this information.

55. White House, "Address to the Nation from Afghanistan."

56. Ibid.

57. Jane Perlez, "$16 Billion in Civilian Aid Pledged to Afghanistan, with Conditions," *New York Times*, July 8, 2012.

58. See detailed analysis in chapter 6.

59. See William Byrd, "When Too Much Is Not Enough," *Foreign Policy.com*, July 2, 2012, http://afpak.foreignpolicy.com/posts/2012/07/02/when_too_much_is_not_enough; William Byrd, "Mutual Accountability: Lessons and Prospects for Afghanistan Post-Tokyo," Peace Brief 132 (Washington: United States Institute of Peace, July 27, 2012).

60. William Byrd, "Keeping Each Other Honest in Afghanistan—Will It Work?" *Foreign Policy.com*, August 6, 2012, http://afpak.foreignpolicy.com/posts/2012/08/06/keeping_each_other_honest_in_afghanistan_will_it_work.

61. Helene Cooper and Thom Shanker, "U.S. Redefines Afghan Success before Conference," *New York Times*, May 17, 2012. On the prior use of "Afghan good

enough" as a moniker for a White House Afghanistan decisionmaking group who sought to narrow the goals in Afghanistan as much as possible, see David Sanger, *Confront and Conceal: Obama's Secret Wars and Surprising Use of American Power* (New York: Crown, 2012), pp. 49–50.

Chapter 3

1. For details, see Barnett Rubin, *Fragmentation of Afghanistan* (Yale University Press, 1995); Ahmed Rashid, *Taliban* (Yale University Press, 2001).

2. Jobin Goodarzi, "Washington and the Taliban, Strange Bedfellows," *Middle East International*, October 25, 1996.

3. Frederik Balfour, "Dark Days for a Black Market: Afghanistan and Pakistan Rely Heavily on Smuggling," *Business Week*, October 15, 2001.

4. For details on the political economy requirements of illicit economies, see Vanda Felbab-Brown, "Rules and Regulations in Ungoverned Spaces: Illicit Economies, Criminals, and Belligerents," in *Ungoverned Spaces: Alternatives to State Authority in an Era of Softened Sovereignty*, edited by Harold Trinkunas and Anne Clunnan (Stanford University Press, 2010).

5. Barnett Rubin, "The Political Economy of War and Peace in Afghanistan," *World Development* 28, no. 10 (2000): 1789–803, http://institute-for-afghan-studies.org/ECONOMY/political_economy_of_war_peace.htm.

6. William Maley, *The Afghanistan Wars* (New York: Palgrave Macmillan, 2002), pp. 223–26, 232.

7. Anthony Davis, "How the Taliban Became a Fighting Force," in *Fundamentalism Reborn: Afghanistan and the Taliban*, edited by William Maley (New York University Press, 1998), p. 46.

8. Ibid., pp. 43–71, for details on the extent of Pakistan's involvement. See also Ahmed Rashid, "Pakistan and the Taliban," in *Fundamentalism Reborn*, pp. 85–86; Steve Coll, *Ghost Wars* (New York: Penguin Press, 2004).

9. Jobin Goodarzi, "Washington and the Taliban, Strange Bedfellows," *Middle East International*, October 25, 1996; and Coll, *Ghost Wars*.

10. For details, see chapter 10 in this volume.

11. For details, see Rashid, "Pakistan and the Taliban"; Davis, "How the Taliban Became a Fighting Force."

12. See chapter 4 in this volume.

13. For details, see Vanda Felbab-Brown, *Shooting Up: Counterinsurgency and the War on Drugs* (Brookings, 2010), chapter 5.

14. Interviews with various Pashtun interlocutors throughout Afghanistan, 2005, 2009, 2010, and 2012.

15. Felbab-Brown, *Shooting Up*, chapter 5.

16. For background on the mujahideen fight against the Soviet occupation, see, for example, Olivier Roy, *Islam and Resistance in Afghanistan* (Cambridge University Press, 1990); Marvin Weinbaum, *Pakistan and Afghanistan: Resistance and Occupation* (Boulder, Colo.: Westview Press, 1994); Ali Ahmad Jalali and Lester W. Grau, *Afghan Guerrilla Warfare: In the Words of the Mujahideen Fighters* (St. Paul: MBI Publishing, 2001).

17. See, for example, Coll, *Ghost Wars*; Bruce Riedel, *The Search for al Qaeda: Its Leadership, Ideology, and Future* (Brookings, 2010); Peter Bergen, *Holy War, Inc: Inside the Secret World of Osama bin Laden* (New York: Free Press, 2001); Peter Bergen, *Manhunt: The Ten-Year Search for Bin Laden—from 9-11 to Abbottabad* (New York: Random House, 2012).

18. For a review of al Qaeda's evolution and trajectories, see also Daniel Byman, "The History of al Qaeda," www.brookings.edu/research/opinions/2011/09/01-al-qaeda-history-byman.

19. For details on Taliban rule and the receptivity of the population to it, see Larry Goodson, *Afghanistan's Endless War* (University of Washington Press, 2001).

20. Interviews with Afghan interlocutors across all walks of life and throughout Afghanistan, 2005, 2009, 2010, and 2012.

21. See Ahmed Rashid, *Descent into Chaos: The U.S. and the Disaster in Pakistan, Afghanistan, and Central Asia* (London: Penguin, 2009); Seth Jones, *The Graveyard of Empires* (New York: Norton, 2009).

22. For a range of data on troop levels, casualties, and governance from 2005 to the present, see the "Afghanistan Index," www.brookings.edu/foreign-policy/afghanistan-index.aspx. For the report, see General Stanley McChrystal, *Commander's Initial Assessment*, August 30, 2009, http://media.washingtonpost.com/wp-srv/politics/documents/Assessment_Redacted_092109.pdf?hpid=topnews.

23. See, for example, Carlotta Gall, "Taliban Hold Sway in Area Taken by U.S., Farmers Say," *New York Times*, May 16, 2010.

24. For details on U.S. military operations and economic efforts in Helmand, see Rajiv Chandrasekaran, *Little America: The War within the War for Afghanistan* (New York: Knopf, 2012).

25. See, for example, Taimoor Shah and Rod Nordland, "Near Kandahar, the Prize Is an Empty Town," *New York Times*, September 1, 2010.

26. In the first six months of 2012, Afghan buyers spent over $53 million on real estate in Dubai, a 27 percent increase compared to the same period in 2011, outpacing the rise in all property transactions in Dubai. For details, see Praveen Menon and Matthew Green, "Afghans Seek Shelter in Dubai Ahead of Pullout," Reuters, September 13, 2012.

27. Based on the author's trip to Afghanistan in April 2012. For a powerful sense of the local mood in the strategically vital Kandahar City and the pulse of the Pashtun areas before the surge, see Alex Strick van Linschoten and Felix Kuehn, "See You Soon, If We're Still Alive," *Foreign Policy*, November 2009, pp.

82–87. See also Rajiv Chandrasekaran, "In Kandahar, a Taliban on the Rise," *Washington Post*, September 14, 2009.

28. Interviews with Afghans throughout Afghanistan, 2009, 2010, and 2012.

29. Ibid.

30. It is also important to note that the distinction between "insurgents" and the rest of the population is not a firm one. Few insurgents are combatants 100 percent of the time; many fight only a few months a year, usually after the poppy harvest when earning opportunities are much fewer.

31. Although the Haqqani insurgents maintain their own identity, history, and operational and leadership structures, they consider themselves part of the Taliban. Indeed, the label Haqqani network is not used by the group itself, which instead refers to itself as the Taliban. See the leaked report from TF 3-10 Bagram, Afghanistan, *State of the Taliban: Detainee Perspectives*, January 6, 2012, p.10, http://s3.documentcloud.org/documents/296489/taliban-report.pdf.

32. For details on fundraising, see Felbab-Brown, *Shooting Up*, chapter 5. Since 2002, fundraising efforts in the Middle East, particularly the Gulf region, have been disguised as religious donations or venture capital, ostensibly to fund Afghan entrepreneurs. For details, see TF 3-10 Bagram, *State of the Taliban*, pp. 12–14.

33. Felbab-Brown, *Shooting Up*, chapter 5; Vanda Felbab-Brown, "Narco-belligerents across the Globe: Lessons from Colombia for Afghanistan?" Working Paper 55-2009 (Madrid: Real Instituto Elcano, October 2009); Gretchen Peters, *Haqqani Network Financing: the Evolution of an Industry* (West Point, N.Y.: Combating Terrorism Center, July 2012); Yaroslav Trofimov, "Taliban Capitalize on Afghan Logging Ban," *Wall Street Journal*, April 10, 2010; Matthew DuPée, "Afghanistan's Conflict Minerals: The Crime-State-Insurgent Nexus," *CTC Sentinel* 5, no.2 (2012): 11–14, www.ctc.usma.edu/posts/afghanistans-conflict-minerals-the-crime-state-insurgent-nexus.

34. For more detail on Pakistan's supporting role, see chapter 10 in this volume.

35. Interrogations of detained Haqqani members revealed little credible evidence of Pakistan's direct funding, training, or equipping the Haqqani network. For details, see TF 3-10 Bagram, *State of the Taliban*, p.12. Other analysts describe a tighter cooperation between the ISI and the Haqqanis. See, for example, Matt Waldman, "The Sun in the Sky: The Relationship between Pakistan's ISI and Afghan Insurgents," Crisis States Research Center Discussion Paper 18 (London School of Economics, June 2010), www.aljazeera.com/mritems/Documents/2010/6/13/20106138531279734lse-isi-taliban.pdf; Steve Coll, "Letter from Afghanistan: War by Other Means," *The New Yorker*, May 24, 2010.

36. See chapter 10 in this volume as well as Bruce Riedel, *Deadly Embrace: Pakistan, America, and the Future of Global Jihad* (Brookings, 2011); Seth G. Jones, "Pakistan's Dangerous Game," *Survival* 49, no. 1 (2007): 15–32.

37. TF 3-10 Bagram, *State of the Taliban*, p. 9.

38. See, for example, Javed Hamdar and Candace Rondeaux, "Suicide Bombing Leaves 40 Dead in Central Kabul," *Washington Post,* July 8, 2008; Karin Brulliard, "Afghan Intelligence Ties Pakistani Group Lashkar-e-Taiba to Recent Kabul Attack," *Washington Post*, March 3, 2010; Maria Abi-Habab and Zia Sultani, "NATO Copter Ends Kabul Hotel Siege," *Wall Street Journal*, June 29, 2011; Emily Wax, "Kabul Attack May Intensify India-Pakistan Proxy War," *Washington Post*, October 11, 2009.

39. Declan Walsh and Eric Schmitt, "New Boldness from Militants Poses Risks to U.S.-Pakistan Ties," *New York Times*, July 30, 2012.

40. TF 3-10 Bagram, *State of the Taliban*, p. 12.

41. Ibid.

42. Ibid., p. 4.

43. Interviews with ISAF military leaders and civilian advisers, Kabul and Kandahar, spring 2009, fall 2010, and spring 2012. See also Dennis Blair, "Annual Threat Assessment of the U.S. Intelligence Community for the Senate Select Committee on Intelligence," February 2, 2010, http://isis-online.org/uploads/conferences/documents/2010_NIE.pdf.

44. See, for example, Antonio Giustozzi, *Koran, Kalashnikov, and Laptop: The Neo-Taliban Insurgency in Afghanistan 2002–2007* (New York: Columbia-Hurst, 2007); Giustozzi, *Decoding the New Taliban: Insights from the Field* (New York: Columbia-Hurst, 2009).

45. For a detailed analysis of the Quetta Shura, see Jeffrey Dressler and Carl Forsberg, "The Quetta Shura Taliban in Southern Afghanistan: Organization, Operations, and Shadow Governance," Backgrounder (Washington: Institute for the Study of War, December 21, 2009), www.understandingwar.org/sites/default/files/QuettaShuraTaliban_1.pdf.

46. For details, see the interview of a senior Taliban commander in Michael Semple, "'Al Qaeda Is a Plague': A Remarkable Insight into the Mind of a Senior Member of the Afghan Taliban Movement," *New Statesman*, July 16, 2012, pp. 32–35.

47. TF 3-10 Bagram, *State of the Taliban*, p. 26.

48. Three senior Taliban negotiators interviewed by NHK World TV, "Today's Close Up," www3.nhk.or.jp/nhkworld/english/tv/todayscloseup/index20120911.html.

49. For several recent incidents, see Matthew Rosenberg and Sangar Rahimi, "In Video Execution, Reign of Taliban Recalled," *New York Times*, July 8, 2012; Rod Nordland, "Portrait of Pain Ignites Debate over Afghan War," *New York Times*, August 4, 2010.

50. For details on the rebellion, see David Young, "The Anatomy of an Anti-Taliban Uprising," *Foreign Policy.com*, September 12, 2012, http://afpak.foreignpolicy.com/posts/2012/09/12/the_anatomy_of_an_anti_taliban_uprising.

51. See, for example, Alia Brahimi, "The Taliban's Evolving Ideology," Global Governance Working Paper 02-2010 (London School of Economics, July 2010), http://eprints.lse.ac.uk/29970/1/WP022010_Brahimi.pdf.

52. See Rod Nordland, "Roadside Bombs Kills 11 in Northern Afghanistan," *New York Times*, November 8, 2011; "Taliban Leader Urges Insurgents to Cut Civilian Deaths," Reuters, August 17, 2012.

53. TF 3-10 Bagram, *State of the Taliban*, p. 3.

54. For the evolution of these bloody tactics by the Taliban, see Brian Glyn Williams, "Mullah Omar's Missiles: A Field Report on Suicide Bombers in Afghanistan," *Middle East Policy* 15, no. 4 (2008): 26–45.

55. Antonio Giustozzi and Christoph Reuter, "The Northern Front: The Afghan Insurgency Spreading beyond the Pashtuns" (Kabul: Afghan Analysts Network, June 2010), http://aan-afghanistan.com/uploads/20100629AGCR-TheNorthernFront1.pdf.

56. TF 3-10 Bagram, *State of the Taliban*, p. 7.

57. See Miriam Abou Zahab and Olivier Roy, *Islamist Networks: The Afghan-Pakistan Connection* (Columbia University Press, 2004); Riedel, *The Search for al Qaeda*.

58. See, for example, Alex van Linschoten and Felix Kuehn, *An Enemy We Created: The Myth of the Taliban/al Qaeda Merger in Afghanistan, 1970–2010* (London: C. Hurst & Co.: 2011).

59. Semple, "'Al Qaeda Is a Plague.'"

60. Brahimi, "Taliban's Evolving Ideology."

61. For details on the Haqqanis, see Jeff Dressler, *The Haqqani Network: From Pakistan to Afghanistan*, Afghanistan Report 6 (Washington: Institute for the Study of War, October 2010), www.understandingwar.org/sites/default/files/Haqqani_Network_0.pdf.

62. See, for example, International Crisis Group, "The Insurgency in Afghanistan's Heartland," Asia Report 207 (Brussels, June 27, 2011); Peters, *Haqqani Network Financing*.

63. Rubin, *Fragmentation of Afghanistan*.

64. See, for example, Thomas Barfield, *Afghanistan: A Cultural and Political History* (Princeton University Press, 2010). The erosion of tribal structures is discussed in detail in chapter 4 of this volume.

65. Larry Goodson, *Afghanistan's Endless War* (University of Washington Press, 2001).

66. Interviews with ISAF officials and political advisers, staff of the UN Assistance Mission in Afghanistan, and Afghan civil society representatives, Uruzgan, spring 2009.

67. Interviews with provincial reconstruction team representatives, Afghan officials, and Afghan and international nongovernmental organizations in Helmand, Kandahar, Zabul, and Uruzgan, Afghanistan, spring 2009.

68. For an analysis of the Taliban campaign in southern Afghanistan, including for Kandahar City, that argues against tribal determinism, see Carl Forsberg, *The Taliban's Campaign for Kandahar*, Afghanistan Report 3 (Washington: Institute for the Study of War, December 1, 2009), www.understandingwar.org/report/talibans-campaign-kandahar.

69. Young, "The Anatomy of an Anti-Taliban Uprising."

70. For some of the intellectual background of this approach, see Jim Gant, "One Tribe at a Time: The Way Forward," *Small Wars Journal,* October 2009, http://smallwarsjournal.com/events/tew/docs/ganttew.pdf; Thomas Johnson and M. Chris Mason, "All Counterinsurgency Is Local," *Atlantic Monthly*, October 2008; Thomas Johnson and M. Chris Mason, "No Sign until the Burst of Fire: Understanding the Pakistan-Afghanistan Frontier," *International Security* 32, no. 4 (2008): 41–77.

71. TF 3-10 Bagram, *State of the Taliban*, p. 14.

72. Interviews in southern Afghanistan, 2009 and 2012. For analyses of motivations among other insurgents, see Roger Petersen, *Resistance and Rebellion: Lessons from Eastern Europe* (Cambridge University Press, 2001); Francisco Gutiérrez Sanín, "Diverging Paths: Comparing Responses to Insurgent Challenges in Colombia and Perú," Paper for the Crisis States Center, London School of Economics, 2006, author's copy, unpublished.

73. See Carl Forsberg, *Politics and Power in Kandahar*, Afghanistan Report 5 (Washington: Institute for the Study of War, April 2010), www.understandingwar.org/sites/default/files/Politics_and_Power_in_Kandahar.pdf.

74. See, for example, Seth G. Jones, "The Rise of the Afghanistan Insurgency: State Failure and Jihad," *International Security* 32, no. 4 (2008): 7–40.

75. See Paula Kantor and Adam Pain, "Securing Life and Livelihoods in Rural Afghanistan: The Role of Social Relationships," Issues Paper (Kabul: Afghan Research and Evaluation Unit [AREU], 2010), www.areu.org.af/Uploads/EditionPdfs/1045E-Securing%20Life%20and%20Livelihoods%20IP%202010%20web.pdf; Martine van Biljert, "Between Discipline and Discretion: Policies Surrounding Senior Subnational Appointments," Briefing Paper (Kabul: AREU, May 2009), www.areu.org.af/UpdateDownloadHits.aspx?EditionId=73&Pdf=923E-Subnational Appointments- BP-print.pdf.

76. See Ernesto Londoño, "Survey of Afghans Points to Rampant Corruption in Government," *Washington Post*, July 8, 2010.

77. Interviews with Afghans across all walks of life, spring 2009, fall 2010, and spring 2012. For some seminal pieces highlighting the role of the warlords in post-Taliban Afghanistan, see, for example, Kathy Gannon, "Afghanistan Unbound," *Foreign Affairs* 83, no. 3 (2004): 35–46; Sarah Chayes, *The Punishment of Virtue: Inside Afghanistan after Taliban* (New York: Penguin Press, 2006); Stephen Carter and Kate Clark, "No Shortcut to Stability: Justice, Politics, and Insurgency in Afghanistan" (London: Chatham House, December 2010), www.chathamhouse.org/sites/default/files/public/Research/Asia/1210pr_afghanjustice.pdf.

78. For how many government administrative positions, such as key law enforcement positions, have been sold for profit and political favoritism, see Barnett Rubin, "Saving Afghanistan," *Foreign Affairs*, 86, no. 1 (2007): 57–78.

79. Many unofficial power brokers sought to legitimize their power and immunize themselves from prosecution by seeking election to Afghanistan's parliament during the September 2010 elections. For details on the election process and the role of the warlords and other power brokers in it, see Jonathan Landay, "Warlord and Killers Seek Re-election to Afghan Parliament," *McClatchy Newspapers*, September 14, 2010; Jonathan Landay and Dion Nissenbaum, "Afghan Elections Panel Reports New Evidence of Serious Fraud,"*McClatchy Newspapers*, September 21, 2010.

80. Transparency International, "2011 Corruption Perceptions Index," http://cpi.transparency.org/cpi2011/results/.

81. Interviews in Afghanistan, September 2010 and April 2012. See also Carter and Clark, "No Shortcut to Stability."

82. This discussion has greatly profited from the author's exchanges on the issue with Paul Fishstein, the former director of the AREU, Kabul, Afghanistan, and now fellow at the Carr Center and Belfer Center at Harvard University.

83. For some of many examples of the Taliban exploiting and inserting itself into local conflicts, see Alissa Rubin, "Taliban Driven from Afghan District," *New York Times*, June 1, 2010.

84. TF 3-10 Bagram, *State of the Taliban*, p. 5.

85. Ibid., pp. 3 and 5.

86. Ibid., p. 6.

87. Ibid., p. 2.

88. James Traub, "Afghanistan's Civic War," *New York Times*, June 15, 2010.

89. Elaborated further in chapters 4 and 9 of this volume.

90. For the macroeconomic effects of the narcotics economy, see Edouard Martin and Steven Symansky, "Macroeconomic Impact of the Drug Economy and Counter-Narcotics Efforts," in *Afghanistan's Drug Industry: Structure, Functioning, Dynamics, and Implications of Counter-Narcotics Policy*, edited by Doris Buddenberg and William A. Byrd (Vienna: UN Office on Drugs and Crime, and Washington: World Bank, 2006), pp. 25–46, www.unodc.org/pdf/afg/publications/afghanistan_drug_industry.pdf.

91. For details on how the sponsorship of the poppy economy allows the Taliban to obtain this key political capital, see Felbab-Brown, *Shooting Up*, chapter 5.

92. Young, "The Anatomy of an Anti-Taliban Uprising."

93. Eric Schmitt, "Allies Restrict Airstrikes against Taliban in Homes," *New York Times*, June 10, 2012.

94. ISAF, "General Petraeus Issues Updated Tactical Directive: Emphasizes 'Disciplined Use of Force,'" August 4, 2010, www.isaf.nato.int/article/isaf-releases/general-petraeus-issues-updated-tactical-directive-emphasizes-disciplined-use-of-force.html.

95. United Nations Mission in Afghanistan (UNAMA), "UNAMA Calls on the Parties to Prioritize Protection of Civilians and Accountability of Security Forces in Transition Period," Press statement, Kabul, Afghanistan, May 31, 2012. For time data series and the Taliban reaction and sensitivity to being exposed as responsible for civilian casualties, see Sayed Salahuddin, "Afghan Taliban Reject U.N. Report on Civilian Deaths," Reuters, December 22, 2010.

Chapter 4

1. For works that take this orientalist view, see, for example, Thomas Johnson and Chris Mason, "No Sign until the Burst of Fire: Understanding the Pakistan-Afghanistan Frontier," *International Security* 32, no. 4 (2008): 41–77; David Ignatius, "Britain's Afghan Wisdom," *Washington Post*, September 24, 2009; David J. Kilcullen, "Terrain, Tribes, and Terrorists: Pakistan, 2006–08," Counterinsurgency and Pakistan Paper 3 (Brookings, 2009). For Kilcullen's seminal work on counterinsurgency, see David Kilcullen, *The Accidental Guerrilla: Fighting Small Wars in the Midst of a Big One* (Oxford University Press, 2009).

2. See, for example, Rory Stewart, "The Irresistible Illusion," *London Review of Books* 31, no. 13 (2009): 3–6; Rory Stewart, "It's Hard to Believe We Can Build a Credible State after So Many Years of Failure," *The Independent*, May 26, 2012.

3. Afghanistan Study Group, *A New Way Forward: Rethinking U.S. Strategy in Afghanistan*, September 2010, www.afghanistanstudygroup.org/read-the-report/.

4. The density of international troops in Afghanistan until late in the first decade of the 2000s was one soldier per 25 square kilometers and per 1,115 inhabitants, thus ranking behind Kosovo, Bosnia, East Timor, Iraq, Somalia, Liberia, Sierra Leone, and Haiti. See Michael Bhatia, Kevin Lanigan, and Philip Wilkinson, "Minimal Investments, Minimal Results: The Failure of Security Policy in Afghanistan," Briefing Paper (Kabul: AREU, June 2004). See also James Dobbins and others, *America's Role in Nation-Building: From Germany to Iraq* (Santa Monica, Calif.: RAND, 2004); Marvin Weinbaum, "Nation-Building in Afghanistan: Impediments, Lessons, and Prospects," Paper prepared for the conference "Nation-Building: Beyond Afghanistan and Iraq," School of Advanced International Studies, Johns Hopkins University, April 13, 2004, www.sais-jhu.edu/sebin/e/x/NationbuildingWeinbaum.pdf.

5. See, for example, United States Institute of Peace, *Establishing the Rule of Law in Afghanistan,* Special Report 117 (Washington: March 2004).

6. For a historical, sociological, and anthropological primer, see Thomas Barfield, *Afghanistan: A Cultural and Political History* (Princeton University Press, 2010).

7. See, for example, Mariam Abou Zahab, "Changing Patterns of Social and Political Life among the Tribal Pashtuns of Pakistan," Instituts d'études politiques–Centre d'études et de recherches internationals and Institut national des langues et civilisations orientales, 2007, unpublished paper available at http://scholar.googleusercontent.com/scholar?q=cache:o7ABbfYBjUUJ:scholar.google.com/+Mariam+Abou+Zahab&hl=en&as_sdt=0,21.

8. See Daniel Markey, "A False Choice in Pakistan," *Foreign Affairs* 86, no. 4 (2007): 85–112; Hassan Abbas, *Pakistan's Troubled Frontier* (Washington: Jamestown Foundation, 2009); Joshua White, *Pakistan's Islamist Frontier: Islamic Politics and U.S. Policy in Pakistan's North-West Frontier* (Arlington, Va.: Center on Faith and International Affairs, 2008).

9. Hamish Nixon, "The 'Subnational Governance' Challenge and the Independent Directorate of Local Governance," in *Snapshots of an Intervention: The Unlearned Lessons of Afghanistan's Decade of Assistance 2001–2011*, edited by Martine van Bijlert and Sari Kouvo (Kabul: Afghanistan Analysts Network, 2012), pp. 117–23.

10. For the seminal work on governance in Afghanistan at that time, see Louis Dupree, *Afghanistan* (Oxford University Press, 1973). See also Barfield, *Afghanistan*.

11. Interviews with current and former officials of the United States and UN Office on Drugs and Crime involved in these development programs in the 1990s, Washington and New York, winter 2006. For details on the programs, see Amir Zada Asad and Robert Harris, *The Politics and Economics of Drug Production on the Pakistan-Afghanistan Border* (Burlington, Vt.: Ashgate, 2003).

12. For how easy it is for such development aid to be usurped by corrupt national elites, see House Committee on Oversight and Government Reform, Subcommittee on National Security and Foreign Affairs, *Hearing on U.S. Aid to Pakistan: Planning and Accountability*, testimony of Andrew Wilder, Research Director, Feinstein International Center, Tufts University, 111 Cong. 1 sess. (December 9, 2009).

13. On the level of civilian casualties, see, for example, Peter Bergen and Katherine Tiedemann, "The Year of the Drone: An Analysis of U.S. Drone Strikes in Pakistan, 2004–2010," Counterterrorism Strategy Initiative Paper (Washington: New America Foundation, February 24, 2010); Peter Bergen and Jennifer Rowland, "CIA Drone War in Pakistan in Sharp Decline," *CNN.com*, March 28, 2012, http://edition.cnn.com/2012/03/27/opinion/bergen-drone-decline/index.html?iref=allsearch; Avery Plaw, Matthew Fricker, and Brian Glyn Williams, "Practice Makes Perfect? The Changing Civilian Toll of CIA Drone Strikes in Pakistan," *Perspectives on Terrorism* 5, no. 5-6 (2011), www.terrorismanalysts.com/pt/index.php/pot/article/view/practice-makes-perfect/html.

14. See Olivier Roy, *Afghanistan: From Holy War to Civil War* (Princeton, N.J.: Darwin Press, 1995).

15. Interview with Ronald Neumann, U.S. ambassador to Afghanistan 2005–07, Washington, D.C., November 8, 2010.

16. For details on Karzai's wheeling and dealing tactics, see Elizabeth Rubin, "Karzai in His Labyrinth," *New York Times*, August 4, 2009.

17. Ahmed Wali Karzai in Kandahar, the famous or notorious (depending on one's perspective) brother of President Hamid Karzai, was especially well known for such interventions to get senior Taliban leaders released from prison, often on pretext of facilitating reconciliation with the Taliban. See Emma Graham-Harrison, "Afghan Officials Free Top Taliban Fighters," Reuters, November 30, 2010.

18. Several of these warlords were killed over the past two years. For an excellent and detailed analysis of major power brokers in southern and western Afghanistan, see Antonio Giustozzi and Noor Ullah, "'Tribes' and Warlords in Southern Afghanistan, 1980–2005," Working Paper 7 (London School of Economics, Crisis States Research Center, September 2006), www.dfid.gov.uk/R4D/PDF/Outputs/CrisisStates/wp7.2.pdf; Antonio Giustozzi, "Genesis of a 'Prince': The Rise of Ismail Khan in Western Afghanistan, 1979–1992," Working Paper 4 (London School of Economics, Crisis States Research Center, September 2006), www.afghanistanica.com/WP4.2.pdf; Sarah Chayes, *The Punishment of Virtue: Inside Afghanistan after Taliban* (New York: Penguin Press, 2006). For an analysis of power brokers in eastern and northern Afghanistan, see Dipali Mukhopadhyay, "Warlords as Bureaucrats: The Afghan Experience," Carnegie Paper 101 (Washington: Carnegie Endowment for International Peace, Middle East Program, August 2009), http://carnegieendowment.org/files/warlords_as_bureaucrats.pdf. See also Dexter Filkins, "Despite Doubt, Karzai Brother Retains Power," *New York Times*, March 30, 2010; Joshua Partlow, "Ahmed Wali Karzai, an Ally and Obstacle to the U.S Military in Afghanistan," *Washington Post,* June 13, 2010; Carlotta Gall, "In Afghanistan's North, a Former Warlord Offers Security," *New York Times*, May 17, 2010; Joshua Partlow and Karin Brulliard, "U.S. Operations in Kandahar Push Out Taliban," *Washington Post*, October 25, 2010.

19. There are exceptions; see chapters 6 and 9 in this volume.

20. See Jan Koehler and Christoph Zürcher, *Conflict Processing and the Opium Poppy Economy in Afghanistan*, PAL Internal Document 5 (Jalalabad, Afghanistan: Project for Alternative Livelihoods in Easter Afghanistan, May 2005), www.giz.de/Themen/de/.../en-DrugsandConflictAfghanistanPAL.pdf; David Mansfield and Adam Pain, "Counternarcotics in Afghanistan: The Failure of Success?" Briefing Paper (Kabul: AREU, December 2008).

21. For a discussion of counterinsurgency metrics, see Michael O'Hanlon, "Assessing Counterinsurgency Operations," in *U.S. Policy in Afghanistan and Iraq: Lessons and Legacies*, edited by Seyom Brown and Robert Scales (Boulder, Colo.: Lynne Rienner, 2012), pp. 129–38; Anthony Cordesman, *Afghanistan: The Failed Metrics of Ten Years of War* (Washington: Center for Strategic and International Studies, February 9, 2012), http://csis.org/publication/afghanistan-failed-metrics-ten-years-war; Ben Connable, *Embracing the Fog*

of War: Assessment and Metrics in Counterinsurgency (Santa Monica, Calif.: RAND, 2012); Joshua Foust, *Measuring Success: Are We Winning? Over 10 Years in Afghanistan* (Washington: American Security Project, May 16, 2012), http://americansecurityproject.org/featured-items/2012/measuring-success-are-we-winning-10-years-in-afghanistan-may-2012-update/.

22. Interviews with Afghans and populations in other violently contested parts of the world, 2004–12.

23. See, for example, Alex Thier, "Introduction: Building Bridges," in *The Future of Afghanistan*, edited by Alex Thier (Washington: United States Institute of Peace, 2009), pp. 1–12.

24. For some of the continuing problems with the ANP, see Ernesto Londoño, "Afghan Forces' Apathy Starts to Wear on U.S. Platoon in Kandahar," *Washington Post*, June 20, 2010.

25. Interviews with ISAF officials, provincial reconstruction team personnel, and ordinary Afghans, southern Afghanistan, spring 2009 and fall 2010. To a surprising degree, the Afghan National Civil Order Police, the elite police unit with most extensive training and widely perceived to be effective and least corrupt, has also been complicit at times in such informal taxing and other abuses. See C. J. Chivers, "Afghan Police Earn Poor Grade for Marja Mission," *New York Times*, June 1, 2010.

26. House Committee on Oversight and Government Reform, Subcommittee on National Security and Foreign Affairs, *Warlord, Inc.: Extortion and Corruption along the U.S. Supply Chain in Afghanistan*, 111 Cong. 2 sess. (June 2010), www.cbsnews.com/htdocs/pdf/HNT_Report.pdf.

27. For details on these insecurity-related transaction costs and other impediments to legal development, see David Mansfield, "Water Management, Livestock, and the Opium Economy—Resurgence and Reductions: Explanations for Changing Levels of Opium Poppy Cultivation in Nangarhar and Ghor in 2006–07," Case Study (Kabul: AREU, May 2008).

28. Extortion along the main highway through Baghlan and Kunduz was subsequently partially reduced in Baghlan as a result of beefed-up ISAF presence and oversight of the Afghan National Security Forces and local militias there. But serious extortion along the road there and in many other parts of Afghanistan still persists. Interviews in Baghlan and with ISAF officials focused on southern Afghanistan, April 2012.

29. Interviews with ISAF officials and nongovernmental organization security officers, Kabul and Jalalabad, April 2012, and with Afghan truckers, Kandahar Air Force Base, spring 2009, and Baghlan, April 2012.

30. See Shahmahmood Miakhel and Noah Coburn, "Many Shuras Do Not a Government Make: International Community Engagement with Local Councils in Afghanistan," Peace Brief 50 (Washington: United States Institute of Peace, September 7, 2010).

31. I am grateful to Erica Gaston of the United States Institute of Peace for her insights on this aspect of the rule of law effort. See Thomas Barfield, "Culture

and Custom in Nation-Building: Law in Afghanistan," *Maine Law Review* 60, no. 2 (2008): 348–73; Noah Coburn, "The Politics of Dispute Resolution and Continued Instability in Afghanistan," Special Report 285 (Washington: United States Institute of Peace, April 16, 2012).

32. Vanda Felbab-Brown, "Rules and Regulations in Ungoverned Spaces: Illicit Economies, Criminals, and Belligerents," in *Ungoverned Spaces: Alternatives to State Authority in an Era of Softened Sovereignty*, edited by Harold Trinkunas and Anne Clunnan (Stanford University Press, 2010), pp. 175–92.

33. Robert B. Charles, "Are British Counternarcotics Efforts Going Wobbly?" Testimony before the House Committee on Government Reform, Subcommittee on Criminal Justice, Drug Policy, and Human Resources, April 1, 2004, http://2001-2009.state.gov/p/inl/rls/rm/31039.htm.

34. "After Victory, Defeat," *The Economist*, July 16, 2005.

35. United Nations Office of Drugs and Crime, "The Opium Situation in Afghanistan as of 29 August 2005" (Vienna, August 2005).

36. David Mansfield, "Pariah or Poverty? The Opium Ban in the Province Nangarhar in 2004/05 Growing Season and Its Impact on Rural Livelihood Strategies," GTZ Policy Brief 1 (Eschborn, Germany: Deutsche Gesellschaft für Technische Zusammenarbeit, September 2005), www.gtz.de/de/dokumente/en-FinalC opingReportStudyPAL20.7.pdf.

37. Michael Griffin, *Reaping the Whirlwind* (London: Pluto Press, 2001), pp.152–53. Other factors that contributed to the decline in opium poppy cultivation were the boom in wheat prices that year and a significant surplus of opium from the bumper harvest in 1994.

38. The $45 million figure comes from Transnational Institute, "Afghanistan, Drugs and Terrorism: Merging Wars," Drugs and Conflict Briefing Series 3 (Amsterdam, December 2001). The $200 million figure comes from Barnett R. Rubin, "The Political Economy of War and Peace in Afghanistan," *World Development* 28, no. 10 (2000): 1789–803.

39. Zareen Naqvi, "Afghanistan-Pakistan Trade Relations" (Islamabad: World Bank, 1999). For details on this illicit economy, see Vanda Felbab-Brown, *Shooting Up: Counterinsurgency and the War on Drugs* (Brookings, 2010), chapter 5.

40. David Mansfield, "Coping Strategies, Accumulated Wealth and Shifting Markets: The Story of Opium Poppy Cultivation in Badakhshan 2000–2003" (Aga Khan Development Network, January 2004), p. 4.

41. See David Mansfield and Adam Pain, "Evidence from the Field: Understanding Changing Levels of Opium Poppy Cultivation in Afghanistan," Briefing Paper (Kabul: AREU, November 2007); Barnet Rubin and Jake Sherman, *Counternarcotics to Stabilize Afghanistan: The False Promise of Crop Eradication* (Center on International Cooperation, New York University, February 2008), www.cic.nyu.edu/afghanistan/docs/counternarcoticsfinal.pdf.

42. For details, see Felbab-Brown, *Shooting Up*, pp. 149–54.

43. See chapter 9 in this volume for details.

Chapter 5

1. This chapter primarily describes power and governance in Nangarhar province in Afghanistan's east and in Kandahar in the south, though it includes some vignettes from other provinces in these two regions. Both eastern and southern Afghanistan, of course, encompass a much larger area and other provinces than just these two.

2. For details on the water disputes, see Robert Wirsing and Christopher Jasparro, "Water Disputes, Resource Insecurity, and Diplomatic Deadlock in South Asia," *Water Policy* 9, no. 3 (2007): 231–51; Sandra Postel and Aaron Wolf, "Dehydrating Conflict," *Foreign Policy*, September 18, 2001, www.irisprojects. umd.edu/ppc_ideas/ebulletin/issue7_pdf/dehydrating_conflict.pdf.

3. For an excellent account of Afghanistan's travel delights and harsh politics, see Rory Stewart, *The Places in Between* (London: Picador, 2004).

4. Interviews in Kabul and Nangarhar, April 2012.

5. Interview with the Logar malik, Kabul, April 2012.

6. Interviews with Afghan businessmen, Kabul and Nangarhar, April 2012.

7. For details, see chapter 9 in this volume. See also David Mansfield, "The Economic Superiority of Illicit Drug Production: Myth and Reality—Opium Poppy Cultivation in Afghanistan," paper prepared for the International Conference on Alternative Development in Drug Control and Cooperation, Feldafing (Munich), January 7–12, 2002.

8. Interviews with contractors for the United States Agency for International Development, Nangarhar, April 2012.

9. The proliferation of mobile phones and the expansion of cell service has been one of the major economic success stories of the post-2002 decade, even though the Taliban loves to shut down the transmission towers. In Helmand, for example, even after the ISAF military surge, the Taliban succeeded in keeping the cell towers shut for several weeks in 2011. For details, see Ismail Sameen, "Taliban Stops Cell Phone Signals in Key Afghan Province," Reuters, March 24, 2011.

10. Interview with an Afghan businessman, Jalalabad, Nangarhar, April 2012.

11. Interviews with Nangarhar businessmen, civil society representatives, and international political analysts, Nangarhar and Kabul, fall 2010 and spring 2012.

12. Gran Hewad, "On the Way to Chicago—Fighting Corruption—and Condoning it?" (Kabul: Afghanistan Analysts Network, April 3, 2012), http://aan-afghanistan.com/print.asp?id=2640.

13. On Shirzai's performance when he was the governor of Kandahar, see Sarah Chayes, *The Punishment of Virtue: Inside Afghanistan after Taliban* (New York: Penguin Press, 2006).

14. For details, see chapter 9 in this volume.

15. For details, see David Mansfield, *Responding to Risk and Uncertainty: Understanding the Nature of Change in the Rural Livelihoods of Opium Poppy*

Growing Households in the 2007/08 Growing Season, Report for the Afghan Drugs Inter Departmental Unit of the UK Government, July 2008, www.david mansfield.org/data/Field_Work/UK/FINAL_UK_DRIVERS_REPORT_08. pdf; Dipali Mukhopadhyay, "Warlords as Bureaucrats: The Afghan Experience," Carnegie Paper 101 (Washington: Carnegie Institute for Peace, Middle East Program, August 2009), http://carnegieendowment.org/files/warlords_as_bureaucrats.pdf.

16. Interviews with ISAF officers and officials of the U.S. Embassy, Kabul, fall 2010.

17. Interviews, Nangarhar, April 2012.

18. Interview with a tribal elder from the Bati Kot district of Nangarhar, April 2012.

19. Interview with a high-level provincial ANP officer, Jalalabad, Nangarhar, April 2012.

20. For details of the conceptual framework, see Vanda Felbab-Brown, *Shooting Up: Counterinsurgency and the War on Drugs* (Brookings, 2010), chapter 2; Felbab-Brown, "Human Security and Crime in Latin America: The Political Capital and Political Impact of Criminal Groups and Belligerents Involved in Illicit Economies" (Florida International University, Western Hemispheric Security Analysis Center, September 2011).

21. See chapter 4 in this volume.

22. Diego Gambetta, *The Sicilian Mafia: The Business of Private Protection* (Harvard University Press, 1993).

23. Ibid., p. 17. See also Herschel I. Grossman, "Rival Kleptocrats: The Mafia versus the State," in *The Economics of Organized Crime*, edited by Gianluca Fiorentini and Sam Peltzman (Cambridge University Press, 1995), pp. 144 and 155; Diego Gambetta and Peter Reuter, "Conspiracy among the Many: The Mafia in Legitimate Industries," in *Economics of Organized Crime*, pp. 116–42. For seminal work on this subject, see Charles Tilly, *From Mobilization to Revolution* (Reading, Mass.: Addison-Wesley, 1978); Tilly, *Coercion, Capital, and European States, AD 990–1990* (Cambridge, Mass.: Blackwell Publishers, 1990); Tilly, "Warmaking and Statemaking as Organized Crime," in *Bringing the State Back In*, edited by Peter Evans, Dietrich Rueschemeyer, and Theda Skocpol (Cambridge University Press, 1985), pp. 169–91.

24. See Enrique Desmond Arias and Corrine Davis Rodrigues, "The Myth of Personal Security: Criminal Gangs, Dispute Resolution, and Identity in Rio de Janeiro's Favelas," *Latin American Politics* 48, no. 4 (2006): 53–81; Ben Pengalese, "The Bastard Child of the Dictatorship: The Comando Vermelho and the Birth of 'Narco-Culture' in Rio de Janeiro," *Luso-Brazilian Review* 45, no. 1 (2008): 118–45.

25. See, for example, Alissa Rubin and Scott Shane, "Assassination in Afghanistan Creates a Void," *New York Times*, July 12, 2011.

26. For an excellent account of the political landscape in Kandahar and its rivalries and power struggles, see Carl Forsberg, *Politics and Power in Kandahar*, Afghanistan Report 5 (Washington: Institute for the Study of War, April 2010), www.understandingwar.org/sites/default/files/Politics_and_Power_in_Kandahar.pdf.

27. For details about Jan Mohammad's governing style and closeness to President Karzai, see Thomas Ruttig, "Who Was Jan Mohammad Khan?" (Kabul: Afghanistan Analysts Network, July 18, 2011), http://aan-afghanistan.com/index.asp?id=1941.

28. See, for example, James Risen, "Afghan Killing Bares a Karzai Family Feud," *New York Times,* December 20, 2009; Joshua Partlow, "In Afghan Village, Fears that Government Can't Provide after Americans Leave," *Washington Post,* July 16, 2012.

29. Interviews with a former high Afghan government official and a confidant of President Karzai, Washington, summer 2011.

30. For an elaboration of this point, see Rajiv Chandrasekaran, *Little America: The War within the War for Afghanistan* (New York: Knopf, 2012).

31. For details, see Forsberg, *Politics and Power in Kandahar.*

32. On other murders and rifts within the Karzai family, see Risen, "Karzai Family Feud." For an excellent study on how critically patronage determines access to economic resources in the post-2002 Afghanistan, see Paula Kantor and Adam Pain, "Securing Life and Livelihoods in Rural Afghanistan: The Role of Social Relationships," Issues Paper (Kabul: Afghan Research and Evaluation Unit, December 2010), www.areu.org.af/Uploads/EditionPdfs/1045E-Securing%20Life%20and%20Livelihoods%20IP%202010%20web.pdf.

33. Dexter Filkins, Mark Mazzetti, and James Risen, "Brother of Afghan Leader Said to Be Paid by the CIA," *New York Times*, October 27, 2009.

34. Interviews with Afghan politicians, journalists, and civil society representatives, Kandahar, fall 2010.

35. James Risen, "Reports Link Karzai's Brother to Heroin Trade," *New York Times*, October 4, 2008, www.nytimes.com/2008/10/04/world/asia/04iht-05afghan.16689186.html.

36. Interviews with ISAF and U.S. military officials, Kandahar, spring 2009 and fall 2010, and with former political advisers of ISAF's military command in Kandahar, Washington, winter 2010 and spring 2011.

37. Interviews in Kandahar, spring 2009 and fall 2010.

38. Interview with a prominent Kandahari businessman, Washington, summer 2010.

39. Afghanistan's Electoral Complaints Commission, composed of both international and Afghan experts, invalidated several hundred thousand votes from several hundred polling stations. As a result, President Karzai did not win in the first round, as he had originally claimed to have done. For details, see

"Karzai 'Stripped of Outright Win,'" *BBC News,* October 19, 2009, http://news. bbc.co.uk/2/hi/south_asia/8314613.stm. For the types of electoral fraud and abuse and the impact of insecurity on elections, see Joshua Partlow and Pamela Constable, "Accusations of Fraud Multiply in Afghanistan," *Washington Post,* August 28, 2009, www.washingtonpost.com/wp-dyn/content/article/2009/08/27/ AR2009082704199.html.

40. Conversation with the leadership of the election observation team, Kabul, September 2010.

41. Interviews with local businessmen, Kandahar, fall 2010, and interview with a prominent Kandahari businessman, Washington, fall 2011.

42. Interview with an ISAF contracting officer, Canadian Provincial Reconstruction Team (PRT), Kandahar, spring 2009. See also Carlotta Gall, "Kandahar, a Battlefield Even before U.S. Offensive," *New York Times,* March 26, 2010.

43. Interview, Kabul, April 2012.

44. Interviews with Kandahari journalists, businessmen, and politicians, Kandahar, fall 2010. See also Carl Forsberg, *The Taliban's Campaign for Kandahar,* Afghanistan Report 3 (Washington: Institute for the Study of War, December 1, 2009), www.understandingwar.org/report/talibans-campaign-kandahar; Forsberg, *Politics and Power in Kandahar.*

45. Interview with a former high official of the U.S. Embassy in Kabul who was intimately involved in efforts to have Wali removed from Kandahar, Washington, spring 2010.

46. Interviews with ISAF and civilian officials in Uruzgan, spring 2009. See also Martine van Bijlert, "Unruly Commanders and Violent Power Struggles: Taliban Networks in Uruzgan," in *Decoding the New Taliban: Insights from the Field,* edited by Antonio Giustozzi (Columbia University Press, 2009), pp. 155–78.

47. Interviews with military officers of the Dutch ISAF command and PRT civilian officials in Uruzgan, spring 2009.

48. For details, see van Bijlert, "Unruly Commanders."

49. Dexter Filkins, "With U.S. Aid, Warlord Builds Afghan Empire," *New York Times,* June 5, 2010.

50. Ibid.

51. Interviews with Afghan civil society leaders and UNAMA officials, Tirin Kot, Uruzgan, spring 2009.

52. Interviews with ISAF officers and political advisers of the Dutch PRT, Tirin Kot, Uruzgan, and with UNAMA officials, Tirin Kot, Urugzan, spring 2009.

53. In western Afghanistan, similarly, the international community succeeded in removing Herat's key power broker, Ismail Khan, from the governorship there. But Khan continues to exercise great influence over the politics and the economy of the province, far greater than its governors, for example.

54. For details on the Akhundzada clan and its basis of power, see Antonio Giustozzi and Noor Ullah, "'Tribes' and Warlords in Southern Afghanistan,

1980–2005," Working Paper 7 (London School of Economics, Crisis States Research Center, September 2006), www.dfid.gov.uk/R4D/PDF/Outputs/Crisis States/wp7.2.pdf.

55. Interviews with U.K. military officers and political advisers to the British ISAF contingent in Camp Bastion, Helmand, spring 2009.

56. Communication with a U.S. Embassy official in Helmand, summer 2012.

57. Interview with an ISAF official, Kandahar, September 2010. See also Joshua Partlow and Karin Brulliard, "U.S. Operations in Kandahar Push out the Taliban," *Washington Post,* October 25, 2010.

58. See, for example, Matthieu Aikins, "Our Man in Kandahar," *The Atlantic,* November 2011.

Chapter 6

1. Michael Flynn, Matt Pottinger, and Paul Batchelor, "Fixing Intel: A Blueprint for Making Intelligence Relevant in Afghanistan," Working Paper (Washington: Center for a New American Security, January 2010).

2. For the basic concept and structure, see Jacob Kipp and others, "The Human Terrain System: A CORDS for the 21st Century," *Military Review,* September-October 2006, pp. 8–15.

3. Interviews with ISAF officials and human terrain team members in Kabul and at various regional commands in Afghanistan, fall 2005, spring 2009, fall 2010, and spring 2012, and at a human terrain team training center at Fort Leavenworth, Kansas, summer 2012.

4. NATO, "The Afghanistan Compact," London Conference on Afghanistan, January 31–February 1, 2006, www.nato.int/isaf/docu/epub/pdf/afghanistan_compact.pdf.

5. "Afghan Anticorruption Chief Sold Heroin in Las Vegas," Associated Press, March 10, 2007.

6. For details, see Heather Barr, "Settling for Nothing: International Support for Anti-Corruption Efforts," in *Snapshots of an Intervention: The Unlearned Lessons of Afghanistan's Decade of Assistance (2001–2011),* edited by Martine van Bijlert and Sari Kouvo (Kabul: Afghan Analysts Network, 2012), pp. 181–86.

7. For a primary analysis of the patron-client versus merit-based appointment system, see Martine van Bijlert, "Between Discipline and Discretion: Policies Surrounding Senior Subnational Appointment," Briefing Paper (Kabul: AREU, May 2009), www.areu.org.af/EditionDetails.aspx?EditionId=73&ContentId=7&ParentId=7&Lang=en-US.

8. Helene Cooper and Thom Shanker, "Aides Say Obama's Afghan Aims Elevate War," *New York Times,* January 28, 2009.

9. See chapter 2 in this volume.

10. This description of Karzai's reaction is based on an interview with a former high official of the U.S. embassy in Kabul, Washington, October 2009.

11. International Crisis Group, "The Insurgency in Afghanistan's Heartland," Asia Report 207 (Brussels, June 27, 2011), www.crisisgroup.org/en/regions/asia/south-asia/afghanistan/207-the-insurgency-in-afghanistans-heartland.aspx.

12. Dexter Filkins and Mark Mazzetti, "Karzai Aide in Corruption Inquiry Is Tied to CIA," *New York Times*, August 25, 2010.

13. Dexter Filkins, "The Afghan Bank Heist," *The New Yorker*, February 14, 2011.

14. Interview with a former official of the Arg Palace and a confidant of President Karzai, October 8, 2010.

15. In this vein, Karzai, for example, fired Fazel Ahmed Faqiryar, one of the attorney generals in the post-2002 Afghanistan that had made some efforts to combat corruption.

16. For such nepotistic behavior in the Afghan Investment Agency, see, for example, Graham Bowley and Jawad Sukhanyar, "7 Officials in Afghan Investment Agency Quit, Protesting Graft," *New York Times*, June 13, 2012.

17. Interviews with ISAF officials, Kabul, fall 2010 and spring 2012.

18. Many analysts believed that Mohammadi was in fact creating a ring of Tajik forces north of Kabul in preparation for a possible civil war. Interviews with Afghan political analysts and political advisers at ISAF and the U.S. and U.K. embassies in Kabul, fall 2010 and spring 2012.

19. Stanley McChrystal, *Commander's Initial Assessment*, unclassified version, August 30, 2009, http://media.washingtonpost.com/wp-srv/politics/documents/Assessment_Redacted_092109.pdf?sid=ST2009092003140.

20. Catherine Dale, "In Brief: Next Steps in the War in Afghanistan: Issues for Congress," Report R42137 (Congressional Research Service, Library of Congress, June 15, 2012).

21. On banking sector corruption and Western anti–money laundering efforts, see Matthew Rosenberg, "Corruption Suspected in Airlift of Billions of Cash from Kabul," *Wall Street Journal*, June 25, 2010; Greg Miller and Ernesto Londoño, "U.S. Officials Say Karzai Aides Are Derailing Corruption Cases Involving Elite," *Washington Post*, June 28, 2010. See also Van Bijlert, "Between Discipline and Discretion."

22. Interview with a former U.S. official, Washington, August 7, 2012. I am grateful to one of the anonymous reviewers for alerting me to this interagency effort.

23. For further elaboration, see chapter 12.

24. See interview with unnamed U.S. officials in Greg Jaffe, "U.S. to Temper Stance on Afghan Corruption," *Washington Post*, September 4, 2010.

25. Dale, "Next Steps in the War," p. 11.

26. See Greg Miller and Joshua Partlow, "CIA Making Secret Payments to Members of Karzai Administration," *Washington Post*, August 27, 2010; Filkins and Mazzetti, "Karzai Aide in Corruption Inquiry."

27. Interview with an ISAF official, Kandahar, September 2010. See also Joshua Partlow and Karin Brulliard, "U.S. Operations in Kandahar Push Out the Taliban," *Washington Post*, October 25, 2010.

28. For more on Raziq's history, see Matthieu Aikins, "Our Man in Kandahar," *The Atlantic*, November 2011.

29. Interview with a former high official of the U.S. Kandahar PRT, Washington, October 2010.

30. Filkins, "Afghan Bank Heist."

31. For some of the latest in the continuing saga, including the struggle of the Afghan government and central bank to recover the stolen and borrowed assets, see Matthew Rosenberg, "Karzai Orders Prosecutor and Tribunal in Scandal over Kabul Bank's Losses," *New York Times*, April 5, 2012; Alissa Rubin, "Bank Case Gets Tribunal at Behest of Karzai," *New York Times*, June 3, 2012; Joshua Partlow, "President Hamid Karzai Calls on Afghans to Fight Corruption," *Washington Post*, June 21, 2012.

32. In the 2010–11 fiscal year alone, the total estimated size of foreign aid was almost $16 billion. World Bank, "Transition in Afghanistan: Looking Beyond 2014. Executive Summary" (Washington, November 18, 2011), p.1, http://siteresources.worldbank.org/AFGHANISTANEXTN/Resources/305984-1297184305854/AFTransition.pdf.

33. See, for example, Rosenberg, "Corruption Suspected in Airlift"; Andrew Higgins, "Officials Puzzle over Millions of Dollars Leaving Afghanistan by Plane for Dubai," *Washington Post*, February 25, 2010. See also Brett Blackledge, Richard Lardner, and Deb Reichmann, "After Years of Rebuilding, Most Afghans Lack Power," *Washington Post*, July 19, 2010.

34. Graham Bowley and Matthew Rosenberg, "In Afghanistan, Businesses Plan Their Own Exits," *New York Times*, March 30, 2012.

35. Yaroslav Trofimov, "Afghan Central Bank Targets Cash Flight," *Wall Street Journal*, February 22, 2012.

36. See, for example, Dexter Filkins, "With U.S. Aid, Warlord Builds Afghan Empire," *New York Times*, June 5, 2010.

37. For how intense such "insecurity pays" dynamics are in central Afghanistan, see International Crisis Group, "Insurgency in Afghanistan's Heartland."

38. Laura Rozen, "'Leveling the Playing Field' in Afghanistan's Upcoming Elections," *Foreign Policy.com*, April 16, 2009, http://thecable.foreign policy.com/posts/2009/04/16/leveling_the_playing_field_in_afghanistans_upcoming_election.

39. Dexter Filkins, "Afghan Leader Outmaneuvers Elections Rivals," *New York Times*, June 24, 2009.

40. See "Karzai 'Stripped of Outright Win,'" *BBC News*, October 19, 2009, http://news.bbc.co.uk/2/hi/south_asia/8314613.stm. For the types of electoral fraud and abuse and the impact of insecurity on elections, see, for example, Joshua Partlow and Pamela Constable, "Accusations of Fraud Multiply in Afghanistan," *Washington Post*, August 28, 2009, www.washingtonpost.com/wp-dyn/content/article/2009/08/27/AR2009082704199.html. For details on the fraud and other electoral problems during the subsequent 2010 parliamentary elections and for the systematic deficiencies of the Afghan electoral system, see Scott Worden,

"Transparency Is the Key to Legitimate Afghan Parliamentary Elections," Brief 61 (Washington: United States Institute for Peace, October 14, 2010); "Afghanistan's Ongoing Elections Drama," May 12, 2011, http://afpak.foreignpolicy.com/posts/2011/05/12/afghanistans_ongoing_election_drama; "Karzai Blinks in Afghan Election Crisis," *Foreign Policy.com*, August 10, 2011, http://afpak.foreign policy.com/posts/2011/08/10/karzai_blinks_in_afghan_election_crisis.

41. John Amick, "Clinton Sets Benchmarks for Progress in Afghanistan," *Washington Post*, November 15, 2009.

42. Interviews with a former high official of the U.S. embassy in Kabul, May 20, 2010, and October 14, 2010.

43. Interviews with former and current high Afghan government officials and political analysts, Washington and Kabul, September 2010 and April 2012.

44. For details, see ISAF, "Afghan Public Protection Force Signs First Contracts," March 2010, www.isaf.nato.int/article/news/afghan-public-protection-force-signs-first-contracts.html.

45. See Rosenberg, "Karzai Orders Prosecutor and Tribunal"; Rubin, "Bank Case Gets Tribunal."

46. On Karzai's threat to join the Taliban, see Alissa Rubin, "Karzai's Words Leave Few Choices for the West," *New York Times*, April 4, 2010. For other Karzai outbursts, see Alissa Rubin and Helene Cooper, "In Afghan Trip, Obama Presses Karzai on Graft," *New York Times*, March 28, 2010; Mark Mazzetti and Rod Nordland, "U.S. Debates Karzai's Place in Fighting Corruption," *New York Times*, September 14, 2010.

47. For the deep linkages of President Karzai's family to key economic activities in Afghanistan and his buildup of his family network as a self-preservation mechanism if the current political order collapses, see James Risen, "Karzai's Kin Use Ties to Gain Power in Afghanistan," *New York Times*, October 5, 2010. See also Alissa Rubin, "Karzai's Isolation Worries Afghans and the West," *New York Times*, June 7, 2010.

48. Iran, in particular, has diligently courted President Karzai; see Dexter Filkins, "Iran Is Said to Give Top Karzai Aide Cash by the Bagful," *New York Times*, October 23, 2010. Iran has tried both to cultivate President Karzai and to develop at least some influence over the Taliban, despite communal rivalries and a strong record of hostilities between the Taliban and Iran.

49. For details on the policy shift, see Helene Cooper and Mark Landler, "U.S. Now Trying Softer Approach toward Karzai," *New York Times*, April 9, 2010.

50. For some of such statements by President Karzai, see Joshua Partlow, Scott Wilson, and William Branigin, "White House Calls Karzai Accusations 'Genuinely Troubling,'" *Washington Post*, April 2, 2010.

51. Shutting down the private security companies, for example, was not just a retaliatory maneuver by Karzai. The measure was widely popular in Afghanistan since many Afghans came to associate the gun-toting public security companies with abuses and arrogance. But the decision also involved political costs for

Karzai since many Afghan power brokers, including his ministers, either directly owned the profitable private security companies or had close relatives who did. Karzai's move to shut the companies down cost them a lot of money.

52. For an endorsement of such an approach, see Stephen Biddle, Fotini Christia, and Alexander Thier, "Defining Success in Afghanistan," *Foreign Affairs* 89, no. 4 (2010): 48–60.

53. For a comprehensive overview of Afghanistan's national and local government structures and international institutions in Afghanistan, see Colin Cookman and Caroline Wadhams, *Governance in Afghanistan: Looking Ahead to What We Leave Behind* (Washington: Center for American Progress, May 2010), www.americanprogress.org/issues/2010/05/afghan_governance.html.

54. Hamish Nixon, "The 'Subnational Governance' Challenge and the Independent Directorate of Local Governance," in Van Bijlert and Kouvo, eds., *Snapshots of an Intervention*, pp. 117–23.

55. Ann Scott Tyson, "New Joint Effort Aims to Empower Afghan Tribes to Guard Themselves," *Washington Post*, March 31, 2008. See also Carlotta Gall, "U.S. Hopes Afghan Councils Will Weaken Taliban," *New York Times*, June 19, 2010.

56. For an excellent discussion of the promise and difficulties of focusing on shuras and other traditional governance structures, see Shahmahmood Miakhel and Noah Coburn, "Many Shuras Do Not a Government Make: International Community Engagement with Local Councils in Afghanistan," Peace Brief 50 (Washington: United States Institute of Peace, September 7, 2010). See also Dexter Filkins, "Inside Corrupt-istan, a Loss of Faith in Leaders," *New York Times*, September 4, 2010.

57. Human Rights Unit, UNAMA, *Afghanistan Midyear Report 2012: Protection of Civilians in Armed Conflict* (Kabul, July 2012), www.ohchr.org/Documents/Countries/AF/UNAMAMidYearReport2012.pdf.

58. Interviews with ISAF and PRT officers and U.S. Embassy officials, spring 2009, fall 2010, and spring 2012. For a similar finding, see Dale, "Next Steps in the War," p. 11.

59. See Serge Michailof, "Review of Technical Assistance and Capacity Building in Afghanistan," discussion paper for the Afghanistan Development Forum, April 26, 2007, www.sergemichailof.fr/?page_id=51. For an excellent discussion of the promises and perils of foreign aid in state building, see Ashraf Ghani and Clare Lockhart, *Fixing Failed States: A Framework for Rebuilding a Fractured World* (Oxford University Press, 2008).

60. This paragraph draws heavily from an excellent evaluation of the capacity growth in the ministry and Atmar's role by Frauke de Weijer in "Capacity Building in MRRD," in Van Bijlert and Kouvo, eds., *Snapshots of an Intervention*, pp. 139–44.

61. For a detailed overview of local governance structures before the creation of the IDLG, see Asia Foundation, *An Assessment of Sub-National Governance*

in Afghanistan (Kabul, 2007), http://asiafoundation.org/pdf/AG-subnational governance.pdf.

62. UNAMA, "Agreement on Provisional Arrangements in Afghanistan Pending the Re-establishment of Permanent Government Institutions" (Bonn, December 5, 2001), http://unama.unmissions.org/Portals/UNAMA/Documents/Bonn-agreement.pdf.

63. Sarah Lister, "Understanding State-Building and Local Government in Afghanistan," Working Paper 14 (London: Crisis States Research Center, 2007), p. 4. See also Greg Jaffe and Karen DeYoung, "Afghanistan's Karzai to Urge Caution as U.S. Pushes to Empower Local Leaders," *Washington Post*, May 12, 2010.

64. Interviews with provincial high officials in Nangarhar and Herat, spring 2012.

65. See, for example, Karin Brulliard, "In Targeting Taliban Stronghold, U.S. Depends on Afghans' Reluctant Support," *Washington Post*, July 16, 2010.

66. Interviews with ISAF officials, influential citizens, and Afghan journalists, Kandahar, September 2010. On the problems with Marja's district governor, Haji Zahir, see Rajiv Chandrasekaran, "'Still a Long Way to Go' for U.S. Operation in Marja, Afghanistan," *Washington Post*, June 10, 2010.

67. Interviews with Afghan journalists, businessmen, and civil society leaders, Kandahar, fall 2010, and Nangarhar and Baghlan, spring 2012.

68. Interviews with U.S., ISAF, U.K., and Afghan officials, Afghanistan, fall 2010 and spring 2012. For a specific case, see Dexter Filkins and Alissa Rubin, "Graft-Fighting Prosecutor Fired in Afghanistan," *New York Times*, August 28, 2010.

69. For an excellent overview of the parliament's powers and efforts to strengthen it, see Marvin Weinbaum, "Toward a More Effective Parliament?" in Van Bijlert and Kouvo, eds., *Snapshots of an Intervention*, pp. 35–40.

70. For a comprehensive analysis of the various decisionmaking structures, see AREU, *The A to Z Guide to Afghanistan Assistance 2010*, 8th ed. (Kabul, 2010), www.areu.org.af/EditionDetails.aspx?EditionId=316&ContentId=7&ParentId=7.

71. For details, see Alissa Rubin, "Two Top Afghan Security Ministers Face Dismissal," *New York Times*, August 4, 2012.

72. Interviews with Pentagon officials, Washington, August 5 and 6, 2012. See also Alissa Rubin, "Afghan Transfer on Pace after Firings, General Says," *New York Times*, August 6, 2012.

73. Interviews and e-mail communications with Afghan politicians and analysts, Washington, August 2012.

74. International Crisis Group, "A Force in Fragments: Reconstituting the Afghan National Army," Asia Report 190 (Brussels, May 12, 2010).

75. "Afghan Governor's Rights Abuses Known in '07," *CBC News*, April 12, 2010.

76. Richard Oppel Jr., "Western and Afghan Officials Split over Karzai Nomination for Spy Chief," *New York Times*, September 11, 2012.

77. For an overview of the CDCs' structure and their undefined relationship with the formal government structures, see Hamish Nixon, "Subnational State-building in Afghanistan," Synthesis Paper (Kabul: AREU, April 2008); Nixon, "The Changing Face of Local Governance? Community Development Councils in Afghanistan," Working Paper (Kabul: AREU, February 2008), www.areu.org.af/ Uploads/EditionPdfs/802E-Changing%20Face%20of%20local%20Governance-WP-print.pdf.pdf.

78. See, for example, John F. McCarthy, "Power and Interest on Sumatra's Rainforest Frontier: Clientelist Coalitions, Illegal Logging and Conservation in the Alas Valley," *Journal of Southeast Asian Studies* 33, no. 1 (2002): 77–106; Ben Jones, *Beyond the State in Rural Uganda* (Edinburgh University Press, 2009).

79. For a first-rate evaluation of the effectiveness of the CDCs and the key role of the local context, see Adam Pain and Paula Kantor, "Understanding and Addressing the Context in Rural Afghanistan: How Villages Differ and Why," Issue Paper (Kabul: AREU, December 2010), www.areu.org.af/Uploads/ EditionPdfs/1046E-Understanding%20and%20Addressing%20Context%20 in%20Rural%20Afghanistan%20IP%202010%20web-1.pdf.

80. Jennifer McCarthy, "Reframing Participatory Development and Livelihoods in Afghanistan's Rural North: A Power Analysis to Understand Variegated Realities of Vulnerability," Ph.D. dissertation, King's College, London, 2011; McCarthy, "Questioning the NSP: Agency and Resource Access in Faryab Province," in Van Bijlert and Kouvo, eds., *Snapshots of an Intervention*, pp. 132–38.

81. Interviews with representatives of an international nongovernmental organization operating in Ghazni, fall 2010, and with ISAF officials, political advisers, and PRT personnel, Kandahar and Uruzgan, spring 2009 and fall 2010.

82. For details, see chapter 2 in this volume.

83. Alissa Rubin, "Afghan President Issues Reforms Aimed at Corruption," *New York Times*, July 26, 2012.

84. Ibid.

Chapter 7

1. For background on these conflicts, in Kunduz in particular, see Nils Wörmer, "The Networks of Kunduz: A History of Conflict and Their Actors, from 1992 to 2001," Thematic Report 02-2012 (Kabul: Afghan Analysts Network, August 2012), http://aan-afghanistan.com/uploads/20120801Woermer-The_Networks_of_Kunduz_FINAL.pdf

2. See, for example, Thomas Ruttig, "A New Taleban Front?" (Kabul: Afghanistan Analysts Network, June 18, 2010), http://aan-afghanistan.com/ index.asp?id=831; Antonio Giustozzi and Christoph Reuter, "The Northern

Front: The Afghan Insurgency Spreading beyond the Pashtuns," Briefing Paper 03-2010 (Kabul: Afghan Analysts Network, June 2010), http://aan-afghanistan.com/uploads/20100629AGCR-TheNorthernFront1.pdf.

3. Leaked report from TF 3-10 Bagram, Afghanistan, *State of the Taliban: Detainee Perspectives*, January 6, 2012, p. 20, http://s3.documentcloud.org/documents/296489/taliban-report.pdf.

4. Ibid., and interviews with ISAF officials, Balkh, April 2012.

5. Interview with a civil society organizer, Pul-e-Khourmi, Baghlan, April 2012. My other Afghan interlocutors in the north included members of the ANP and ALP, government officials, lawyers, businessmen, shopkeepers, and street vendors.

6. For a more thorough discussion, see chapter 11 in this volume.

7. Ibid.

8. For details, see chapter 10 in this volume and also Alissa Rubin and Salman Masood, "After Strike in Pakistan, Rage and Damage Control," *New York Times*, November 2011.

9. Craig Whitlock and Karen DeYoung, "Northern Land Routes to Be Crucial in U.S. Withdrawal from Afghanistan," *Washington Post*, July 4, 2012.

10. The lengthy, frustrating, and complicated negotiations between the United States and Pakistan are recounted in chapter 10 of this volume.

11. Rod Nordland, "U.S.-Pakistan Freeze Chokes Fallback Route in Afghanistan," *New York Times*, June 2, 2012.

12. House Committee on Oversight and Government Reform, Subcommittee on National Security and Foreign Affairs, *Warlord, Inc.: Extortion and Corruption along the U.S. Supply Chain in Afghanistan*, 111 Cong. 2 sess. (June 2010), www.cbsnews.com/htdocs/pdf/HNT_Report.pdf.

13. The U.S. military did not provide further details. See "Taliban Happy Pakistan Reopened NATO Supply Line," Associated Press, July 31, 2012.

14. Interviews with Taliban commanders in Ghazni, cited in ibid.

15. Ibid.

16. Interview with a high-level ISAF officer, ISAF headquarters, Kabul, April 2012.

17. Whitlock and DeYoung, "Northern Land Routes."

18. U.S. Congress, Senate, *Senate Appropriations Subcommittee on Defense Holds Hearing on the Proposed Fiscal 2013 Appropriations for the Defense Department*, CQ Congressional Transcript, 112 Cong. 2 sess. (June 13, 2012), www.ngaus.org/ngaus/files/ccLibraryFiles/Filename/000000008054/SAC-D%20DoD%20Posture%20Hearing%20Transcript_06%2013%202012.pdf.

19. Mike Mount, "U.S. and NATO Secure Exit Route from Afghanistan," *CNN.com*, June 4, 2012.

20. Marcus Weisberger, "Tab for Alternate Afghan Supply Route Hits $2.1 Billion," *USA Today*, June 30, 2012.

21. Tony Capaccio, "Pentagon Freeing $1.1. Billion Withheld from Pakistan," *Bloomberg.com*, July 5, 2012.

22. Whitlock and DeYoung, "Northern Land Routes."

23. Ibid.

24. For the geopolitical dimensions, see Andrew Kuchins and Thomas Sanderson, *The Northern Distribution Network: Geopolitical Challenges and Opportunities* (Washington: Center for Strategic and International Studies, January 2010), http://csis.org/files/publication/091229_Kuchins_NDNandAfghan_Web.pdf.

25. For more on Russia's role in the region, see chapter 10 in this volume.

26. Nordland, "U.S.-Pakistan Freeze."

27. See, for example, Nilanjana Roy, "Improving Women's Status, One Bathroom at a Time," *New York Times*, March 15, 2011; Jim Yardley, "In Mumbai, A Campaign against Restroom Injustice," *New York Times*, June 14, 2012.

28. For details, see Kenneth Katzman, "Afghanistan: Politics, Elections, and Government Performance," Report RS21521 (Congressional Research Service, Library of Congress, June 5, 2012).

29. For an excellent discussion of women's conditions in Afghanistan, their improvement and retrogression, see Sippi Azarbaijani-Moghaddam, "The Arrested Development of Afghan Women," in *The Future of Afghanistan*, edited by Alex Their (Washington: United States Institute of Peace, 2009), pp. 63–72.

30. Alex Pearlman, "5 Questions with Manizha Naderi," *Global Post*, May 22, 2012. For some of the latest issues, such as women's rights in the context of negotiations with the Taliban, see "Hamid Karzai under Fire on Afghan Women's Rights," *The Telegraph*, March 8, 2012.

31. The majority of cases of sexual violence in Afghanistan continue to go on unreported. For several recent dramatic examples that show the complexity of rigid mores within families and externally perpetrated violence, see Alissa Rubin, "Afghan Rape Case Turns Focus on Afghan Local Police," *New York Times*, June 27, 2012; Graham Bowley, "Wed and Tortured at 13, Afghan Girl Finds Rare Justice," *New York Times*, August 11, 2012; "Bomb Kills Head of Women's Affairs in Afghan East," Reuters, July 13, 2012.

32. Azarbaijani-Moghaddam, "Arrested Development of Afghan Women."

33. For a dramatic case, see "Afghan Girl, 15, Tortured by In-laws for Refusing Prostitution," *Guardian*, January 2, 2012.

34. Information about restrictions on women in the media comes from interviews in Kabul, fall 2010 and spring 2012. With regard to other repressive gender-based policies, see, for example, Alissa Rubin, "Afghan Proposal Would Clamp Down on Women's Shelters," *New York Times*, February 10, 2011; Rod Nordland, "Moral Crimes Land Afghan Women in Jail," *New York Times*, March 28, 2012.

Indeed, Afghan politics has been characterized by periodic swings between moderate governance that enables the expansion of women's rights and conservative governance that restricts them. See Maliha Zulfacar, "The Pendulum of Gender Politics in Afghanistan," *Central Asian Survey* 25, no. 1- 2 (2006): 27–59.

35. TF 3-10 Bagram, *State of the Taliban*, p. 7.

36. Interview with a Pashtun businessman, Pul-e-Khourmi, Baghlan, April 2012.

37. Interview with a Tajik medical doctor, Baghlan, April 2012.

38. Dipali Mukhopadhyay, "Warlords as Bureaucrats: The Afghan Experience," Carnegie Papers 101 (Washington: Carnegie Institute for Peace, Middle East Program, August 2009), http://carnegieendowment.org/files/warlords_as_bureaucrats.pdf.

39. For details on Noor's rent-seeking activities, see Carlotta Gall, "In Afghanistan's North, Ex-Warlord Offers Security," *New York Times*, May 17, 2010; Paul Fishstein and Andrew Wilder, *Winning Hearts and Minds? Examining the Relationship between Aid and Security in Afghanistan* (Tufts University, Feinstein International Center, 2011). Allegations of power abuse are based on interviews with ISAF and UNAMA officials, political advisers, and NGO representatives, Balkh, April 2012. See also Graham Bowley, "Lucrative Afghan Oil Deal Was Awarded Properly, Karzai Says," *New York Times*, June 24, 2012.

40. For more details, see Enayat Najafizada, "Under Atta's Shadow: Political Life in the Afghan North" (Kabul: Afghanistan Analysts Network, October 26, 2011), http://aan-afghanistan.com/index.asp?id=2190.

41. For a flavor of Afghanistan's crony capitalism and war economy, see Jonathan Landay, "Factory, Coal Mine Show Connections Matter Most in Afghan Business," *McClatchy Newspapers,* November 14, 2010; Dexter Filkins, "Convoy Guards in Afghanistan Face Inquiry," *New York Times*, June 6, 2010.

42. For details about the sons of the power brokers, see Mujib Mashal, "Afghanistan's Princelings: Are the Children of the Mujahideen Ready to Rule?" *Time*, August 13, 2012.

43. See, for example, Matthew Rosenberg, "Outspoken Afghan Rights Official Ousted," *New York Times*, December 22, 2011.

44. See David Zucchino, "Afghanistan Faces Growing Addiction Problem," *Los Angeles Times*, July 31, 2009; United Nations Office on Drugs and Crime, *Drug Use in Afghanistan: 2009 Survey, Executive Summary* (Vienna: September 2009), www.unodc.org/documents/data-and-analysis/Studies/Afghan-Drug-Survey-2009-Executive-Summary-web.pdf.

45. Interview with a businessman from a village west of Pul-e-Khourmi, April 2012.

46. Several weeks later, a Taliban bomb in Samangan—on the same road where we had traveled to our picnic—set on fire eighteen fuel trucks and another four supply vehicles. See "Taliban Bomb Destroys 22 NATO Supply Trucks in Afghan North," Reuters, July 18, 2012.

47. Mustafa Andalib and Mirwais Harooni, "Afghan Girls' School Shut Down, Taliban Blamed," Reuters, May 9, 2012.

48. On how erecting physical buildings does not constitute effective economic development or improvements in human security, see J. Brian Atwood, M. Peter McPhearson, and Andrew Natsios, "Arrested Development: Making Foreign Aid a More Effective Tool," *Foreign Affairs* 87, no. 6 (2008): 123–32.

Chapter 8

1. For a background on the historic arbakai, see Mohammed Osman Tariq, "Tribal Security System (Arbakai) in Southeast Afghanistan," Occasional Paper 7 (London School of Economics, Crisis States Research Center, December 2008), www2.lse.ac.uk/internationalDevelopment/research/crisisStates/download/op/OP7Tariq.pdf.

2. Interviews with high-level ISAF officials and members of the U.S. Special Operations Forces responsible for the ALP, Kabul, Kandahar, Herat, and Balkh, fall 2010 and April 2014. For details on the Anbar Awakening and its relationship to the U.S. military surge in Iraq, see Stephen Biddle, "Lessons Learned in Afghanistan and Iraq," in *U.S. Policy in Afghanistan and Iraq: Lessons and Legacies*, edited by Seyom Brown and Robert Scales (Boulder, Colo.: Lynne Rienner, 2012), pp. 89–98. See also Marc Lynch, "Explaining the Awakening: Engagement, Publicity, and the Transformation of Iraqi Sunni Political Attitudes," *Security Studies* 20, no. 1 (2011): 36–72; John McCary, "The Anbar Awakening: An Alliance of Incentives," *Washington Quarterly* 32, no. 1 (2009): 43–59.

3. Inspector General, Department of Defense, *Assessment of U.S. Government and Coalition Efforts to Develop the Afghan Local Police*, Report DODIG-2012-109, July 9, 2012, www.dodig.mil/SPO/Reports/DODIG-2012-109.pdf; David Young, "The Anatomy of an Anti-Taliban Uprising," *Foreign Policy.com*, September 12, 2012, http://afpak.foreignpolicy.com/posts/2012/09/12/the_anatomy_of_an_anti_taliban_uprising.

4. Alissa Rubin and Sangar Rahimi, "Afghan Officials Cite Revenge Killings in Latest Outbreak of Ethnic Hatred," *New York Times*, August 3, 2012.

5. The efforts to stand up the Afghan National Army and the Afghan National Police are described in detail in chapter 11 of this volume.

6. Ministry of Interior documents establishing the AP3 and LDI, cited in Mathieu Lefèvre, "The Afghanistan Public Protection Program and the Local Defense Initiative," in *Snapshots of an Intervention: The Unlearned Lessons of Afghanistan's Decade of Assistance (2001–2011)*, edited by Martine van Bijlert and Sari Kouvo (Kabul: Afghanistan Analysts Network, 2012), pp. 74–79.

7. Interviews about the ALP and other self-defense programs in Afghanistan with ISAF and U.S. military officials at different levels of the chain of command in Kabul and in various ISAF regional commands, Kandahar, Helmand, Uruzgan, Nangarhar, Baghlan, and Zabul, spring 2009, fall 2010, and April 2012.

8. Interview with a SOF official in charge of a local ALP outfit, Herat, April 2012.

9. Interview with a street vendor in Pul-e-Khourmi who lived in a nearby village, Baghlan, September 2010. This section overall is based on interviews with Afghan officials at all levels of the government, ANP officers, ALP members, maliks, Afghan civil society organizers, businessmen, as well as ordinary Afghans such as shopkeepers, Kandahar, Helmand, Uruzgan, Nangarhar, Baghlan, and

Zabul, spring 2009, fall 2010, and April 2012. For a recent, highly visible case of such abuse attributed to the ALP, see Alissa Rubin, "Rape Case, in Public, Cites Abuse by Armed Groups in Afghanistan," *New York Times*, June 1, 2012.

10. Interview, Kandahar, fall 2010. For a comprehensive documentation of recent cases of abuse by irregular pro-government forces in Afghanistan—both the ALP and others—see Human Rights Watch, *Just Don't Call It a Militia: Impunity, Militias, and the "Afghan Local Police"* (New York, 2011), www.hrw.org/sites/default/files/reports/afghanistan0911webwcover.pdf.

11. Apparently, General McChrystal and General Petraeus had to spend considerable time persuading Karzai to concede to the efforts. Interviews with ISAF officials, Kandahar, spring 2009, and Kabul, fall 2010. See also Matthew Rosenberg and Alissa Rubin, "Afghanistan to Disband Irregular Police Force Set Up under NATO," *New York Times*, December 26, 2011; David Cloud, "U.S. Plans to Beef Up Rural Afghan Forces," *Los Angeles Times*, August 18, 2012.

12. Interview in Baghlan, April 2012.

13. See Geraint Hughes, "The Soviet-Afghan War, 1978–1989: An Overview," *Defense Studies* 8, no. 3 (2008): 326–50.

14. Interviews with maliks, civil society leaders, and businessmen, Kandahar, Nangarhar, and Baghlan, fall 2010 and spring 2012.

15. For an overview of these various efforts, see David Axe, "War Is Boring: Fourth Time the Charm for NATO's Afghan Militia Plan?" *World Politics Review*, July 21, 2010.

16. For more on ASOP, see chapter 6 in this volume.

17. Lefèvre, "Afghanistan Public Protection Program," p. 74. For a background on Hotak and his willingness to change sides repeatedly depending on who the stronger local force was, see Chris Sands, "Former Taliban Chief Who Became Top Policeman Says Peace Will Never Come," *The National*, May 25, 2010.

18. Lefèvre, "Afghanistan Public Protection Program," p. 74.

19. Ibid., p. 76.

20. On some of the security difficulties in the province, see International Crisis Group, "The Insurgency in Afghanistan's Heartland," Asia Report 207 (Brussels: June 27, 2011), www.crisisgroup.org/en/regions/asia/south-asia/afghanistan/207-the-insurgency-in-afghanistans-heartland.aspx.

21. House Armed Services Committee, Subcommittee on Oversight and Investigations, *Hearing on Afghan National Security Forces and Security Lead Transition: The Assessment Process, Metrics and Efforts to Build Capacity*, testimony of Kenneth Moorefield, Deputy Inspector General for Special Plans and Office of Inspector General, Operations, Department of Defense, 112 Cong. 2 sess. (July 24, 2012).

22. Lefèvre, "Afghanistan Public Protection Program," p. 77.

23. Interview with International Relief and Development officials, Kandahar, fall 2010. For a detailed analysis of the Arghandab LDI, see Lefèvre, "Afghanistan Public Protection Program," p. 78.

24. Lefèvre, "Afghanistan Public Protection Program," pp. 78–79.

25. Interviews with NDS and ANP officials, Kabul and Baghlan, September 2010 and April 2012.

26. Interviews with Ministry of Interior officials, Baghlan, April 2012.

27. Interviews with ISAF, U.S. Embassy, UNAMA, and Afghan government officials, Kabul, fall 2010 and spring 2012.

28. For contradictions within the effort to disarm illegal armed groups (DIAG), see Robin Edward-Poulton, *DIAG Evaluation—Disbandment of Illegal Armed Groups in Afghanistan, A Project of the United Nations Development Programme and Afghanistan's New Beginnings Programme (ANBP)* (Oxford: EPES Mandala Consulting, April 2009), http://erc.undp.org/evaluationadmin/downloaddocument.html?docid=3451; Michael Vinay Bhatia and Robert Muggah, "The Politics of Demobilization in Afghanistan," in *Security and Post-Conflict Reconstruction: Dealing with Fighters in the Aftermath of War*, edited by Robert Muggah (New York: Routledge, 2009), pp. 126–64.

29. For details, see Craig Whitlock and Greg Miller, "U.S. Covert Paramilitary Presence in Afghanistan Much Larger than Thought," *Washington Post*, September 22, 2010. See also Bob Woodward, *Obama's Wars* (New York: Simon and Schuster, 2010).

30. Whitlock and Miller, "U.S. Covert Paramilitary Presence."

31. Interviews with ISAF and SOF officials, Kabul, Kandahar, Herat, and Balkh, fall 2010 and spring 2012.

32. Cited in Inspector General, *Assessment of U.S. Government and Coalition Efforts*, p. ii.

33. See David Flynn, "Extreme Partnership in Afghanistan: Arghandab District, Kandahar Province, 2010–2011," *Military Review*, March-April 2012, pp. 27–35.

34. Interviews with ANP officer in change of the local ALP, Baghlan, and with political advisors to ISAF, Regional Command-North, fall 2010 and spring 2012.

35. Amie Ferris-Rotman, "Afghanistan: Hundreds of Soldiers Detained, Fired for Insurgent Links," Reuters, September 5, 2012.

36. "Afghanistan: Fears over Child Recruitment, Abuse by Pro-government Militias," IRIN (UN Office for the Coordination of Humanitarian Affairs news service), January 20, 2011.

37. See, for example, Barnett Rubin, "Saving Afghanistan," *Foreign Affairs* 86, no. 1 (2007): 57–78.

38. Interviews with MoI, NDS, and provincial government officials and non-governmental organization (NGO) representatives, Baghlan, September 2010 and April 2012.

39. Interviews with a SOF officer, Herat, April 2012.

40. For details, see Human Rights Watch, *Just Don't Call It a Militia*, pp. 97–98.

41. Ibid.

42. Interview with an Afghan civil society organizer, Baghlan, April 2012.

43. See, for example, Graham Bowley, "Afghan Police in Spotlight after Foiling Taliban Strike," *New York Times*, May 10, 2012.

44. I am grateful to Ambassador Ronald Neumann for this piece of information.

45. Interviews with ALP members, ANP officers, civil society representatives, and local residents, Baghlan, April 2012.

46. Interviews with former and current political advisers in ISAF's Regional Command-North, Balkh, April 2012. See also Rosenberg and Rubin, "Afghanistan to Disband."

47. Ibid.

48. For details on how the police handled the rape case against the ALP commander, see Alissa Rubin, "Afghan Rape Case Turns Focus on Afghan Local Police," *New York Times,* June 27, 2012.

49. On one such instance of a village-level self-generated uprising against the Taliban in Daikundi, see Rajiv Chandrasekaran, "U.S. Eager to Replicate Afghan Villagers' Successful Revolt against Taliban," *Washington Post,* June 21, 2010.

50. For further details on this uprising, see "The Worm Turns," *The Economist*, August 18, 2012.

51. David Young, "An 'Afghan Summer' of Revolt," *Foreign Policy.com,* September 12, 2012, http://afpak.foreignpolicy.com/posts/2012/09/12/an_afghan_summer_of_revolt.

52. Ibid.

53. Ibid.

54. Ibid.

55. Lefèvre, "Afghanistan Public Protection Program," p. 75.

56. On the positive side, the Wardak AP3 militias showed considerable restraint by avoiding involvement in local tribal disputes, such as those between the Hazaras and the Kuchis over grazing lands. See Axe, "War Is Boring."

57. Interview with an ALP commander, Baghlan, April 2012.

58. Sayed Salahuddin, "Afghan Local Police Group Deserts to Taliban-Led Insurgents," *Washington Post*, July 4, 2012.

59. Interviews with ISAF and UNAMA officials, Kabul, Kandahar, Herat, Balkh, and Baghlan, fall 2010 and spring 2012. See also Kenneth Moorefield's testimony in House Armed Services Committee, Subcommittee on Oversight and Investigations, *Hearing on Afghan National Security Forces.*

60. Interviews with ANP officers, ALP members, foreign NGO security officers, and representatives of civil society, Baghlan, April 2012.

61. See Flynn, "Extreme Partnership in Afghanistan."

62. I am grateful to Ambassador Ronald Neumann for this information and insights on the ALP based on his visits to the Arghandab ALP units.

63. For a detailed description of their successes against the Taliban and for a contrast with the problems that have plagued the ALP in the north, see Luke

Mogelson, "Bad Guys vs. Worse Guys in Afghanistan," *New York Times*, October 19, 2011.

64. Cited in Inspector General, *Assessment of U.S. Government and Coalition Efforts*, p. 7.

65. The U.S. Army's Nangarhar initiative apparently did not involve SOFs at the beginning.

66. For a description of this rivalry, see David Mansfield, "The Ban on Opium Production—A Risk Too Far?" (Harvard University, March 08, 2010), pp. 13–16, www.hks.harvard.edu/cchrp/sbhrap/research/pdf/Mansfield_RiskTooFar. pdf. See also Alissa Rubin, "Afghan Tribal Rivalries Bedevil a U.S. Plan," *New York Times*, March 11, 2010.

67. Interviews with Afghan government officials, community representatives from several districts, and foreign NGO security officers and political analysts, Nangarhar, April 2012.

68. Interviews with ANP officers, ALP members, foreign NGO security officers, and representatives of civil society, Baghlan, April 2012.

69. Ibid.

70. For other human rights abuses and acts of crime perpetrated by the ALP and other self-defense militias in other parts of Afghanistan, see Lynn Yoshikawa and Matt Pennington, "Afghan Local Police: When the Solution Becomes the Problem," *Foreign Policy.com*, October 27, 2011, http://afpak.foreignpolicy.com/posts/2011/10/27/afghan_local_police_when_the_solution_becomes_the_problem.

71. Cited in Dexter Filkins, "Afghan Militias Battle with Aid of U.S.," *New York Times*, November 22, 2009.

72. I am grateful to Philipp Rotmann of the Global Public Policy Institute for sharing detailed information and for his other invaluable input into this chapter.

73. Bethany Little, "600 ALP Recruits Validated in Takhar," NATO-ISAF, April 21, 2012, www.isaf.nato.int/article/news/district-conducts-validation-shura.html.

74. Interviews with ISAF officials, UNAMA officers, and local community representatives, Uruzgan, spring 2009, and with ISAF and U.S. Embassy officials and U.S. journalists, Kabul, September 2010. For a more recent example of problems with ALP units in Uruzgan, see Rod Nordland, "Afghan Officer Sought in the Killing of 9 Colleagues," *New York Times,* March 8, 2012.

75. Alissa Rubin and Sangar Rahimi, "Afghan Officials Cite Revenge Killings in Latest Outbreak of Ethnic Hatred," *New York Times*, August 3, 2012.

76. For details, see Abdul Matin Sarfraz and Rod Nordland, "Afghan Protest Vengeful Militias," *New York Times*, September 2, 2012.

77. For a recent case in which a Hazara man, apparently a member of the ALP, slaughtered eleven Pashtuns, see Rubin and Rahimi, "Afghan Officials Cite Revenge Killings." Some Afghan officials have disputed that the offender was in fact a member of the ALP and instead emphasized that although he wanted to join, he was rejected for his criminal record.

78. Personal communication from a U.S. political adviser in Helmand, July 2012. See also Ryan Evans, "The Once and Future Civil War in Afghanistan," *ForeignPolicy.com*, July 26, 2012.

79. Interviews with U.S. military and ISAF officers, Kabul, Kandahar, Baghlan, Herat, and Balkh, September 2010 and April 2012.

80. For more details, see Mogelson, "Bad Guys."

81. Interviews with Afghan government, MoI, and NDS officials and with ALP members, Baghlan, September 2010.

82. Afghankush was assassinated by a suicide bomber in 2011.

83. Interviews with UNAMA, MoI, and NDS officials, Baghlan, September 2010, and a security officer of a Western development agency, Baghlan, April 2012. I am also grateful to Philipp Rotmann for further details.

84. For a nuanced discussion of how broader insecurity impinges on the determination of local communities to embrace the counterinsurgency effort and generate self-defense forces, see John Nagl, "A Better War in Afghanistan," Statement to Senate Foreign Relations Committee, September 16, 2009, www.cnas.org/files/documents/publications/CNASTestimony_Nagl_SFRC_September_16_2009.pdf.

85. Author's interviews with maliks from Logar, September 2010.

86. Interview with an ALP commander, Baghlan, April 2012.

87. The state of the ANSF and the challenges they face are analyzed in detail in chapter 11 of this volume.

88. On this point, see Philipp Rotmann, "Afghanistan: Urgent Investments in the Long Transition," Policy Brief (Berlin: Global Public Policy Institute, March 2012), www.gppi.net/fileadmin/media/pub/2012/rotmann_2012_policy-brief_afghanistan-urgent-investments.pdf.

Chapter 9

1. At various points over the past two decades, including during the 2000s, the illicit drug sector as a percentage of GDP surpassed 30 percent. See, for example, Christopher Ward and William Byrd, *Afghanistan's Opium Drug Economy*, World Bank Report SASPR-5 (Washington, December 2004); United Nations Office on Drugs and Crime (UNODC), "Opium Amounts to Half of Afghanistan's GDP in 2007, Reports UNODC," November 16, 2007, www.unodc.org/india/afghanistan_gdp_report.html. Since 2002 the drug sector as a percentage of GDP has oscillated between 60 and 30 percent, as the illicit economies contracted and expanded several times over the decade and also because Afghanistan's legal economy expanded.

2. For details on the evolution of poppy cultivation and the drug trade in Afghanistan since the 1980s, see Vanda Felbab-Brown, *Shooting Up: Counterinsurgency and the War on Drugs* (Brookings, 2010), chapter 5.

3. Ibid., for details on the Taliban ban and its multiple and complex effects. See also UNODC, *Afghanistan Opium Survey 2011: Summary Findings* (Vienna:

October 2011), www.unodc.org/documents/crop-monitoring/Afghanistan/ Executive_Summary_2011_web.pdf.

4. For a comprehensive and comparative analysis of the various factors, see David Mansfield, "The Economic Superiority of Illicit Drug Production: Myth and Reality—Opium Poppy Cultivation in Afghanistan," paper prepared for the International Conference on Alternative Development in Drug Control and Cooperation, Feldafing (Munich), January 7–12, 2002.

5. For the top estimates, see Gretchen Peters, *Seeds of Terror: How Heroin Is Bankrolling the Taliban and al Qaeda* (New York: Thomas Dunne, 2009). A Congressional Research Service report put the estimate at about $100 million a year, a number that many drug experts (myself included) find most plausible. For this report, see Kenneth Katzman, "Afghanistan: Post-Taliban Governance, Security, and U.S. Policy," Report RL30588 (Library of Congress, Congressional Research Service, May 3, 2012), www.fas.org/sgp/crs/row/RL30588.pdf. For further discussions on the size of the Afghan narcotics economy and Taliban profits, see also Christopher M. Blanchard, "Afghanistan: Narcotics and U.S. Policy," Report RL32686 (Library of Congress, Congressional Research Service, July 2009), www.fas.org/sgp/crs/row/RL32686.pdf; Letizia Paoli, Victoria A. Greenfield, and Peter Reuter, *The World Heroin Market: Can Supply Be Cut?* (Oxford University Press, 2009), pp. 41–83 and 111–14.

6. Department of Defense, *Report on Progress toward Security and Stability in Afghanistan* (April 2012), p. 55, www.defense.gov/pubs/pdfs/Report_Final_SecDef_04_26_10.pdf.

7. Leaked report from TF 3-10 Bagram, Afghanistan, *State of the Taliban: Detainee Perspectives*, January 6, 2012, p. 14.

8. The case for bankrupting the Taliban via counternarcotics initiatives is presented in Thomas Schweich, Department of State, *U.S. Counternarcotics Strategy for Afghanistan*, August 2007, http://2001-2009.state.gov/p/inl/rls/rpt/90561.htm.

For details on the positions of the U.S., U.K., and other militaries in Afghanistan and contentions within and among allied governments about the best counternarcotics policy, see Felbab-Brown, *Shooting Up*, chapter 5.

9. For details, see Vanda Felbab-Brown, "Afghanistan: When Counternarcotics Undermine Counterterrorism," *Washington Quarterly* 28, no. 4 (2005): 55–72.

10. For details, see Adam Pain, "Opium Trading Systems in Helmand and Ghor," Issue Paper (Kabul: Afghan Research and Evaluation Unit [AREU], January 2006), www.areu.org.af/publications/Opium%20Trading%20Systems.pdf.

11. Mark Shaw, "Drug Trafficking and the Development of Organized Crime in Post-Taliban Afghanistan," in *Afghanistan's Drug Industry: Structure, Functioning, Dynamics, and Implications for Counter-narcotics Policy*, edited by Doris Buddenberg and William Byrd (Vienna: UNODC and Washington: World Bank, 2006), pp. 189–214, www.unodc.org/pdf/Afgh_drugindustry_Nov06.pdf.

12. For some of the early protection arrangements emerging between the Taliban and drug trafficking groups in the first part of the post-2001 decade, see Carlotta Gall, "Taliban Rebels Still Menacing Afghan South," *New York Times,* March 2, 2006.

13. For details, see Felbab-Brown, *Shooting Up*, chapter 5.

14. For analysis of the social control structures, see Olivier Roy, *Islam and Resistance in Afghanistan* (Cambridge University Press, 1990). For the impact of counternarcotics policies on the tribal structures, see David Mansfield, "The Ban on Opium Production across Nangarhar—A Risk Too Far?" (Harvard University, March 08, 2010), www.hks.harvard.edu/cchrp/sbhrap/research/pdf/Mansfield_RiskTooFar.pdf.

15. Interviews with U.S. counternarcotics officials and ISAF officers, Kabul, Kandahar, and Washington, fall 2010, winter 2011, and spring 2012.

16. TF 3-10 Bagram, *State of the Taliban*, p. 14.

17. Ibid., p. 15.

18. For a critique of the raids to target middle-level commanders and the interdiction policy's loss of selectivity, see Open Society Foundations and the Liaison Office, *The Cost of Kill/Capture: Impact of the Night Raid Surge on Afghan Civilians* (New York: September 19, 2011), www.soros.org/sites/default/files/Night-Raids-Report-FINAL-092011.pdf.

19. For details on counternarcotics policies in Helmand, see David Mansfield, "Between a Rock and a Hard Place: Counter-narcotics Efforts and Their Effects in Nangarhar and Helmand in the 2010–11 Growing Season," Case Study (Kabul: AREU, October 2011).

20. See Dmitry Solovyov, "Russia Gives U.S. Afghan Drugs Data, Criticizes NATO," Reuters, May 23, 2010.

21. For eradication levels over the past decade, see UNODC, *Afghanistan Opium Survey 2011*, p. 15.

22. See, for example, Barnett Rubin and Jake Sherman, *Counternarcotics to Stabilize Afghanistan: The False Promise of Crop Eradication* (New York: Center on International Cooperation, February 2008), www.cic.nyu.edu/afghanistan/docs/counternarcoticsfinal.pdf; David Mansfield and Adam Pain, "Evidence from the Field: Understanding Changing Levels of Opium Poppy Cultivation in Afghanistan," Briefing Paper (Kabul: AREU, November 2007).

23. Interviews with Afghan provincial government officials and ISAF officers, Herat, April 2012.

24. For background on the findings, history, and varied effectiveness of counternarcotics efforts in the aforementioned countries, see Felbab-Brown, *Shooting Up.*

25. For analysis of possible countries and areas where poppy cultivation would likely shift if cultivation in Afghanistan somehow collapsed or was suppressed, see Vanda Felbab-Brown, "The Drug-Conflict Nexus in South Asia: Beyond Taliban Profits and Afghanistan," in *The Afghanistan-Pakistan Theater:*

Militant Islam, Security, and Stability, edited by Daveed Gartenstein-Ross and Clifford May (Washington: Foundation for Defense of Democracies, May 2010), pp. 90–112.

26. For details, see Mansfield, "Between a Rock and a Hard Place."

27. UNODC, *Afghanistan Opium Survey 2012* (Vienna: April 2012), p. 30.

28. Mansfield, "The Ban on Opium Production across Nangarhar."

29. David Mansfield, "Pariah or Poverty? The Opium Ban in the Province Nangarhar in 2004/05 Growing Season and Its Impact on Rural Livelihood Strategies," GTZ Policy Brief 1 (Eschborn, Germany: Deutsche Gesellschaft für Technische Zusammenarbeit, September 2005), www.gtz.de/de/dokumente/en-Final CopingReportStudyPAL20.7.pdf.

30. Mansfield, "The Ban on Opium Production across Nangarhar."

31. Interviews with poppy farmers, maliks, and provincial government officials, Nangarhar, April 2012.

32. UNODC, *Afghanistan Opium Survey 2012*, p. 30.

33. Interviews with maliks and poppy farmers, Nangarhar, April 2012.

34. Paula Kantor and Adam Pain, "Rethinking Rural Poverty Reduction in Afghanistan," Policy Note Series (Kabul: AREU, October 2011), www.areu.org.af/UpdateDownloadHits.aspx?EditionId=564&Pdf=1127E-Rethinking Rural Poverty Reduction in Afghanistan PN October 2011.pdf.

35. Interviews with poppy farmers and maliks, Nangarhar, and maliks and shopkeepers, Baghlan, fall 2010 and spring 2012. For an excellent analysis detailing the effects of economic stress on social cohesion and patronage networks, see Kantor and Pain, "Rethinking Rural Poverty."

36. Interviews in Uruzgan and Kandahar, spring 2009; Kandahar and Baghlan, fall 2010; and Herat and Nangarhar, spring 2012.

37. Interviews with Nangarhar government officials, businessmen, and maliks, April 2012. See also Kantor and Pain, "Rethinking Rural Poverty."

38. Interview with provincial government official, Nangarhar, April 2012.

39. See Joel Hafvenstein, *Opium Season: A Year on the Afghan Frontier* (Guilford, Conn.: Lyons Press, 2007); Holly Barnes Higgins, "The Road to Helmand," *Washington Post*, February 4, 2007.

40. World Bank, "Afghanistan: Priorities for Agriculture and Rural Development," 2011, http://web.worldbank.org/WBSITE/EXTERNAL/COUNTRIES/SOUTHASIAEXT/EXTSAREGTOPAGRI/0,,contentMDK:20273762~menuPK:548212~pagePK:34004173~piPK:34003707~theSitePK:452766,00.html. As of 2009, the Microfinance Investment Support Facility had approximately 450,000 clients, of which only 28 percent were in the rural areas. See Adam Pain and Paula Kantor, "Beyond the Market: Can the AREDP Transform Afghanistan's Rural Nonfarm Economy?" AREU Briefing Paper Series, February 2011, p. 7, www.areu.org.af/Uploads/EditionPdfs/1106E-Beyond%20the%20Market%20BP%202011%20web.pdf.

41. Ibid.

42. On the travails of getting the Kajaki Dam to produce electricity at full capacity, see Carlotta Gall, "Deep in Taliban Territory, a Push for Electricity," *New York Times*, November 8, 2008; Jean MacKenzie, "Watershed of Waste: Afghanistan's Kajaki Dam and USAID," *Global Post*, October 11, 2011.

43. Katzman, "Afghanistan: Post-Taliban Governance."

44. Department of Defense, *Report on Progress*, p. 91.

45. Ibid., and interviews with USAID officials, Kabul, fall 2010, and Washington, fall 2011. See also data from AVIPA's implementing partner—International Relief and Development—in Senate Committee on Foreign Relations, *Evaluating U.S. Foreign Assistance to Afghanistan*, Majority Staff Report, 112 Cong. 1 sess. (June 8, 2011), p. 8.

46. Gayle Tzemach Lemmon, "New Hope for Afghan Raisin Farmers," *New York Times*, October 9, 2010.

47. Senate Committee on Foreign Relations, *Evaluating U.S. Foreign Assistance*, p. 11.

48. In 2010 approximately $1 billion was appropriated to CERP. See Colin Cookman and Caroline Wadhams, *Governance in Afghanistan: Looking Ahead to What We Leave Behind* (Washington: Center for American Progress, May 12, 2010), p. 30, www.americanprogress.org/issues/2010/05/pdf/afghangovernance.pdf.

49. Rajiv Chandrasekaran, "In Afghan Region, U.S. Spreads the Cash to Fight the Taliban," *Washington Post*, May 31, 2010; Karen DeYoung, "Results of Kandahar Offensive May Affect Future U.S. Moves," *Washington Post*, May 23, 2010.

50. Ibid.

51. Interviews with U.S. and Canadian government officials and representatives of the international development companies charged with the economic stabilization programs, Kandahar and Helmand, spring 2009 and fall 2010.

52. Kantor and Pain, "Rethinking Rural Poverty Reduction."

53. Paul Fishstein and Andrew Wilder, *Winning Hearts and Minds? Examining the Relationship between Aid and Security in Afghanistan* (Tufts University, Feinstein International Center, January 2012); Andrew Wilder, "A 'Weapons System' Based on Wishful Thinking," *Boston Globe*, September 16, 2009.

54. TF 3-10 Bagram, *State of the Taliban*, p. 14.

55. Interviews with U.S. and Canadian government officials and representatives of the international development companies charged with the economic stabilization programs, Kandahar, Helmand, and Nangarhar, spring 2009, fall 2010, and spring 2012.

56. Barbara Stapleton, "A Means to What End? Why PRTs Are Peripheral to the Bigger Political Challenges in Afghanistan," *Journal of Military and Strategic Studies* 10, no. 1 (2007), www.jmss.org/jmss/index.php/jmss/article/view/38/36.

57. See Andrew Natsios, "The Nine Principles of Reconstruction and Development," *Parameters* 35, no. 3 (Autumn 2005): 4–20.

58. See, for example, Hamish Nixon, "The 'Subnational Governance' Challenge and the Independent Directorate of Local Governance," in *Snapshots of an Intervention: The Unlearned Lessons of Afghanistan's Decade of Assistance (2001–2011)*, edited by Martine van Bijlert and Sari Kouvo (Kabul: Afghan Analysts Network, 2012), pp. 117–23; World Bank, "Service Delivery and Governance at the Sub-National Level in Afghanistan," Report 40617 (Kabul, July 2007), www-wds.worldbank.org/external/default/WDSContentServer/WDSP/IB/2007/08/28/000020953_20070828101004/Rendered/INDEX/406170AF0Service0delivery01PUBLIC1.txt.

59. Nick Horne, "Throwing Money at the Problem: US PRTs in Afghanistan," in Van Bijlert and Kouvo, *Snapshots of an Intervention*, pp. 111–15.

60. Tim Kock and Jerry Turnbull, "Rural Development Centers (Farm Stores) in Afghanistan, Do They Work? The Business Owners' Perspectives," *Journal of International Agricultural and Extension Education* 18, no. 3 (2011): 35–44.

61. Interviews with a top Mercy Corps representative, Kabul, April 2012.

62. See Ward and Byrd, *Afghanistan's Opium Drug Economy.*

63. See Mansfield, "Between a Rock and a Hard Place."

64. David Mansfield, *Responding to Risk and Uncertainty: Understanding the Nature of Change in the Rural Livelihoods of Opium Poppy Growing Households in the 2007/08 Growing Season*, July 2008, www.davidmansfield.org/data/Field_Work/UK/FINAL_UK_DRIVERS_REPORT_08.pdf.

65. Interviews with ISAF and USAID officials in charge of the program, Kandahar Air Force Base, spring 2009.

66. Ronald Neumann, "Afghan Aid Project Not a Road to Nowhere," *Washington Post*, August 3, 2012.

67. Interviews with ISAF officers; USAID, Canadian, and U.S. PRT officials; and Afghan government officials, Kandahar and Zabul, spring 2009 and fall 2010.

68. Joel Hafvenstein, "The Helmand Food Zone Fiasco," Registan.net, August 26, 2010, http://registan.net/index.php/2010/08/26/helmand-food-zone-fiasco/.

69. Interview with the captain of the U.S. PRT, Zabul, spring 2009.

70. Interviews with officials of the U.S., U.K., and Canadian government development agencies, Kabul and Kandahar, fall 2010, and Washington, fall 2011.

71. Senate Committee on Foreign Relations, *Evaluating U.S. Foreign Assistance*, p. 10.

72. Joshua Partlow, "In Afghan Village, Fears That Government Can't Provide after Americans Leave," *Washington Post*, July 16, 2012.

73. Department of Defense, *Report on Progress*, p. 87.

74. Mark Moyar, "Development in Afghanistan's Counterinsurgency: A New Guide," *Small Wars Journal*, March 2011, p. 5, http://smallwarsjournal.com/documents/development-in-afghanistan-coin-moyar.pdf.

75. Interviews with USAID personnel, U.S. Embassy, Kabul, fall 2010, and with high officials of ISAF's Regional Command-South, Kandahar Air Force Base, fall 2010.

76. Partlow, "In Afghan Village."

77. See Rajiv Chandrasekaran, "U.S. Construction Projects in Afghanistan Challenged by Inspector General's Report," *Washington Post*, July 30, 2012; Matthew Rosenberg, "U.S. Fund to Rebuild Afghanistan Is Criticized," *New York Times*, July 30, 2012; Special Inspector General for Afghanistan Reconstruction, *Fiscal Year 2011 Afghanistan Infrastructure Fund Projects Are behind Schedule and Lack Adequate Sustainment Plans* (July 2012), www.sigar.mil/pdf/audits/2012-07-30audit-12-12Revised.pdf.

78. Interviews with Afghan government officials, international development firm representatives, international NGO representatives, Afghan businessmen, tribal elders, and ISAF officials, Uruzgan, Helmand, Zabul, and Kandahar, spring 2009 and fall 2010, and Nangarhar, spring 2012.

79. United Nations Office of the High Commissioner for Human Rights, *Human Rights Dimension of Poverty in Afghanistan* (Kabul, March 2010), http://unama.unmissions.org/Portals/UNAMA/human%20rights/Poverty%20Report%2030%20March%202010_English.pdf.

80. Horne, "Throwing Money."

81. See, for example, Graham Bowley and Matthew Rosenberg, "In Afghanistan, Businesses Plan Their Own Exits," *New York Times*, March 30, 2012.

82. Jane Perlez, "$16 Billion in Civilian Aid Pledged to Afghanistan, with Conditions," *New York Times*, July 8, 2012.

83. The original effort with grape cultivation was to convert farmers to using wire, as is done in the West, but the wire would rapidly be stolen. Interviews with U.S. and Canadian development workers and international NGO employees, Zabul, spring 2009; Kandahar, fall 2010; and Baghlan, fall 2010.

84. Department of Defense, *Report on Progress*, p. 84.

85. World Bank, "Building on Basics in Health Care" (June 2009), http://web.worldbank.org/WBSITE/EXTERNAL/EXTABOUTUS/IDA/0,,contentMDK:21289162~menuPK:3266877~pagePK:51236175~piPK:437394~theSitePK:73154,00.html.

86. Department of Defense, *Report on Progress*, p. 85.

87. Ibid.

88. Ibid., p. 86.

89. Senate Committee on Foreign Relations, *Evaluating U.S. Foreign Assistance*, p. 28.

90. Discussed in chapter 6 in this volume.

91. For the complexities of the whole-of-government approach, see Ronald Neumann, "The Hole in Whole of Government Needs Leadership and Learning Organizations," in *Strategic Realism and Irregular Conflict*, edited by Frank Kramer (Washington: CNA, and Marine Corps University Press, forthcoming).

92. Senate Committee on Foreign Relations, *Evaluating U.S. Foreign Assistance*, p. 17.

93. Department of State, Office of Inspector General, "Report of Inspection," ISP-I-10-32A (February 2010), p. 11, http://oig.state.gov/documents/organization/138084.pdf.

94. House of Representatives, Committee on Appropriations, Subcommittee on State, Foreign Operations, and Related Programs, "Foreign Operations: Key Issues for Congressional Oversight," testimony of Jacquelyn Williams-Bridgers, U.S. Government Accountability Office, 112 Cong. 1 sess. (March 3, 2011).

95. For such guiding principles beyond Afghanistan, see USAID, *The Development Response to Violent Extremism and Insurgency: Putting Principles into Practice* (September 2011), http://transition.usaid.gov/our_work/policy_planning_and_learning/documents/VEI_Policy_Final.pdf.

96. See "Afghanistan and the International Community: From Transition to the Transformation Decade, Conference Conclusions," International Afghanistan Conference in Bonn, December 5, 2011, http://eeas.europa.eu/afghanistan/docs/2011_11_conclusions_bonn_en.pdf.

97. For a fascinating account of the difficulties in translating formulated policy into programs and outcomes on the ground, see Ronald Neumann's excellent *The Other War: Winning and Losing in Afghanistan* (Dulles, Va.: Potomac Books, 2009).

98. For such an argument, see Ashraf Ghani and Clare Lockhart, *Fixing Failed States* (Oxford University Press, 2008).

99. Karen DeYoung and Joshua Partlow, "Karzai Pledges Reforms in Exchange for International Backing at Afghan Conference," *Washington Post*, July 20, 2010.

100. Curt Tarnoff, "Afghanistan: U.S. Foreign Assistance," Report R40699 (Congressional Research Service, Library of Congress, August 19, 2011), p. 5.

101. For details on the Kabul Bank, see chapter 6 in this volume.

102. Government of the Islamic Republic of Afghanistan, *Towards a Self-Sustaining Afghanistan: An Economic Transition Strategy* (November 29, 2011), www.auswaertiges-amt.de/cae/servlet/contentblob/604482/publication File/162938/Economic_Side_Event_Towards_a_Self_Sustaining_Afghanistan. pdf; "Afghanistan and the International Community: From Transition to the Transformation Decade."

103. For data on the ARTF, see World Bank, *ARTF—Administrator's Report on Financial Status As of August 21, 2012 (end of Asad 5th month of SY1391)*, http://siteresources.worldbank.org/INTAFGHANISTAN/Resources/Afghanistan-Reconstructional-Trust-Fund/ARTF_Financial_Status_Report_August_21_2012. pdf. For total U.S. and international spending, see Rosenberg, "U.S. Fund to Rebuild." Although not specifying whether the following amount included U.S. spending (which indeed would contradict the number reported in Rosenberg's article), the Japanese government announced at the Tokyo Conference that the "international community" had spent $35 billion on Afghan reconstruction over the past decade. Cited in Perlez, "$16 Billion."

104. William Byrd, "Keeping Each Other Honest in Afghanistan—Will It Work?" *Foreign Policy.com*, August 6, 2012, http://afpak.foreignpolicy.com/posts/2012/08/06/keeping_each_other_honest_in_afghanistan_will_it_work.

105. For an early call to focus on the growth of the Afghan economy after 2014, see Nathaniel Fick and Clare Lockhart, "The Economic Imperative: Stabilizing Afghanistan through Economic Growth," Policy Brief (Washington: Center for a New American Security, April 2010), http://67.192.225.242/files/documents/publications/Economic%20Imperative_FickLockhart_April2010_code507_policybrief.pdf.

106. World Bank, *Transition in Afghanistan: Looking Beyond 2014: Executive Summary* (Washington, November 18, 2011), p. 1, http://siteresources.worldbank.org/AFGHANISTANEXTN/Resources/305984-1297184305854/AFTransition.pdf.

107. Ibid., p. 2.

108. Interviews with USAID officials, Kabul, fall 2010.

109. World Bank, *Transition in Afghanistan*.

110. Bowley and Rosenberg, "Businesses Plan Their Own Exits."

111. Jon Boone and Nooruddin Bakhshi, "Boom Time for Afghanistan's People Smugglers," *The Guardian*, January 19, 2012.

112. Abid Amiri, "Why Are Afghans Leaving Afghanistan?" *Diplomatic Courier*, January 31, 2012.

113. Bowley and Rosenberg, "Businesses Plan Their Own Exits."

114. Ibid.

115. Miriam Arghandiwal, "Entrepreneurs Serving Afghan Expats See Good Times Ending," Reuters, August 6, 2012.

116. Interviews with Afghans in Kabul, Kandahar, Baghlan, and Nangarhar, fall 2010 and spring 2012.

117. The mineral deposits were estimated at $1 trillion by the United States Geological Survey in 2010.

118. Ministry of Mines, Government of Afghanistan, "Sustaining Afghanistan's Economy after the Transition," PowerPoint presentation, Center for American Progress, Washington, February 2011.

119. Interviews with officials of the Chinese Embassy in Washington, winter 2011.

120. See chapter 1 of this volume, as well as Matthew Rosenberg, "Afghan Cabinet Raises Concern about Mining Legislation, to West's Unease," *New York Times*, July 25, 2012.

121. Matthew Rosenberg, "As Exxon Mobil Weighs Oil Bid, Afghans Move Closer to a Foreign Investment Goal," *New York Times*, July 5, 2012.

122. I am grateful to my colleague Erica Down of the Brookings Institution, an expert on China's resource extraction policies around the world, for her insights.

123. For an argument strongly in support of such a policy, see Frederick Starr and Andrew Kuchins, "The Key to Success in Afghanistan: A Modern Silk Road

Strategy," Silk Road Paper (Washington: Central Asia-Caucasus Institute, May 2010), www.silkroadstudies.org/new/docs/silkroadpapers/1005Afghan.pdf

124. Marvin Weinbaum, "The Regional Dimension in Afghan Stability," in *Afghanistan in Transition: Crafting A Strategy for Enduring Stability*, edited by Beata Górka-Winter and Bartosz Wiśniewski (Warsaw: PISM [Polish Institute of International Affairs], 2012), pp. 81–92.

Chapter 10

1. For the geopolitical struggles in the region, see Peter Hopkirk, *The Great Game: The Struggle for Empire in Central Asia* (New York: Kodansha America, 1994).

2. For details, see Ahmed Rashid, *Taliban: Militant Islam, Oil, and Fundamentalism* (Yale University Press, 2000); Steve Coll, *Ghost Wars: The Secret History of the CIA, Afghanistan and bin Laden, from the Soviet Invasion to September 10, 2001* (London: Penguin Books, 2005).

3. For seminal work on the Durand Line, see Louis Dupree, "The Durand Line of 1893: A Case Study in Artificial Political Boundaries and Culture Areas," in *Current Problems in Afghanistan* (Princeton University Press, 1961), pp. 77–93. For analysis of how the border, which is not recognized by Afghanistan, undermines the possibility of improved relations between Afghanistan and Pakistan, see Barnett Rubin and Abubakar Siddique, "Resolving the Pakistan-Afghanistan Stalemate," Special Report 176 (Washington: United States Institute of Peace, October 2006), www.usip.org/files/resources/SRoct06.pdf.

4. Marvin Weinbaum and Haseeb Humayoon, "The Intertwined Destinies of Afghanistan and Pakistan," in *The Future of Afghanistan*, edited by Alexander Thier (Washington: United States Institute of Peace, 2009), pp. 93–103.

5. For a recent such episode, see Kevin Sieff, "Afghan Refugees Forced to Return Home," *Washington Post,* June 20, 2012.

6. For details of the 2011 FATA reforms, see Shehryar Fazli, "A New Dawn for Pakistan's Tribal Areas?" *Foreign Policy.com,* August 12, 2011, http://afpak. foreignpolicy.com/posts/2011/08/12/a_new_dawn_for_pakistans_tribal_areas.

7. See International Crisis Group, "Countering Militancy in FATA," Asia Report 178 (Brussels: October 21, 2009); Joshua White, "Pakistan's Islamist Frontier: Islamic Politics and U.S. Policy in Pakistan's North-West Frontier," in *The Afghanistan-Pakistan Theater: Militant Islam, Security, and Stability*, edited by Daveed Gartenstein-Ross and Clifford May (Washington: Foundation for Defense of Democracies, May 2010), pp. 41–74.

8. See Stephen Cohen, *The Idea of Pakistan* (Brookings, 2004); Anatol Lieven, *Pakistan: A Hard Country* (New York: PublicAffairs Books, 2012).

9. Of course, many Afghan elites have also been educated in Pakistan.

10. For details on India's projects in Afghanistan, see Kenneth Katzman, "Afghanistan: Post-Taliban Governance, Security, and U.S. Policy," Report

RL30588 (Library of Congress, Congressional Research Service, May 3, 2012). For an overview of India's broader interests in Afghanistan, see also Christine Fair, "India in Afghanistan and Beyond: Constraints and Opportunities" (New York: Century Foundation, September 28, 2010), http://tcf.org/publications/2010/9/india-in-afghanistan-and-beyond-opportunities-and-constraints.

11. See the leaked report from TF 3-10 Bagram, Afghanistan, *State of the Taliban: Detainee Perspectives*, January 6, 2012, p. 8, http://s3.documentcloud.org/documents/296489/taliban-report.pdf.

12. For details on the terrorist attacks and Indian suspicions of an ISI role see, for example, Javed Hamdar and Candace Rondeaux, "Suicide Bombing Leaves 40 Dead in Central Kabul," *Washington Post,* July 8, 2008. See also Karin Brulliard, "Afghan Intelligence Ties Pakistani Group Lashkar-e-Taiba to Recent Kabul Attack," *Washington Post*, March 3, 2010; Maria Abi-Habab and Zia Sultani, "NATO Copter Ends Kabul Hotel Siege," *Wall Street Journal*, June 29, 2011; Emily Wax, "Kabul Attack May Intensify India-Pakistan Proxy War," *Washington Post*, October 11, 2009; Alissa Rubin, Graham Bowley, and Sangar Rahimi, "Complex Attack by Taliban Sends Message to the West," *New York Times*, April 15, 2012.

13. Interviews with ISAF officials, Kabul, April 2012.

14. Elisabeth Bumiller and Jane Perlez, "Pakistan's Spy Agency Is Tied to Attack on U.S. Embassy," *New York Times*, September 22, 2011.

15. See chapter 3 in this volume.

16. Matt Waldman, "The Sun in the Sky: The Relationship between Pakistan's ISI and Afghan Insurgents," Discussion Paper 18 (London School of Economics, Crisis States Research Center, June 2010), www.aljazeera.com/mritems/Documents/2010/6/13/20106138531279734lse-isi-taliban.pdf.

17. TF 3-10 Bagram, *State of the Taliban*, p. 8.

18. See chapter 3.

19. TF 3-10 Bagram, *State of the Taliban*, p. 8.

20. Musharraf cited in Taimoor Shah and Carlotta Gall, "Afghan Rebels Find Aid in Pakistan, Musharraf Admits," *New York Times*, August 13, 2007.

21. See, for example, Ahmed Rashid, *Descent into Chaos: The United States and the Failure of Nation Building in Pakistan, Afghanistan, and Central Asia* (London: Penguin Books, 2008).

22. Bruce Riedel, *Deadly Embrace: Pakistan, America, and the Future of Global Jihad* (Brookings, 2011).

23. Ibid. See also Jacob Shapiro and C. Christine Fair, "Understanding Support for Islamist Militancy in Pakistan," *International Security* 34, no. 3 (2009–10): 79–118.

24. For details on Pakistan's calculations regarding and military operations against jihadi militants, see Christine Fair and Seth Jones, "Pakistan's War Within," *Survival* 51, no. 2 (2009): 161–88.

25. TF 3-10 Bagram, *State of the Taliban*, pp.12 and 17. Baitullah Mehsud, the now deceased leader of one powerful anti-Pakistan group, Tehrik-i-Taliban Pakistan, began his jihadi career as a low-level commander in the Haqqani network.

26. Hussain Nadim, "The Quiet Rise of the Quetta Shura," *Foreign Policy.com*, August 14, 2012, http://afpak.foreignpolicy.com/posts/2012/08/14/the_quiet_rise_of_the_quetta_shura.

27. See Ismail Khan and Declan Walsh, "Taliban Kill 13 Soldiers in Pakistan Raid," *New York Times*, June 25, 2012; Matthew Rosenberg and Eric Schmitt, "Allies Rebuke Pakistan on Cross-Border Attacks," *New York Times*, July 29, 2012.

28. "Pakistan Accuses Afghanistan of Backing Taliban Enemy," *New York Times*, August 5, 2012. For background on TNSM, see Hassan Abbas, "The Rise of the Black-Turban Brigade: The Rise of TNSM in Pakistan," *Terrorism Monitor* 4, no. 23 (2006), www.jamestown.org/programs/gta/single/?tx_ttnews%5Btt_news%5D=986&tx_ttnews%5BbackPid%5D=181&no_cache=1; Hassan Abbas, *Pakistan's Troubled Frontier* (Washington: Jamestown Foundation, 2009); Smruti S. Pattanaik, "'Old' Islamists and 'New' Radicals: Understanding the Politics of Religious Radicalization in Pakistan and Its Implications," *Strategic Analysis* 35, no. 4 (2011): 581–94; Justine Fleischner, "Governance and Militancy in Pakistan's Swat Valley" (Washington: Center for Strategic and International Studies, November 2011), http://ancien.operationspaix.net/IMG/pdf/CSIS_Fleischner_SwatValley__14-10-2011_.pdf. For the resurgence of Mullah Fazlullah's forces, see Michael Georgy and Jibran Ahmad, "Pakistan's Fazlullah Re-emerges as a Security Threat," Reuters, June 28, 2012.

29. Interviews with former high officials of the Arg Palace, NDS, and Afghan members of parliament, Kabul and Washington, summer 2009, summer 2010, fall 2010, and spring 2012.

30. For an illustrative incident, see "Afghanistan-Pakistan Border Guards Trade Fire: Afghan Officials," *Express Tribune*, August 14, 2012.

31. Pew Research Center, *Pakistani Public Opinion Ever More Critical of U.S.* (Washington: June 2012), www.pewglobal.org/files/2012/06/Pew-Global-Attitudes-Project-Pakistan-Report-FINAL-Wednesday-June-27-2012.pdf.

32. For background, see Dennis Kux, *The United States and Pakistan 1947–2000: Disenchanted Allies* (Washington: Woodrow Wilson Center Press, 2001.)

33. Interviews with officials of Pakistan's embassy in Washington, summer 2009 and fall 2011.

34. This section draws heavily on Bruce Riedel's analysis of the U.S.-Pakistan relations since Pakistan's independence. See Riedel, *Deadly Embrace*.

35. Ibid., p. x.

36. For details, see John Schmidt, *The Unraveling: Pakistan in the Age of Jihad* (New York: Farrar, Strauss, and Giroux, 2011); Shuja Nawaz, "Ungovernable," *American Interest* 7, no. 1 (2011): 60–71; Cohen, *The Idea of Pakistan*;

Lieven, *A Hard Country*; Feisal Khan, "Corruption and the Decline of the State in Pakistan," *Asian Journal of Political Science* 15, no. 2 (2007): 219–47.

37. For details about the nuclear deal, see Moeed Yusuf, "The Indo-U.S. Nuclear Deal: An Impact Analysis," *Journal on Science and World Affairs* 3, no. 2 (2007): 47–56.

38. Interviews with Pakistani diplomats, Washington, spring 2009. For details on the A.Q. Khan nuclear smuggling network, see Samina Ahmed, "Pakistan's Nuclear Weapons Program: Turning Points and Nuclear Choices," *International Security* 23, no. 4 (1999): 178–204; Gordon Corera, *Shopping for Bombs: Nuclear Proliferation, Global Insecurity, and the Rise and Fall of the A.Q. Khan Network* (Oxford University Press, 2006); David Albright and Corey Hinderstein, "Unraveling the A.Q. Khan and Future Proliferation Networks," *Washington Quarterly* 28, no. 2 (2005): 111–28.

39. For details of the proposed initiative, see Bruce Riedel, "Expand the U.S. Agenda toward Pakistan: Prospects for Peace and Stability Can Brighten," *Opportunity 08: Independent Ideas for America's Next President*, edited by Michael E. O'Hanlon (Brookings, May 2008), www.brookings.edu/research/papers/2008/05/~/me+dia/Research/Files/Papers/2008/5/06%20pakistan%20riedel%20opp08/PB_Pakistan_Riedel.pdf; Barnett Rubin and Ahmed Rashid, "From Great Game to Grand Bargain," *Foreign Affairs* 87, no. 6 (2008): 30–44.

40. For a history of U.S. difficulties in assisting the resolution of the Kashmir dispute, see Howard Schaffer, *Limits of Influence* (Brookings, 2009); Moeed Yusuf and Adil Najam, "Kashmir: Ripe for Resolution?" *Third World Quarterly* 30, no. 8 (2009): 1503–28.

41. Interviews with Indian diplomats, Washington, spring 2009.

42. For the evolution of U.S. policy toward India during the Bush administration, when India was indeed decoupled from Pakistan, see Ashley Tellis, "The Merits of Dehyphenation: Explaining U.S. Success in Engaging India and Pakistan," *Washington Quarterly* 31, no. 4 (2008): 21–42.

43. See, for example, Harsh Pant, "A Rising India's Search for a Foreign Policy," *Orbis* 53, no. 2 (2009): 250–64; Harsh Pant, "The Pakistan Thorn in China-India-U.S. Relations," *Washington Quarterly* 35, no. 1 (2012): 83–95; David Malone, *Does the Elephant Dance: Contemporary Indian Foreign Policy* (Oxford University Press, 2011); Stephen Cohen and Sunil Dasgupta, *Arming without Aiming: India's Military Modernization* (Brookings, 2012).

44. See, for example, Christine Fair, "The U.S.-Pakistan Relations after a Decade of the War on Terror," *Contemporary South Asia* 20, no. 2 (2012): 243–53.

45. For background, see Daniel Markey, *Securing Pakistan's Tribal Belt*, Special Report 36 (New York: Council on Foreign Relations, August 2008); Fleischner, "Governance and Militancy"; Ayesha Siddiqa, "Pakistan's Counterterrorism Strategy: Separating Friends from Enemies," *Washington Quarterly* 34, no. 1 (2011): 149–62.

46. For a detailed account of U.S. anti–al Qaeda efforts prior to the Abbottabad attack and of the attack itself, see Eric Schmitt and Thom Shanker, *Counterstrike: The Untold Story of America's Secret Campaign against Al Qaeda* (New York: Times Books, 2011).

47. White House, Office of the Press Secretary, "Remarks by the President in Address to the Nation on the Way Forward in Afghanistan and Pakistan," U.S. Military Academy at West Point, December 1, 2009, www. whitehouse.gov/the-press-office/remarks-president-address-nation-way-forward-afghanistan-and-pakistan.

48. See, for example, Thomas Perry Thornton, "Pakistan: Fifty Years of Insecurity," in *India and Pakistan: The First Fifty Years*, edited by Selig Harrison, Paul Kreisberg, and Dennis Kux (Cambridge University Press, 1999), pp. 170–88; Ayesha Siddiqa, *Military Inc.: Inside Pakistan's Military Economy* (Oxford University Press, 2007); Shuja Nawaz, *Crossed Swords: Pakistan, Its Army, and the Wars Within* (Oxford University Press, 2008).

49. On Pakistan's diplomatic engagement with the United States and its evasive response to U.S. efforts to commit it to steady action, see Teresita Schaffer and Howard Schaffer, *How Pakistan Negotiates with the United States* (Washington: United States Institute of Peace, 2011).

50. For the effectiveness of U.S. economic aid in Pakistan, see House Committee on Oversight and Government Reform, Subcommittee on National Security and Foreign Affairs, *Hearing on U.S. Aid to Pakistan: Planning and Accountability*, testimony of Andrew Wilder, Research Director, Feinstein International Center, Tufts University, 111 Cong. 1 sess. (December 9, 2009), www.hks. harvard.edu/cchrp/sbhrap/news/Wilder_PakistanAidTestimony_12_9_09.pdf; International Crisis Group, "Aid and Conflict in Pakistan," Asia Report 227 (Brussels: June 27, 2012); Nancy Birdsall, Wren Elhai, and Molly Kinder, "A New Strategy for Aid to Pakistan," *Foreign Policy.com*, June 1, 2011, http:// afpak.foreignpolicy.com/posts/2011/06/01/a_new_strategy_for_aid_to_pakistan.

51. Susan Epstein and Alan Krondstadt, "Pakistan: U.S. Foreign Assistance," Report R41856 (Library of Congress, Congressional Research Service, July 7, 2011).

52. See, for example, Peter Bergen and Katherine Tiedemann, "The Year of the Drone: An Analysis of U.S. Drone Strike in Pakistan, 2004–2010," Counterterrorism Strategy Initiative Paper (Washington: New America Foundation, February 24, 2010); Peter Bergen and Jennifer Rowland, "CIA Drone War in Pakistan in Sharp Decline," *CNN.com*, March 28, 2012, http://edition.cnn. com/2012/03/27/opinion/bergen-drone-decline/index.html?iref=allsearch; Avery Plaw, Matthew Fricker, and Brian Glyn Williams, "Practice Makes Perfect? The Changing Civilian Toll of CIA Drone Strikes in Pakistan," *Perspectives on Terrorism 5*, no. 5-6 (2011), www.terrorismanalysts.com/pt/index.php/pot/article/ view/practice-makes-perfect/html; David Kilcullen and Andrew Exum, "Death from Above, Outrage from Below," *New York Times*, May 17, 2009.

53. Mike Mount, "U.S. and NATO Secure Exit Route from Afghanistan," *CNN.com*, June 4, 2012.

54. For details of the negotiations, see Declan Walsh, "Notions of Honor Color High-Stakes Haggling over NATO Supply Routes," *New York Times*, June 8, 2012; Declan Walsh, "Quiet Duo Forged Road Deal for U.S. and Pakistan," *New York Times*, July 26, 2012.

55. "Pakistan to Scan All NATO Containers," Agence France-Presse, July 3, 2012.

56. "Pakistan Begins to Speed Up Processing of NATO Supplies at Border Crossing," *The National*, July 9, 2012.

57. See, for example, Teresita Schaffer, "U.S. Influence on Pakistan: Can Partners Have Divergent Priorities?" *Washington Quarterly* 26, no. 1 (2002): 169–83; Paul Staniland, "Caught in the Muddle: America's Pakistan Strategy," *Washington Quarterly* 34, no. 1 (2011): 133–48.

58. For recent militant grumbling in Punjab, Pakistan's most prosperous, but also highly unequal, province, see Waqar Gillani and Salman Masood, "Gunmen in Pakistan Kill 6 Soldiers and a Policeman," *New York Times*, July 9, 2012.

59. See, for example, Steve Inskeep, *Instant City: Life and Death in Karachi* (London: Penguin, 2011); Hassan Abbas, ed., *Stabilizing Pakistan through Police Reforms* (New York: Asia Society, July 2012), http://asiasociety.org/files/pdf/as_pakistan_police_reform.pdf.

60. For an excellent analysis of the Istanbul summit and regional dynamics, see Marvin Weinbaum, "The Regional Dimension in Afghan Stability," in *Afghanistan in Transition: Crafting A Strategy for Enduring Stability*, edited by Beata Górka-Winter and Bartosz Wiśniewski (Warsaw: PISM [Polish Institute of International Affairs], 2012), pp. 81–92.

61. TF 3-10 Bagram, *State of the Taliban*, p. 19.

62. Josh White, "A Shortage of Troops in Afghanistan: Iraq War Limits U.S. Options, Says Chairman of Joint Chiefs," *Washington Post*, July 3, 2008.

63. See, for example, James Dobbins, *After Taliban: Nation-Building in Afghanistan* (Washington: Potomac Books, 2008); Mohsen Milani, "Iran's Policy toward Afghanistan," *Middle East Journal* 60, no. 2 (2006): 235–56; Alireza Nader and Joya Laha, "Iran's Balancing Act in Afghanistan," Occasional Paper (Santa Monica, Calif.: RAND, 2011).

64. Matthew Rosenberg, "Iranian Currency Traders Find a Haven in Afghanistan," *New York Times*, August 17, 2012.

65. Interviews with Afghan government officials, journalists, and security analysts and with ISAF officials, Kabul and Herat, April 2012.

66. For details on Russia's views, see John Burns, "An Old Afghanistan Hand Offers Lessons of the Past," *New York Times*, October 19, 2008; William Maley, "Afghanistan and Its Region," in Thier, *Future of Afghanistan*, pp. 93–103.

67. See "Russia under Putin: The Making of a Neo-KGB State," *The Economist*, August 23, 2007. For a nuanced discussion of President Putin's worldview and the competing objectives he is balancing in his rule over Russia, see Fiona Hill and Clifford Gaddis, *Mr. Putin: Operative in the Kremlin* (Brookings, 2013).

68. My analysis of Russia's foreign policy toward to the United States profited greatly from my conversation with my colleague Steven Pifer of the Brookings Institution. See also Steven Pifer, "Squaring U.S. Policy toward Russia with U.S. Interests in the Larger Post-Soviet Space," paper presented at the Conference on U.S.-Russia Relations: Policy Challenges for the Congress, Madrid, February 15–21, 2010, www.amacad.org/russia/russiaConference.pdf; Oksana Antonenko, "The Central Asian States and Russia," *Adelphi Series* 51, no. 425–26 (2011): 199–218.

69. Joshua Foust, "Post-Soviet Central Asian National Interests in Afghanistan" (New York: Century Foundation, September 28, 2010), www.humansecurity gateway.com/documents/CF_PostSovietCentralAsianNationalInterestsin Afghanistan.pdf.

70. Maley, "Afghanistan and Its Region."

71. See Ahmed Rashid, *Jihad: The Rise of Militant Islam in Central Asia* (Yale University Press, 2002).

72. Fozil Mashrab, "Kyrgyzstan Takes on the Kremlin," *Asia Times*, February 24, 2012.

73. Jane Perlez, "China Shows Interest in Afghan Security, Fearing Taliban Would Help Separatists," *New York Times*, June 8, 2012. See also Raffaello Pantucci, "China's Afghan Dilemma," *Survival* 52, no. 4 (2010): 21-27.

74. For the China-Pakistan relationship, see, for example, Mathieu Duchâtel, "The Terrorist Risk and China's Policy toward Pakistan: Strategic Reassurance and the 'United Front,'" *Journal of Contemporary China* 20, no. 71 (2011): 543–61; Evan A. Feigenbaum, "China's Pakistan Conundrum: The End of the All-Weather Friendship," *Foreign Affairs*, December 4, 2011, www.foreignaffairs.com/articles/136718/evan-a-feigenbaum/chinas-pakistan-conundrum; Lisa Curtis, "China's Military and Security Relationship with Pakistan," testimony before the U.S.–China Economic and Security Review Commission, May 20, 2009, www.uscc.gov/hearings/2009hearings/written_testimonies/09_05_20_wrts/09_05_20_curtis_statement.pdf.

75. Interviews with Afghan officials and international political analysts, Baghlan and Balkh, September 2010 and April 2012.

Chapter 11

1. "UN: Afghan Civilian Deaths Down, but Trend Eroding," Associated Press, August 8, 2012; Alissa Rubin, "Afghan Attacks Kill Dozens in Deadliest Day for Civilians This Year," *New York Times*, August 14, 2012.

2. See Rajiv Chandrasekaran, *Little America: The War within the War for Afghanistan* (New York: Knopf, 2012).

3. White House, Office of the Press Secretary, "Remarks by President Obama in Address to the Nation from Afghanistan," May 1, 2012, www.whitehouse.gov/the-press-office/2012/05/01/remarks-president-address-nation-afghanistan.

4. House Armed Services Committee, Subcommittee on Oversight and Investigations, "Afghan National Security Forces: A Glass 55% Full," testimony of Michael O'Hanlon, Brookings Institution, 112 Cong. 2 sess. (June 29, 2012), www.brookings.edu/research/testimony/2012/06/29-afghanistan-security-ohanlon.

5. For early calls to expand the ANSF, particularly the ANA, to match the demands of intensifying insurgency, see Ronald Neumann, "Afghans, Report for Duty," *New York Times*, January 14, 2008. See also Kimberly Kagan, "Afghan Army and Police Forces Must Grow Much Larger," *Washington Examiner*, August 8, 2009.

6. Antonio Giustozzi, "The Afghan National Army: Marching in the Wrong Direction?" in *Snapshots of an Intervention: The Unlearned Lessons of Afghanistan's Decade of Assistance (2001–2011)*, edited by Martine van Bijlert and Sari Kouvo (Kabul: Afghanistan Analysts Network, 2012), p. 64.

7. Kenneth Katzman, "Afghanistan: Post-Taliban Governance, Security, and U.S. Policy," Report RL30588 (Library of Congress, Congressional Research Service, May 3, 2012), p. 34.

8. Ibid.

9. See leaked report from TF 3-10 Bagram, Afghanistan, *State of the Taliban: Detainee Perspectives*, January 6, 2012, p. 22, http://s3.documentcloud.org/documents/296489/taliban-report.pdf.

10. Katzman, "Afghanistan: Post-Taliban Governance," p. 32.

11. Ibid.

12. Ibid.

13. NATO, "Chicago Summit Declaration on Afghanistan," May 21, 2012, www.nato.int/cps/en/natolive/official_texts_87595.htm. The cost estimate is from Katzman, "Afghanistan: Post-Taliban Governance," p. 32.

14. For more on the sustainability of the ANSF, see Anthony Cordesman, *Transition in the Afghanistan-Pakistan War: How Does This War End?* (Washington: Center for Strategic and International Studies, January 11, 2012), pp. 98–99, http://csis.org/files/publication/120111_Afghanistan_Aspen_Paper.pdf.

15. Department of Defense, *Report on Progress toward Security and Stability in Afghanistan* (April 2012), www.defense.gov/pubs/pdfs/Report_Final_SecDef_04_26_10.pdf.

16. See "U.S. Drawdown in Afghanistan Includes Many Trainers," Associated Press, July 2, 2012.

17. See Richard Leiby, "2 More NATO Troops Killed in Afghanistan," *Washington Post*, September 15, 2012; "Taliban Leader Urges Insurgents to Cut Civilian Deaths," Reuters, August 17, 2012; Alissa Rubin, "End Sought to Attacks on Allies by Afghans," *New York Times*, August 13, 2012.

18. Leiby, "2 More NATO Troops Killed."

19. Amie Ferris-Rotman, "Afghanistan: Hundreds of Soldiers Detained, Fired for Insurgent Links," Reuters, September 5, 2012.

20. Richard Oppel Jr. and Graham Bowley, "Afghan Attacks on Allied Troops Prompt NATO to Shift Policy," *New York Times*, August 18, 2012.

21. Matthew Rosenberg, "Coalition Sharply Reduces Joint Operations with Afghan Troops," *New York Times*, September 18, 2012.

22. "ISAF Officials: Reports on Partnering Change 'Not Accurate,'" American Forces Press Service, September 18, 2012; David Stringer and Slobodan Lekic, "NATO: Change in Afghanistan Ops Won't Hurt Strategy," Associated Press, September 18, 2012.

23. TF 3-10 Bagram, *State of the Taliban*, p. 21.

24. Interviews with ISAF officials, Kabul, April 2012.

25. Alissa Rubin, "Afghan Strike Shows Force and Restraint of Taliban," *New York Times*, August 3, 2012.

26. NATO, "Transition to Afghan Lead: Inteqal," Media Backgrounder, May 16, 2012, www.nato.int/nato_static/assets/pdf/pdf_topics/20120516_media_backgrounder_transition_en.pdf.

27. Interviews with Afghan government and NATO officials, Kabul, Balkh, and Baghlan, April 2012.

28. Catherine Dale, "In Brief: Next Steps in the War in Afghanistan: Issues for Congress," Report R42137 (Library of Congress, Congressional Research Service, June 15, 2012), p. 8.

29. This paragraph is drawn from Kevin Sieff, "Months after Americans Leave, an Afghan Base in Disrepair," *Washington Post*, August 2, 2012.

30. TF 3-10 Bagram, *State of the Taliban*, pp. 4, 21–22, 27.

31. Ibid.

32. Ibid.

33. Ibid., p. 21.

34. NATO, "Chicago Summit Declaration."

35. For details on the continuing discussion as to what lead means, see Dale, "Next Steps in the War."

36. Department of Defense, "DoD News Briefing with General John Allen from the Pentagon," May 23, 2012, www.defense.gov/transcripts/transcript.aspx?transcriptid=5040.

37. White House, "Address to the Nation from Afghanistan."

38. Ibid.

39. See David Barno and Andrew Exum, *Responsible Transition: Security U.S. Interests in Afghanistan Beyond 2014* (Washington: Center for a New American Security, December 2010), www.cnas.org/files/documents/publications/CNAS_ResponsibleTransition_BarnoExum_2.pdf.

40. Interviews with ISAF officers in northern Afghanistan and Kabul, April 2012.

41. Interviews with officials of the Afghan Ministry of Interior, Ministry of Defense, and National Directorate of Security and with ISAF and U.S. Embassy officials, Kabul, Kandahar, and Baghlan, fall 2010 and spring 2012.

42. Antonio Giustozzi, "Afghanistan's National Army: The Ambiguous Prospects of Afghanization," *Terrorism Monitor* 6, no. 9 (2008): 1–3.

43. Communication with NTM-A officials, July 2012. In its April 2012 *Report on Progress toward Security and Stability in Afghanistan*, the Department of Defense did not report on the ethnic composition. In its April 2010 *Report*, the following numbers were given: 42 percent Pashtun, 41 percent Tajik, 8 percent Hazara, 4 percent Uzbek, and 5 percent others. Department of Defense, *Report on Progress toward Security and Stability in Afghanistan* (April 2010), p.104, www.defense.gov/pubs/pdfs/Report_Final_SecDef_04_26_10.pdf.

44. Interviews with ISAF officials, Afghanistan, spring 2009, fall 2010, and spring 2012.

45. Interviews with Afghan military officers, Kandahar, Baghlan, and Kabul, fall 2010. For ethnic rifts in the ANA, especially at the command level, see International Crisis Group, "A Force in Fragments: Reconstituting the Afghan National Army," Asia Report 190 (Brussels: May 12, 2010). For other performance problems, such as drug abuse; inability and unwillingness to operate independently of ISAF support; attrition, desertion, and retention issues; corruption; and illiteracy, see Elisabeth Bumiller, "Report Criticizes U.S. System for Evaluating Afghan Forces," *New York Times*, June 28, 2010. ISAF maintains that it carefully monitors the emergence of such ethnic factionalization and patronage networks and takes actions to counteract them.

46. Giustozzi, "Marching in the Wrong Direction," pp. 63–66.

47. Interviews with ISAF officers and ANA and ANP rank-and-file recruits as well as officers, Afghanistan, spring 2009 and fall 2010. For regional balance problems in the ANA, see Bumiller, "Report Criticizes U.S. System."

48. Interviews with ISAF officers and ANA and ANP rank-and-file recruits as well as officers, Afghanistan, spring 2009 and fall 2010. Interviews with ISAF officers, Kabul, April 2012.

49. TF 3-10 Bagram, *State of the Taliban*, pp. 21, 26.

50. See chapters 3 and 4 in this volume. See also International Crisis Group, "Reforming Afghanistan's Police," Asia Report 138 (Brussels: August 30, 2007), www.crisisgroup.org/~/media/Files/asia/south-asia/afghanistan/138_reforming_afghanistan_s_police.pdf; Andrew Wilder, *Cops or Robbers? The Struggle to Reform the Afghan National Police*, Issues Paper (Kabul: Afghan Research and Evaluation Unit, July 2007), www.areu.org.af/Uploads/EditionPdfs/717E-Cops%20or%20Robbers-IP-print.pdf.

51. Katzman, "Afghanistan: Post-Taliban Governance," p. 36.

52. Ibid.

53. Department of Defense, *Report on Progress* (April 2012), p. 32.

54. Alissa Rubin and Habib Zahori, "Police Official Went to Fight for Taliban, Afghans Say," *New York Times*, July 24, 2012.

55. Seth G. Jones, *Counterinsurgency in Afghanistan* (Santa Monica, Calif.: RAND, 2008), www.rand.org/pubs/monographs/2008/RAND_MG595.pdf.

56. David Ward, "Afghan Civilian Police: Police Instead of Soldiers" (U.S. Army War College, March 23, 2010), www.dtic.mil/cgi-bin/GetTRDoc?AD= ADA521797.

57. Department of Defense, *Report on Progress* (April 2012), p. 32.

58. Katzman, "Afghanistan: Post-Taliban Governance," p. 36.

59. Joanna Buckley, "Building the Police through the Focused District Development Programme," in Van Bijlert and Kouvo, *Snapshots of an Intervention*, pp. 81–89.

60. Interviews with ISAF officials, including ISAF trainers of the ANP, Afghanistan, fall 2010 and spring 2012. For details on the ANSF's performance, Habib Zahori, Rod Nordland, and Alissa Rubin, "Witnesses Describe Brazen Attack on Resort Hotel near Kabul," *New York Times*, June 22, 2012; Alissa Rubin, Graham Bowley, and Sangar Rahimi, "Complex Attack Sends Message to the West," *New York Times*, April 15, 2012; Alissa Rubin and Rod Nordland, "Raid by Afghan Forces and NATO Ends Attack on Hotel in Kabul," *New York Times*, June 28, 2011.

61. For one recent example where the population exhibited some level of trust in the police with respect to counterterrorism functions, see Matthew Rosenberg and Alissa Rubin, "8 Civilians Killed in Bombing near Kabul," *New York Times*, August 7, 2012.

62. Ward, "Afghan Civilian Police."

63. International Crisis Group, "Reforming Afghanistan's Police."

64. Among the power brokers associated with the border police is Kandahar's General Abdul Raziq, discussed in detail in chapter 5 in this volume.

65. Department of Defense, *Report on Progress* (April 2012), pp. 31–32.

66. Presentation by a high-level ISAF official, Washington, August 2012.

67. See chapter 2 in this volume. See also Rajiv Chandrasekaran, "'Little America': Infighting on Obama Team Squandered Chance for Peace in Afghanistan," *Washington Post*, June 24, 2012.

68. For a strong argument that labeling the Haqqani network a terrorist group will undermine negotiations not just with the Haqqanis, but with the Taliban overall and hamper efforts toward peace in Afghanistan, see Alex Strick van Linschoten and Felix Kuehn, "A Pointless Blacklisting," *New York Times*, September 11, 2012.

69. On the various efforts so far, see, for example, International Crisis Group, "Talking about Talks: Toward a Political Settlement in Afghanistan," Asia Report 221 (Brussels: March 26, 2012).

70. Based on a TV interview with three senior members of the Taliban negotiating team, NHK World TV, "Today's Close Up," www3.nhk.or.jp/nhkworld/english/tv/todayscloseup/index20120911.html.

71. Interviews with high-level ISAF officers, Kabul, April 2012. See also Stephen Hadley and John Podesta, "The Right Way out of Afghanistan," *Foreign Affairs* 91, no. 4 (2012): 41–53.

72. See Rod Nordland and Matthew Rosenberg, "Taliban Call Off Talks as Karzai Urges Faster U.S. Transition," *New York Times*, March 15, 2012.

73. "Key Taliban Member Calls for End to War," *Dawn*, August 16, 2012.

74. Missy Ryan, "U.S. Sweetens Taliban Prisoner Proposal in Bid to Revive Peace Talks," Reuters, August 7, 2012.

75. For example, the Republican members of the House Armed Services Committee released a report indicating that more than 25 percent of the 600 former detainees at Guantanamo that were moved to countries like Afghanistan, Saudi Arabia, or Yemen were confirmed or suspected in engaging in "terrorist activity." House Armed Services Committee, Subcommittee on Oversight and Investigations, *Leaving Guantanamo: Policies, Pressures, and Detainees Returning to the Fight*, 112 Cong. 2 sess. (January 2012), Committee Print 112-4, http://armedservices.house.gov/index.cfm/files/serve?File_id=dd0b4c6e-528e-4138-9755-86bae92e1cdb.

76. Deb Riechmann, "Some at Gitmo Could Go to Afghanistan," Associated Press, June 29, 2012.

77. NHK World TV, "Today's Close Up." Four Taliban commanders interviewed by a team of Western scholars publicly adopted the same attitude. See Michael Semple and others, *Taliban Perspectives on Reconciliation*, Briefing Paper (London: Royal United Services Institute, September 2012), www.rusi.org/downloads/assets/Taliban_Perspectives_on_Reconciliation.pdf.

78. Michael Semple, "'Al Qaeda Is a Plague': A Remarkable Insight into the Mind of a Senior Member of the Afghan Taliban Movement," *New Statesman*, July 16, 2012, pp. 32–35.

79. TF 3-10 Bagram, *State of the Taliban*, pp. 18, 20, 23–25. These findings also confirm the analysis in Alex van Linschoten and Felix Kuehn, *An Enemy We Created: The Myth of the Taliban/al Qaeda Merger in Afghanistan, 1970–2010* (London: C. Hurst, 2011).

80. TF 3-10 Bagram, *State of the Taliban*, p. 3.

81. For the former position, see NHK World TV, "Today's Close Up." For the latter, see Semple and others, *Taliban Perspectives*.

82. NHK World TV, "Today's Close Up."

83. Ibid.

84. Semple, "'Al Qaeda Is a Plague.'"

85. Interviews with senior level ISAF commanders, Kabul, April 2012.

86. For these and other concerns about negotiating with the Taliban, see Lisa Curtis, "The U.S. Must Move Cautiously on Taliban Reconciliation" (Washington: Heritage Foundation, April 26, 2012), www.heritage.org/research/reports/2012/04/the-us-must-move-cautiously-on-taliban-reconciliation.

87. Kamran Yousaf, "Afghan Reconciliation: Pakistan May Release 'Former Chief of Quetta Shura,'" *Express Tribune*, August 8, 2012; "Afghan Officials Met with Jailed Taliban Leader," Associated Press, August 12, 2012.

88. For details, see Kathy Gannon and Anne Gearan, "Hamid Karzai's Office Scuttled Secret U.S.-Taliban Talks," Associated Press, August 29, 2011.

89. See discussions in chapters 6, 7, and 8 in this volume.

90. TF 3-10 Bagram, *State of the Taliban*, p. 20.

91. See, for example, Paul Richter, "Status of Afghan Women Threatens Hillary Clinton's Legacy," *Los Angeles Times*, April 8, 2012.

92. For a cross-section of Afghan societal attitudes toward the negotiations, see Hamish Nixon, "Afghan Perspectives on Achieving a Durable Peace," Peace Brief 94 (Washington: United States Institute of Peace, June 3, 2011).

93. TF 3-10 Bagram, *State of the Taliban*, pp. 2, 26.

94. Semple, "'Al Qaeda Is a Plague.'"

95. Ibid.

96. TF 3-10 Bagram, *State of the Taliban*, p. 26.

97. NHK World TV, "Today's Close Up."

98. Semple, "'Al Qaeda Is a Plague.'"

99. NHK World TV, "Today's Close Up."

100. For details on the Taliban's considerations in the negotiations, see Michael Semple, *Reconciliation in Afghanistan* (Washington: United States Institute of Peace, 2009); Michael Semple and Fotini Christia, "Flipping the Taliban: How to Win in Afghanistan," *Foreign Affairs* 88, no. 4 (2009): 34–45.

101. For a comprehensive analysis of the many different elements that could be considered in a negotiated deal and the structuring of the peace process, see Semple, *Reconciliation in Afghanistan*; Hamish Nixon and Caroline Hartzell, *Beyond Power Sharing: Institutional Options for an Afghan Peace Process* (Washington: United States Institute of Peace, 2011).

102. Semple, "'Al Qaeda Is a Plague.'"

103. Dexter Filkins, "After America: Will Civil War Hit Afghanistan When the U.S. Leaves?" *New Yorker*, July 9, 2012, www.newyorker.com/reporting/2012/07/09/120709fa_fact_filkins.

104. These numbers are drawn from Ryan Evans, "The Once and Future Civil War in Afghanistan," *Foreign Policy.com*, July 26, 2012, http://afpak.foreign policy.com/posts/2012/07/26/the_once_and_future_civil_war_in_afghanistan.

105. Ibid.

106. Interviews with a broad range of Afghans—from shopkeepers to maliks—Afghanistan, fall 2010 and spring 2012.

Chapter 12

1. Interviews with officials of ISAF, UNAMA, and various embassies in Kabul, Afghanistan, April 2012.

2. For more on the possibilities of an earlier election, see Ben Farmer, "Hamid Karzai Considering Early Afghan Presidential Elections in 2013, *The Telegraph*, April 12, 2012.

3. Interviews with Afghan candidates, members of parliament, and voters, Kandahar and Baghlan, fall 2010.

4. For an analogous argument, see Ronald Neumann, "Response to Hadley and Podesta," *Foreign Affairs*, November-December 2012. For a strongly argued opposite opinion—that Washington should specifically designate at least which potential presidential candidates it finds intolerable, if not which it prefers—see Michael O'Hanlon, "Life after Karzai," *ForeignPolicy.com*, June 13, 2012. Stephen Hadley and John Podesta similarly call for making it clear that U.S. support for Afghanistan, including the Strategic Partnership Agreement, is conditioned on Karzai ceding power in 2014 to a legitimately elected successor. See Stephen Hadley and John Podesta, "The Right Way Out of Afghanistan," *Foreign Affairs* 91, no. 4 (2012): 41–53.

5. See, for example, Hadley and Podesta, "The Right Way Out."

6. Neumann, "Response to Hadley and Podesta."

7. "Rocking the boat" is indeed the phrase that President Karzai supposedly used in a meeting with about sixty prominent maliks and businessmen in August 2010 to counter their demands to facilitate business operation by undertaking anticorruption measures in line ministries. Interview with one of the maliks present at the meeting at the Arg Palace, Kabul, fall 2010.

8. Interview with a U.S. Embassy official, Kabul, fall 2010.

9. The expression "Afghan good enough" was adopted by officials of the U.S. government in advance of NATO's Chicago Summit in May 2012. See Helene Cooper and Thom Shanker, "U.S. Redefines Afghan Success before Conference," *New York Times*, May 17, 2012. On the prior use of "Afghan good enough" as a moniker for a White House Afghanistan decisionmaking group who sought to narrow the goals in Afghanistan as much as possible, see David Sanger, *Confront and Conceal: Obama's Secret Wars and Surprising Use of American Power* (New York: Crown, 2012), pp. 49–50.

Index

Abdullah, Abdullah, 107

Accountability: of Afghan Local Police, 268–69; of local officials, 113; media's role in, 3; of power brokers, 16, 266; under Strategic Partnership Agreement, 34

Advisory services, 21, 218, 250, 257–60

Afghan Border Police, 231–32, 260

Afghan Infrastructure Fund, 180

Afghanistan Compact (2006), 98

Afghanistan Investment Support Agency, 187

Afghanistan Reconstruction Trust Fund, 185

Afghanistan Vouchers for Increased Production in Agriculture (AVIPA-Plus), 173

Afghan Local Police (ALP), 138–60; abuses by, 69, 153–54; accountability of, 268–69; control mechanisms for, 144–48; demobilization of, 159, 269; effectiveness of, 136, 148–57; extortion by, 69; future prospects for, 157–60; history of, 140–43; and military transition, 242; in northern Afghanistan, 132–34; objectives for, 139–40; political impact of, 151–52;

recommendations for, 21, 268–70; recruitment for, 145–46; supervision of, 145–46; and Taliban, 134, 156–57

Afghan National Army (ANA): capacity building in, 250–51, 257–60; corruption in, 227–28; desertion rate, 215–16; and insider attacks, 218–19; and military transition, 215–28, 242–43; recruitment for, 215; specialty enablers lacking in, 220–21, 250; target strength for, 215; training for, 217, 249

Afghan National Auxiliary Police, 141

Afghan National Civil Order Police (ANCOP), 229–30

Afghan National Police (ANP): corruption and crime in, 54, 159–60; counterterrorism capacity of, 8–9, 230–31; crime prevention capacity of, 67–68, 231–32, 259; and military transition, 228–33, 242, 269; target strength for, 215

Afghan National Security Forces (ANSF): and anticorruption initiatives, 112; capabilities of, 20, 246; ISAF partnering with, 9, 249; and military transition, 242, 249; in northern Afghanistan, 122; and

Uruzgan, local militias in, 154
USAID. *See* United States Agency for International Development
Uzbekistan: regional cooperation role of, 211; transshipment agreements with, 124, 125
Uzbeks: in Afghan National Army, 226, 228; in Afghan National Police, 155; and ethnic conflict, 121, 129, 130; and Taliban negotiations, 237

Value-added chains, 176

Wardak, Abdul Rahim, 115
Warlords: accountability of, 248–49; and governance, 64, 65; intelligence and logistical support provided by,

98, 251; ISAF reliance on, 251; recommendations for reining in, 21, 265–68; and Taliban, 40, 41. *See also* Power brokers
Wasifi, Izzatullah, 98
Wesa, Tooryalai, 86, 113
Wheat as poppy replacement crop, 177
Whole-of-government approach, 182
Women for Afghan Women organization, 131
Women's rights: in northern Afghanistan, 126–28; and Taliban, 42, 238, 274; and U.S. policy objectives, 25–26
World Bank, 186, 262

Zardari, Asif Ali, 191, 202, 207
Zia ul-Haq, Mohammad, 199